SOMETHING ABOUT THE AUTHOR®

Something about
the Author *was named
an "Outstanding
Reference Source,"
the highest honor given
by the American
Library Association
Reference and Adult
Services Division.*

ISSN 0276-816X

something ABOUT THe AUThor®

**Facts and Pictures about Authors
and Illustrators of Books for Young People**

volume 212

GALE
CENGAGE Learning™

Detroit • New York • San Francisco • New Haven, Conn • Waterville, Maine • London

Something about the Author, Volume 212

Project Editor: Lisa Kumar

Editorial: Laura Avery, Pamela Bow, Jim Craddock, Amy Fuller, Andrea Henderson, Margaret Mazurkiewicz, Tracie Moy, Jeff Muhr, Kathy Nemeh, Mary Ruby, Mike Tyrkus

Permissions: Savannah Gignac, Jackie Jones, Barb McNeil

Imaging and Multimedia: Savannah Gignac, John Watkins

Composition and Electronic Capture: Amy Darga

Manufacturing: Drew Kalasky

Product Manager: Janet Witalec

For product information and technology assistance, contact us at **Gale Customer Support, 1-800-877-4253.** For permission to use material from this text or product, submit all requests online at **www.cengage.com/permissions.** Further permissions questions can be emailed to **permissionrequest@cengage.com**

Since this page cannot legibly accommodate all copyright notices, the acknowledgments constitute an extension of the copyright notice.

While every effort has been made to ensure the reliability of the information presented in this publication, Gale, a part of Cengage Learning, does not guarantee the accuracy of the data contained herein. Gale accepts no payment for listing; and inclusion in the publication of any organization, agency, institution, publication, service, or individual does not imply endorsement of the editors or publisher. Errors brought to the attention of the publisher and verified to the satisfaction of the publisher will be corrected in future editions.

EDITORIAL DATA PRIVACY POLICY: Does this publication contain information about you as an individual? If so, for more information about our editorial data privacy policies, please see our Privacy Statement at www.gale.cengage.com.

Gale
27500 Drake Rd.
Farmington Hills, MI, 48331-3535

LIBRARY OF CONGRESS CATALOG CARD NUMBER 62-52046

ISBN-13: 978-1-4144-4225-9
ISBN-10: 1-4144-4225-4

ISSN 0276-816X

This title is also available as an e-book.
ISBN-13: 978-1-4144-6444-2
ISBN-10: 1-4144-6444-4
Contact your Gale sales representative for ordering information.

Printed in the United States of America
1 2 3 4 5 6 7 14 13 12 11 10

Contents

Authors in Forthcoming Volumes

Below are some of the authors and illustrators that will be featured in upcoming volumes of *SATA*. These include new entries on the swiftly rising stars of the field, as well as completely revised and updated entries (indicated with *) on some of the most notable and best-loved creators of books for children.

*Francesca Lia Block ❚ With her book *Weetzie Bat,* Block created a new type of young-adult novel: one that reflected the Los Angeles punk scene of the 1990s. Living in a culture steeped in sex, drugs, and rock 'n' roll, Weetzie and her boyfriend, My Secret Agent Lover Man, follow their punk-rock destiny in books that include *Baby Be-Bop, Witch Baby,* and *Necklace of Kisses.* In 2009, *Weetzie Bat,* was awarded the prestigious Phoenix Award, an honor given to books that have proven to be influential over time.

*David Bouchard ❚ Of Métis ancestry, Canadian poet and writer Bouchard celebrates the landscape and rural lifestyle he experienced while growing up on the Manitoba prairie. His award-winning books for young readers include *The Great Race, A Barnyard Bestiary, If You're Not from the Prairie,* and *Voices from the Wild: An Animal Sensagoria.* A former educator, Bouchard has been named to the Order of Canada for his writing and literacy advocacy.

David Ellwand ❚ Ellwand is a British illustrator and photographer whose books for children include *Emma's Elephant; and Other Favorite Animal Friends, The Big Book of Beautiful Babies,* and *Ten in the Bed: A Counting Book.* Turning to fantasy, he has also worked with his wife, writer Ruth Ellwand, to craft the graphic novel *The Mystery of the Fool and the Vanisher.* Apart from his books for children, Ellwand is best known for his whimsical photography books *Fairie-ality: The Fashion Collection from the House of Ellwand* and its companion volume, *Fairie-ality Style: A Sourcebook of Inspirations from Nature.*

*Katharine Holabird ❚ Holabird is the author of the beloved "Angelina" stories about an endearing dancing mouse. An American living in England, Holabird has also written popular picture books about Little Mouse and a boy named Alexander, but it is Angelina, the mouse in dancing shoes, that remains her most popular creation. A prolific writer, she continues to work with long-time collaborator, artist Helen Craig, and her "Angelina" stories have been adapted as ballets, television programs, and even as a series of picture-book adaptations.

Terry Golson ❚ From her home in New England, Golson combines a passion for raising goats and chickens with a talent for both cooking and writing to build a career as an author and establish a backyard farm that stars in its very own Web site. Golson's cookbooks, which include *Wholehearted Cooking* and *The Farmstead Egg Cookbook,* share her recipes for creative and healthy cuisine, and she shares her passion for backyard farming in her many presentations for schools and libraries. Golson also engages children with a warmhearted story in her engaging picture book *Tillie Lays an Egg.*

Kazuo Iwamura ❚ A prolific author and illustrator of both picture books and comic books, Japanese artist Iwamura shares his love of nature in his work. In addition to creating artwork for other writers, his original, self-illustrated books include the "Family of Fourteen" stories: simple and endearing tales that capture the antics of a group of fieldmice in the books *The Fourteen Forest Mice and the Winter Sledding Day* and *The Fourteen Forest Mice and the Summer Laundry Day,* among others. While most of Iwamura's books have been published in Japan and France, his "Family of Fourteen" books have sold more than six million copies around the world.

*Barbara McClintock ❚ McClintock's lushly detailed ink and watercolor art often features expressive animals dressed in nineteenth-century costume and settings featuring minute period details. Frequently compared to British artist Randolph Caldecott, she sometimes sets her characters upon the pages as if they were actors upon a stage. In addition to her work for other writers, McClintock takes readers to Paris in her book *Adéle and Simon,* and retells traditional stories in books such as *The Little Red Hen, Animal Fables from Aesop,* and *Cinderella.*

Danica McKellar ❚ Although author and writer McKellar is perhaps best known for her performance as Winnie Cooper on the popular television program *The Wonder Years,* many of her readers were not yet born when she played the iconic teen role. While pursuing an acting career—McKellar has appeared on television's *The West Wing* among other roles—she took a different direction in college, graduating summa cum laude in mathematics. In addition to launching a Web site offering advice and encouragement to young people, she also produced the teen-friendly primer *Math Doesn't Suck: How to Survive Middle-School Math without Losing Your Mind or Breaking a Nail.*

*Sue Porter ❚ A British author and artist, Porter has designed, illustrated, and sometimes written dozens of books for children, among them the interactive nursery rhyme book *Baa, Baa, Black Sheep* and *Little Wolf and the Giant.* In addition, her "Parsnip" series of interactive board books have captured the affection of legions of toddlers through their playful design and stories featuring the antics of a cuddly lamb and its friends.

*Laurence Yep ❚ Yep is the author of such award-winning novels as *Dragonwings, Child of the Owl, Sea Glass,* and *Dragon Steel,* as well as of illustrated stories for younger readers. His fiction brings the history and culture of Chinese Americans into realistic view, replacing the exaggerated, stereotyped images of characters such as Dr. Fu Manchu and Charley Chan with realistic portraits of Chinese-American men and women who have enriched North American society with both their determination to succeed and their willingness to share their cultural heritage.

Introduction

Something about the Author (*SATA*) is an ongoing reference series that examines the lives and works of authors and illustrators of books for children. *SATA* includes not only well-known writers and artists but also less prominent individuals whose works are just coming to be recognized. This series is often the only readily available information source on emerging authors and illustrators. You'll find *SATA* informative and entertaining, whether you are a student, a librarian, an English teacher, a parent, or simply an adult who enjoys children's literature.

What's Inside *SATA*

SATA provides detailed information about authors and illustrators who span the full time range of children's literature, from early figures like John Newbery and L. Frank Baum to contemporary figures like Judy Blume and Richard Peck. Authors in the series represent primarily English-speaking countries, particularly the United States, Canada, and the United Kingdom. Also included, however, are authors from around the world whose works are available in English translation. The writings represented in *SATA* include those created intentionally for children and young adults as well as those written for a general audience and known to interest younger readers. These writings cover the entire spectrum of children's literature, including picture books, humor, folk and fairy tales, animal stories, mystery and adventure, science fiction and fantasy, historical fiction, poetry and nonsense verse, drama, biography, and nonfiction. Obituaries are also included in many volumes of *SATA* and are intended not only as death notices but also as concise overviews of people's lives and work. Additionally, each edition features newly revised and updated entries for a selection of *SATA* listees who remain of interest to today's readers and who have been active enough to require extensive revisions of their earlier biographies.

Autobiography Feature

Beginning with Volume 103, many volumes of *SATA* feature one or more specially commissioned autobiographical essays. These unique essays, averaging about ten thousand words in length and illustrated with an abundance of personal photos, present an entertaining and informative first-person perspective on the lives and careers of prominent authors and illustrators profiled in *SATA*.

Two Convenient Indexes

In response to suggestions from librarians, *SATA* indexes no longer appear in every volume but are included in alternate (odd-numbered) volumes of the series, beginning with Volume 57.

SATA continues to include two indexes that cumulate with each alternate volume: the Illustrations Index, arranged by the name of the illustrator, gives the number of the volume and page where the illustrator's work appears in the current volume as well as all preceding volumes in the series; the Author Index gives the number of the volume in which a person's biographical sketch, autobiographical essay, or obituary appears in the current volume as well as all preceding volumes in the series.

These indexes also include references to authors and illustrators who appear in *Gale's Yesterday's Authors of Books for Children, Children's Literature Review,* and *Something about the Author Autobiography Series.*

Easy-to-Use Entry Format

Whether you're already familiar with the *SATA* series or just getting acquainted, you will want to be aware of the kind of information that an entry provides. In every *SATA* entry the editors attempt to give as complete a picture of the person's life and work as possible. A typical entry in *SATA* includes the following clearly labeled information sections:

PERSONAL: date and place of birth and death, parents' names and occupations, name of spouse, date of marriage, names of children, educational institutions attended, degrees received, religious and political affiliations, hobbies and other interests.

ADDRESSES: complete home, office, electronic mail, and agent addresses, whenever available.

CAREER: name of employer, position, and dates for each career post; art exhibitions; military service; memberships and offices held in professional and civic organizations.

MEMBER: professional, civic, and other association memberships and any official posts held.

AWARDS, HONORS: literary and professional awards received.

WRITINGS: title-by-title chronological bibliography of books written and/or illustrated, listed by genre when known; lists of other notable publications, such as plays, screenplays, and periodical contributions.

ADAPTATIONS: a list of films, television programs, plays, CD-ROMs, recordings, and other media presentations that have been adapted from the author's work.

WORK IN PROGRESS: description of projects in progress.

SIDELIGHTS: a biographical portrait of the author or illustrator's development, either directly from the biographee—and often written specifically for the *SATA* entry—or gathered from diaries, letters, interviews, or other published sources.

BIOGRAPHICAL AND CRITICAL SOURCES: cites sources quoted in "Sidelights" along with references for further reading.

EXTENSIVE ILLUSTRATIONS: photographs, movie stills, book illustrations, and other interesting visual materials supplement the text.

How a *SATA* Entry Is Compiled

SATA editors examine a wide variety of published sources to gather information for an entry. Biographical and bibliographic sources are consulted, as are book reviews, feature articles, published interviews, and material sometimes obtained from the biographee's family, publishers, agent, or other associates. Whenever possible, the author or illustrator is sent a copy of the entry to check for accuracy and completeness.

Entries that have not been verified by the biographees or their representatives are marked with an asterisk (*).

Contact the Editor

We encourage our readers to examine the entire *SATA* series. Please write and tell us if we can make *SATA* even more helpful to you. Give your comments and suggestions to the editor:

Editor
Something about the Author
Gale, Cengage Learning
27500 Drake Rd.
Farmington Hills MI 48331-3535

Toll-free: 800-877-GALE
Fax: 248-699-8070

Something about the Author Product Advisory Board

The editors of *Something about the Author* are dedicated to maintaining a high standard of excellence by publishing comprehensive, accurate, and highly readable entries on a wide array of writers for children and young adults. In addition to the quality of the content, the editors take pride in the graphic design of the series, which is intended to be orderly yet inviting, allowing readers to utilize the pages of *SATA* easily and with efficiency. Despite the longevity of the *SATA* print series, and the success of its format, we are mindful that the vitality of a literary reference product is dependent on its ability to serve its users over time. As literature, and attitudes about literature, constantly evolve, so do the reference needs of students, teachers, scholars, journalists, researchers, and book club members. To be certain that we continue to keep pace with the expectations of our customers, the editors of *SATA* listen carefully to their comments regarding the value, utility, and quality of the series. Librarians, who have firsthand knowledge of the needs of library users, are a valuable resource for us. The *Something about the Author* Product Advisory Board, made up of school, public, and academic librarians, is a forum to promote focused feedback about *SATA* on a regular basis. The nine-member advisory board includes the following individuals, whom the editors wish to thank for sharing their expertise:

SOMETHING ABOUT THE AUTHOR

BALIT, Christina 1961-

Personal

Surname pronounced "Ba-*leet*"; born August 5, 1961, in Manchester, England; daughter of Georges Michelle (an architect) and Patricia (a teacher, cook, actress, and homemaker; current surname Price) Balit; married Brian Croucher (an actor), May 8, 1992; children: Sean Georges, Billie George (daughter). *Education:* Chelsea School of Art, B.A.; Royal College of Art, M.A.; also attended Morley Theatre School and Questors Theatre School.

Addresses

Home—Shottenden, Kent, England. *Agent*—Lisa Eveliegh, 26-A Rochester Sq., London NW1 9SA, England. *E-mail*—contact@christinabalit.co.uk.

Career

Illustrator, author, and playwright. City and Guilds School of Art, London, England, tutor.

Awards, Honors

Travel grant from Thames Television, 1982; award for Outstanding Children's Book, Primary English, 1995; Best Books selection for junior education, 1996; Kate Greenaway Medal shortlist, 1996, for *Blodin the Beast* by Michael Morpurgo, and commendation, 1997, for *Ishtar and Tammuz* by Christopher J. Moore; English Association Award for Nonfiction, and U.S. Parents Guide to Children's Media Award, both 2002, both for *Kingdom of the Sun* by Jacqueline Mitton; Brave New Roles Award, 2006, for *Needle*.

Writings

SELF-ILLUSTRATED

An Arabian Home: Leila and Mustapha's Story, Hampstead Press (New York, NY), 1988.
Atlantis: The Legend of a Lost City, introduction by Geoffrey Ashe, Henry Holt (New York, NY), 2000.
Escape from Pompeii, Henry Holt (New York, NY), 2003.

Author's works have been translated into Gaelic.

ILLUSTRATOR

Michael Morpurgo, *Blodin the Beast,* Fulcrum Publishing (Golden, CO), 1995.
Christopher J. Moore, *Ishtar and Tammuz: A Babylonian Myth of the Seasons,* Kingfisher (New York, NY), 1996.
James Riordan, *The Twelve Labors of Hercules,* Millbrook Press (Brookfield, CT), 1997.
Jacqueline Mitton, *Zoo in the Sky,* Frances Lincoln (London, England), 1998.

1

Mary Hoffman, *Women of Camelot: Queens and Enchantresses at the Court of King Arthur,* Abbeville Press (New York, NY), 2000.

Robert Leeson, *My Sister Shahrazad: Tales from the Arabian Nights,* Frances Lincoln (London, England), 2001.

Jacqueline Mitton, *Kingdom of the Sun: A Book of the Planets,* National Geographic Society (Washington, DC), 2001.

Lois Rock, *Everlasting Stories: A Family Bible Treasury,* Chronicle Books (San Francisco, CA), 2001, published as *The Lion Bible: Everlasting Stories,* Lion (Oxford, England), 2001.

Jacqueline Mitton, *Once upon a Starry Night: A Book of Constellation Stories,* National Geographic (Washington, DC), 2003.

Lois Rock, *The Lion Book of Tales and Legends,* Lion (Oxford, England), 2003, published as *Saintly Tales and Legends,* Pauline Books & Media (Boston, MA), 2004.

Lois Rock, *Easter: The Everlasting Story,* Lion Children's (Oxford, England), 2004.

Hugh Lupton and Daniel Morden, *The Adventures of Odysseus,* Barefoot Books (Cambridge, MA), 2006.

Nick Would, *The Scarab's Secret,* Walker (New York, NY), 2006.

Jacqueline Mitton, *Zoo in the Sky: A Book of Animal Constellations,* National Geographic Society (Washington, DC), 2006.

Mary Hoffman, *Kings and Queens of the Bible,* Henry Holt (New York, NY), 2008.

Jacqueline Mitton, *The Planet Gods: Myths and Facts about the Solar System,* National Geographic (Washington, DC), 2008.

David Self, *The Lion Book of Wisdom Stories from around the World,* Trafalgar (London, England), 2009.

PLAYS

Agony for Beginners, produced in London, England, 1989.
Woman with Upturned Skirt, produced in London, England, 1992.
The Sentence, produced in London, England, 1996.
Needle, produced in London, England, 2006.

Sidelights

British-born writer and illustrator Christina Balit grew up in the Middle East, and her experiences living in this exotic culture are especially evident in her first published writing, *An Arabian Home: Leila and Mustapha's Story,* as well as in her illustrations for Arabian tales. In addition, even her illustrations of Bible stories are "reminiscent of ancient Near Eastern art," in the opinion of *Booklist* critic Todd Morning, reviewing her work for Lois Rock's *Everlasting Stories: A Family Bible Treasury.* The location of the tale she is illustrating also has an affect on Balit's style; in her self-illustrated titles *Atlantis: The Legend of a Lost City* and *Escape from Pompeii,* for example, she draws on Greek and Mediterranean art styles, respectively, to better place readers inside the setting of each story.

Early in her career in children's books Balit began creating illustrations for picture books by other authors, most dealing with mythology, fairy tales, or Biblical stories. Working with Rock, Balit illustrated stories retold from the Bible, such as the story of Easter, as well

In her art, Christina Balit captures the ancient legends that weave into the plot of Jacqueline Mitton's Once upon a Starry Night. (Illustration copyright © 2003 by Christina Balit. Reproduced by permission of Frances Lincoln Ltd., 4 Torriano Mews, Torriano Ave., London NW5 2RZ, England, and National Geographic Society.)

The story of Moses is one of several tales recreated by Balit in her art for Mary Hoffman's **Kings and Queens of the Bible.** (Illustration copyright © 2008 by Christina Balit. Reprinted by permission of Henry Holt & Company, LLC.)

as Rock's accounts of the lives of the saints. One of these collaborations, *Everlasting Stories,* includes one hundred different tales enhanced by "stunning illustrations and borders on every page," according to Linda Beck in a review for *Library Journal.* Morning, in his *Booklist* review of the same book, praised Balit's artwork for its "vitality."

Balit's work with astrophysicist and author Jacqueline Mitton includes *Zoo in the Sky: A Book of Animal Constellations*, *Kingdom of the Sun: A Book of the Planets,* and *Once upon a Starry Sky: A Book of Constellations,* all which introduce young readers to constellations and the solar system by referencing the stories and legends of the ancient world. Reviewing *Zoo in the Sky* for *Booklist,* Carolyn Phelan commented that the book "certainly has eye appeal," while *Once upon a Starry Sky* features a "text as dynamic as Balit's striking pictures." Although Phelan found Mitton's text for *Zoo in the Sky* less informative than some, she concluded that Balit's illustrations make "a visually dynamic introduction to the animal constellations." In *School Library Journal,* Dona Ratterree enjoyed Mitton's retelling of ten Greek

and Roman stories in *Once upon a Starry Night,* describing Balit's accompanying characteristic gold-foiled images as containing "an enticing riot of color and detail." In *Zodiac: Celestial Circle of the Sun,* another collaboration between author and artist, Mitton's examination of the ancient Babylonian system of prognostication is enhanced by what Phelan described as "large, striking" images mixing "brilliant colors" and "silver foil."

Several of the titles Balit has illustrated have been retellings of traditional myths or stories, from Hercules's Labors to Shahrazad's Arabian tales. In Christopher J. Moore's *Ishtar and Tammuz: A Babylonian Myth of the Seasons,* her artwork brings to life the Babylonian goddess of creation, Ishtar, and Ishtar's son, Tammuz, the god of fertility. When Ishtar realizes that her son is more popular than she is, she jealously banishes him to the land of the dead, only to beg him to return when she realizes that his banishment caused the earth to become lifeless. The goddess of death agrees to release Tammuz, but only for half of the year. "The visual impact of these highly stylized illustrations underscores the dramatic nature of Moore's retelling," commented a reviewer for *Publishers Weekly,* while Karen Morgan, writing in *Booklist,* described Balit's "sumptuous double-page spreads as visually exciting and dramatic."

In *Kings and Queens of the Bible,* a book by Mary Hoffmann, Balit contributes what *School Library Journal* contributor Heidi Estrin described as "jewel-toned, stylized" artwork that creates a "fairy-tale atmosphere" reflecting Hoffman's formal text. In *Kirkus Reviews* a contributor noted the Egyptian influences in Balit's art, citing her use of "glowing highlights of gold and . . . imaginative touches" of red and turquoise. "Using flattened perspectives and backgrounds filled with Egyptian motifs, Balit creates kaleidoscopically patterned illustrations" to bring to life another ancient tale in Nick Would's picture book *The Scarab's Secret,* wrote a *Kirkus Reviews* writer. In *School Library Journal* Coop Renner also praised this work, writing that "vivid illustrations" featuring "long, lean bodies, skewed architectural perspectives, and vibrant Egyptian motifs" combine with Would's "languid and detailed" text to produce an "unusual tale of the bond between a prince of Egypt and a scarab beetle."

Other retellings featuring Balit's art includes Hugh Lupton and Daniel Morden's *The Adventures of Odysseus* as well as *The Lion Book of Wisdom Stories from around the World,* the latter an anthology of fifteen folktales spanning time and culture that are collected and retold by David Self. Described by *Booklist* contributor Hazel Rochman as "an exciting introduction to the classic story" first recounted in Homer's Odyssey, *The Adventures of Odysseus* features artwork that captures the original stories' "power and drama," according to *School Library Journal* critic Grace Oliff, the critic adding that Balit's watercolor and gouache images "incorporate traditional Greek [and] . . . contemporary elements." Although Self's text was characterized as somewhat unfocused, Heidi Estrin nonetheless described the artwork in *The Lion Book of Wisdom Stories from around the World* as "lush and beautiful," while Rochman appraised the work as a combination of "simple, chatty storytelling" and "richly colored collages."

Balit also draws on mythology in her original, self-illustrated works. In *Atlantis,* she uses Plato's legend of the titular sunken city to tell the story of how Poseidon, god of the sea, falls in love with a human woman and marries her. When he comes to live on his new wife's small island, he transforms it into a beautiful and fertile land that their children will rule for generations. When Poseidon's heirs eventually become corrupt, however, the god creates a storm that sinks the island, Atlantis, to the bottom of the sea. "Balit captures the elemental forces that create Atlantis and then destroy it," praised Ilene Cooper in her *Booklist* review. A reviewer for *Publishers Weekly* wrote that the author/illustrator "gracefully retells the story" by using a "sumptuous palette," while Laura Scott commented in *School Library Journal* that Balit's "boldly colored illustrations extend the text with pleasing design."

Balit's self-illustrated *Escape from Pompeii* is inspired more by history than mythology, retelling the story of the eruption of Mount Vesuvius in A.D. 79. Here her tale focuses on two children, Tranio and Livia, who only barely make their way out of Pompeii before the doomed coastal city is completely destroyed. Setting the stage for the disaster through Traino's eyes, Balit explains that Mount Vesuvius was once thought of as the protector of Pompeii. The boy travels throughout the city on his daily errands, only noticing the tremors of the ground beneath him as he reaches his father's theater group. When he realizes the extent of the danger, Traino runs to find his friend Livia to make sure she is safe. Years later, Traino and Livia return to Pompeii and stand on top of layers of ash, beneath which Balit shows the buried city.

Wendy Lukehart, reviewing *Escape from Pompeii* for *School Library Journal,* recommended the book to "children who thrive on disasters" and commented on the the art illustrating the eruption of Mount Vesuvius, calling it "a dramatic spread with a firey-red center." A *Kirkus Reviews* writer noted that the work is "elaborately illustrated," and that Balit's use of stylized poses and period clothing works to make the ancient setting come to life for young readers. A critic for *Publishers Weekly* noted that, while "illustrations dominate this vivid story," *Escape from Pompeii* is "a dramatic, visually exciting look at a cataclysmic event."

Balit once told *SATA:* "I remember the books I kept as a child, and it was always perfectly clear that I was going to make my own. The Middle East left its mark. The world is littered with it. It made sense to surround myself with reference to history and proto-history of the ancient Near East. I had wandered around those ruins often. They were regular weekend picnics, thanks to my parents.

"When one of my books is published, I pick it up and read it to my children. That's when I notice the pictures I worry about, that I wish I had more time to make, that I imagine re-doing. But it's over. The deadline rules us all, as do book fairs and sales trips and proofs by October. Finally the art work goes back in a drawer, rarely on a wall, because it doesn't belong on one.

"So I move on to the next book, trying always to remember that, like an actor, it is my job to honor the text, and not the other way around. I live with an actor, and I feel for him desperately. He can only work when asked, and he shoulders all responsibility for our well-being and upkeep. I can do what I do whether I'm asked or not. I climb that ladder to the loft and just keep doing it. I yearn to write a beautiful play, to paint the perfect book. I blame my parents, of course. They encouraged me not to limit myself to anything, to be confident and go do—go work. If I told them tomorrow that I wanted to drive a train, they'd say 'Great! Why not? Fax us from Mexico.'

"My need to make something from nothing is the reason my blood runs, and I need to keep it thick. I read somewhere that Jacques-Yves Cousteau said 'If we didn't die, we would not appreciate life as we do.' I don't fear dying, but I can't imagine how people live if they don't 'make' things."

Biographical and Critical Sources

PERIODICALS

Booklist, September 1, 1996, Karen Morgan, review of *Ishtar and Tammuz: A Babylonian Myth of the Seasons,* p. 123; November 1, 1998, Carolyn Phelan, review of *Zoo in the Sky: A Book of Animal Constellations,* p. 498; May 15, 2000, Ilene Cooper, review of *Atlantis: The Legend of a Lost City,* p. 1754; July, 2001, Stephanie Zvirin, review of *Atlantis,* p. 2011; January 1, 2002, Todd Morning, review of *Everlasting Stories: A Family Bible Treasury,* p. 854; January 1, 2004, Carolyn Phelan, review of *Once upon a Starry Night,* p. 868; November 15, 2005, Carolyn Phelan, review of *Zodiac: Celestial Circle of the Sun,* p. 49; March 15, 2006, Gillian Engberg, review of *The Scarab's Secret,* p. 53; December 1, 2006, Hazel Rochman, review of *The Adventures of Odysseus,* p. 40; October 1, 2008, Ian Chipman, review of *Kings and Queens of the Bible,* p. 50; July 1, 2009, Hazel Rochman, review of *The Lion Book of Wisdom Stories from around the World,* p. 64.
Kirkus Reviews, October 1, 2003, review of *Escape from Pompeii,* p. 1220; April 15, 2006, review of *The Scarab's Secret,* p. 419; September 15, 2008, review of *Kings and Queens of the Bible.*
Publishers Weekly, July 22, 1996, review of *Ishtar and Tammuz,* p. 242; June 19, 2000, review of *Atlantis,* p. 78; December 15, 2003, review of *Escape from Pompeii,* p. 72.
School Library Journal, May, 2000, Laura Scott, review of *Atlantis,* p. 160; April, 2002, Linda Beck, review of *Everlasting Stories,* p. 140; November, 2003, Wendy Lukehart, review of *Escape from Pompeii,* p. 88; January, 2004, Dona Ratterree, review of *Once upon a Starry Night,* p. 120; January, 2006, Rosalyn Pierini, review of *Zodiac,* p. 121; April, 2006, Coop Renner, review of *The Scarab's Secret,* p. 122; November, 2006, Grace Oliff, review of *The Adventures of Odysseus,* p. 162; November, 2008, Heidi Estrin, review of *Kings and Queens of the Bible,* p. 108; August, 2009, Heidi Estrin, review of *The Lion Book of Wisdom Stories from around the World,* p. 84.

ONLINE

Christina Balit Home Page, http://www.christinabalit.co.uk (January 10, 2010).

Frances Lincoln Web site, http://www.franceslincoln.com/ (January 10, 2010), "Christina Balit."*

*   *   *

BEN-ZVI, Rebeccca Tova
See O'CONNELL, Rebecca

*   *   *

BROOKS, Ron 1948-

Personal

Born April 12, 1948, in Pambula, New South Wales Australia. *Education:* Attended Bairnsdale Technical School, Swinburne Technical School, and Swinburne Institute of Technology; Royal Melbourne Institute of Technology, degree (illustration). *Hobbies and other interests:* Gardening.

Career

Author and illustrator of books for children. Freelance graphic designer and commercial illustrator; teacher; consultant with Australian Children's Television Association; presenter at schools.

Awards, Honors

Best Picture Book of the Year designation, Children's Book Council of Australia (CBCA), 1974, for *The Bunyip of Berkeley's Creek,* 1978, for *John Brown, Rose, and the Midnight Cat,* 2000, for *Fox;* CBCA Picture Book of the Year Highly Commended designation, 1975, and Best Children's Visual Arts Book of the Year Award, 1976, both for *Annie's Rainbow;* CBCA Picture Book of the Year shortlist, Young Australians' Best Books Awards shortlist, and Ashton Scholastic Award for Best Designed Children's Book, all 1996, all for *Old Pig;* Queensland Premier's Literary Award, and Patricia Wrightson Prize, New South Wales Premier's Literary Award, both 2001, both for *Fox.*

Writings

SELF-ILLUSTRATED

Annie's Rainbow, Collins (Sydney, New South Wales, Australia), 1975.
Timothy and Gramps, Collins (Sydney, New South Wales, Australia), 1978.

ILLUSTRATOR

Joan Phipson, *Bass and Billy Martin,* Macmillan of Australia (South Melbourne, Victoria, Australia), 1972.
David Martin, *Hughie,* Blackie (Glasgow, Scotland), 1972.

Jenny Wagner, *The Bunyip of Berkeley's Creek,* Kestrel (Harmondsworth, England), 1973.

Jenny Wagner, *Aranea: A Story about a Spider,* Kestrel (Harmondsworth, England), 1975.

Valerie Weldrick, *Time Sweep,* Hutchinson (Richmond South, Victoria, Australia), 1977.

Jenny Wagner, *John Brown, Rose, and the Midnight Cat,* Kestrel (Harmondsworth, England), 1977.

Ted Greenwood, *The Pochetto Coat,* Hutchinson (Richmond, Victoria, Australia), 1978.

(With Shane McGowan) *The Story of Australia,* Nelson (Melbourne, Victoria, Australia), 1984.

(With others) Mitsumasa Anno, *All in a Day,* Philomel (New York, NY), 1986.

Maurice Burns, *Go Ducks Go!,* Scholastic, Inc. (New York, NY), 1987.

Rosalind Price and Walter McVitty, compilers, *The Macquarie Bedtime Story Book*, Maquarie (Chatswood, New South Wales, Australia), 1987, published as *The Puffin Bedtime Story Book,* Puffin (Ringwood, Victoria, Australia), 1990.

Julia McClelland, *This Baby,* Oxford University Press (Melbourne, Victoria, Australia), 1992, Houghton Mifflin (Boston, MA), 1994.

Jenny Wagner, *Motor Bill and the Lovely Caroline,* Viking (Ringwood, Victoria, Australia), 1994, Ticknor & Fields (London, England), 1995.

Margaret Wild, *Old Pig,* Allen & Unwin (St. Leonards, New South Wales, Australia), 1995, Dial Books (New York, NY), 1996.

Margaret Perversi, *Henry's Bath,* Viking (Ringwood, Victoria, Australia), 1997, Candlewick Press (Cambridge, MA), 2008.

Margaret Perversi, *Henry's Bed,* Viking (Ringwood, Victoria, Australia), 1997, Candlewick Press (Cambridge, MA), 2008.

Ursula Dubosarsky, *Honey and Bear,* Viking (Ringwood, Victoria, Australia), 1998.

Margaret Wild, *Rosie and Tortoise,* DK Pub. (New York, NY), 1999.

Odo Hirsch, *Frankel Mouse,* Allen & Unwin (St. Leonards, New South Wales, Australia), 2000.

Margaret Wild, *Fox,* Allen & Unwin (St. Leonards, New South Wales, Australia), 2000, Kane/Miller (La Jolla, CA), 2001.

Odo Hirsch, *Frankel Mouse and the Bestish Lair,* Allen & Unwin (St. Leonards, New South Wales, Australia), 2002.

Ursula Dubosarsky, *Special Days with Honey and Bear,* Viking (Ringwood, Victoria, Australia), 2002.

Adaptations

Fox was adapted as a stage play by the Monkey Baa Theatre for Young People and produced in New South Wales, Australia, 2008.

Sidelights

In 1974, author-illustrator Ron Brooks received the top honor from the Australian Children's Book Council for the illustrations he contributed to *The Bunyip of Berkeley's Creek,* a book written by Jenny Wagner. This initial success—the first of several awards Brooks has received—convinced him to concentrate his efforts on children's literature full time. One of the first illustrators in Australia to see his books published in other

Ron Brooks teams up with Margaret Wild to produce the humorous picture book Old Pig. (Dial Books for Young Readers, 1996. Illustration © 1995 by Ron Brooks. Reproduced by permission.)

countries, Brooks has since collaborated with several noted Australian authors, among them Margaret Wild, Walter McVitty, and Margaret Perversi. In addition to working as an illustrator, he has also created the original, self-illustrated picture books *Annie's Rainbow* and *Timothy and Gramps,* and also works as a sculptor and educator.

Brooks was born in Pambula, New South Wales, Australia, in 1948. He lived in several remote locations in Australia during his childhood years, including the Gippsland Lakes region located on the continent's south coast. In comments provided to Grace Allen Hogarth for *Illustrators of Children's Books, 1967-76,* Brooks noted that the freedom he experienced as a boy strongly influenced his decision to write and illustrate books for children: "When I wasn't in school, I was out on the sand dunes, creeks, lakes, islands, exploring the miles of beautiful coastline." He recalled building numerous forts and tree houses, and floating on nearby rivers and lakes using homemade rafts and canoes.

At age fifteen, Brooks moved to Melbourne to study art, and he attended several schools and colleges over the next six years. After working as a freelance graphic designer for clients in the advertising and publishing industries, he began writing and illustrating picture books in 1972 and has never looked back. The most satisfying aspect of writing for children, as Brooks explained to Hogarth, is that young readers have the ability to enter and become a part of his stories. "I like to view my art as like that of a maker of windows," he noted, "which each reader, once having entered, is then able to explore, use and reapply his experiences in his own individual way."

In Brooks's first self-illustrated book, *Annie's Rainbow,* Annie is a prim little girl in a white dress who longs to capture a rainbow. She spends most of her time in the garden, waiting for a rainbow to appear and then trying in vain to catch it. One day, she sees a particularly beautiful rainbow and ventures into the woods to find its source, a shining fountain. There Annie meets a sympathetic artist who helps her to achieve her dream by giving her a picture of the rainbow. A *Publishers Weekly* reviewer praised Brooks's "simple story" and "lovely paintings," noting that "misty colors accentuate the dreaminess" of the tale. Similarly, a *Booklist* commentator called *Annie's Rainbow* "a visual treat plus a curiously satisfying tale."

In *Timothy and Gramps* Brooks tells the story of a young boy who feels like an outsider at his school in Dorset, England. Timothy finds relief from his loneliness and isolation by taking long walks with his lively grandfather and exchanging imaginative stories with the older man. Finally, Timothy persuades his grandfather to accompany him to school and speak to his class for "show and tell." After his grandfather entertains the class with colorful tales, Timothy begins to feel more comfortable in relating to his classmates and gains ac-

The childish antics of the young hero of Julia McClelland's **This Baby** *are captured in Brooks' engaging illustrations.* (Illustration copyright © 1992 by Ron Brooks. Reproduced by permission of Houghton Mifflin Harcourt Publishing Company. All rights reserved.)

ceptance as well. Reviewing *Timothy and Gramps, School Library Journal* critic Janet French praised Brooks's pen-and-ink drawings, noting that they are "warmed with the soft colors of the English countryside." Writing in *Growing Point,* Margery Fisher also commended the illustrations in *Timothy and Gramps,* writing that, with "elegant precision," Brooks communicates the "zest and richness" of the relationship between the two main characters.

Brooks's illustration projects for books by other authors include *This Baby* by Julia McClelland, *Henry's Bath* by Perversi, and *Old Pig* and *Fox,* the last two written by popular Australian children's writer Wild. *This Baby* concerns a family of bear-like wombats that is preparing for the arrival of a new baby. Only wombat-child Andrew is alternately angry, frightened, and jealous as his parents' attention is diverted to the upcoming event. He reacts by throwing tantrums, sulking, and having bad dreams, while his loving parents try to reassure him. Finally, when they make Andrew realize how small and helpless the infant will be, he begins to look forward to becoming a big brother. In a review for *School Library Journal,* Susan Hepler praised Brooks's decision to show the family from a position above their den

Continuing his collaboration with Wild, Brooks employs unique perspectives in his dramatic pastel images for the picture book Fox. (Kane/Miller, 2001. Illustration copyright © 2000 by Ron Brooks. Reproduced by permission.)

in his watercolor illustrations, which gave "the fat ursines an even more compressed and cozy look. It's as if readers are looking in on this family drama." Jo Goodman, writing in *Magpies,* called *This Baby* a "sheer delight," adding that the "text and illustrations complement each other perfectly."

Reviewing Brooks's contribution to Jenny Wagner's *Motor Bill and the Lovely Caroline,* a *Publishers Weekly* critic wrote that the artist's "sheer watercolors in ethereal summertime hues lend the story a gentle lyricism." In *Henry's Bath,* one of several books that pair Brooks's art with a story by Perversi, the artist creates pictures that, "full of activity and emotion," capture the "energy and spirit" of a determined young toddler, according to *School Library Journal* reviewer Linda Staskus.

Brought to life in Brooks's pastel watercolor illustrations, *Old Pig* is a poignant story that follows a grandmother pig as she prepares to face the end of her life. After living happily with her granddaughter for many years, one day Old Pig has trouble getting up in the morning to begin the day's routine. When she realizes that her death is near, she prepares herself by returning books to the library, closing her bank account, and paying her bills. Then she takes a walk with her granddaughter in order to enjoy the wonders of nature—such as the play of light on the trees and the taste of rain—one last time. The book's final picture shows the granddaughter alone. In a review for *Booklist,* Ilene Cooper noted that "the soft watercolors are entirely childlike and unpretentious, but Brooks manages to mix the everyday with a beauty that transcends chores and meals." Likewise, as Betsy Hearne noted in the *Bulletin of the Center for Children's Books,* Brooks's illustrations "cast a golden glow over this gentle farewell to life and love,"

while Christina Dorr added in *School Library Journal* that the drawings "successfully extend the unspoken portions of the story." A *Publishers Weekly* reviewer called *Old Pig* "a winning addition to the many books that help children cope with the loss of a loved one."

Other collaborations between Brooks and Wild include *Fox* and *Rosie and Tortoise.* A young rabbit worries about the fragility of her new premature baby brother in *Rosie and Tortoise,* while *Fox* tells a darker story about a wounded magpie whose desire to feel the joy of flight once again exacts a terrible cost. Unable to fly since it was injured in a brush fire, Magpie now perches on the back of her loyal friend, a one-eyed dog, where she can feel the familiar rush of the wind as Dog trots along. However, Magpie wants more, and when a wily fox lures her away from Dog, he leads the bird into danger while also teaching a lesson about the nature of true contentment. In a review of *Fox,* a *Kirkus Reviews* writer cited Brooks for the "expressionistic art" he creates to capture the dark-edged drama in Wild's critically acclaimed story. An Australian Children's Book Council picture book of the year, *Fox* was described by a *Pub-*

Margaret Perversi's family-centered story in **Henry's Bed** *is captured in Brooks's gestured art.* (Illustration copyright © 1997 by Ron Brooks. Reproduced by permission of the publisher Candlewick Press, Inc., Cambridge, MA.)

lishers Weekly reviewer as a "haunting look at friendship and cruelty" in which Brooks's coarsely crafted and "stark" collage artwork features "thick applications of mostly dark paint." In *Booklist* Gillian Engberg deemed Wild's story "bleak and unsetting" as well as "haunting," and Susan Scheps concluded in *School Library Journal* that the book's "dramatic" images in dark, ashy shades, "allow . . . readers to sense the excitement and danger" when the bright orange fox appears in the pages of Wild's resonant allegory.

Biographical and Critical Sources

BOOKS

Kingman, Lee, Grace Allen Hogarth, and Harriet Quimby, compilers, *Illustrators of Children's Books, 1967-1976,* Horn Book (Boston, MA), 1978.

PERIODICALS

Booklist, January 1, 1977, review of *Annie's Rainbow,* p. 663; January 15, 1995, Julie Corsaro, review of *Motor Bill and the Lovely Caroline,* p. 940; May 15, 1996, Ilene Cooper, review of *Old Pig,* p. 1587; December 1, 1999, Michael Cart, review of *Rosie and Tortoise,* p. 715; November 15, 2001, Gillian Engberg, review of *Fox,* p. 585.

Bulletin of the Center for Children's Books, March, 1996, Betsy Hearne, review of *Old Pig,* p. 247.

Growing Point, January, 1979, Margery Fisher, review of *Timothy and Gramps,* p. 3448.

Kirkus Reviews, September 15, 2001, review of *Fox,* p. 1371.

Magpies, July, 1993, Jo Goodman, review of *This Baby.*

Publishers Weekly, June 3, 1996, review of *Old Pig,* p. 82; December 13, 1976, review of *Annie's Rainbow,* p. 62; January 9, 1995, review of *Motor Bill and the Lovely Caroline,* p. 62; September 20, 1999, review of *Rosie and Tortoise,* p. 87; October 8, 2001, review of *Fox,* p. 65.

School Library Journal, September, 1979, Janet French, review of *Timothy and Gramps,* p. 104; August, 1994, Susan Hepler, review of *This Baby,* p. 140; April, 1996, Christina Dorr, review of *Old Pig,* p. 121; December, 2001, Susan Scheps, review of *Fox,* p. 114; August, 2008, Linda Staskus, review of *Henry's Bath,* p. 100.

ONLINE

Allen & Unwin Web site, http://www.allenandunwin.com/ (January 10, 2010), "Ron Brooks."

Aussie Reviews Web site, http://www.ausiereviews.com/ (January 10, 2010), review of *Fox.**

BUTZER, C.M. 1974-

Personal

Born 1974, in Portland, OR. *Education:* Cornish College of the Arts, B.F.A., 1996; School of Visual Arts, M.F.A., 2005.

Addresses

Home and office—Brooklyn, NY. *E-mail*—chris@cmbutzer.com.

Career

Cartoonist, illustrator, and publisher. Wizards of the Coast, Redmond, WA, illustrator and designer; Studio Galante, Florence, Italy, illustrator, 1997-2003; Rabid Rabbit comic anthology, New York, NY, editor-in-chief, 2005—. Lecturer at St. John's University, New York, NY, and School of Visual Arts, New York, NY, beginning 2009.

Writings

(Self-illustrated) *Gettysburg: The Graphic Novel,* Bowen Press/HarperCollins (New York, NY), 2009.

Author and illustrator of *Pow No. 1* (comic anthology); contributor to "Rapid Rabbit" comic anthologies. Contributor of illustrations to publications by Harcourt Brace, Dorling Kindersley, Anness Publishing, Miles Kelly Publishing, and others.

Sidelights

C.M. Butzer, a New York City-based illustrator who co-created the "Rabid Rabbit" series of comic anthologies, is the author of *Gettysburg: The Graphic Novel,* a highly regarded look at one of the pivotal battles of the U.S. Civil War. "I wanted this book to be an introduction for anyone to the story of Gettysburg in 1863," Butzer told Katie Monnin in an online interview for *Graphic Novel Reporter.* "Most books on Gettysburg tend to either focus on the battle or the speech; in this book, I've tried to show that they are interconnected."

In *Gettysburg* Butzer examines both the prologue and the aftermath of the pivotal civil-war battle, focusing not only on the soldiers who saw combat but also the residents of the small Pennsylvania town who bore witness to the incredible events. "Clearly defined art and sharply delineated panels portray all of the horrors of battle," observed a contributor in *Kirkus Reviews,* and Douglas P. Davey, writing in *School Library Journal,* similarly noted that Butzer's "bold images—a slow rain of cannonballs, a solitary corpse on the battlefield—enliven the gray-toned art."

Butzer's attention to detail is a major strength of *Gettysburg,* Monnin noted, the critic stating that the author and illustrator "has done astounding research and went to extraordinary visual lengths to pay tribute to this moment in our national history." "The war has been so well documented that it's almost too much information to process," Butzer remarked in his *Graphic Novel Reporter* interview. "Since it is so rich in primary sources, I did my best to use those directly in the text and as inspiration for the drawings," he explained. "I tried to make up as little as possible—for me, that is the beauty and the challenge of nonfiction comics: to preserve the content as much as possible through my interpretation."

Biographical and Critical Sources

PERIODICALS

Booklist, December 1, 2008, Jesse Karp, review of *Gettysburg: The Graphic Novel,* p. 46.

Kirkus Reviews, December 1, 2008, review of *Gettysburg.*

School Library Journal, November, 2008, Douglas P. Davey, review of *Gettysburg,* p. 150.

ONLINE

C.M. Butzer Home Page, http://www.cmbutzer.com (January 1, 2010).

C.M. Butzer Web log, http://cmbutzer.blogspot.com (January 1, 2010).

Graphic Novel Reporter Online, http://www.graphicnovel reporter.com/ (January 1, 2010), Katie Monnin, interview with Butzer

Rabid Rabbit Web site, http://www.rabidrabbit.org/ (January 1, 2010), "C.M. Butzer."

C

CHABRIAN, Deborah
See CHABRIAN, Deborah L.

*   *   *

CHABRIAN, Deborah L.
(Deborah Chabrian)

Personal

Born in IL; married Ed Martinez (an artist); children: two. *Education:* Parsons School of Design, degree, 1980; attended Art Institute of Chicago and School of Visual Arts; studied with painter Burton Silverman.

Addresses

Home and office—South Kent, CT. *E-mail*—deborah@chabrian.com.

Career

Painter and illustrator. *Exhibitions:* Works exhibited at Morrison Gallery, Kent, CT, 2006; Forbes Gallery, New York, NY, 2007; and in annual exhibitions of the American Watercolor Society, New York, NY, National Watercolor Society, Fullerton, CA, National Academy of Design, New York, NY, National Portrait Institute, New York, NY, Catherine Lorillard Wolfe Art Club, New York, NY, and Society of Illustrators, New York, NY.

Member

American Watercolor Society, National Watercolor Society, Catharine Lorillard Wolfe Art Club.

Awards, Honors

Hallmark Cards National Gold Medal and honor prizes; National Galleries Endowment Award, National Watercolor Society; National Portrait Institute Competition finalist; *Watercolor* cover competition winner, 2008; several awards in juried exhibitions.

Illustrator

Jan Gleiter and Kathleen Thompson, *Pocahontas,* Raintree Children's Books (Milwaukee, WI), 1985.

Peggy Parish, *The Ghosts of Cougar Island,* Dell (New York, NY), 1986.

(As Deborah Chabrian) Dandi Daley Mackall, *The Gift of the Christmas Cookie: Sharing the True Meaning of Jesus' Birth,* Zonderkidz (Grand Rapids, MI), 2008.

Contributor to *Easy Solutions: Color Mixing: How to Mix the Right Colors for the Subject Every Time,* edited by M. Stephen Doherty, Rockport Publishers, 1998.

Sidelights

An accomplished fine artist, Deborah L. Chabrian has earned numerous awards and honors for her sensitive and engaging watercolor paintings. Working from her home studio in an eighteenth-century Connecticut farmhouse, Chabrian primarily creates still lifes and figurative art, often drawing inspiration from her immediate surroundings. "Many of the objects I paint are ones I bought for my home because I appreciated the shape, color, and style," Chabrian remarked in a *Watercolor* magazine interview with M. Stephen Doherty. "I feel passionate about home—I think of mine as my own Giverny—and what it represents to me: a place where I nourish my soul and grow my dreams. I strive to make a life in which it is possible for art to happen, and when it does, I race with the changing light to capture it."

Working in pen and ink as well as water color, Chabrian has also served as the illustrator of several children's picture books, including *The Gift of the Christmas Cookie: Sharing the True Meaning of Jesus' Birth* by Dandi Daley Mackall. Set during the Great Depression of the 1930s, Mackall's story focuses on a young boy named Jack whose father has left home to search for work. On Christmas Eve, Jack and his mother prepare a batch of cookies to give to the needy. As the cookies bake, Jack's mother explains the origin of the holiday treats to her son, noting that woodcarvers during the

Deborah L. Chabrian's illustration projects include The Ghost of Cougar Island *by Peggy Parrish.* (Illustration copyright © 1986 by Deborah Chabrian. Used by permission of Yearling Books, an imprint of Random House Children's Books, a division of Random House, Inc.)

Middle Ages created molds in shapes that told the story of the Nativity. His mother's endearing tale inspires Jack, who offers a gift to a destitute stranger on Christmas morning. According to Joanna K. Fabicon in *School Library Journal,* Chabrian's pictures for *The Gift of the Christmas Cookie* "depict Jack's kitchen as spare but welcoming. The mouthwatering cookies look as if they can satisfy both physical and spiritual hunger." Writing in *Kirkus Reviews,* a contributor also praised Chabrian's work, noting that her "sensitive watercolor illustrations . . . convey Jack's range of emotions."

Describing her art in a *Watercolor* interview, Chabrian stated: "I push the medium . . . to create paintings that are perhaps richer and denser than one would normally expect from a watercolor painting." "I am always searching for the elusive quality created by light that causes something in my gut to react," she explained to Doherty. "I document these fleeting moments in time, not as historical records of fact, but as moods that evoke a sense of time and place. It is important for me to determine what I find most interesting and appealing about a subject so I can emphasize that in my paintings."

Biographical and Critical Sources

PERIODICALS

American Artist, March, 2007, "Into the Heart of the Southwest—Twenty Painters Interpret the Forbes Trinchera Ranch."
Kirkus Reviews, November 1, 2008, review of *The Gift of the Christmas Cookie: Sharing the True Meaning of Jesus' Birth.*
School Library Journal, October, 2008, Joanna K. Fabicon, review of *The Gift of the Christmas Cookie,* p. 96.
Watercolor, winter, 2004, M. Stephen Doherty, "Speaking through Pictures: Connecticut Artist Deborah L. Chabrian First Decides What She Wants to Say in a Watercolor, Then Prioritizes the Elements of the Picture," p. 88; summer, 2008, interview with Chabrian, p. 38.

ONLINE

Deborah L. Chabrian Home Page, http://chabrian.com (January 1, 2010).
Artnet Web site, http://www.artnet.com/ (January 1, 2010), "Deborah L. Chabrian."*

*   *   *

CHAMBERLAIN, Margaret 1954-

Personal

Born June 11, 1954, in London, England; daughter of Sidney George and Rose Myra Chamberlain; married Ian Dicks (an illustrator), May 13, 1978. *Education:* Canterbury College of Art, B.A. (with honors), 1976, Royal College of Art, M.A., 1979.

Addresses

Home—Dorset, England. *E-mail*—marg@margaret chamberlain.co.uk.

Career

Illustrator, beginning 1979.

Awards, Honors

National Federation of Children's Books Award, 1982, for *Fair's Fair* by Leon Garfield; Most Valued Person Award, American Motorcycles Association, for *A Busy Day for a Good Grandmother.*

Writings

SELF-ILLUSTRATED

Touch and Feel ABC Book, Methuen (London, England), 1986.
Playtime Rhymes, Ladybird (Lewiston, ME), 1987.

Margaret Chamberlain (Photograph by Lisa Chillingworth. Reproduced by permission.)

Bedtime Rhymes, Ladybird (Lewiston, ME), 1987.

ABC Rhymes, Ladybird (Loughborough, England), 1988.

Number Rhymes, Ladybird (Loughborough, England), 1988.

Please Don't Torment Tootsie, Hodder Children's (London, England), 2008.

ILLUSTRATOR

Sid Fleischman, *Humbug Mountain,* Gollancz (London, England), 1980.

Jean Watson, *Martha Is Afraid of the Dark,* Lion Pub. Corp. (Belleville, MI), 1980.

Jean Watson, *Matthew Goes to Market,* Lion Pub. Corp. (Belleville, MI), 1980.

Jean Watson, *Dan the Shepherd,* Lion Pub. Corp. (Belleville, MI), 1980.

Jean Watson, *Martha's Busy Morning,* Lion Pub. Corp. (Belleville, MI), 1980.

Sid Fleischman, *The Man on the Moon-eyed Horse,* Gollancz (London, England), 1980.

Brian Ball, *Dennis and the Flying Saucer,* Heinemann London, England), 1980.

Leon Garfield, *Fair's Fair,* Macdonald & Janes (London, England), 1981.

Sing a Song of Sixpence, Blackie (Edinburgh, Scotland), 1981, Harper & Row (New York, NY), 1982.

Jeanne Willis, *The Tale of Georgie Grub,* Andersen (London, England), 1981, Holt, Rinehart & Winston (New York, NY), 1982.

John Inman, *Curtain Up!,* Heinemann (London, England), 1981.

Jeanne Willis, *The Tale of Fearsome Frit,* Andersen (London, England), 1982, Holt, Rinehart & Winston (New York, NY), 1983.

Jasper Hood and Christopher Hood, *Contact with Maldonia,* Heinemann (London, England), 1982.

Gwen Grant, *The Lily Pickle Band Book,* Heinemann (London, England), 1982.

Alison McMorland, collector, *Brown Bread and Butter: Seventy Songs, Rhymes, and Games for Children,* Ward Lock Educational (London, England), 1982.

Mary Hoffman and Chris Callery, *The Buttercup Buskers' Rainy Day,* Heinemann (London, England), 1982.

Georgie Adams, *Mr. Bill and the Runaway Sausages,* Blackie (London, England), 1983.

Margaret Mahy, *The Pirates' Mix-up Voyage: Dark Doings in the Thousand Islands,* J.M. Dent (London, England), 1983, Dial Books for Young Readers (New York, NY), 1993.

Jeanne Willis, *The Thief of Mucky Mabel,* Andersen (London, England), 1984.

Margaret Mahy, *Leaf Magic and Five Other Favourites,* J.M. Dent (London, England), 1984.

Teresa Verschoyle, reteller, *Puss in Boots,* Macmillan Children's Books (London, England), 1984.

Margaret Mahy, *The Birthday Burglar; and A Very Wicked Headmistress,* J.M. Dent (London, England), 1984, David R. Godine (Boston, MA), 1988.

Helen East, *A Cat for a Noisy Day,* Macdonald (London, England), 1984.

Helen East, *A Crocodile out Shopping,* Macdonald (London, England), 1984.

Helen East, *A Tortoise for Bedtime,* Macdonald (London, England), 1984.

Helen East, *A Caterpillar at Breakfast,* Macdonald (London, England), 1984.

Bel Mooney, *I Don't Want To!* (also see below), Methuen Children's (London, England), 1985.

Margaret Mahy, *The Man Whose Mother Was a Pirate,* J.M. Dent (London, England), 1985.

George Adams, *Mr. Bill and the Flying Fish,* Blackie (London, England), 1985.

Bill Graham, *Dear Monster,* Methuen (London, England), 1986.

Bill Graham, *All By Myself: The Toilet Training Book,* Methuen (London, England), 1986.

Catherine Sefton, *Flying Sam,* Hamilton (London, England), 1986.

Janet Matarasso, *Why Can't You Grow Up?,* Cambridge University Press (Cambridge, England), 1986.

Linda Dearsley, *Gordon the Ghost and Sarah Jane,* Macdonald (London, England), 1987.

Helen Cresswell, *Trouble,* Gollancz (London, England), 1987, E.P. Dutton (New York, NY), 1988.

Janet Matarasso, *Angela's New Sister,* Cambridge University Press (Cambridge, England), 1988.

Tony Bradman, *Look Out, He's Behind You!,* Putnam (New York, NY), 1988.

Bel Mooney, *I Can't Find It!* (also see below), Methuen Children's (London, England), 1988.

Bill Graham, *Our Baby Sleeps Anywhere,* Methuen (London, England), 1988.

Bill Graham, *Cinderella Doesn't Live Here Any More,* Methuen (London, England), 1988.

Bill Graham, *Play Safe,* Little Mammoth (London, England), 1989.

André Syson, *Blob's the World,* Fourth Estate (London, England), 1989.

Bel Mooney, *It's Not Fair!* (also see below), Methuen Children's (London, England), 1989.

Mick Gowar, *A Hard Day's Work,* Delacorte Press (New York, NY), 1989.

Tony Bradman, *Who's Afraid of the Big Bad Wolf?,* Aladdin Books (New York, NY), 1989.

Pat Thomson, *The Best Thing of All,* Gollancz (London, England), 1990.

Margaret Greaves, reteller, *Tattercoats,* Clarkson N. Potter (New York, NY), 1990.

Bel Mooney, *Why Not?* (also see below), Methuen Children's (London, England), 1990.

Bel Mooney, *But You Promised!* (also see below), Methuen Children's (London, England), 1990.

Angela McAllister, *The Enchanted Flute,* Aurum (London, England), 1990.

Bel Mooney, *I Know!* (also see below), Methuen Children's (London, England), 1991.

Bel Mooney, *Here's Kitty* (includes *It's Not Fair!, But You Promised!* and *Why Not?*), Methuen Children's (London, England), 1992.

Bel Mooney, *Oh, Kitty!?* (includes *I Don't Want To!, I Can't Find It!,* and *It's Not Fair!*), Methuen Children's (London, England), 1992.

Antonia Barber, reteller, *Tales from Grimm,* Frances Lincoln (London, England), 1992.

Tony Bradman, *Has Anyone Seen Jack?,* Frances Lincoln (London, England), 1992.

Kaye Umansky, *Pass the Jam, Jim,* Red Fox (London, England), 1993.

Margaret Mahy, *A Busy Day for a Good Grandmother,* Margaret K. McElderry Books (New York, NY), 1993.

Sheila Lavelle, *Calamity with the Fiend,* Hamish Hamilton (London, England), 1993.

Judy Hindley, *A Piece of String Is a Wonderful Thing,* Candlewick Press (Cambridge, MA), 1993.

Linda Allen, *Mrs Simkin and the Wishing Well,* Hamish Hamilton (London, England), 1993.

Jackie Vivelo, *Mr. Scatter's Magic Spell,* Dorling Kindersley (London, England), 1993, Houghton Mifflin (New York, NY), 1994.

Malcolm Yorke, *Ritchie F. Dweebly Thunders On!,* Houghton Mifflin (New York, NY), 1994.

Malcolm Yorke, *Miss Butterpat Goes Wild!,* Houghton Mifflin (New York, NY), 1994.

Malcolme Yorke, *Molly the Mad Basher,* Houghton Mifflin (New York, NY), 1994.

Judy Hindley, *The Wheeling and Whirling-around Book,* Candlewick Press (Cambridge, MA), 1994.

Bel Mooney, *I'm Scared,* Methuen (London, England), 1994.

Marjorie Darke, *Imp,* Mammoth (London, England), 1994.

Bel Mooney, *I Wish!,* Methuen (London, England), 1994.

Sheila Lavelle, *The Fiend Next Door,* Puffin (London, England), 1995.

Sheila Lavelle, *My Best Friend,* Puffin (London, England), 1995.

Sheila Lavelle, *Revenge of the Fiend,* Hamish Hamilton (London, England), 1995.

Diana Hendry, *Dog Dottington,* Walker Books (London, England), 1995, published as *Dog Donovan,* Candlewick Press (Cambridge, MA), 1995.

Bel Mooney, *Why Me?,* Methuen Children's (London, England), 1996.

Martin Waddell, *Bears Everywhere,* Candlewick Press (Cambridge, MA), 1996.

Bel Mooney, *I'm Bored!,* Methuen Children's (London, England), 1997.

Thelma Lambert, *The Surprise Disguise,* Hamish Hamilton (London, England), 1997.

Judy Hindley, *Princess Rosa's Winter,* Kingfisher (London, England), 1997, Kingfisher (Boston, MA), 2005.

Kaye Umansky, *You Can Swim, Jim,* Bodley Head (London, England), 1997.

Bel Mooney, *I Don't Want to Say Yes!,* Methuen Children's (London, England), 1998.

Kaye Umansky, *Need a Trim, Jim,* Bodley Head (London, England), 1999.

Bel Mooney, *It's Not My Fault!,* Methuen Children's (London, England), 1999.

Bel Mooney, *Promise You Won't Be Cross,* Methuen Children's (London, England), 1999.

Judy Hindley, *The Little Book of Dogs,* Red Fox (London, England), 2000.

Judy Hindley, *The Little Book of Cats,* Red Fox (London, England), 2000.

Margaret Ryan, *Doris's Brilliant Birthday,* A. & C. Black (London, England), 2001.

Margaret Ryan, *Smudger and the Smelly Fish,* A. & C. Black (London, England), 2001.

Margaret Ryan, *Kevin and the Pirate Test,* A. & C. Black (London, England), 2001.

Margaret Ryan, *Captain Motley and the Pirate's Gold,* A. & C. Black (London, England), 2001.

Jeanne Willis, *New Shoes,* Andersen (London, England), 2002.

Kaye Umansky, *This Is Jane, Jim,* Red Fox (London, England), 2002.

Bel Mooney, *Kitty's BIG Ideas,* Egmont (London, England), 2002.

Judy Hindley, *Dogs Are My Favourite Things,* Random House (London, England), 2002.

Fiona Water, selector, *Wizard Poems,* Macmillan (London, England), 2004.

Bel Mooney, *Mr. Tubs Is Lost!,* Blue Bananas (London, England), 2004, Crabtree Pub. Co. (New York, NY), 2006.

Sally Grindley, *A Big Kiss for Alice,* Bloomsbury Children's (London, England), 2005, published as *It's My School,* Walker & Company (New York, NY), 2006.

Tabitha Black, *Mona Lisa Mystery,* Hodder Children's (London, England), 2007.

Tabitha Black, *Toil and Trouble,* Hodder Children's (London, England), 2007.

Floella Benjamin, *My Two Grannies,* Frances Lincoln (London, England), 2007.

Kaye Umansky, *I Don't Like Gloria!*, Candlewick Press (Cambridge, MA), 2007.

Lynne Rickards, *Pink!*, Chicken House (Frome, England), 2008, Chicken House (New York, NY), 2009.

Fiona Tierney, *Lion's Lunch?*, Chicken House (New York, NY), 2010.

Also illustrator of educational materials and comic strips.

Sidelights

Margaret Chamberlain is a British illustrator whose colorful cartoon art has appeared in the pages of dozens of picture books and beginning readers since the late 1970s. The list of authors whose stories have been brought to life in her artwork includes Sid Fleishman, Margaret Mahy, Kaye Umansky, Tony Bradman, Floella Benjamin, Judy Hindley, and Bel Mooney. Chamberlain's collaboration with popular writer Mahy includes the light-hearted picture books *A Busy Day for a Good Grandmother, Leaf Magic and Five Other Favourites,* and *The Pirates' Mixed-up Voyage: Dark Doings in the Thousand Islands.* Reviewing *The Pirates' Mixed-up Voyage* for *Publishers Weekly,* a critic cited the engaging mix of "goofy, good-natured humor, cartoony characters and a convoluted mystery" as comparable to the work of Roald Dahl, a noted artist/illustrator who was also Chamberlain's tutor during her art studies.

Chamberlain's work for Diana Hendry's *Dog Donovan* was praised by *Booklist* critic Stephanie Zvirin as "cartoonlike watercolors that nicely reflect both the story's comedy and its seriousness." The artist's "loose-lined pictures . . . showcase the expressive characters" in

***Chamberlain's illustration projects include Diana Hendry's amusing story in* Dog Donovan.** (Illustration copyright © 1995 by Margaret Chamberlain. Reproduced by permission of Walker Books Ltd. Published in the U.S. by Candlewick Press, Inc., Cambridge, MA.)

Sally Grindley's *It's My School,* according to Gillian Engberg in the same periodical. *Pink!,* a quirky story by Lynne Rickards about a penguin who wakes up one morning to find that it has turned a very un-penguinish color, features "comical illustrations" by Chamberlain that "suit the exclamatory tone of the text," according to a *Publishers Weekly* contributor.

A new generation of grandmas take center stage in several books illustrated by Chamberlain, among them Mahy's *A Busy Day for a Good Grandmother* and Benjamin's *My Two Grannies.* As Hazel Rochman noted in *Booklist,* Mahy "challenges homey stereotypes" about apron-clad, cookie-baking, grey-haired grannies by following an adventurous grandma who balances babysitting with skateboarding and trail-biking adventures that involve everything from alligators to avalanches. In her pen-and-watercolor illustrations, Chamberlain "pick[s] up the nonsense" of the grandma's activities, Rochman added, while a *Publishers Weekly* contributor noted that Mahy's "sprightly alliterative" text pairs well with art that mirrors "the story's madcap humor and breathless pace . . . with warmth and wit." Benjamin's story finds a young girl working to find a bridge between her calypso-loving Trinidadian grandma Vero and her veddy, veddy British grandmother Alvina. The girls' efforts are enriched by what Mary N. Oluonye described as "humorous cartoons . . . full of bright, vivid colors," while a *Kirkus Reviews* writer concluded that Chamberlain's "childlike" images "add a gently humorous touch" to Benjamin's multicultural story.

Chamberlain often includes dogs in her picture-book art, and in Umansky's *I Don't Like Gloria!* a black-and-white pup is the star of the story. The pup is sulking now that a fluffy, attention-stealing Persian cat has been welcomed into its family. Citing the artist's skill in capturing "facial expressions" in her retro-styled colored-pencil art, Maryann H. Owen added in *School Library Journal* that *I Don't Like Gloria!* addresses "the age-old predicament of feeling supplanted by an unwelcome newcomer." Also featuring dogs—and described by *School Library Journal* contributor Rachael Vilmar as "a tongue-in-cheek look at the proper care of pets"— *Please Don't Tease Tootsie* pairs humorous art with Chamberlain's first original story. In the book, the author/illustrator crafts a sequence of alliterative pleas urging a succession of heavy-handed youngsters to treat their respective pets with gentleness. She pairs each phrase with a "droll and stylized" image featuring her signature bright colors, according to Vilmar. Also reviewing *Please Don't Tease Tootsie,* a *Kirkus Reviews* critic wrote that animals ranging from cats and dogs to newts and rabbits are affectionately captured in "charming, expressive" images that "are both hilarious and sweet."

"Since my childhood I have really been interested in nothing but drawing," Chamberlain once told *SATA,* "so it's just as well I have a talent and have been able to make a career of it. I believe my talent and use of it to be pretty un-self-conscious. I direct my ideas toward

Chamberlain captures the closeness of a multigenerational and multi-ethnic family in her artwork for Floella Benjamin's **My Two Grannies.** (Frances Lincoln Children's Books, 2009. Illustration copyright © Margaret Chamberlain 2007. Reproduced by permission.)

nobody but myself. Ideas have always come to me straight from my imagination. I have always enjoyed escapist 'cosy' stories and have been very lucky to find authors whose vision of the world is similar to mine. I enjoy small, trivial, amusing detail.

"There is a side of my nature that revels in the grotesque and 'Victorianesque.' I illustrated a book by Leon Garfield who is a well-known and respected author of children's tales: he writes in a similar style to [that of nineteenth-century English novelist Charles] Dickens. In working on *Fair's Fair*, I enjoyed capturing the poverty and absolute misery of life in Dickensian London. This book won an award through votes from children of all ages for their favourite book. However 'grown-up' publishers and the U.S. market seem afraid of this type of unidealised thing and I have not been asked to work in this style again.

"I have always enjoyed the pathos of such writers as Hans Andersen and Grimm. These stories do not seem popular with publishers nowadays. Although I believe

children are still fascinated and moved by the misery of others, I think it is a shame that children are too protected by their parents and teachers.

"These thoughts probably give the impression that I am a macabre illustrator which I definitely am not. I think it's very easy for illustrators to be too sentimental in our ideas about what it is like to be a child. We forget how difficult it is and that it's not all easy.

"I have been very lucky that the self-indulgent flights of fancy I enjoy illustrating are enjoyed by enough other people for me to make my living from it."

Biographical and Critical Sources

PERIODICALS

Booklist, October 15, 1993, Hazel Rochman, review of *A Busy Day for a Good Grandmother,* p. 453; March 1,

1995, Stephanie Zvirin, review of *Dog Donovan,* p. 1248; August 1, 2006, Gillian Engberg, review of *It's Not My School,* p. 95.

Horn Book, May-June, 1993, Elizabeth J. Watson, review of *The Pirates' Mixed-up Voyage,* p. 334; July-August, 1993, Ellen Fader, review of *A Piece of String Is a Wonderful Thing,* p. 478.

Kirkus Reviews, June 1, 2006, review of *It's My School,* p. 572; May 15, 2008, review of *Please Don't Tease Tootsie;* September 1, 2008, review of *My Two Grannies;* November 15, 2008, review of *Pink!*

Publishers Weekly, February 15, 1993, review of *The Pirates' Mixed-up Voyage,* p. 239; July 12, 1993, Rochman, review of *A Busy Day for a Good Grandmother,* p. 79; November 15, 1993, reviews of *Mr. Scatter's Magic Spell* and *Miss Butterpat Goes Wild,* both p. 79; February 6, 1995, review of *Dog Donovan,* p. 85; June 12, 2006, review of *It's My School,* p. 51; February 12, 2007, review of *I Don't Like Gloria!,* p. 84; January 5, 2009, review of *Pink!,* p. 49.

School Library Journal, July, 2006, Lisa Gangemi Kropp, review of *Sally, It's My School,* p. 78; May, 2007, Maryann H. Owen, review of *I Don't Like Gloria!,* p. 109; August, 2008, Rachael Vilmar, review of *Please Don't Tease Tootsie,* p. 84; December, 2008, Mary N. Oluonye, review of *My Two Grannies,* p. 84; January, 2009, Amy Lilien-Harper, review of *Pink,* p. 84.

ONLINE

Chicken House Web site, http://doublecluck.com/ (January 15, 2010), "Margaret Chamberlain."

Margaret Chamberlain Home Page, http://www.margaret chamberlain.co.uk (January 15, 2010).

* * *

CHAPMAN, Jane
(Jack Tickle)

Personal

Born 1970, in England; married Tim Warnes (an illustrator); children: Noah, one other son. *Education:* Attended Yeovil Art College; Brighton University, B.A. (graphic design II, first class). *Religion:* Christian. *Hobbies and other interests:* Quilting, embroidery, patchwork, cinema.

Addresses

Home—Somerset, England.

Career

Author and illustrator, 1995—. Worked as a portrait painter, 1995-96; soft-toy designer for Russ Berrie, 1995-97.

Awards, Honors

Times Educational Supplement Junior Information Award, 1999, for *The Emperor's Egg* by Martin Jenkins.

Writings

FOR CHILDREN; SELF-ILLUSTRATED

Peter and Pickle's Puzzling Presents, Magi (London, England), 1995.

Mary's Baby, Artists & Writers Guild Books (New York, NY), 1995.

Hey Diddle, Diddle, and Other Nursery Rhymes, Walker/Early Learning Centre (London, England), 1997.

The Three Little Pigs, and Other Nursery Tales, Walker/Early Learning Centre (London, England), 1997.

Old MacDonald Had a Farm, edited by Gale Pryor, Candlewick Press (Cambridge, MA), 1999.

We Went to Visit a Farm One Day, Walker/Early Learning Centre (London, England), 1999.

Let's Go! (board book), Candlewick Press (Cambridge, MA), 2003.

Let's Build! (board book), Candlewick Press (Cambridge, MA), 2003.

Sing a Song of Sixpence: A Pocketful of Nursery Rhymes and Tales, Candlewick Press (Cambridge, MA), 2004.

ILLUSTRATOR

A.H. Benjamin, *What If?,* Little Tiger Press (Wauwatosa, WI), 1996, published as *Baa, Moo: What Will We Do?,* Little Tiger Press (London, England), 2003.

Susan Akass, *Grizzly Bears,* ABC, 1996.

Julie Sykes, *Dora's Eggs,* Little Tiger Press (Wauwatosa, WI), 1997.

Linda Jennings, *Penny and Pup,* Little Tiger Press (Wauwatosa, WI), 1997.

Tony Mitton, *Where's My Egg?,* Candlewick Press (Cambridge, MA), 1998.

Phyllis Root, *One Duck Stuck,* Candlewick Press (Cambridge, MA), 1998.

Caroline Pitcher, *Don't Be Afraid, Little Foal,* Magi (London, England), 1998.

Caroline Pitcher, *Run with the Wind,* Little Tiger Press (Wauwatosa, WI), 1998.

Vivian French, *The Story of Christmas,* Candlewick Press (Cambridge, MA), 1999.

Julie Sykes, *Smudge,* Little Tiger Press (Wauwatosa, WI), 1999.

Martin Jenkins, *The Emperor's Egg,* Candlewick Press (Cambridge, MA), 1999.

Diana Hendry, *The Very Noisy Night,* Dutton (New York, NY), 1999.

Vivian French, *Noah's Ark, and Other Bible Stories,* Walker/Early Learning Centre (London, England), 2000.

Linda Cornwell, *Two Hungry Bears,* NP, 2000.

Nicola Davies, *One Tiny Turtle,* Walker (London, England), 2000, Candlewick Press (Cambridge, MA), 2001.

Karma Wilson, *Bear Snores On,* Simon & Schuster (New York, NY), 2000, board-book edition, 2005.

David Bedford, *Touch the Sky, My Little Bear,* Handprint Books (Brooklyn, NY), 2001.

Diana Hendry, *The Very Busy Day,* Little Tiger (London, England), 2001.

Julie Sykes, *Dora's Chicks,* Tiger Tales (Wilton, CT), 2002.

Peter Kavanagh, *Love like This,* Little Tiger Press (London, England), 2002.

Peter Kavanagh, *I Love My Mama,* Simon & Schuster (New York, NY), 2003.

Karma Wilson, *Bear Wants More,* Margaret K. McElderry Books (New York, NY), 2003.

Claire Freedman, *Dilly Duckling,* Margaret K. McElderry Books (New York, NY), 2004.

Nick Dowson, *Tigress,* Candlewick Press (Cambridge, MA), 2004.

Karma Wilson, *Bear Stays up for Christmas,* Margaret K. McElderry Books (New York, NY), 2004.

Diana Hendry, *The Very Snowy Christmas,* Tiger Tales (Wilton, CT), 2005.

Karma Wilson, *Mortimer's Christmas Manger,* Margaret K. McElderry Books (New York, NY), 2005.

Tim Warnes, *Mommy Mine,* HarperCollins (New York, NY), 2005.

Sally Lloyd Jones, *Time to Say Goodnight,* HarperCollins (New York, NY), 2006.

Karma Wilson, *Bear's New Friend,* Margaret K. McElderry Books (New York, NY), 2006.

Christine Leeson, *The Snow Angel,* Little Tiger (London, England), 2006.

Karma Wilson, *Bear Feels Sick,* Margaret K. McElderry Books (New York, NY), 2007.

Tim Warnes, *Daddy Hug,* HarperCollins (New York, NY), 2007.

Elizabeth Baguley, *A Long Way from Home,* Little Tiger (London, England), 2007, Tiger Tales (New York, NY), 2008.

Karma Wilson, *Where Is Home, Little Pip?,* Margaret K. McElderry Books (New York, NY), 2008.

Karma Wilson, *Bear Feels Scared,* Margaret K. McElderry Books (New York, NY) 2008.

Karma Wilson, *Bear Stays Up for Christmas,* Margaret K. McElderry Books (New York, NY), 2008.

Paul Bright, *The Bears in the Bed and the Great Big Storm,* Good Books (Intercourse, PA) 2008

M. Christina Butler, *The Dark, Dark Night,* Good Books (Intercourse, PA), 2008.

Karma Wilson, *Don't Be Afraid, Little Pip,* Margaret K. McElderry Books (New York, NY), 2009.

Paul Bright, *Grumpy Badger's Christmas,* Good Books (Intercourse, PA), 2009.

Claire Freedman, *When We're Together,* Good Books (Intercourse, PA) 2009.

Karma Wilson, *What's in the Egg, Little Pip?,* Margaret K. McElderry Books (New York, NY) 2010.

ILLUSTRATOR; "HAPPY HONEY" BEGINNING READERS

Laura Godwin, *Happy and Honey,* Margaret K. McElderry Books (New York, NY), 2000.

Laura Godwin, *Honey Helps,* Margaret K. McElderry Books (New York, NY), 2000.

Laura Godwin, *The Best Fall of All,* Margaret K. McElderry Books (New York, NY), 2002.

Laura Godwin, *Happy Christmas, Honey!,* Margaret K. McElderry Books (New York, NY), 2002.

ILLUSTRATOR; UNDER PSEUDONYM JACK TICKLE

Isobel Finn, *The Very Lazy Ladybird,* Little Tiger Press (Wauwatosa, WI), 1999.

Sheridan Cain, *The Crunching, Munching Caterpillar,* Little Tiger Press (Wauwatosa, WI), 2000.

Julie Sykes, *Little Rocket's Special Star,* Little Tiger (London, England), 2000.

Andrew Murray, *The Very Sleepy Sloth,* Little Tiger (London, England), 2003.

Sam Lloyd, *Yummy Yummy Food for My Tummy!,* Little Tiger (London, England), 2003.

Sheridan Cain, *The Teeny Weeny Tadpole,* Little Tiger (London, England), 2005.

ILLUSTRATOR; POP-UP BOOKS; UNDER PSEUDONYM JACK TICKLE

The Very Lazy Lion, Little Tiger (London, England), 2004.

The Very Bouncy Bear, Little Tiger (London, England), 2004.

The Very Happy Hen, Little Tiger (London, England), 2004.

The Very Silly Shark, Little Tiger (London, England), 2004.

The Very Clever Crocodile, Little Tiger (London, England), 2006.

The Very Friendly Firefly, Little Tiger (London, England), 2006.

The Very Smiley Snowman, Little Tiger (London, England), 2006.

Adaptations

One Duck Stuck was adapted as an animated segment of the BBC television program *Words and Pictures.* Several books featuring Chapman's illustrations have been paired with audiocassettes, among them *The Crunching Munching Caterpillar,* Little Tiger, 2005.

Sidelights

A prolific illustrator, British artist Jane Chapman shares her gift for creating engaging animal characters in the pages of picture books such as Tony Mitton's *Where's My Egg?,* Nick Dowson's *Tigress,* Martin Jenkins' award-winning *The Emperor's Egg,* and Karma Wilson's popular *Bear Snores On* and its sequels. Chapman's work features bright colors balanced by realistic details, and she uses subtle variations in hue to both complement and augment the storyline she is illustrating. "I've always loved working in acrylic paint," the artist once explained to *SATA;* "Sometimes I whack it on thickly with lots of textured brushstrokes."

Jane Chapman captures the antic energy of a flummoxed fowl in her artwork for Phillis Root's picture book **One Duck Stuck.** (Illustration copyright © 1998 by Jane Chapman. Reproduced by permission of Walker Books, Ltd. Published in the U.S. by Candlewick Press, Inc., Cambridge, MA.)

Born in Plymouth, England, and raised in a middle-class English family, Chapman graduated from Brighton University with a degree in graphic design, having specialized in illustration. Although she began her career as a portrait painter, she soon realized that she would have to change track. As the artist recalled to *SATA,* "Although my work was commercial, I was never going to be anything other than a penniless artist unless I got some royalties coming in!" Reassessing her career path, Chapman decided to follow in the footsteps of her husband, fellow artist Tim Warnes, and change her focus to children's book illustration.

One of Chapman's first illustration projects was the picture book *Mary's Baby,* which features an original story recounting the tale of Christ's birth. Jane Marino, reviewing the work for *School Library Journal,* com-

mented that Chapman's "controlled vocabulary and short sentences" pair with her "round, childlike figures, with button eyes and little black circles for mouths" to "emphasize the simplicity of the story."

While Chapman has produced several more original self-illustrated picture books, and also creates the art accompanying the traditional rhymes and stories in both *Sing a Song of Sixpence: A Pocketful of Nursery Rhymes and Tales* and *Old Macdonald Had a Farm,* most of her time is spent creating artwork for texts written by others. In her work for Julie Sykes' books *Dora's Eggs* and *Dora's Chicks,* about a mother hen focused on raising a family, Chapman was praised for using bold yet simple forms to convey a harmonious impression and a sense of trust. Jane Doonan, writing in *School Librarian,* took particular note of the illustrator's use of colors and "nuances of textures" in her art for *Dora's Eggs,* while in *School Library Journal* Marlene Gawron deemed the artwork in *Dora's Chicks* "large and bright."

Because animal characters are a staple of picture books for young children, Chapman has had the opportunity to bring to life a varied menagerie through her illustrations for stories by an equally varied group of writers that include Phyllis Root, Nick Dowson, Wilson, Laura Godwin, and even her husband, Warnes, with whom she has created *Mommy Mine* and *Daddy Hug.* Calling *Mommy Mine* "a salute to mothers of all types," a *Kirkus Reviews* writer added that as Warnes' text ranges in focus from insect mothers to giraffes to humans, Chapman brings to life each type of mother with affection and a "spirit of whimsy."

While many of Chapman's illustration projects feature cuddly animal characters with human attributes, her work for Dowson's *Tigress* showcases her versatility. In reviewing the book, which introduces young readers to the growth of a tiger cub living in its natural environment, a *Publishers Weekly* contributor praised Chapman's "lifelike, closely focused renderings" of the mother tiger and its growing offspring. In *Booklist* Hazel Rochman cited the illustrator's ability to capture a mother's gentle nurturing in her "bright, clear, double-page acrylic pictures."

Chapman likes to use strong, bright colors, noting that it gives her work a contemporary feel that makes it appealing to her young audience. A *Publishers Weekly* reviewer, commenting on Chapman's work for Phyllis Root's *One Duck Stuck,* noted that "the illustrator revels in juxtaposing strong colors," an assessment the artist would approve of. In *The Emperor's Egg,* an award-winning collaboration with writer Martin Jenkins, her artwork "balances realistic details with the penguin's implicit charm," according to a *Publishers Weekly* reviewer. The same critic credited Chapman with creating "naturalistic acrylics of the frozen environment, against cold violet or warm orange backdrops," and *Times Educational Supplement* reviewer Diana Hinds praised the penguin protagonists in *The Emperor's Egg* as "engaging and characterful without being in the least cute."

In addition to strong color, Chapman emphasizes texture in her art. Her illustrations for *The Very Noisy Night* and *The Very Busy Day* add a new dimension to Diana Hendry's stories by detailing every aspect of the book's setting and integrating these details into the world of Hendry's two mouse protagonists. Thread spools become tables and playing cards are used as beds in the miniature world she creates; postage-stamp pictures, matchbox dresser drawers with button handles, and birthday cake candles for bedside lights spark the imagination of young readers and reveal new discoveries upon each successive turn of the page. In a review of *The Very Busy Day, School Library Journal* contributor Linda M. Kenton cited Chapman's art as "inno-

vative and inviting," adding that "it is delightful to examine how resourceful these mice are" in finding new uses for common household objects. In *Booklist* Helen Rosenberg agreed, writing that the book's "bold, colorful paintings contain clever details that will delight youngsters."

In her work for M. Christina Butler's *The Dark, Dark Night,* the story of a foolish frog that becomes frightened upon seeing its own shadow, Chapman creates "lush swamp paintings" that highlight the story's "animal stars," according to Gay Lynn Van Vleck in *School Library Journal,* while a *Kirkus Reviews* writer noted that the story's characters "pop with bold color and apt detail." The action moves from swamp to forest in Sally Lloyd-Jones' *Time to Say Goodnight,* as night falls and creatures big and small find a cozy place to sleep. In *Booklist* Karin Snelson praised Lloyd-Jones' "rhythmic, . . . hypnotic language" and Chapman's "irresistibly cute" baby animal characters, calling *Time to Say Goodnight* "warm and reassuring." The "sweetly expressive" animal characters in the book's soft-toned illustrations "will be a surefire winner with children and parents alike," concluded a *Kirkus Reviews* writer.

A creative collaboration that has yielded particular riches has been Chapman's work with Wilson. The popularity of their first book, *Bear Snores On,* has inspired several more volumes featuring the good-natured brown bear and its affectionate and fun-loving forest friends. In *Bear Snores On* a brown bear, sleeping snugly in its cave during a winter snowstorm, is quietly

Chapman's original illustrations team with several well-known nursery rhymes in **Sing a Song of Sixpence.** (Illustration copyright © 2004 by Jane Chapman. Reproduced by permission of the publisher Candlewick Press, Inc., Cambridge, MA.)

In her colorful digital art, Chapman echoes the tenderness in her story for **The Bears in the Bed and the Great Big Storm.** (Illustration copyright © 2008 by Jane Chapman. Reproduced by permission of Little Tiger Press.)

joined by Mouse. The small fire that Mouse lights attracts the notice of other chilly animals, and soon Squirrel, Hare, Gopher, and Raven have crowded into the toasty-warm cave, sharing snacks and stories. Finally, Bear is awakened from his sleep, but the good-natured creature quickly forgives its friends for interrupting its winter nap. Chapman's "delightful illustrations . . . depicting the animals' party are the perfect accompaniment to [Wilson's] . . . lyrical text," wrote a *Kirkus Reviews* writer of *Bear Snores On,* Heather E. Miller adding in *School Library Journal* that the artist's renderings of the story's animal characters are "infused with warmth and humor."

Other books in the "Bear" chronicles include *Bear Stays up for Christmas, Bear's New Friend,* and *Bear Wants More,* the last which takes place in spring and finds the friends of the newly awoken bear scurrying around as they arrange a post-hibernation feast for their famished friend. "Bear is rendered as appealing as ever," noted a *Kirkus Reviews* writer of the title character in *Bear Wants More,* adding that "this lovable lump of soft brown fur is as cozy and comforting as a well-loved teddy." Another "Bear" story, *Bear Feels Scared,* focuses on Bear's fear of getting lost while on a walk in the woods, and here author and illustrator "once again tap into the psychology of preschoolers," according to a *Publishers Weekly* contributor. Chapman's paintings for the book "perfectly mesh realism with emotional ex-

pression," noted *School Library Journal* contributor Amy Lilien-Harper, the critic adding that the "large, richly colored" artwork in *Bear Feels Scared* make the book an effective choice for group story hours.

Wilson and Chapman introduce another endearing character, a penguin named Little Pip, in the stories *Where Is Home, Little Pip?, Don't Be Afraid, Little Pip,* and *What's in the Egg, Little Pip?* In *Where Is Home, Little Pip?* the baby penguin finds itself lost after a succession of playful activities lead it into unknown territory. In capturing the penguin's search for home, Wilson's "well-structured text" and Chapman's "beautiful" paintings in tones of cool Arctic blue highlighted by warm pink and tan, combine to produce "a wonderful story of a loving family," according to *School Library Journal* critic Mane Marino.

Discussing her work habits on the Walker Books Web site, Chapman explained: "I like to draw and organize roughs in the winter, when the light is bad, and paint all through the summer. I work in acrylic paint, which has been the only medium for me, since I was introduced to it by an art teacher at school. The good thing about acrylic is that you can paint over your mistakes, wiping them clean." The illustrator, who sometimes uses the pseudonym Jack Tickle when publishing her work, once told *SATA* that, "in terms of inspiration, I find my husband a great model! He spends so much time on the research and rough stage, perfecting every little detail, that I feel shamed into trying to follow suit!" The illustrator added that, "although this career wasn't my first choice when I first left college it certainly is now. . . . Now I'm happy to say that I wouldn't do anything else."

Biographical and Critical Sources

PERIODICALS

Booklist, December 1, 1999, Marta Segal, review of *The Very Noisy Night,* p. 711; January 1, 2000, Linda Perkins, review of *The Emperor's Egg,* p. 932; November 1, 2002, Ilene Cooper, review of *Happy Christmas, Honey!,* p. 507; December 1, 2002, Ilene Cooper, review of *Happy and Honey,* p. 97; April 15, 2001, Amy Brandt, review of *Touch the Sky, My Little Bear,* p. 1563; December 1, 2001, Hazel Rochman, review of *One Tiny Turtle,* p. 656; January 1, 2002, Ellen Mandel, review of *Bear Snores On,* p. 868; February 15, 2002, Helen Rosenberg, review of *The Very Busy Day,* p. 1019; December 1, 2002, Kathy Broderick, review of *The Best Fall of All,* p. 674; April 15, 2003, Connie Fletcher, review of *Bear Wants More,* p. 1479; March 1, 2004, Ilene Cooper, review of *Dilly Duckling,* p. 1194; June 1, 2004, Hazel Rochman, review of *Tigress,* p. 1740; September 1, 2004, Hazel Rochman, review of *Sing a Song of Sixpence: A Pocketful of Nursery Rhymes and Tales,* p. 126; May 15, 2005, Hazel Rochman, review of *Mommy Mine,* p. 1667;

February 1, 2006, Karin Snelson, review of *Time to Say Goodnight*, p. 56; November 1, 2008, Daniel Kraus, review of *Where Is Home, Little Pip?*, p. 50.

Bulletin of the Center for Children's Books, November, 2001, review of *One Tiny Turtle*, p. 99; March, 2003, review of *Bear Wants More*, p. 294; July-August, 2004, Hope Morrison, review of *Tigress*, p. 460.

Guardian Education, August 31, 1999, Vivian French, review of *The Very Noisy Night*, p. 5.

Horn Book, July-August, 2004, Margaret A. Bush, review of *Tigress*, p. 466.

Kirkus Reviews, August 15, 2001, review of *One Tiny Turtle*, p. 1210; November 15, 2001, review of *Bear Snores On*, p. 1616; November 1, 2002, review of *Happy Christmas, Honey!*, p. 1618; December 1, 2002, review of *Bear Wants More*, p. 1776; March 1, 2003, review of *I Love My Mama*, p. 389; December 15, 2003, review of *Dilly Duckling*, p. 1450; May 15, 2004, review of *Tigress*, p. 490; July 1, 2004, review of *Sing a Song of Sixpence*, p. 626; November 1, 2004, review of *Bear Stays up for Christmas*, p. 1055; February 15, 2005, review of *Mommy Mine*, p. 237; November 1, 2005, review of *Mortimer's Christmas Manger*, p. 1197; February 15, 2006, review of *Time to Say Goodnight*, p. 186; September 15, 2007, review of *Bear Feels Sick;* April 15, 2008, review of *Daddy Hug;* May 15, 2008, review of *The Dark, Dark Night;* September 15, 2008, reviews of *A Long Way from Home* and *The Bears in the Bed and the Great Big Storm*.

Publishers Weekly, September 18, 1995, review of *Mary's Baby*, p. 98; May 4, 1998, review of *One Duck Stuck*, p. 211; November 15, 1999, reviews of *The Very Noisy Night*, p. 64, and *The Emperor's Egg*, p. 65; October 9, 2000, review of *Honey Helps*, p. 86; November 26, 2001, review of *Bear Snores On*, p. 60; September 23, 2002, review of *Happy Christmas, Honey!*, p. 39; September 30, 2002, review of *The Emperor's Egg*, p. 75; January 20, 2003, review of *I Love My Mama*, p. 80; January 26, 2004, review of *Dilly Duckling*, p. 252; July 5, 2004, review of *Tigress*, p. 55; September 17, 2004, review of *Bear Stays up for Christmas*, p. 61; September 26, 2005, review of *Mortimer's Christmas Manger*, p. 86; February 13, 2006, review of *Time to Say Goodnight*, p. 88; July 21, 2008, review of *Bear Feels Scared*, p. 158.

School Librarian, August, 1997, Jane Doonan, review of *Dora's Eggs*, p. 134; winter, 1999, Lucinda Jacob, review of *The Very Noisy Night*.

School Library Journal, October, 1995, Jane Marino, review of *Mary's Baby*, p. 36; September, 1998, Heide Piehler, review of *Run with the Wind*, p. 179; November, 1999, Robin L. Gibson, review of *The Very Noisy Night;* December, 2000, Wendy S. Carroll, reviews of *Happy and Honey* and *Honey Helps*, p. 108; May, 2001, Linda M. Kenton, review of *Touch the Sky, My Little Bear*, p. 109; December, 2001, Margaret Bush, review of *One Tiny Turtle*, p. 120; January, 2002, Heather E. Miller, review of *Bear Snores On*, p. 114; March, 2002, Linda M. Kenton, review of *The Very Busy Day*, p. 189; July, 2002, Marlene Gawron, review of *Dora's Chicks*, p. 100; October, 2002, Mara Alpert, review of *Happy Christmas, Honey!*, p. 59, and Pamela K. Bomboy, review of *The Best Fall of All*, p. 111; February, 2003, Amy Lilien-Harper, review of *Bear Wants More*, p. 124; April, 2003, Lisa Gangemi Kropp, review of *I Love My Mama*, p. 129; April, 2004, Judith Constantinides, review of *Dilly Duckling*, p. 110; July, 2004, Patricia Manning, review of *Tigress*, p. 69; October, 2004, Jane Marino, review of *Sing a Song of Sixpence*, p. 139; July, 2005, Linda M. Kenton, review of *Mommy Mine*, p. 84; March, 2006, Robin L. Gibson, review of *Time to Say Goodnight*, p. 196; July, 2006, Julie Roach, review of *Bear's New Friend*, p. 90; September, 2007, Susan E. Murray, review of *Bear Feels Sick*, p. 178; October, 2007, Diane Olivo-Posner, review of *The Snow Angel*, p. 101; May, 2008, Anne Parker, review of *Daddy Hug*, p. 111; July, 2008, Gay Lynn Van Vleck, review of *The Dark, Dark Night*, p. 67; September, 2008, Amy Lilien-Harper, review of *Bear Feels Scared*, and Jane Marino, review of *Where Is Home, Little Pip?*, both p. 161; December, 2008, Laura Butler, review of *A Long Way from Home*, p. 84, and Donna Atmur, review of *The Bears in the Bed and the Great Big Storm*, p. 85.

Times Educational Supplement, March 10, 2000, Diana Hinds, review of *The Emperor's Egg*.

ONLINE

Walker Books Web site, http://www.walkerbooks.co.uk/ (January 15, 2010), "Jane Chapman."*

*   *   *

CHAST, Roz 1954-

Personal

Born November 26, 1954, in Brooklyn, NY; daughter of George (a teacher of French and Spanish) and Elizabeth (an assistant principal) Chast; married William Franzen (a writer), September 22, 1984; children: Ian, Nina. *Education:* Attended Kirkland College and Manhattan Art Students League; Rhode Island School of Design, B.F.A., 1977.

Addresses

Home—Ridgefield, CT. *Office*—New Yorker Cartoonists, 25 W. 23rd St., New York, NY 10036.

Career

Cartoonist and book illustrator. *New Yorker,* New York, NY, cartoonist, 1979—. Has also provided art for advertising agencies. *Exhibitions:* Works included in exhibitions at Illustration Gallery, New York, NY, and at Julie Saul Gallery, New York, NY.

Awards, Honors

Pratt Institute, honorary Ph.D., 1998; Museum of Cartoon and Comic Art Festival Award, 2004.

Roz Chast (Photograph by Anne Hall. Reproduced by permission.)

Writings

ILLUSTRATOR; FOR CHILDREN

Jane Read Martin and Patricia Marx, *Now Everybody Really Hates Me,* Harper (New York, NY), 1993.

Alfa-Betty Olsen and Marshall Efron, *Gabby the Shrew,* Random House (New York, NY), 1994.

Jane Read Martin and Patricia Marx, *Now I Will Never Leave the Dinner Table,* HarperCollins (New York, NY), 1995.

Patricia Marx, *Meet My Staff,* HarperCollins (New York, NY), 1998.

Steve Martin, *The Alphabet from A to Y with Bonus Letter, Z!,* Flying Dolphin Press (New York, NY), 2007.

Patricia Marx, *Dot in Larryland: The Big Little Book of An Odd-sized Friendship,* Bloomsbury Children's Books (New York, NY), 2009.

CARTOON COLLECTIONS

Unscientific Americans, Dial (New York, NY), 1982.

Parallel Universes: An Assortment of Cartoons, Harper (New York, NY), 1984.

Mondo Boxo: Cartoon Stories, Harper (New York, NY), 1987.

The Four Elements, Harper (New York, NY), 1988.

Proof of Life on Earth, HarperCollins (New York, NY), 1991.

Childproof: Cartoons about Parents and Children, Hyperion (New York, NY), 1997.

The Party, after You Left, Bloomsbury (New York, NY), 2004.

Theories of Everything: Selected, Collected, and Health-inspected Cartoons, 1978-2006, Bloomsbury (New York, NY), 2006.

ILLUSTRATOR

Allia Zobel, *The Joy of Being Single,* Workman Publishing (New York, NY), 1992.

Henry Beard, Andy Borowitz, and John Boswell, *Rationalizations to Live By,* Workman Pub. (New York, NY), 2000.

Erin McKean, editor, *Weird and Wonderful Words,* foreword by Simon Winchester, Oxford University Press (New York, NY), 2002.

Esther Cohen, *Don't Mind Me, and Other Jewish Lies,* Hyperion (New York, NY), 2008.

Contributor to anthology *Sex and Sensibility: Ten Women Examine the Lunacy of Modern Love,* edited by Liza Donnelly, Twelve (New York, NY), 2008. Contributor of cartoons to periodicals, including *New Yorker, Christopher Street, Village Voice, Money,* and *National Lampoon.*

Sidelights

Hailed by William Goldstein in *Publishers Weekly* as "probably the funniest woman in the world," Roz Chast is a cartoonist whose humorous, offbeat drawings about the absurdities of everyday life have made her popular with readers of the *New Yorker,* where she serves as a staff cartoonist. In addition, Chast has collected her cartoons in books such as *Unscientific Americans, Proof of Life on Earth,* and the succinctly titled *Theories of Everything: Selected, Collected, and Health-inspected Cartoons, 1978-2006,* and has also provided the illustrations for picture books for young readers that feature distinctive human and animal characters. Blending sophisticated ideas with a drawing style that is often described as childlike, Chast "looks at the world with a child's fixity and a child's fears," according to Pope Brock in *People.* According to *Time* writer Lev Grossman, Chast's wiggly lined cartoon drawings "are like entire novels compressed into 4-in. by 3-in. rectangles."

Reviewers often laud Chast as an especially gifted observer of humanity. In his *Booklist* review of her first cartoon collection, *Unscientific Americans,* Alan Moores noted that Chast is "wise in her sense of the absurdities of modern life," while Ben Reuven of the *Los Angeles Times Book Review* called the book "outrageous, inspired, ever-so-slightly demented." Chast's collection *Parallel Universes* was deemed "wickedly funny" by Jonathan Yardley in the *Washington Post Book World.*

In his review of *Proof of Life on Earth,* Ralph Sassone noted that Chast "can be counted on to decode and re-contextualize the small talk, inflated claims, and petty impulses that make up life on this planet—and to make it a hoot." He summed up the cartoonist's work as "a sharp yet democratic vision in which everything under the sun gets a chance to fulfill its absurd potential."

Chast was born in Brooklyn, New York, and grew up as an only child in the Flatbush area of the city. She started drawing as a child, later recalling in *People:* "My first and biggest cartoon love was Charles Addams. I like the creepiness in his cartoons." Addams, the creator of "The Addams Family," was one of the *New Yorker*'s most famous cartoonists. Chast recounted an important grade-school experience for Goldstein in *Publishers Weekly:* "The teacher had some kind of contest for drawing, I don't know what it was. But you know those things that when ladies would put their sweater over their shoulders, to keep them from falling off, there'd be this little kind of chain attached? Well I won one of those! So that kind of really inspired me—'Wow, if this is what drawing can do, I'll just stay with it.'" Chast was also a fan of comics, but remembers that her parents, educators in the Brooklyn public schools, forbade her to read the "*Archie and Veronica* variety; they

weren't educational enough." Instead, her parents would buy her "Classics Illustrated"—"you know, *The Ox-Box Incident* in living color," she said—which she disliked intensely. Fortunately, Chast had a friend with a stack of comics three feet high who exposed her to *Mad* and other less-highbrow publications.

While she was in high school, Chast attended classes at the Art Students League in Manhattan. Considering a career as a painter, she earned a bachelor's degree in fine arts at the Rhode Island School of Design (RISD); however, after graduating, Chast "knew what I really loved to do was cartoons and stuff like that, but I thought that was completely impractical and I'd never be able to do it." Nonetheless, she compiled a portfolio of her work and sought a position as a magazine illustrator, a career she abandoned after a few months when she started to draw cartoons. Riding home on the subway one day, she saw a copy of *Christopher Street* and was pleased to discover that it included cartoons as a regular feature. A short time later, Chast sold her first cartoon to *Christopher Street* for ten dollars. In 1978, she sold her first drawing to the *New Yorker,* eventually procuring a contract from them for first rights to all of her works and, in the early 1990s, becoming one of only two female staff cartoonists at the magazine. At the *New Yorker,* Chast met her husband, William Franzen, who was working on the staff first as a messenger and later as a humor writer. At the prestigious magazine, which is noted for its cartoons, Chast produces several new ideas each week, but only one in six or seven actually makes it into publication.

After publishing five collections of her cartoons and illustrating Allia Zobel's humorous book *The Joy of Being Single,* Chast entered the field of children's literature when she provided the pictures for Jane Read Martin and Patricia Marx's collaboration *Now Everybody Really Hates Me,* published in 1993. In the story, Patty Jane Pepper is sent to her room for assaulting her younger brother during his birthday party. The book explores Patty Jane's fantasies of staying in her room forever—except maybe for visits to her friends. Critics generally appreciated *Now Everybody Really Hates Me* for capturing a familiar childhood experience as well as for the portrayal of stubborn Patty Jane; in addition, reviewers praised Chast for her line-and-wash drawings, which are credited for successfully mirroring the events of the story while adding humorous details and funny asides. *Booklist* reviewer Stephanie Zvirin maintained that Chast "uses expressive, snappy, slightly sophisticated drawings, washed in watercolor, to interpret Patty's tale of childhood woe." Writing in *School Library Journal,* Caroline Parr claimed that it is "Chast's cartoons that make this book stand out." *New York Times* reviewer Andrea Barnet noted that "the marriage of text and pictures is so seamless it seems surprising that Ms. Chast . . . has never done a children's book before."

Chast contributes her quirky cartoon art to **Now I Will Never Leave the Dinner Table,** *an amusing story by Jane Read Martin and Patricia Marx.* (Illustration copyright © 1999 by Roz Chast. Used by permission of HarperCollins Children's Books, a division of HarperCollins Publishers. In the British Commonwealth with permission of The Wylie Agency, LLC.)

Chast's next illustration project was creating art for *Gabby the Shrew.* In this story by Alfa-Betty Olsen and

Marshall Efron a young shrew's constant hunger leads it into a situation where it disrupts a human family before being discovered by its mother. *School Library Journal* reviewer Marilyn Taniguchi asserted that "Chast's clever cartoon illustrations are in tune with the text's hyperbole," while *Booklist* critic Lauren Peterson observed that the book's "delightfully silly cartoons with occasional sound effects . . . nicely reflect the story's slapstick flavor."

With *I Will Never Leave the Dinner Table,* Chast again joins forces with Martin and Marx, creating a sequel to *Now Everybody Really Hates Me.* Patty Jane is now stranded at the dinner table facing a huge pile of spinach at the insistence of her baby-sitter, perfect older sister Joy, who has accused Patty Jane of hiding her portion of spinach in her pocket. Patty Jane digs in her heels, and while she sulks, she freely assassinates her sister's character while imagining how she can get Joy out of her life forever. Mary M. Burns, writing in *Horn Book,* called *Now I Will Never Leave the Dinner Table* "a guffaw-a-minute sitcom with no laugh track needed" and added that Chast's "watercolor-and-line illustrations effectively augment the deadpan text with flamboyant, detailed images to match Patty Jane's unbridled style." In *Booklist* Stephanie Zvirin wrote that "Chast's sophisticated cartoonlike artwork . . . evokes Patty Jane in all her disagreeable glory and provides fine reinforcement for the sardonic humor of the tale," while a *Publishers Weekly* contributor concluded that "Chast makes hay with the hyperbolic text."

Marx and Chast have continued to collaborate on books for children, and their creations include *Meet My Staff* and *Dot in Larryland: The Big Little Book of an Odd-sized Friendship.* Featuring one of the tiniest characters in picture-book history, *Dot in Larryland* follows a girl who is smaller than a raindrop, as well as a giant whose head is literally in the clouds. Although both are lonely, their loneliness ends when they encounter each other and become fast friends. In her illustrations for Marx's offbeat tale, Chast "does a great job of showing the world through the [characters'] two extreme perspectives," according to *Booklist* contributor Hazel Rochman. In *School Library Journal* Kim T. Ha noted that Marx's affinity for made-up words echos that of Dr. Seuss, and Chast contributes additional "wisecracking fun" through her "pen-and-ink and watercolor artwork . . . filled with clever detail and touches" such as dialogue balloons. *Meet My Staff* focuses on a boy named Walter and the servants who do everything that the child does not want to do, from practicing the piano to losing at board games and eating vegetables. Here Chast contributes what *Booklist* critic Stephanie Zvirin described as "a freewheeling cast of dorky characters . . . that match [Marx's] . . . text to perfection," while a *Publishers Weekly* contributor praised the cartoonist for "incorporat[ing] . . . witty details into her rollicking . . . art."

Dubbed a "nutty abecedary" by a *Publishers Weekly* critic, *The Alphabet from A to Y with Bonus Letter Z!* is the result of Chast's collaboration with actor Steve Martin. The book features an alphabet's worth of "surreal situations," each described in Martin's quasi-rhyming couplets and brought to life in Chast's "customary cast of homely, anxious figures," according to a *Kirkus Reviews* writer. In her illustrations, the artist goes beyond the text, adding jottings depicting other thing beginning with the letter in question. According to the *Publishers Weekly* critic, author and illustrator "show their mettle as each other's wacky sidekicks" while transforming *The Alphabet from A to Y with Bonus Letter Z!* into "a dizzying combination of words and pictures." "It's hard not to giggle at the way Chast goes all out with the artwork," Cooper added, recommending the picture book to adults even more than children.

Biographical and Critical Sources

BOOKS

Legends in Their Own Time, Prentice Hall, 1994.
Newsmakers 92, Gale (Detroit, MI), 1992.

PERIODICALS

Booklist, November 15, 1982, Alan Moores, review of *Unscientific Americans,* p. 420; October 15, 1993, Stephanie Zvirin, review of *Now Everybody Really Hates Me,* p. 453; January 1, 1995, Lauren Peterson, review of *Gabby the Shrew,* p. 826; April 1, 1996, Stephanie Zvirin, review of *Now I Will Never Leave the Dinner Table,* pp. 1371-1372; August, 1998, Stephanie Zvirin, review of *Meet My Staff,* p. 2015; November 15, 2007, Ilene Cooper, review of *The Alphabet from A to Z with Bonus Letter Z!,* p. 42; November 15, 2008, Hazel Rochman, review of *Dot in Larryland: The Big Little Book of an Odd-sized Friendship,* p. 49.
Horn Book, September-October, 1996, Mary M. Burns, review of *I Will Never Leave the Dinner Table,* pp. 582-83.
Kirkus Reviews, May 15, 2006, review of *Theories of Everything: Selected, Collected, and Health-inspected Cartoons, 1978-2006* p. 3; April 1, 2008, review of *The Alphabet from A to Y with Bonus Letter Z!*
Los Angeles Times Book Review, October 3, 1982, Ben Reuven, review of *Unscientific Americans,* p. 6; March 14, 1997, Molly Selvin, "Wry Anxiety," p. E1.
New York Times, December 5, 2006, Michiko Katutani, review of *Theories of Everything,* p. E1; June 14, 2009, Cara Buckley, interview with Chast.
New York Times Book Review, April 24, 1994, Andrea Barnet, review of *Now Everybody Really Hates Me,* p. 24.
People, December 2, 1991, Pope Brock, "Drawing on Anxiety," pp. 169-70, 172.
Publishers Weekly, August 14, 1987, William Goldstein, "Chast-Izing the World: An Interview with *The New Yorker*'s Funniest Cartoonist," pp. 82-83; March 11,

1996, review of *Now I Will Never Leave the Dinner Table,* p. 63; August 10, 1998, review of *Meet My Staff,* p. 386; May 24, 2004, review of *The Party, after You Left,* p. 47; October 1, 2007, review of *The Alphabet from A to Z, with Bonus Letter Z!,* p. 55; November 17, 2008, review of *Dot in Larryland,* p. 57.

School Library Journal, March, 1994, Caroline Parr, review of *Now Everybody Really Hates Me,* p. 205; February, 1995, Marilyn Taniguchi, review of *Gabby the Shrew,* p. 78; March, 2003, Linda Wadleigh, review of *Weird and Wonderful Words,* p. 254; February, 2009, Kim T. Ha, review of *Dot in Larryland,* p. 78.

Time, November 13, 2006, Lev Grossman, "Drawing Conclusions," p. 147.

Village Voice Literary Supplement, December, 1991, Ralph Sassone, review of *Proof of Life on Earth,* p. 10.

Washington Post Book World, September 23, 1984, Jonathan Yardley, review of *Parallel Universes: An Assortment of Cartoons,* p. 12.

Women's Wear Daily, November 20, 2006, Emily Holt, interview with Chast.

ONLINE

Julia Saul Gallery Web site, http://www.saulgallery.com/ (January 10, 2010), "Roz Chast."

New Yorker Online, http://www.newyorker.com/ (January 10, 2010), "Roz Chast."*

* * *

COLEMAN, Wim 1926-
(Cole Perriman, a joint pseudonym)

Personal

Born 1926, in IA; married Pat Perrin (a writer); children: Monse. *Education:* Drake University, degrees (theatre, literature, education).

Addresses

Home—San Miguel de Allende, Gto., Mexico. *E-mail*—wim-pat@playsonideas.com.

Career

Author and playwright. Worked variously as an actor, director, waiter, editor, and bartender.

Member

PEN (San Miguel de Allende chapter).

Writings

FOR CHILDREN

(Editor) *Othello,* Perfection Form Co. (Logan, IA), 1987.

(Adaptor with Pat Perrin) *Marilyn Ferguson's Book of Pragmagic: Pragmatic Magic for Everyday Living: Ten Years of Scientific Breakthroughs, Exciting Ideas, and Personal Experiments That Can Profoundly Change Your Life,* illustrated by Kristin Ferguson, Pocket Books (New York, NY), 1990.

(With Pat Perrin) *The Jamais Vu Papers; or, Misadventures in the Worlds of Science, Myth, and Magic,* Harmony Books (New York, NY), 1991.

(Reteller) Mark Twain, *Huckleberry Finn,* Perfection Learning (Logan, IA), 1993.

(Reteller) Stephen Crane, *The Red Badge of Courage,* Perfection Learning (Logan, IA), 1993.

(Reteller with Pat Perrin) Charles Dickens, *A Tale of Two Cities,* Perfection Learning (Logan, IA), 1994.

(Reteller) Mary Shelley, *Frankenstein,* Perfection Learning (Logan, IA), 1994.

(Compiler, as William S.E. Coleman) *Massacre at Wounded Knee: A Collective Autobiography,* Cool Hand Communications (Boca Raton, FL), 1996 published as *Voices of Wounded Knee,* University of Nebraska Press (Lincoln, NE), 2000.

(With Pat Perrin) *Retold Classic Chillers,* illustrated by Sue Cornelison, Perfection Learning (Logan, IA), 1997.

(Editor and author of introduction) *American Quakers,* Discovery Enterprises (Carlisle, MA), 1998.

(With Pat Perrin; editor and author of introduction) *Crime and Punishment: The Colonial Period to the New Frontier,* Discovery Enterprises (Carlisle, MA), 1998.

(With Pat Perrin; editor and author of introduction) *Aviation: Early Flight in America,* Discovery Enterprises (Carlisle, MA), 1999.

(Editor) *The Constitution and the Bill of Rights,* Discovery Enterprises, Ltd. (Carlisle, MA), 1999, second edition, History Compass (Boston, MA), 2006.

(With Pat Perrin) *Sister Anna,* Discovery Enterprises, Ltd. (Carlisle, MA), 2000.

(With Pat Perrin; editor and author of introduction) *The Declaration of Independence,* Discovery Enterprises (Carlisle, MA), 2000.

British Literature 449-1798: In Classic and Modern English, Perfection Learning (Logan, IA), 2001.

(Adaptor) *Nine Muses: Modern Plays from Classic Myths,* Perfection Learning (Logan, IA), 2001.

(With Pat Perrin) *George Washington: Creating a Nation,* Enslow Publishers (Berkeley Heights, NJ), 2004.

(Adaptor) *King Lear,* Perfection Learning Corp. (Logan, IA), 2004.

(Adaptor) *Macbeth,* Perfection Learning Corp. (Logan, IA), 2004.

(Adaptor *Othello,* Perfection Learning Corp. (Logan, IA), 2004.

(With Pat Perrin) *The Mystery of the Piltdown Skull,* Perfection Learning (Logan, IA), 2004.

(With Pat Perrin) *The Mystery of the Cardiff Giant,* Perfection Learning (Logan, IA), 2004.

(With Pat Perrin) *The Mystery of the Murdered Playwright,* Perfection Learning (Logan, IA), 2004.

(With Pat Perrin) *The Mystery of the Vanishing Slaves,* Perfection Learning (Logan, IA), 2004.

(With Pat Perrin) *Colonial Williamsburg,* MyReportLinks.
com Books (Berkeley Heights, NJ), 2005.

(With Pat Perrin) *Martin Luther King, Jr., National Historic Site,* MyReportLinks.com Books (Berkeley Heights, NJ), 2005.

(With Pat Perrin) *The Alamo,* MyReportLinks.com Books (Berkeley Heights, NJ), 2005.

(With Pat Perrin) *The American Civil War,* Greenhaven Press (San Diego, CA), 2005.

(With Pat Perrin) *Iraq in the News: Past, Present, and Future,* MyReportLinks.com Books (Berkeley Heights, NJ), 2006.

(With Pat Perrin) *Osama Bin Laden,* Greenhaven Press (Farmington Hills, MI), 2006.

(With Pat Perrin) *The Amazing Erie Canal and How a Big Ditch Opened Up the West,* MyReportLinks.com Books (Berkeley Heights, NJ), 2006.

(With Pat Perrin) *The Rebellious Californians and the Brave Struggle to Join the Nation,* MyReportLinks.com Books (Berkeley Heights, NJ), 2006.

(With Pat Perrin) *The Transcontinental Railroad and the Great Race to Connect the Nation,* MyReportLinks.com Books (Berkeley Heights, NJ), 2006.

(With Pat Perrin) *What Made the Wild West Wild,* MyReportLinks.com Books (Berkeley Heights, NJ), 2006.

(Reteller with Pat Perrin) Robert Louis Stevenson, *Treasure Island* (graphic novel), illustrated by Greg Rebis, Stone Arch Books (Mankato, MN), 2007.

(With Pat Perrin) *Anna's World,* Chiron, 2008.

(With Pat Perrin) *Racism on Trial: From the Medgar Evers Murder Case to "Ghosts of Mississippi",* Enslow Publishers (Berkeley Heights, NJ), 2009.

Contributor to books, *Retold Northern European Myths,* and *Retold World Myths,* Perfection Learning (Logan, IA), 1993; *Retold Edgar Allan Poe,* Perfection Learning, 2000; *Retold Jack London,* 2001; *Retold Classics: O. Henry,* 2002; and *World War II Chronicle,* Publications International (Lincolnwood, IL), 2007.

OTHER

(With Pat Perrin, under joint pseudonym Cole Perriman) *Terminal Games* (adult mystery novel), Bantam (New York, NY), 1994.

Author of plays produced in New York, NY, and Los Angeles, CA.

Sidelights

An author and playwright, Wim Coleman produces most of his writing in collaboration with his wife, Pat Perrin. Although the couple has produced a science-fiction novel, *Terminal Games,* under the joint pseudonym Cole Perriman, most of their books focus on history and current issues as part of nonfiction series. Geared for high-school students, books such as *George Washington: Creating a Nation, The Alamo, What Made the Wild West Wild,* and *The Amazing Erie Canal and How a Big*

Ditch Opened Up the West gather relevant facts into a readable, well-organized format, while *Osama bin Laden,* which the couple edited, gathers speeches, journal articles, and other documents about the Muslim extremist leader. *What Made the Wild West Wild* was described by *School Library Journal* contributor Deanna Romriell as "a competent introduction to the topic," while in *Booklist* Roger Leslie praised the "succinct chapters" and "clear" text in *The Amazing Erie Canal and How a Big Ditch Opened up the West.*

In addition to their nonfiction works, Coleman and Perrin have also produced illustrated retellings of well-known works of literature that are designed to attract reluctant readers. Reviewing *Treasure Island,* a retelling of the novel by Robert Louis Stevenson, *School Library Journal* critic Joel Bangilan wrote that the book's "narrative, dialogue, and description are rudimentary," allowing the story to be told primarily by the books comic-book-style art. An original novel, *Anna's World,* takes readers back to the 1840s and the life of a young teen growing up in a Shaker community. To break up the tedium of her days spent working as part of the community, Anna meets such famous individuals as Henry David Thoreau and Nathaniel Hawthorne, and also comes to appreciate the values underlying Shaker life. Praising *Anna's World* as "well written" and featuring "good character development," *School Library Journal* contributor Sharon Morrison recommended the novel as "an excellent . . . choice for social-studies classes."

Biographical and Critical Sources

PERIODICALS

Booklist, August, 2005, Hazel Rochman, review of *The Alamo,* p. 2013; October, 2006, Roger Leslie, review of *The Amazing Erie Canal and How a Big Ditch Opened up the West,* p. 66.

Kirkus Reviews, November 1, 2008, review of *Anna's World.*

School Library Journal, March, 2005, Andrew Medlar, review of *George Washington: Creating a Nation,* p. 226; May, 2005, Jody Kopple, review of *The Alamo,* p. 146; April, 2006, Ann W. Moore, review of *Osama bin Laden,* p. 152; December, 2006, Kathleen Gruver, review of *Iraq in the News: Past, Present, and Future,* p. 160; January, 2007, Deanna Romriell, review of *What Made the Wild West Wild,* p. 146, and Joel Bangilan, review of *Treasure Island,* p. 159; March, 2009, Sharon Morrison, review of *Anna's World,* p. 142.

ONLINE

Pat Perrin and Wim Coleman Home Page, http://www. playsonideas.com (January 10, 2010).*

CONNELLY, Gwen 1952-

Personal

Born 1952; married.

Addresses

Home—Chicago, IL; Boca Raton, FL. *E-mail*—info@gwenconnellystudios.com.

Career

Illustrator and fine artist.

Illustrator

Trudy Madler, *Why Did Grandma Die?,* Raintree Children's Books (Milwaukee, WI), 1980.

Margaret Hillert, *Little Red Riding Hood,* Follett (Chicago, IL), 1982, revised and expanded library edition, Norwood House Press (Chicago, IL) 2006.

Rochelle Nielsen Barsuhn, *Afraid,*, Child's World (Elgin, IL), 1982, revised edition published as *Feeling Afraid,* 1983.

Colleen L. Reece, *Thank You,* Child's World (Elgin, IL), 1982, special revised edition published as *Saying Thank You,* 1983.

Phylliss Adams, Eleanore Hartson, and Mark Taylor, *Pippin at the Gym,* Follett (Chicago, IL), 1983.

Phylliss Adams, Eleanore Hartson, and Mark Taylor, *Pippin Cleans Up,* Follett (Chicago, IL), 1983.

Phylliss Adams, Eleanore Hartson, and Mark Taylor, *Pippin Eats Out,* Follett (Chicago, IL), 1983.

Phylliss Adams, Eleanore Hartson, amd Mark Taylor, *Pippin Goes to Work,* Follett (Chicago, IL), 1983.

Phylliss Adams, Eleanore Hartson, and Mark Taylor, *Pippin Learns a Lot,* Follett (Chicago, IL), 1983.

Phylliss Adams, Eleanore Hartson, and Mark Taylor, *Pippin's Lucky Penny,* Follett (Chicago, IL), 1983.

Diane Dow Suire, compiler, *Adventures,* Child's World (Elgin, IL), 1984.

Mary Thornton Blanton, *Knock on a Door,* Dandelion House (Elgin, IL), 1984.

Jane Belk Moncure, *My First Thanksgiving Book,* Childrens Press (Chicago, IL), 1984.

Dotti Hannum and others, *Thanksgiving Handbook,* Child's World, Inc. (Elgin, IL), 1985.

Rochelle Nielsen Barsuhn, *Sometimes I Feel—,* Dandelion House (Elgin, IL), 1985.

Charles Colson with William Coleman, *Being Good Isn't Easy,* Chariot Books (Elgin, IL), 1986.

Charles Colson with William Coleman, *Guess Who's at My Party,* Chariot Books (Elgin, IL), 1986.

Charles Colson with William Coleman, *Trouble in the School Yard,* Chariot Books (Elgin, IL), 1986.

Charles Colson with William Coleman, *Watch out for Becky,* Chariot Books (Elgin, IL), 1986.

(With Krystyna Stasiak) Jane Belk Moncure, *Our Christmas Book,* Child's World (Elgin, IL), 1986.

Mary Lewis Wang, *The Frog Prince,* Children's Press (Chicago, IL), 1986.

Sandra Ziegler, *Our St. Patrick's Day Book,* Child's World (Elgin, IL), 1987.

Dandi Daley Knorr, *Me First,* Standard Publishing (Cincinnati, OH), 1987.

Dandi Daley Knorr, *A Secret Birthday Gift,* Standard Publishing (Cincinnati, OH), 1987.

Dandi Daley Knorr, *A Super Friend,* Standard Publishing (Cincinnati, OH), 1987.

Patricia and Fredrick McKissack *The King's New Clothes,* Children's Press (Chicago, IL), 1987.

Valerie Pankow, *No Bigger than My Teddy Bear,* Abingdon Press (Nashville, TN), 1987.

Madeleine Yates, *Mommy Says It's Nap Time,* Abingdon Press (Nashville, TN), 1988.

Madeleine Yates, *Mommy's Coming Back,* Abingdon Press (Nashville, TN), 1988.

Brendan Patrick Paulsen, *The Luck of the Irish,* Raintree Publishers (Milwaukee, WI), 1989.

Diane Dow Suire, compiler, *Seasons: Favorite Poems,* Child's World (Elgin, IL), 1989.

Sandra Brooks, *I Can Pray to God,* Standard Publishing Company (Cincinnati, OH), 1989.

Janet Riehecky, *Please,* Child's World (Elgin, IL), 1989.

Janet Riehecky, *Thank You,* Child's World (Elgin, IL), 1989.

Janet Riehecky, *After You,* Child's World (Elgin, IL), 1989.

Janet Riehecky, *Excuse Me,* Child's World (Elgin, IL), 1989.

Janet Riehecky, *I'm Sorry,* Child's World (Elgin, IL), 1989.

Janet Riehecky, *May I?,* Child's World (Elgin, IL), 1989.

Janet McDonnell, *Wind: What Can It Do?,* Child's World (Elgin, IL), 1990.

Margaret Driscoll Timmons, reteller, *The Gingerbread Man: A Folk Tale,* Silver Burdett & Ginn (Morristown, NJ), 1990.

El Alfabeto, Passport Books (Lincolnwood, IL), 1991.

Jane Belk Moncure, *Caring for My Home,* Child's World (Mankato, MN), 1991.

Jean Warren, *Ellie the Evergreen,* activity illustrations by Barb Tourtillotte, Warren Publishing House (Everett, WA), 1993.

Henry and Melissa Billings, compilers, *Young People's Stories of Sharing,* Young People's Press (San Diego, CA), 1995.

Henry and Melissa Billings, compilers, *Young People's Stories of Truthfulness,* Young People's Press (San Diego, CA), 1995.

Evangeline Nicholas, *Chicago Winds,* Wright Group (Bothell, WA), 1997.

Connie and Peter Roop, *Let's Celebrate Thanksgiving,* Millbrook Press (Brookfield, CT), 1999.

Connie and Peter Roop, *Let's Celebrate Earth Day,* Millbrook Press (Brookfield, CT), 2001.

Peter and Connie Roop, *Let's Celebrate Presidents' Day,* Millbrook Press (Brookfield, CT), 2001.

Peter and Connie Roop, *Let's Celebrate St. Patrick's Day,* Millbrook Press (Brookfield, CT), 2003.

Maxine Rose Schur, reteller, *The Story of Ruth,* Kar-Ben Publishing (Minneapolis, MN), 2005.

Carol Boyd Leon, *Dayenu!: A Passover Haggadah for Families and Children,* KTAV Publishing House (Jersey City, NJ), 2008.

Also illustrator of various handbooks, activity books, textbooks, and sticker books for children.

Sidelights

In a career that has spanned more than thirty years, artist Gwen Connelly has created illustrations for dozens of books for children. Beginning her career in advertising, Connelly quickly found a niche in illustration, where her colorful oil paintings have enriched everything from fairy tales to nonfiction books about holidays. Turning to fine art as a way to express her feelings in the wake of the September 11, 2001, terrorist attacks, Connelly also creates large-scale oil paintings and mixed-media collage, and she has also worked in the fiber arts.

Characteristic of Connelly's illustration projects, Peter and Connie Roop's picture book *Let's Celebrate Thanks-*

giving features "delightful" images that "increase the appeal of a book," according to Helen Rosenberg in *Booklist*. In the same authors' *Let's Celebrate Earth Day,* Connelly's art helps in "breaking up the text and clarifying information," *Booklist* critic Kay Weisman noted.

Connelly has also lent her talents to several religious-themed books for children. Maxine Rose Schur's *The Book of Ruth* retells the Old Testament story of a young widow who leaves her own people behind to follow her mother-in-law Naomi to Naomi's homeland. A *Publishers Weekly* critic noted that the artist "balances a palette of lush greens, dusty browns and bold jewel tones in her softly lined watercolors." For Carol Boyd Leon's *Dayenu!: A Passover Haggadah for Families and Children,* Connelly's images are paired with readings in-

Gwen Connelly's illustration projects includes creating art for Peter and Connie Roop's **Let's Celebrate St. Patrick's Day.** (Illustration copyright © 2003 by Gwen Connelly. Reproduced by Millbrook Press, a division of Lerner Publishing Group.)

tended to be shared during the Jewish holiday that celebrates the Hebrews' escape from slavery in Egypt. *School Library Journal* contributor Heidi Estrin commented that these illustrations are a "colorful, child-friendly" addition to this book and CD package.

Biographical and Critical Sources

PERIODICALS

Booklist, September 15, 1999, Helen Rosenberg, review of *Let's Celebrate Thanksgiving,* p. 264; May 1, 2001, Kay Weisman, review of *Let's Celebrate Earth Day,* p. 1687.

Publishers Weekly, June 27, 2005, review of *The Story of Ruth,* p. 67.

School Library Journal, October, 2005, Rachel Kamin, review of *The Story of Ruth,* p. 146; March, 2009, Heidi Estrin, review of *Dayenu!: A passover Haggadah for Families and Children,* p. 136.

ONLINE

Gwen Connelly Home Page, http://gwenconnellystudios. com (January 20, 2010).*

D

DANTZ, William R.
See PHILBRICK, Rodman

*   *   *

DAVIS, Tanita S.

Personal

Born in San Francisco, CA; married; husband's name David. *Education:* Mills College, M.F.A., 2004.

Addresses

Home—Glasgow, Scotland. *Agent*—The Chudney Agency, 72 N. State Rd., Ste. 501, Briarcliff Manor, NY 10510.

Career

Writer. Former teacher of juvenile offenders.

Awards, Honors

Coretta Scott King Honor Book citation, American Library Association, 2010, for *Mare's War.*

Writings

Summer of Friends, Review and Herald Pub. Association (Hagerstown, MD), 1999.
Summer of Memories, Review and Herald Pub. Association (Hagerstown, MD), 2000.
A la Carte, Alfred A. Knopf (New York, NY), 2008.
Mare's War, Alfred A. Knopf (New York, NY), 2009.

Sidelights

The author of several young-adult novels, Tanita S. Davis grew up in the San Francisco area and started writing at the age of five, when her mother told her to put on paper everything she wanted to say instead of talking so much. "It was only when I started school that I realized that I was flying solo," Davis recalled to Amy Bowllan on a *School Library Journal* Web log. "As the only African American girl in my first grade class at a private Christian school, for which my parents scrimped and saved, I became shy and silent." Reflecting on her childhood experience as an outsider, the author noted that this "often pushes us to be observers, to sink down into ourselves and become the walls. I was overlooked, but I observed. I listened, I wrote."

In her novel *A la Carte,* Davis introduces seventeen-year-old Lainey, who aspires to be the first African-American vegetarian celebrity chef. Lainey turns to the kitchen for comfort when her friend Simeon disappears and the loan of money she made to him becomes the subject of arguments with her mother. Lainey keeps working toward her goal, entering cooking contests and developing recipes even as she comes to understand the limits of Simeon's friendship. "The tone of the book is sad and lonely, reflecting Lainey's life," and her frustration "is convincingly drawn," KaaVonia Hinton remarked a *Kliatt* review of *A la Carte.* While Davis's debut "at times suffers from awkward wording and slow moments, it's still a book with a lot of heart," Jennifer Barnes wrote in *School Library Journal,* adding that "readers will relate to Lainey." "Davis's first novel shows much promise for good things to come," observed *Booklist* contributor Heather Booth, citing the story's "well-drawn" characters. A *Kirkus Reviews* critic enjoyed the book's "evocative language" and "seamless structure" and concluded that *A la Carte* "is as delightful and fulfilling as the handwritten recipes-in-progress" that are included.

Davis's own family history inspired her novel *Mare's War,* which includes a young African-American woman's experiences serving in the Women's Army Corps (WAC) during World War II. In the novel, teenage sisters Octavia and Tali learn about their grandmother Mare's time in the WAC while on a cross-country trip together. The novel "chronicles a part of our history

Cover of Tanita S. Davis's middle-grade novel **A la Carte,** *featuring artwork by Robert Rodriguez.* (Illustration copyright © 2008 by Robert Rodriguez. Used by permission of Alfred A. Knopf, an imprint of Random House Children's Books, a division of Random House, Inc.)

that is seldom written about but compelling to discover, and Tanita Davis makes it come alive," Augusta Scattergood commented in the *Christian Science Monitor.* "A steady travelogue, realistic banter, memorable characters, and moments of tension, insight, and understanding make this an appealing selection," Gerry Larson remarked in a *School Library Journal* review of *Mare's War,* and a *Kirkus Reviews* critic observed that "the parallel travel narratives are masterfully managed" in a novel that is "absolutely essential reading." In 2010 *Mare's War* was named a Coretta Scott King honor book and was also nominated for an NAACP Image award as an outstanding literary work for youth or teens.

Davis hopes to explore many themes and genres in her work, and by doing so, expand the horizons of her readers. "Stories take me beyond tolerance into the first steps of understanding," she told Bowllan. "And when I walk into my world, I don't feel like I don't know the people around me. I look at them and think, yeah, I have a corner of the quilt that covers you. We're all in the same bed, and the more we can stick together, the more we can keep warm."

Biographical and Critical Sources

PERIODICALS

Booklist, August 1, 2008, Heather Booth, review of *A la Carte,* pp. 57-58.
Christian Science Monitor, July 6, 2009, Augusta Scattergood, review of *Mare's War,* p. 25.
Kirkus Reviews, May 1, 2008, review of *A la Carte;* May 1, 2009, review of *Mare's War.*
Kliatt, July, 2008, KaaVonia Hinton, review of *A la Carte,* pp. 10-11.
School Library Journal, December, 2008, Jennifer Barnes, review of *A la Carte,* pp. 120-121; July, 2009, Gerry Larson, review of *Mare's War,* p. 81.

ONLINE

Brown Bookshelf Web site, http://thebrownbookshelf.com/ (February 11, 2009), "Tanita S. Davis."
School Library Journal Web log, http://www.schoollibrary journal.com/blog/ (September 6, 2009), Amy Bowllan, interview with Davis.
Tanita S. Davis Home Page, http://www.tanitasdavis.com (January 12, 2010).*

*   *   *

DIXON, Ann 1954-
(Ann Renee Dixon)

Personal

Born February 26, 1954, in Richland, WA; daughter of David S. (an engineer) and Barbara (a homemaker) Dixon; married Walter R. Pudwill (a carpenter), May 30, 1982; children: Linnea C. Pudwill, Noranna N. *Education:* University of Washington, B.A. (Swedish language and literature; magna cum laude), 1976; participated in University of Alaska courses, 1987-97. *Religion:* Christian. *Hobbies and other interests:* Reading, writing, swimming, skiing, biking, gardening, basketball.

Addresses

Office—P.O. Box 1009, Willow, AK 99688. *E-mail*—ann@anndixon.com.

Career

Writer, storyteller, and librarian. Storyteller, 1976—; Hoedads, Inc., Eugene, OR, reforestation contractor, 1977-81; freelance writer, 1981—; Willow Public Library, Willow, AK, vice president and member of Willow Library Board, 1981-87, librarian, 1987-97. Willow Elementary School, reading volunteer, 1990-96; presenter at conferences.

Member

Society of Children's Book Writers and Illustrators, Authors Guild, Authors League of America, Alaska Library Association, Alaska Center for the Book, Phi Beta Kappa.

Awards, Honors

Pacific Northwest Booksellers Award for Children's Books, 1994, for *The Sleeping Lady;* Parents Guide to Children's Media award, 1999, National Outdoor Book Award, 2000, and Alaska Battle of the Books selection, 2000-01, all for *Blueberry Shoe;* Literacy in Alaska award, 2000; Notable Social Studies Trade Books for Young People designation, National Council for the Social Studies/Children's Book Council, Benjamin Franklin Award, and Alaska Battle of the Books selection, all 2002, all for *Alone across the Arctic;* Patricia Gallagher Award, Oregon Reading Association, Volunteer State Book Award, Tennessee Library Association/Tennessee Association of School Librarians, and Alaska Battle of the Books selection, all 2003, all for *Big-enough Anna.*

Writings

PICTURE BOOKS

(Reteller) *How Raven Brought Light to People*, illustrated by James Watts, Margaret K. McElderry (New York, NY), 1992.

(Reteller) *The Sleeping Lady,* illustrated by Elizabeth Johns, Alaska Northwest (Portland, OR), 1994.

Merry Birthday, Nora Noël, illustrated by Mark Graham, Eerdmans (Grand Rapids, MI), 1996, new edition published as *Waiting for Noël: An Advent Story,* 2000.

Trick-or-Treat!, illustrated by Larry Di Fiori, Cartwheel/Scholastic (New York, NY), 1998.

Blueberry Shoe, illustrated by Evon Zerbetz, Alaska Northwest (Portland, OR), 1999.

Winter Is, illustrated by Mindy Dwyer, Alaska Northwest (Portland, OR), 2002.

(With Pam Flowers) *Big-enough Anna: The Little Sled Dog Who Braved the Arctic,* illustrated by Bill Farnsworth, Alaska Northwest (Anchorage, AK), 2003.

When Posey Peeked at Christmas, illustrated by Anne Kennedy, Albert Whitman (Morton Grove, IL), 2008.

OTHER

(With Pam Flowers) *Alone across the Arctic: One Woman's Epic Journey by Dog Team* (nonfiction), illustrated with photographs by Flowers, Alaska Northwest (Portland, OR), 2001.

Contributor of poetry to anthology *Once upon Ice, and Other Frozen Poems,* edited by Jane Yolen, Boyds Mills Press, 1997. Contributor to periodicals, including *Country Journal, Cricket, Harrowsmith,* and *Ladybug.*

Adaptations

Author's song "Two Little Feet," first published in *Ladybug* magazine, was recorded on *Sing and Swing with Ladybug,* 1999.

Sidelights

Ann Dixon is the author of several award-winning picture books for children, including *How Raven Brought Light to People* and *Blueberry Shoe.* A resident of Alaska, Dixon has also served as the coauthor of *Alone across the Arctic: One Woman's Epic Journey by Dog Team,* which follows Pam Flowers' trip across the frozen north. One of Alaska's most talented writers for children, Dixon often includes topics and themes from that state in her books. "I love sharing the wonders of reading, writing, and imagination with children," she noted in an essay on her home page.

Born in Richland, Washington, in 1954, Dixon developed a love for reading at an early reading age. "As a child I was hooked on the combination of fresh air and books by riding my bicycle several miles to the local one-room library," she once remarked to *SATA.* "Reading and writing stories were my favorite subjects in school." Dixon attended the University of Washington, majoring in Swedish language and literature. "I spent much of my college time working in or otherwise hanging around libraries," she admitted, and "it was there that I discovered 'formal' storytelling, as opposed to the informal, family storytelling I'd grown up with. I also rediscovered folktales and children's books. At the same

Ann Dixon's story When Posey Peeked at Christmas *is brought to life in Anne Kennedy's humorous art.* (Albert Whitman & Company, 2008. Illustration copyright © 2008 by Anne Kennedy. Reproduced by permission.)

time, while living in a large city I learned that proximity to clean air and water, mountains, trees, birds, dirt, rocks, etc., was essential to my soul."

Out of college, Dixon worked as a reforestation contractor in Oregon before deciding to move north. "I began learning about other cultures, first by learning languages, then by traveling," she explained. "Eventually I settled in Alaska, where nature abounds and numerous cultural influences are at work (and play). As the world shrinks due to increasing opportunities for communication and transportation, I continue to be fascinated with the myriad ways people express their beliefs and imaginations through story."

After moving to Alaska, Dixon became a freelance writer, married, and had two children. She later served as the director of the Willow, Alaska, Public Library, and she credits her work there for rekindling her desire to write. "Because I spent so much time in libraries and around children, reading stacks of picture books, my interest turned naturally back to children's books," Dixon noted on her home page.

Dixon's first published children's book, *How Raven Brought Light to People,* is a retelling of a Native American legend, as is *The Sleeping Lady.* "Alaska's Mount Susitna is the inspiration for this affecting pourquoi story with a pacifist twist," wrote a contributor for *Publishers Weekly* about *The Sleeping Lady.* In Dixon's story, Susitna and Nekatla are among the race of giants residing in the region of Alaska in ancient times, and when news comes of fierce warriors approaching, their wedding is put on hold until Nekatla can teach the invaders peace. Meanwhile, Susitna remains behind sewing and gathering fruits. She waits for her intended, but he never returns as he has been murdered by the invading warriors. Weary of waiting, Susitna slumbers and is soon covered in snow from the frozen tears of her friends, thus creating the mountain that Alaskans know today. "Dixon's serene presentation [in *The Sleeping Lady*] resonates with the simplicity of a Native American legend," noted the *Publishers Weekly* critic.

Other books by Dixon include *Blueberry Sue, Merry Birthday, Nora Noël,* and *Trick-or-Treat!* In *Blueberry Shoe* a baby's lost shoe is at the center of a story about the cycle of life. The baby's family merely thinks of the tennis shoe as lost, but it proves to be a thing of value to a vole and a bear in turn. The next summer, when the baby—now a toddler—finds the shoe while the family is out picking berries, it has become the home of a blueberry plant. A contributor for *Publishers Weekly* found *Blueberry Shoe* to be as "comforting as a serving of warm blueberry cobbler," while *Booklist* critic Linda Perkins wrote that Dixon's "spare narrative introduces indigenous Alaskan animals, contrasting seasons, the joy of rediscovery, and the idea of growth."

In *Winter Is,* a work told in verse, Dixon centers on three young children who enjoy a variety of familiar cold-weather pastimes, such as making snow angels and ice skating on a frozen lake. In addition, the youngsters delight in a host of activities specific to their region, including watching the northern lights and rushing home on a dogsled. Lauren Peterson, writing in *Booklist,* observed that Dixon's "bouncy, rhyming verse describes the action," and *ForeWord* contributor Linda Salisbury similarly noted that the author's "deceptively simple text for *Winter Is* is poetic and packed with details about winter experiences common to anyone who lives where snow can be enjoyed in the country." Writing in *School Library Journal,* Linda Ludke called *Winter Is* "a poetic choice for a seasonal storytime."

A group of mice learns the history of a family heirloom in *When Posey Peeked at Christmas,* a book by Dixon that was described as "a sweet but purposeful storytime filler" by *School Library Journal* critic Anne Connor. With her grandchildren gathered around her under the Christmas tree, an elderly mouse holds a faded red box as she recounts the tale of Posey, a youngster who once spoiled the holiday by giving in to temptation and secretly unwrapping her Christmas presents while her family was out caroling. The next morning, a guilt-ridden Posey finds one last gift in her stocking and decides to leave it unwrapped as a reminder that surprises can bring joy. Writing in *Kirkus Reviews,* a contributor described *When Posey Peeked at Christmas* as a "gracefully written story, which subtly makes the point that peeking at presents doesn't pay off."

Dixon collaborated with Pam Flowers on *Alone across the Arctic,* the true story of Flowers' solo attempt to recreate, in reverse, Norwegian explorer Knud Rasmussen's 1923-24 expedition, a 2,500-mile journey through Alaska and Canada using a team of sled dogs. "This is an engaging survival story with broad appeal," wrote Lee Bock in *School Library Journal,* while *Booklist* contributor David Pitt called *Alone across the Arctic* "an inspiring story" that is "well told." Dixon and Flowers also join forces on *Big-enough Anna: The Little Sled Dog Who Braved the Arctic,* a picture book that focuses on the adventurer's favorite canine, the lead dog during Flowers' 1993 expedition. "More than once," Dixon noted on her home page, "this young dog's incredible persistence not only saved the lives of her team mates and musher, but enabled them to finish the expedition despite nearly overwhelming difficulties." According to *School Library Journal* reviewer Maryann H. Owen, "dog lovers will appreciate this real-life adventure tale starring a loyal and intrepid canine."

Asked why she enjoys writing, Dixon explained on her home page: "Because I like to read. Because writing makes me feel good. Because it's something I can do well, at least some of the time. Because it's satisfying to watch nothing but words and ideas turn into something beautiful I can hold in my hand. Because it makes me happy to think about people enjoying my books and that I might be contributing something useful to the world after all."

Biographical and Critical Sources

PERIODICALS

Booklist, October 15, 1999, Linda Perkins, review of *Blueberry Shoe,* p. 451; September 15, 2001, David Pitt, review of *Alone across the Arctic: One Woman's Epic Journey by Dog Team,* p. 188; January 1, 2003, Lauren Peterson, review of *Winter Is,* p. 905.

ForeWord, January-February, 2003, Linda Salibury, review of *Winter Is.*

Kirkus Reviews, November 1, 2008, review of *When Posey Peeked at Christmas.*

Library Journal, March 1, 2002, John Kenny, review of *Alone across the Arctic,* p. 128.

New York Times Book Review, May 23, 1993, John Bierhorst, review of *How Raven Brought Light to People,* p. 27.

Publishers Weekly, November 14, 1994, review of *The Sleeping Lady,* p. 66; August 23, 1999, review of *Blueberry Shoe,* p. 57.

School Library Journal, April, 1992, Yvonne Frey, review of *How Raven Brought Light to People,* p. 104; May, 1995, Roz Goodman, review of *The Sleeping Lady,* p. 113; October, 1996, Jane Marino, review of *Merry Birthday, Nora Noël,* p. 35; December, 1999, Mollie Bynum, review of *Blueberry Girl,* p. 94; January, 2004, Maryann H. Owen, review of *Big-enough Anna: The Little Sled Dog Who Braved the Arctic,* p. 114; October, 2008, Anne Connor, review of *When Posey Peeked at Christmas,* p. 93.

ONLINE

Ann Dixon Home Page, http://www.anndixon.com (January 1, 2010).*

*   *   *

DIXON, Ann Renee
See DIXON, Ann

*   *   *

DURRANT, Lynda 1954-

Personal

Born December 17, 1954, in Cleveland, OH; daughter of Oliver (an engineer) and Shirley (a teacher) Durrant; married Wesley Lemmon (an executive), May 27, 1989; children: Jonathan. *Education:* University of Washington—Seattle, B.A., 1979, M.A., 1982, M.A.T. *Politics:* "Moderate." *Religion:* Congregationalist. *Hobbies and other interests:* Horses.

Addresses

Home and office—P.O. Box 123, Bath, OH 44210.

Career

Writer and teacher.

Member

Society of Children's Book Writers and Illustrators.

Awards, Honors

Young-Adult Choice designation, International Reading Association, and Books for the Teen Age selection, New York Public Library, both 1996, both for *Echohawk;* Notable Children's Trade Book in the Field of Social Studies selection, National Council for the Social Studies/Children's Book Council, 1998, Ohioana Book Award (juvenile category), Ohioana Library Association, 1999, and Books for the Teen Age selection, New York Public Library, all for *The Beaded Moccasins;* Ohioana Book Award (juvenile category), Quick Picks selection, American Library Association, and Books for the Teen Age selection, New York Public Library, all 2001, all for *Betsy Zane, the Rose of Fort Henry.*

Writings

Echohawk, Clarion Books (New York, NY), 1996.

The Beaded Moccasins: The Story of Mary Campbell, Clarion Books (New York, NY), 1998.

Turtle Clan Journey, Clarion Books (New York, NY), 1999.

Betsy Zane, the Rose of Fort Henry, Clarion Books (New York, NY), 2000.

The Sun, the Rain, and the Apple Seed: A Novel of Johnny Appleseed's Life, Clarion Books (New York, NY), 2003.

My Last Skirt: The Story of Jennie Hodgers, Union Soldier, Clarion Books (New York, NY), 2006.

Imperfections, Clarion Books (New York, NY), 2008.

Contributor to periodicals, including *Jack and Jill* and *Beehive.*

Sidelights

Lynda Durrant's historical young-adult novels focus on pioneer days and on the lives, legends, and hardships of those who traveled and settled the United States in the eighteenth and nineteenth century and the Native Americans who encountered them. Her novels *Echohawk* and *Turtle Clan Journey,* as well as *The Beaded Moccasins: The Story of Mary Campbell* and *Betsy Zane, the Rose of Fort Henry,* all focus on the years leading up to the American Revolution, while both *My Last Skirt: The Story of Jennie Hodgers, Union Soldier* and *Imperfections* are set during the U.S. Civil War.

In *Echohawk,* Durrant's first novel, Jonathan is kidnapped and his family slain by a tribe of Mohicans that fully adopts the boy and teaches him its language and its ways. Renamed Echohawk, Jonathan gradually adopts the Mohican culture and strives to reconcile the two worlds that have figured in his short life. Jonathan's story continues in *Turtle Clan Journey,* as his adopted father and brother are forced to flee to the Ohio Territory. The last of their clan, the trio must keep ahead of the government-sponsored hunters who are now seeking to reclaim any white captives from Native-American bands. Inevitably, Jonathan/Echohawk is ambushed by soldiers and sent to live with his aunt Ruth in a white settlement in Albany, New York. He soon realizes that the material comforts of the white man are no substitute for the freedom and independence of the Mohican. "Durrant does what she does best, sympathetically balancing the differences between Mohican and colonial attitudes," wrote a *Kirkus Reviews* critic, and *Book Report* writer Roger Helmer noted that the author's "wonderful attention to historic detail take[s *Turtle Clan Journey*] . . . to a level beyond the traditional captivity story." Calling Jonathan "a sympathetic protagonist," Michael Cart predicted in his *Booklist* review of *Turtle Clan Journey* that "readers who enjoyed Durrant's first novel will want to read the sequel."

Cover of Lynda Durrant's young-adult novel Turtle Clan Journey, *illustrated by George Pratt.* (Illustration copyright © 1999 by George Pratt. Reprinted by permission of Clarion Books, an imprint of Houghton Mifflin Harcourt Publishing Company. All rights reserved.)

In *The Beaded Moccasins* Durrant presents what *Booklist* contributor Hazel Rochman described as a "strong fictionalization" of the real-life kidnapping of twelve-year-old Mary Campbell by Delaware Indians in 1759 Pennsylvania. Intended to replace the deceased granddaughter of the Delaware chief, Mary is snatched from her family farm in Connecticut and taken on a grueling trip across Pennsylvania, New York, and Ohio into Delaware territory. Together with neighbor Mary Stewart and her toddler son, Mary is forced to walk the many miles to the Dakota reservation. Along the way, the toddler is killed and scalped because he slows the party's progress, and Mary Stewart is traded to a French merchant near Lake Erie. After Mary Campbell is adopted into her new Dakota family, she struggles to adjust to the difficult life and physical hardships of the tribe. Although she yearns for the comforts of her former life and searches for ways to escape, the preteen eventually comes to accept the Dakota lifestyle. Elizabeth Bush, reviewing *The Beaded Moccasins* for the *Bulletin of the Center for Children's Books,* remarked that "Durrant's exceptionally graceful prose and nonjudgmental description of the cultural chasm between the colonists' and Delawares' worlds set this novel apart" from similar works. "The abundant details of the daily habits of the tribe will be beneficial for students," commented Joyce Sparrow in *Voice of Youth Advocates,* the critic adding that "the story of an adolescent forced to adapt to a different culture is fascinating." Durrant's audience "will be moved by the psychological truth of [Mary's] adjustment and her yearning to prove herself and belong," concluded Rochman.

Another brave frontier girl is the focus of *Betsy Zane, the Rose of Fort Henry,* which *School Library Journal* critic Catherine T. Quattlebaum called "a compelling work of period fiction strongly rooted in fact." Twelve-year-old Betsy lives with her great aunt Elizabeth in Revolutionary War-era Philadelphia. Although Betsy's brothers had sent her there to avoid the dangers of war in their home state of Virginia, when Elizabeth dies, the girl has no choice but to rejoin her family. After her great aunt's funeral, Betsy deals with the woman's business affairs and then heads off to join her brothers near Fort Henry. The girl quickly proves herself of value in the war zone: she single-handedly delivers a critical shipment of gunpowder to the soldiers at Fort Henry, sustaining the fort during the siege that proved to be the final battle of the war. Returning to her former life, Betsy encounters cultural prejudices against women, reconsiders her own ideas about slavery, and learns more about herself, her family, and her new fledgling nation. Durrant "has delved deeply into the complex, shifting relations between European settlers and native populations, and she depicts a wide range of attitudes among the Zane family," observed John Peters in a *Booklist* review of *Betsy Zane, the Rose of Fort Henry.* "Exhaustively researched, Durrant's story successfully brings the remarkable Zane family members to life," Quattlebaum remarked, while in *Kliatt* Claire Rosser wrote that Durrant's inclusion of "numerous notes . . . help[s] the reader understand what part of the story is historical fact."

Cover of Durrant's fictional biography **The Sun, the Rain, and the Apple Seed,** *featuring artwork by Stefano Vitale.* (Illustration copyright © 2003 by Stefano Vitale. Reprinted by permission of Clarion Books, an imprint of Houghton Mifflin Harcourt Publishing Company.)

The Sun, the Rain, and the Apple Seed: A Novel of Johnny Appleseed's Life is Durrant's fictionalized biography of John Chapman, the famed historical figure whose sometimes bizarre behavior and single-minded determination gave life to the legend of Johnny Appleseed. Chapman's early childhood experiences of planting apple seeds with his father and watching the apple trees grow and bear fruit led to his adult mission in life, when he decided in 1799 that he would travel the frontiers in Illinois, Indiana, and Ohio, planting apple seeds and ensuring a supply of fruit for later settlers. Chapman's goals were admirable, but sometimes his behavior was odd. He occasionally wore a stew pot for a hat; he talked to angels and spirits; he claimed to be married to a pair of stars he called his spirit wives; and even his casual conversation with other people was filled with Biblical quotations and verses. However, Chapman was also known to be brave and concerned for others, reportedly once running nonstop for three days and nights to warn some settlers of an impending native attack. Eventually, his sincerity and charm won over many of the people concerned about his odd behavior. In an afterword, Durrant expands on

the historical details of Chapman's life. Gillian Engberg, writing in *Booklist,* remarked that the author "creates a vivid portrayal of a historical legend with a powerful vision," and Kristen Oravec noted in *School Library Journal* that Durrant's portrait of Chapman "is well delineated."

Based on a true story, *My Last Skirt* follows Irish immigrant Jennie Hodgers as she disguises herself as a young man named Albert Cashier and sails with her brother to America to escape the poverty created by the Irish potato famine. Having grown accustomed to the freedom to be had in living as a man, Jennie continues the ruse, even joining an Illinois regiment during the Union Army. Despite her success on the battlefield, Jennie is stricken by an unrequited love for a fellow soldier; continuing to pass for a man into her later years, she becomes the first woman to earn a soldier's pension. In *Booklist* Jennifer Mattson praised *My Last Skirt* as a valuable work of historical fiction that "sheds welcome light on an obscure but fascinating . . . figure." Praising the "gripping" story and "vivid details," *School Library Journal* contributor Christina Carey maintained that Jennie/Albert's "loneliness, longing, and missed opportunities will resonate deeply with readers," and a *Kirkus Reviews* writer concluded that "Durrant succeeds brilliantly" in bringing to life a woman who dared to break with convention and then wrestled with the consequences.

Another Civil War-era story, *Imperfections,* follows fifteen-year-old Rosemary Elizabeth Lipking as she and her mother and two other siblings find refuge in a Kentucky Shaker community after escaping from the home they shared with Rosemary's abusive father. Within weeks, Rosemary's mother has gone. Separated from her younger brother and baby sister, the teen is now expected to fully participate in the community. As Sister Bess, she worships, dresses, eats, and sleeps in the Shaker manner, all the while hoping to achieve the perfection that is the goal of that community. As time goes on, Rosemary realizes that her creative nature will not allow her to remain a Shaker forever, and Durrant's "theme of finding oneself will resonate with many teens," according to *School Library Journal* contributor Shannon Seglin. Noting Rosemary's "homespun, present-tense" narration, a *Kirkus Reviews* writer dubbed *Imperfections* a "lovely and thought-provoking" novel, and in *Booklist* Kathleen Isaacs wrote that Durrant's story "rewards readers with an unusual glimpse into a rarely portrayed religion."

"Even when I was a young reader, I knew that I wanted to write for young readers," Durrant once told *SATA*. "I write to a child's enthusiasm, curiosity, and more than anything else, a child's willingness to suspend his disbelief. A children's book could seem outlandish, even repulsive, in any other medium. Children give the writer the benefit of the doubt. That's what makes children's books so special."

Biographical and Critical Sources

PERIODICALS

Booklist, March 15, 1998, Hazel Rochman, review of *The Beaded Moccasins: The Story of Mary Campbell,* pp. 1233-1234; May 1, 1999, Michael Cart, review of *Turtle Clan Journey,* p. 1585; September 15, 2000, John Peters, review of *Betsy Zane, the Rose of Fort Henry,* p. 240; May 15, 2003, Gillian Engberg, review of *The Sun, the Rain, and the Appleseed: A Novel of Johnny Appleseed's Life,* p. 1665; February 15, 2006, Jennifer Mattson, review of *My Last Skirt: The Story of Jennie Hodgers, Union Soldier,* p. 108; November 15, 2008, Kathleen Isaacs, review of *Imperfections,* p. 38.

Book Report, November, 1999, Roger Helmer, review of *Turtle Clan Journey,* p. 60.

Bulletin of the Center for Children's Books, May, 1998, Elizabeth Bush, review of *The Beaded Moccasins,* p. 319; April, 1999, Elizabeth Bush, review of *Turtle Clan Journey,* p. 277.

Kirkus Reviews, April 1, 1999, review of *Turtle Clan Journey,* p. 532; March 15, 2003, review of *The Sun, the Rain, and the Appleseed,* p. 465; February 1, 2006, review of *My Last Skirt,* p. 130; November 1, 2008, review of *Imperfections.*

Kliatt, July, 1998, Claire Rosser, review of *The Beaded Moccasins,* p. 6; March, 2003, Claire Rosser, review of *Betsy Zane, the Rose of Fort Henry,* p. 22.

Publishers Weekly, February 24, 2003, review of *The Sun, the Rain, and the Appleseed,* p. 73.

School Library Journal, June, 1998, Gerry Larson, review of *The Beaded Moccasins,* p. 145; June, 1999, Renee Steinberg, review of *Turtle Clan Journey,* p. 129; April, 2001, Catherine T. Quattlebaum, review of *Betsy Zane, the Rose of Fort Henry,* p. 140; May, 2003, Kristen Oravec, review of *The Sun, the Rain, and the Appleseed,* p. 150; April, 2006, Christina Stenson-Carey, review of *My Last Skirt,* p. 138; April, 2009, Shannon Seglin, review of *Imperfections,* p. 132.

Voice of Youth Advocates, December, 1998, Joyce Sparrow, review of *The Beaded Moccasins,* p. 353.*

Durrant takes readers back to the civil-war era in her novel **Imperfections,** *which features cover art by Alison Jay.* (Illustration copyright © 2008 by Alison Jay. Reprinted by permission of Clarion Books, an imprint of Houghton Mifflin Harcourt Publishing Company.)

*　　*　　*

DYER, Sarah 1978-
(Sarah L. Dyer)

Personal

Born September 3, 1978, in Brighton, England. *Education:* Kingston University, B.A. (illustration), 2001.

Addresses

Home—Hove, E. Sussex, England. *Agent*—Sophie Hicks, Ed Victor, Ltd., 6 Bayley St., Bedford Sq., London WC1B 3HE, England. *E-mail*—sarah@sarahdyer.com.

Career

Writer and illustrator. Kingston University, London, England, part-time instructor.

Awards, Honors

Bronze Smarties' Prize, 2001, and United Kingdom Reading Award, 2002, both for *Five Little Fiends.*

Writings

SELF-ILLUSTRATED

Five Little Fiends, Bloomsbury Children's Books (New York, NY), 2002.

Clementine and Mungo, Bloomsbury (New York, NY), 2004.

Princess for a Day: A Clementine and Mungo Story, Bloomsbury (London, England), 2007.

Mrs. Muffly's Monster, Frances Lincoln (New York, NY), 2008.

The Girl with the Bird's-Nest Hair, Bloomsbury (London, England), 2009.

Monster Day at Work, Frances Lincoln (London, England), 2010.

Sidelights

Sarah Dyer is a British illustrator and children's book writer whose self-illustrated picture books include *Five Little Fiends, Mrs. Muffly's Monster, The Girl with the Bird's-Nest Hair,* and the "Clementine and Mungo" books. Trained at Kingston University, Dyer has taught foundation art courses and illustration classes at the university in addition to establishing her own illustration career. Dyer's debut book, *Five Little Fiends,* won both a Bronze Smarties' prize and a United Kingdom reading award.

Five Little Fiends centers on the greed of five imps who decide to take the things in life they most enjoy. The five individually take the sea, land, sky, sun, and moon. Although they used to discuss how beautiful the world was, their selfish actions show them that each of the objects they took needs the other to work properly, and they eventually restore these stolen objects to the world. *Booklist* contributor Kathy Broderick called the impish characters "appealing" and added that "even the youngest child will recognize feelings of personal greed and group sharing." A contributor to *Publishers Weekly* wrote that, although Dyer's "wordless closing image . . . suggests that wholehearted optimism is premature," this ending "doesn't quash the hopefulness of the narrative."

Dyer introduces two engaging monster siblings in her books *Clementine and Mungo* and *Princess for a Day:*

Sarah Dyer pairs her whimsical stylized artwork with an engaging story in her picture book **Princess for a Day.** (Bloomsbury Children's Books, 2008. Illustration copyright © 2007 by Sarah Dyer. All rights reserved. Reproduced by permission.)

A Clementine and Mungo Story. Clementine and Mungo takes place in a single day, as brother Mungo asks older sister Clementine about everything the siblings encounter. He learns, in the process, that fall leaves change color due to the work of painting pigs, that dragons live inside indoor plumbing systems to heat the water, and that cats unzip their fur coats in the summer to stay cool. A contributor to *Publishers Weekly* described *Clementine and Mungo* as a "quirky tale of childhood imagination and sibling love," and added that "Dyer's illustrations convey both a sophisticated and naive quality, much like Clementine's answers." In *Childhood Education,* Nicole Vosper praised the story for illustrating "the strong bond between siblings," and in *Booklist* Ilene Cooper called Dyer's "uncluttered design . . . a very appealing format" in which to develop her characters. "Dyer gets the sibling relationship just right," Cooper concluded, while in *School Library Journal,* Jane Marino dubbed *Clementine and Mungo* a "short but sweet" story that combines a "spare text and quiet humor" into "an irresistible storytime choice."

Monsters also take center stage in *Mrs. Muffly's Monster,* an imaginative story about an eccentric older woman whose actions convince a young neighbor that she must be sharing her house with a hungry monster. After all, her shopping list for the past week has included dozens of dozens of eggs, pounds of butter, and a wheelbarrow-sized supply of sugar. As readers eventually learn, Mrs. Muffly has competitive baking on her mind, but the little girl's monster fantasy is nonetheless brought to life in "mixed-media" illustrations that "are certain to entertain children," according to *School Library Journal* contributor Donna Atmur. "Childhood logic and a preference for the impossible explodes" in Dyer's "enjoyable tale," concluded a *Kirkus Reviews* writer.

Biographical and Critical Sources

PERIODICALS

Booklist, September 1, 2002, Kathy Broderick, review of *Five Little Fiends,* p. 136; August, 2004, Ilene Cooper, review of *Clementine and Mungo,* p. 1941.
Childhood Education, fall, 2005, Nicole Vosper, review of *Clementine and Mungo.*
Kirkus Reviews, July 15, 2004, review of *Clementine and Mungo,* p. 684; September 15, 2008, review of *Mrs. Muffly's Monster.*
Magpies, November, 2001, review of *Five Little Fiends,* p. 28.
Publishers Weekly, April 29, 2002, review of *Five Little Fiends,* p. 70; July 26, 2004, review of *Clementine and Mungo,* p. 53.
School Library Journal, September, 2002, Heather E. Miller, review of *Five Little Fiends,* p. 189; September, 2004, Jane Marino, review of *Clementine and Mungo,* p. 158; December, 2008, Donna Atmur, review of *Mrs. Muffly's Monster,* p. 86.

ONLINE

Bloomsbury Web site, http://www.bloomsbury.com/ (December 9, 2007), interview with Dyer.
Sarah Dyer Home Page, http://sarahdyer.com (January 10, 2010).

*   *   *

DYER, Sarah L.
See DYER, Sarah

E-F

ELY, Lesley

Personal
Born in England. *Education:* Attended college.

Addresses
Home—Northamptonshire, England.

Career
Educator and writer. Headmistress and teacher of autistic children.

Writings
Looking after Louis, illustrated by Polly Dunbar, Albert Whitman (Morton Grove, IL), 2004.
Measuring Angels, illustrated by Polly Dunbar, Frances Lincoln (New York, NY), 2008.

Sidelights
In *Looking after Louis* British writer Lesley Ely joins illustrator Polly Dunbar to tell a story about a young autistic boy named Louis and his affect on the students who share his classroom. To the story's young narrator, the boy who sits next to her in class is often distracted and communicates in an odd way. However, when Louis joins them in a game of soccer with unusual rules, all the children find a common ground. Featuring an afterword by a clinical psychologist that discusses how teachers, parents, and children can best deal with and help autistic children, *Looking after Louis* was described by a *Kirkus Reviews* writer as a "lesson in tolerance" that is brought to life in Dunbar's "sketch," naïf cartoon drawings. In *Booklist* Connie Fletcher noted that younger children might not understand what makes Louis different than the other characters in Ely's story. Nonetheless, according to Fletcher, *Looking after Louis*

is a "big-hearted" picture book that "is more about creative kindness and inclusion." In *School Library Journal* Kathleen Kelly MacMillan deemed the story an "upbeat look at mainstreaming" that encourages "the development of sensitivity" to school children with special needs.

A second collaboration between Ely and Dunbar, *Measuring Angels* finds that a falling out between a young girl and her best friend can not only bring down their spirits: it even causes plants to wilt! In Miss Miles'

Lesley Ely's humorous story for Measuring Angels *is enhanced by Polly Dunbar's energetic cartoon art.* (Lincoln Children's Books, 2008. Illustration copyright © 2008 by Polly Dunbar. Reproduced by permission.)

class, the two girls are teamed up in a sunflower-growing contest, but while planting and caring for the baby plant the two girls barely speak. Consequently, their seedling seems spindly and listless compared to the more-robust plants of the other teams of young gardeners. When Miss Miles advises them to talk to their plant, the girls gradually turn plant talk into a conversation, mending their friendship and causing their sunflower to flourish. Enlivened by Dunbar's "sunny collage illustrations," *Measuring Angels* effectively captures "the rocky emotional terrain of feuding friends," according to *School Library Journal* contributor Linda Ludke.

Biographical and Critical Sources

PERIODICALS

Booklist, April 15, 2004, Connie Fletcher, review of *Looking after Louis,* p. 1445.
Kirkus Reviews, March 15, 2004, review of *Looking after Louis,* p. 268; December 1, 2008, review of *Measuring Angels.*
School Library Journal, April, 2004, Kathleen Kelly MacMillan, review of *Looking after Louis,* p. 109; March, 2009, Linda Ludke, review of *Measuring Angels,* p. 112.

ONLINE

Frances Lincoln Web site, http://www.franceslincoln.com/ (January 15, 2010), "Lesley Ely."*

* * *

ERNST, Lisa Campbell 1957-

Personal

Born March 13, 1957, in Bartlesville, OK; daughter of Paul Everton (a chemical engineer) and Mardell (an owner of a decorating store) Campbell; married Lee R. Ernst (an art director in advertising), December 27, 1978; children: two daughters. *Education:* University of Oklahoma, B.F.A., 1978. *Hobbies and other interests:* Reading, drawing, gardening.

Addresses

Home—Kansas City, MO. *Office*—207 Westport Rd., Kansas City, MO 64111.

Career

Author and illustrator. Ogilvy & Mather (advertising agency), New York, NY, assistant art director, 1978; writer, illustrator, and book designer, beginning 1978. *Exhibitions: Mirror Magic* included in American Institute of Graphic Arts Book Show, 1981.

Lisa Campbell Ernst (Photograph by Lee Ernst. Reproduced by permission.)

Awards, Honors

Children's Books of the Year designation, Child Study Association of America, 1986, for both *A Colorful Adventure of the Bee* and *Up to Ten and down Again;* Missouri Show-Me Readers Award, 1999, for *Duke, the Dairy Delight Dog;* Bill Martin, Jr., Picture Book Award, 2000, for *Stella Louella's Runaway Book; Parenting* Best Books of the Year designation, 2000, for both *Bear's Day* and *Cat's Play;* Edgar Wolfe Literary Award, Friends of the Library (Kansas City, KS), 2001.

Writings

FOR CHILDREN; SELF-ILLUSTRATED

Sam Johnson and the Blue Ribbon Quilt, Lothrop (New York, NY), 1983.
The Prize Pig Surprise, Lothrop (New York, NY), 1984.
Up to Ten and down Again, Lothrop (New York, NY), 1986.
Hamilton's Art Show, Lothrop (New York, NY), 1986.
(With husband, Lee Ernst) *A Colorful Adventure of the Bee, Who Left Home One Monday Morning and What He Found along the Way,* Lothrop (New York, NY), 1986.

The Rescue of Aunt Pansy, Viking Kestrel (New York, NY), 1987.

Nattie Parsons' Good-Luck Lamb, Viking Kestrel (New York, NY), 1988.

When Bluebell Sang, Bradbury (New York, NY), 1989.

(With husband, Lee Ernst) *The Tangram Magician,* Abrams (New York, NY), 1990.

Ginger Jumps, Bradbury (New York, NY), 1990.

Miss Penny and Mr. Grubbs, Bradbury (New York, NY), 1991.

Walter's Tail, Bradbury (New York, NY), 1992.

Zinnia and Dot, Viking (New York, NY), 1992.

Squirrel Park, Bradbury (New York, NY), 1993.

The Luckiest Kid on the Planet, Bradbury (New York, NY), 1994.

Little Red Riding Hood: A Newfangled Prairie Tale, Simon & Schuster (New York, NY), 1995.

Duke, the Dairy Delight Dog, Simon & Schuster (New York, NY), 1996.

The Letters Are Lost!, Viking (New York, NY), 1996.

Bubba and Trixie, Simon & Schuster (New York, NY), 1997.

Bear's Day, Penguin Putnam (New York, NY), 2000.

Cat's Play, Penguin Putnam (New York, NY), 2000.

Goldilocks Returns, Simon & Schuster (New York, NY), 2000.

Stella Louella's Runaway Book, Simon & Schuster (New York, NY), 2001.

Potato: A Tale from the Great Depression, National Geographic Society (Washington, DC), 2002.

The Three Spinning Fairies: A Tale from the Brothers Grimm, Dutton (New York, NY), 2002.

Hannah Mae O'Hannigan's Wild West Show, Simon & Schuster (New York, NY), 2003.

Spring, HarperCollins (New York, NY), 2004.

Sylvia Jean, Drama Queen, Penguin Putnam (New York, NY), 2004.

Wake up, It's Spring!, HarperCollins (New York, NY), 2004.

The Turn-around Upside-down Alphabet Book, Simon & Schuster (New York, NY), 2004.

This Is the Van That Dad Cleaned, Simon & Schuster (New York, NY), 2005.

The Gingerbread Girl, Dutton Children's Books (New York, NY), 2006.

Round like a Ball!, Chronicle Books (Maplewood, NJ), 2008.

Snow Surprise, Harcourt (Orlando, FL), 2008.

Sylvia Jean, Scout Supreme, Dutton Children's Books (New York, NY), 2010.

ILLUSTRATOR

Alice Siegel and Margo McLoone, *It's a Girl's Game, Too,* Holt (New York, NY), 1980.

Burton Marks and Rita Marks, *Kites for Kids,* Lothrop (New York, NY), 1980.

Louise Murphy, *My Garden: A Journal for Gardening around the Year,* Scribner (New York, NY), 1980.

Seymour Simon, *Mirror Magic,* Lothrop (New York, NY), 1980.

David Cleveland, *The Frog on Robert's Head,* Coward (New York, NY), 1981.

Marks and Marks, *The Spook Book,* Lothrop (New York, NY), 1981.

Charles L. Blood, *American Indian Games and Crafts,* F. Watts (New York, NY), 1981.

Harriet Ziefert, *Dress Little Bunny,* Viking Penguin (New York, NY), 1986.

Harriet Ziefert, *Play with Little Bunny,* Viking Penguin (New York, NY), 1986.

Harriet Ziefert, *Good Morning, Sun!,* Viking (New York, NY), 1988, reprinted, Chronicle Books (Maplewood, NJ), 2006.

Harriet Ziefert, *Breakfast Time!,* Viking (New York, NY), 1988, reprinted, Chronicle Books (Maplewood, NJ), 2006.

Harriet Ziefert, *Let's Get Dressed,* Viking (New York, NY), 1988.

Harriet Ziefert, *Bye-Bye, Daddy!,* Viking (New York, NY), 1988.

Harriet Ziefert, *Count with Little Bunny,* Viking (New York, NY), 1988.

Harriet Ziefert, *Feed Little Bunny,* Viking (New York, NY), 1988.

Mary DeBall Kwitz, *Gumshoe Goose, Private Eye,* Dial (New York, NY), 1988.

Harriet Ziefert, *Little Bunny's Melon Patch,* Puffin (New York, NY), 1990.

Harriet Ziefert, *Little Bunny's Noisy Friends,* Puffin (New York, NY), 1990.

Ruth Young, *Who Says Moo?,* Viking (New York, NY), 1994.

Kate Lied, *Potato: A Tale from the Great Depression,* National Geographic Society (Washington, DC), 1997.

Alex Moran, *Come Here Tiger!,* Harcourt (San Diego, CA), 2001.

Patricia Hubbel, *Sea, Sand, Me!,* HarperCollins (New York, NY), 2001.

Alex Moran, *Boots for Beth,* Harcourt (San Diego, CA), 2003.

Claire Daniel, *The Chick That Wouldn't Hatch,* Harcourt (San Diego, CA), 2003.

Angela Shelf Medearis, *Lucy's Quiet Book,* Harcourt (Orlando, FL), 2004.

Sidelights

Recognized both for her self-illustrated stories and for the books she has illustrated for other authors, Lisa Campbell Ernst creates picture and concept books for younger readers, among them *Duke, the Dairy Delight Dog, Sylvia Jean, Drama Queen,* and the exuberant *Wake up, It's Spring!* Consistently lauded for her skill as an artist and graphic designer, Ernst has been praised as the creator of delightful stories that feature engaging characters and clever concepts. In her illustrations, she uses pen-and-ink and colors her drawn images with layers of pastel and colored pencil.

Born in Bartlesville, Oklahoma, in 1957, Ernst attended the University of Oklahoma, receiving a bachelor of fine arts degree in 1978. She began her career as an as-

Ernst's original self-illustrated picture books include the alphabet story
The Letters Are Lost. (Illustration copyright © 1996 by Lisa Campbell Ernst. Reproduced by permission of Puffin Books, a division of Penguin Putnam Books for Young Readers.)

sistant art director in a New York City advertising firm, and this brief job provided her with a background in design that proved invaluable when she began to illustrate professionally shortly thereafter.

Providing pictures for the works of such authors as Harriet Ziefert and Seymour Simon brought Ernst success as an illustrator and opened the way for the publication of her first self-illustrated picture book, *Sam Johnson and the Blue Ribbon Quilt,* in 1983. Set near the turn of the twentieth century, the book presents a comic inversion of the equal-rights argument as farmer Sam Johnson discovers that he has a talent for quilting. When Sam's wife will not let him join the Women's Quilting Club, Sam organizes a quilting club for men. Through a challenge at the county fair, both clubs eventually cooperate and produce a stunning quilt that combines designs from each camp. Noting the quaint and nostalgic charm of *Sam Johnson and the Blue Ribbon Quilt,* a *Publishers Weekly* reviewer called Ernst "an original and beguiling author," and *School Library Journal* contributor Elizabeth Simmons dubbed the work "a very special addition to the growing list of non-sexist books for children."

Many of Ernst's picture books feature charming animals and teach simple but significant lessons to younger readers. In *The Rescue of Aunt Pansy,* a picture book described as "fun for all" by a *Publishers Weekly* reviewer, Joanne the mouse mistakenly believes that Rus-

sell the cat has captured Joanne's aunt when in fact the cat is playing with a toy mouse. A playful circus dog named Ginger seeks nothing more than the love of a little girl in *Ginger Jumps,* while *When Bluebell Sang* follows the rise to stardom of Bluebell, a singing cow, as Farmer Swenson discovers the cow's vocal talent and greedy talent agent Big Eddie takes both farmer and cow on a world tour. Praising *Ginger Jumps,* Ilene Cooper observed in *Booklist* that "Ernst's quiet wit works well with the story's strong message," while *School Library Journal* contributor Phyllis G. Sidorsky called *When Bluebell Sang* "an amusing, lighthearted tale."

Ernst introduces an engaging young pig in *Sylvia Jean, Drama Queen,* and the porcine Sylvia Jean returns in *Sylvia Jean, Scout Supreme.* When readers first meet the piglet in *Sylvia Jean, Drama Queen,* she demonstrates her fashion sense: Sylvia has the perfect costume for every event in her busy day. The ultimate challenge comes when she decides to attend a costume party, and she brags to her friends that she will easily win. As the day of the party comes, Sylvia has still not decided upon the perfect costume . . . until she hits upon one that none of her friends will recognize. Citing the author's use of "lively" prose and colorful art in her *Booklist* review, Gillian Engberg recommended *Sylvia Jean, Drama Queen* for its "reassuring message about exploring creativity and overcoming creative blocks." Lisa Gangemi Kropp agreed in her *School Library Journal* review, hailing Ernst's "enjoyable tale" for illustrating "how special it is to be true to oneself."

In addition to creating likeable animal characters, Ernst features humans as protagonists in several of her self-illustrated, lesson-filled tales. In *Miss Penny and Mr. Grubbs* an annual competition escalates into sabotage as Mr. Grubbs releases hungry rabbits into Miss Penny's prize-winning vegetable garden. When the county fair comes around, the irrepressible Miss Penny wins—for the forty-ninth year in a row—by entering some well-fed rabbits rather than vegetables. Carolyn Noah, reviewing the work for *School Library Journal,* commented that "the book's buoyancy and infectious visual humor make Miss Penny not only a county-fair winner, but a story time and read-alone prize as well."

The title character in *The Luckiest Kid on the Planet,* "Lucky" Morgenstern, has amazing good fortune until he learns that his real name, given to him by his grandfather, is actually Herbert. When Lucky sees his winning streak come to an abrupt end after his grandfather becomes ill, he starts to worry, but grandfather eventually recovers and the boy's pessimism fades. A *Publishers Weekly* critic remarked of the book that "Ernst's sage commentary on the correlation between attitude and experience comes delightfully gift-wrapped, with well-timed comic writing and rounded, pastel cartoons glistening with good humor."

Stella Louella's Runaway Book and *Hannah Mae O'Hannigan's Wild West Show* are two rather different adventures that also feature human characters: this time, young girls. The first book centers on an experience familiar to most readers: the search for a missing library book. Stella Louella is dismayed to find that her book has been enjoyed and passed on by her brother to the postman, a police officer, and many others. To the girl's relief, however, the book eventually makes its way back into the hands of the librarian. Deborah Stevenson wrote in the *Bulletin of the Center for Children's Books* that Ernst's "diverting sequence" of events includes hints that will amuse young readers, while a *Kirkus Reviews* critic added that the author's illustrations "stage the action beautifully, advancing the text and supplying plenty of funny details."

In *Hannah Mae O'Hannigan's Wild West Show* Ernst's protagonist has a rather more surprising task at hand: wrangling hamsters. Cowgirl wannabe Hannah lives in the city, where she rides her pony in a park and practices roping her other pets. When she finally visits Uncle Coot's ranch out in the country, Hannah's cowgirl skills prove to be exceptional. Described by Susan Dove Lempke in *Horn Book* as a "rootin'-tootin' picture book about living out your dream," *Hannah Mae O'Hannigan's Wild West Show* contains what *School Library Journal* critic Andrea Tarr described as a "subtle sense of irony" and "irresistible" humor.

Animal and human characters team up in Ernst's picture book *Squirrel Park*. Young Stuart's father, an architect, allows his son to design a new park for the city. However, the man insists that the plan should be organized geometrically, with only straight paths, and he provides a ruler and T-square to expedite the accomplishment of this task. Such a layout, Stuart realizes, will put a great oak tree centered in the middle of the park site in jeopardy. So, with the help of his pet squirrel Chuck, who gnaws the T-square into a more favorable shape, Stuart creates a curvy scheme with paths that meander gently around the tree. As a *Kirkus Reviews* critic concluded, Ernst, with her "usual wit and panache . . . vigorous pen . . . and cheerfully assertive colors," achieves still another picture-book success with *Squirrel Park.*

In addition to penning original tales, Ernst had brought her quirky humor to bear on several traditional tales. *Little Red Riding Hood: A Newfangled Prairie Tale* is set in contemporary times, and presents readers with a bicycle-riding Red Riding Hood, a robust grandma who does not need any saving at all, and an unpleasantly surprised wolf. In *The Gingerbread Girl,* the traditional story about the cookie who escapes from the baker only to be captured by a hungry fox has a happier ending when the cookie has long licorice-string hair that Gingerbread Girl uses to lasso her foxy captor. Reviewing *Little Red Riding Hood* for *Horn Book,* Margaret A. Bush noted: "As in her earlier books, Ernst demonstrates her mastery over the picture-book form, with inventive plot and enjoyable characters succinctly drawn in the narrative and beautifully extended in the illustrations."

Another "fractured fairytale" by Ernst is served up in *Goldilocks Returns.* All grown up, Goldilocks runs a home-security business, and is still riddled with guilt over the trouble she made for the three bears decades ago, when she was a girl. Despite the guilt, however, Goldilocks has not changed all that much, and she once again winds up trespassing while the bears are cooling their porridge, this time to improve their diet, redecorate their house, and otherwise make a mess of things. A *Publishers Weekly* reviewer found Ernst "at her wittiest when depicting the mild-mannered bears" and remarked on the "satirical edge" of her pastel color scheme. Writing for *Booklist,* Ilene Cooper judged that "the text is forced in places, but there's plenty of humor in Ernst's rollicking art."

A contemporary sensibility also transforms *The Three Spinning Fairies: A Tale from the Brothers Grimm.* This story tells of Zelda, the lazy daughter of the royal baker, who is overheard whining by the queen. Her mother tries to protect her by saying that Zelda was actually begging to spin string because she loved the work so much. The queen is impressed and pronounces that the girl can wed the prince if she can spin three rooms full of flax. Only the intervention of three unusual fairies, Anita, Benita, and Bob, can make this happen. However, Zelda gets her due in a plot twist added by Ernst: her new mother-in-law soon decides that she should take over her mother's bakery and all the hard work it entails. *Booklist* reviewer Susan Dove Lempke enjoyed the "fresh, zany feel" in *The Three Spinning Fairies,* which she credited to both the art work and the story's modern language. A *Kirkus Reviews* writer noted that Ernst's illustrations "invest each character with great personality" and concluded that the "general silliness keeps didacticism from the story."

Ernst has also created concept books for the very young. *Up to Ten and down Again* finds a lone duck swimming in a pond where it observes an increasing number of boys, girls, dogs, cars, and clouds. *School Library Journal* contributor Susan Scheps called the work "a counting book extraordinaire" while a *Bulletin of the Center for Children's Books* reviewer added that *Up to Ten and down Again* "fulfills almost every requirement for a teaching tool."

Teaching children about colors is the subject of *A Colorful Adventure of the Bee, Who Left Home One Monday Morning and What He Found Along the Way.* Simple, yet handsomely designed, this concept book, illustrated by Ernst's husband Lee Ernst, details the various colors encountered by an adventurous insect. Writing in *School Library Journal,* Luann Toth claimed that preschoolers "will ask for it time and time again." Another concept book by Ernst is *The Letters Are Lost!* While the text begins with all the letters "neat and tidy" in a wooden box, each letter departs, in turn, on an alphabetical adventure in what *Horn Book* contributor Margaret A. Bush dubbed "a quite traditional alphabet book beautifully rendered." A *Kirkus Reviews* critic called *The Letters Are Lost!* "invaluable" as a teaching tool and a "worth adding even to the most extensive collections of alphabet books."

In *Round like a Ball!* Ernst takes up an earth-friendly theme, drawing readers into a guessing game that involves round objects and a series of rhymed phrases hinting at each object to come. As the pages turn, everyone in the narrator's family takes a turn solving the riddle, from Grandma and Grandpa and aunts and uncles to family pets. Featuring fold-outs and cut-out elements that add to the puzzle, the author/illustrator's brightly colored and "distinctive collage . . . illustrations . . . will appeal to a young audience," noted *School Library Journal* contributor Piper Nyman. A *Kirkus Reviews* writer praised the large-format picture book for its "dappled brushwork . . . and artfully placed text." *Round like a Ball!* "displays an uncommon narrative and visual harmony," the *Kirkus Reviews* critic concluded, and in *Booklist* Randall Enos advised that Ernst's "showstopping foldout of the Earth will work well for . . . group viewing."

Biographical and Critical Sources

PERIODICALS

Booklist, May 15, 1990, Ilene Cooper, review of *Ginger Jumps,* p. 1799; March 1, 1992, Stephanie Zvirin, review of *Walter's Tail,* p. 1286; July, 1995, Ilene Cooper, review of *Little Red Riding Hood: A Newfangled Prairie Tale,* p. 1881; April 1, 2000, Ilene Cooper, review of *Goldilocks Returns,* p. 1468; January 1, 2002, Susan Dove Lemke, review of *The Three Spinning Fairies,* p. 861; September 15, 2005, Gillian Engberg, review of *Sylvia Jean, Drama Queen,* p. 71; September 1, 2006, Ilene Cooper, review of *The Gingerbread Girl,* p. 135; April 1, 2008, Randall Enos, review of *Round like a Ball!,* p. 57.
Bulletin of the Center for Children's Books, December, 1998, Deborah Stevenson, review of *Stella Louella's Runaway Book,* p. 129; January 1, 2004, Karin Snelson, review of *Wake up, It's Spring,* p. 874.
Horn Book, January-February, 1996, Margaret A. Bush, review of *Little Red Riding Hood,* pp. 80-81; March-April, 1996, Margaret A. Bush, review of *The Letters Are Lost!,* p. 187; July-August, 2003, Susan Dove Lempke, review of *Hannah Mae O'Hannigan's Wild West Show,* p. 441; November-December, 2006, Susan P. Bloom, review of *The Gingerbread Girl,* p. 698.
Kirkus Reviews, March 15, 1993, review of *Squirrel Park,* p. 370; December 15, 1995, review of *The Letters Are Lost!,* p. 769; July 1, 1998, review of *Stella Louella's Runaway Book,* p. 966; January 1, 2002, review of *The Three Spinning Fairies,* p. 45; January 15, 2004, review of *Wake up, It's Spring,* p. 82; May 1, 2005, review of *This Is the Van That Dad Cleaned,* p. 538; March 15, 2008, review of *Round like a Ball!*
New York Times Book Review, November 13, 1983, Karla Kuskin, review of *Sam Johnson and the Blue Ribbon Quilt,* p. 55.
Publishers Weekly, August 12, 1983, review of *Sam Johnson and the Blue Ribbon Quilt,* p. 67; September 21, 1984, review of *The Prize Pig Surprise,* p. 96; June 12, 1987, review of *The Rescue of Aunt Pansy,* p. 83; April 28, 1989, review of *When Bluebell Sang,* p. 76; August 15, 1994, review of *The Luckiest Kid on the Planet,* p. 94; June 12, 2000, review of *Goldilocks Returns,* p. 72; February 9, 2003, review of *Wake up, It's Spring!,* p. 80.
School Library Journal, December, 1983, Elizabeth Simmons, review of *Sam Johnson and the Blue Ribbon Quilt,* p. 54; November, 1986, Luann Toth, review of *A Colorful Adventure of the Bee, Who Left Home One Monday Morning and What He Found along the Way,* pp. 75-76; August, 1986, Susan Scheps, review of *Up to Ten and down Again,* p. 80; April, 1989, Phyllis G. Sidorsky, review of *When Bluebell Sang,* p. 82; June, 1991, Carolyn Noah, review of *Miss Penny and Mr. Grubbs,* p. 76; July, 1992, Jane Marino, review of *Zinnia and Dot,* p. 58; July, 2003, Andrea Tarr, review of *Hannah Mae O'Hannigan's Wild West Show,* p. 95; February, 2004, Judith Constantinides, review of *Wake up, It's Spring!,* p. 112; May, 2005, Rachael Vilmar, review of *This Is the Van That Dad Cleaned,* p. 82; September, 2005, Lisa Gangemi Kropp, review of *Sylvia Jean, Drama Queen,* p. 169; November, 2006, Susan Scheps, review of *The Gingerbread Girl,* p. 92; February, 2009, Piper Nyman, review of *Round like a Ball!,* p. 91.

ONLINE

Missouri Center for the Book Web site, http://authors. missouri.org/ (March 1, 2003), Sue Thomas, interview with Ernst.*

*　　　*　　　*

FORD, Bernette
(B.G. Ford, Bernette G. Ford)

Personal

Born in New York, NY; married George Ford (an illustrator); children: Olivia. *Education:* Connecticut College, degree, 1972.

Addresses

Home—Brooklyn, NY. *Office*—Color-Bridge Books, 2732 Bedford Ave., Ste. 3, Brooklyn, NY 11210. *E-mail*—colorbridgebooks@verizon.net.

Career

Author, publishing consultant, and book packager. Random House Books for Young Readers, New York, NY, 1972-79, began as editorial assistant; Western Publishing, 1979-83, began as senior editor at Golden Press, became editorial director; Grosset & Dunlap, New York, NY, 1983-89, began as editor-in-chief, became vice

Bernette Ford (Photograph by M.C. Gillis. Reproduced by permission.)

president and publisher; Scholastic, Inc., New York, NY, vice president and editorial director of Cartwheel Books, 1989-2002; Color-Bridge Books, LLC, Brooklyn, NY, founder, 2003—.

Writings

(As B.G. Ford) *Do You Know?*, illustrated by Harry Mc-Naught, Random House (New York, NY), 1979.

(As B.G. Ford) *Don't Forget the Oatmeal!: A Supermarket Word Book, Featuring Jim Henson's Sesame Street Muppets,* illustrated by Jean Chandler, Western Publishing Co. (Racine, WI), 1980.

(As B.G. Ford) *Grover's Book of Cute Little Baby Animals: Featuring Jim Henson's Sesame Street Muppets,* illustrated by Tom Leigh, Western Publishing Co. (Racine, WI), 1980.

(Reteller as B.G. Ford) *Little Red Riding Hood,* illustrated by Elve Fortis de Hieronymis, Grosset & Dunlap (New York, NY), 1985.

(As Bernette G. Ford, with Cheryl Willis Hudson) *Bright Eyes, Brown Skin,* illustrated by husband, George Ford, Just Us Books (Orange, NJ), 1990.

The Hunter Who Was King, and Other African Tales, illustrated by George Ford, Hyperion Books for Children (New York, NY), 1994.

(Editor) *Real Mother Goose Christmas Carols,* Cartwheel Books (New York, NY), 1994.

Hurry Up!, illustrated by Jennifer Kindert, Scholastic, Inc. (New York, NY), 2003.

Don't Hit Me!, illustrated by Gary Grier, Scholastic, Inc. (New York, NY), 2004.

First Snow, illustrated by Sebastien Braun, Holiday House (New York, NY), 2005.

(Adapter as B.G. Ford) *Albuquerque Turkey,* illustrated by Lucinda McQueen, Sterling Publishing (New York, NY), 2005.

No More Diapers for Ducky! illustrated by Sam Williams, Boxer Books (New York, NY), 2006, published as *Nappy Duck and Potty Piggy,* Boxer Books (London, England), 2006.

No More Bottles for Bunny!, illustrated by Sam Williams, Boxer (London, England), 2007, Boxer Books (New York, NY), 2008.

Ballet Kitty, illustrated by Sam Williams, Boxer (London, England), 2007.

Ballet Kitty: Ballet Class, illustrated by Sam Williams, Boxer (London, England), 2008.

No More Pacifier for Piggy!, illustrated by Sam Williams, Boxer (New York, NY), 2008, published as *No More Dummy for Piggy!,* Boxer (London, England), 2008.

No More Blanket for Lambkin!, illustrated by Sam Williams, Boxer (New York, NY), 2009.

Series editor for Boxer "Concept" series, including *A Big Dog, A Starfish, A Teddy Bear, A Red Train, A Happy Home,* and *A Black Cat,* Boxer (London England), 2008.

Sidelights

In a career that has spanned almost four decades, Bernette Ford has devoted herself to producing quality books for children as both author and publisher. She began working as an editorial assistant at Random House and eventually became a vice president at, first, Grosset & Dunlap and later at Scholastic's Cartwheel Books. Since 2003 Ford has run her own consulting and book-packaging business, Color-Bridge Books, which specializes in multicultural children's books. In choosing projects to produce, she told Shannon Maughan of *Publishers Weekly,* "I try to do commercial books that are fun—things that really jump out and grab children. It's important to hook them at a very young age; when children have an early relationship to books, we build lifetime readers."

Throughout her years working as an editor or publisher, Ford has made it a point to not only develop books that can appeal to a wide range of readers, but also books for under-served audiences, such as African Americans. On example is *Bright Eyes, Brown Skin,* which is written with Cheryl Willis Hudson and illustrated by Ford's husband, George Ford, the first illustrator to win the American Library Association's Coretta Scott King Award. The subject is simple: a day full of preschool activities, and Ford's "gentle, catchy rhyme meanders through the pages," Diane Roback and Richard Donahue remarked in *Publishers Weekly.* The reviewers added that *Bright Eyes, Brown Skin* "goes a long way" toward filling the need for more positive children's books featuring black children. Ford has also teamed up with her husband for the pop-up book *The Hunter Who Was King, and Other African Tales.* In her retelling of three African folktales, Ford's "straightforward language retains the storyteller's cadences," a *Publishers Weekly* critic noted of *The Hunter Who Was King.*

Developed through Color-Bridge Books, Ford has also overseen the "Just for You!" series, which is designed for African-American youngsters and features everyday stories written by both noted and upcoming black authors and illustrators. "I believe it is absolutely critical that children of color see themselves doing things all children do," Ford told Suzanne Rust in *Black Issues Book Review.* "These books validate our children's existence; they say, 'You are important enough to be in a book and this book is just for you.'" Ford has also authored two books in the "Just for You!" series: *Hurry Up!* and *Don't Hit Me!* In a *School Library Journal* review of several books in the series, Corrina Austin noted that the "stories are engaging, even though the language is quite simple."

Many of Ford's books are geared to very young readers, and her picture book *First Snow* uses simple language to show a young bunny's introduction to winter snow. "Ford's text has a poetic rhythm that emphasizes the senses," *School Library Journal* contributor Maura Bresnahan remarked. While a *Kirkus Reviews* critic found the book to be a "sometimes clashing" if "interesting combination of nature and picture book," *Booklist* critic Ilene Cooper concluded that Ford and illustrator Sebastien Braun "get it just right." "Ford's artful text is both fluid and evocative," the critic added, "yet it's right at a child's level."

Ford demonstrates her understanding of the development of very young children in a book series that deals with "graduating" from babyish things such as diapers, pacifiers, bottles, and blankies. *No More Diapers for Ducky!* finds Ducky deciding it is time to leave diapers behind so that she can use the potty like her friend Piggy. A *Publishers Weekly* writer noted of this work that Ford's story has "a freshness apparent in both the language and the artwork" by Sam Williams. The text and art "are simple and endearing," Martha Topol remarked in *School Library Journal,* adding that the story's "message is clear, yet subtle." A similar lesson is "handled subtly" in *No More Bottles for Bunny!,* according to Linda Zeilstra Sawyer in *School Library Journal.* In the story, Bunny finds his bottle gets in the way during a tea party with Ducky and Piggy, so he decides to have his tea in a big-boy cup. The way Bunny deals with the problem makes for "an endearing tale," Sawyer concluded.

Piggy is the friend who has trouble giving up something in *No More Pacifier for Piggy!* Piggy is learning to play peekaboo with friend Ducky, but his pacifier keeps getting in the way. He learns to put it aside while they play and has fun anyway. Ford's "simple text and [Williams'] engaging illustrations will attract the intended audience," Amy Lilien-Harper observed in *School Library Journal.* In *No More Blanket for Lambkin!* a beloved blankie hinders Ducky and Lambkin's unfettered playtime. Ducky suggests that they play laundry, but washing Lambkin's blanket leaves it shrunken and filled with holes. Luckily, Ducky turns the blanket into a lamb-shaped toy for her friend. *School Library Journal* contributor Kate Neff called *No More Blanket for Lambkin!* "a sweet book about two different friendships, one that fades away with age, and one that is strengthened with time and caring."

Biographical and Critical Sources

PERIODICALS

Black Issues Book Review, September-October, 2004, Suzanne Rust, "Let Every Child Relate," p. 58.

Booklist, November 1, 2005, Ilene Cooper, review of *First Snow,* p. 40.

Kirkus Reviews, August 15, 2005, review of *First Snow,* p. 913.

Publishers Weekly, November 16, 1990, Diane Roback and Richard Donahue, review of *Bright Eyes, Brown Skin,* p. 55; March 29, 1991, Shannon Maughan, "Turning Cartwheels at Scholastic," pp. 70-71; December 20, 1993, review of *The Hunter Who Was King, and Other African Tales,* p. 71; March 27, 2006, review of *No More Diapers for Ducky!,* p. 77.

School Library Journal, January, 2005, Corrina Austin, review of *Hurry Up!* and *Don't Hit Me!,* p. 85; September, 2005, Maura Bresnahan, review of *First Snow,* p. 170; August, 2006, Martha Topol, review of *No More Diapers for Ducky!,* p. 87; May, 2007, Linda Zeilstra Sawyer, review of *No More Bottles for Bunny!,* p. 91; August, 2008, Amy Lilien-Harper, review of *No More Pacifier for Piggy!,* pp. 88-89; August, 2009, Kate Neff, review of *No More Blanket for Lambkin!,* p. 75.

Ford teams up with illustrator Sam Williams to create a humorous toddler-themed story in No More Pacifier for Piggy! *(Boxer Books, 2009. Illustration copyright © 2008 by Sam Williams, Ltd. Reproduced by permission.)*

ONLINE

Color-Bridge Books Web site, http://www.color-bridge-books.com/ (January 15, 2010).

Missouri Writers Guild 91st Annual Conference Web site, http://home.earthlink.net/~mwgconference, "Bernette Ford—Color-Bridge Books" (January 15, 2010).*

FORD, Bernette G.
 See FORD, Bernette

*   *   *

FORD, B.G.
 See FORD, Bernette

G

GOLDMAN, Judy 1955-

Personal

Born 1955, in Mexico City, Mexico; married; children: Ilán, one other son. *Education:* Universidad Iberoamerica (Mexico City, Mexico), degree.

Addresses

Home—Mexico City, Mexico. *E-mail*—rabkey@alestra. net.mx.

Career

Writer, editor, and translator.

Member

Society of Children's Book Writers and Illustrators.

Awards, Honors

Third-place award, International Board on Books Mexico Premio Antionorrobles, 1984, for *Una rana en un árbol;* Best Books of the Year shortlist, Bank Street College of Education, 2008, for *Uncle Monarch and the Day of the Dead.*

Writings

FOR CHILDREN

Judy Goldman (Photograph by Ilán Rabchinskey. Reproduced by permission.)

Una rana en un árbol, illustrated by María Teresa Romero, Editorial Trillas (Mexico City, Mexico), 1986.

Pepe, Sandra y la barda, illustrated by Maribel Suírez, Editorial Trillas (Mexico City, Mexico), 1987.

Eugenio y la botella verde, illustrated by Gerardo Suzán, Editorial Trillas (Mexico City, Mexico), 1989.

Desastre en la cocina, illustrated by Gerardo Suzán, Editorial Trillas (Mexico City, Mexico), 1989.

Porfirio y el sarampión, illustrated by Gerardo Suzán, Editorial Trillas (Mexico City, Mexico), 1989.

Michi y la fiesta de disfraces, illustrated by María Teresa Romero, Editorial Trillas (Mexico City, Mexico), 1990.

Los huesos sagrados (title means "The Sacred Bones"), illustrated by Fabricio Vanden Broeck, Ediciones SM (Mexico City, Mexico), 2003.

Te cuento? (short stories), illustrated by Humberto García, Norma Ediciones (Mexico City, Mexico), 2004.

El brebaje de Pánfilo, illustrated by Iker Vicente, Editorial Porrúa (Mexico City, Mexico), 2006.

Uncle Monarch and the Day of the Dead, illustrated by René King Moreno, Boyds Mills Press (Honesdale, PA), 2008.

Amol iz gevén/Érase una vez (Jewish folk tales), illustrated by Aurea Freniere, Editorial Porrúa (Mexico City, Mexico), 2009.

Sapo y Yuki (Yaqui folk tale), illustrated by Arno Avilés, Editorial Progreso (Mexico City, Mexico), 2009.

Muyal (Mayan folk tale), illustrated by Mónica Padilla, Editorial Progreso (Mexico City, Mexico), 2009.

Creator, with son and photographer Ilán Rabchinskey, of nature-themed books for private publishers. Also author of *¡Vamos a comer. . . flores!* Translator of numerous children's books into Spanish for Mathew Price Ltd. (Dallas, TX). Contributor to periodicals, including *Highlights for Children* and *Spider;* editor of electronic periodical *La cometa.*

Sidelights

An author and translator, Judy Goldman was born in Mexico City, Mexico, and was raised in a bilingual, bicultural household where there was a library with books of many kinds. Since she was a child, Goldman often had her nose in a book, something she believes led her to writing, especially for her sons when they were small. She has written original works for children in both English and Spanish, and has also translated numerous children's books for the growing Spanish-language market in the United States. Her books for children, which include *Uncle Monarch and the Day of the Dead* and *El*

Goldman weaves an important Mexican holiday into her story **Uncle Monarch and the Day of the Dead,** *featuring artwork by René King Moreno.*
(Boyds Mills Press, 2008. Illustration copyright © 2008 by Rene King Moreno. Reproduced by permission.)

brebaje de Pánfilo, share Mexico's rich traditions and culture, as well as the traditions of her Jewish faith. Goldman's son, Ilán Rabchinskey, is a well-known photographer and they have teamed up to create several books about Mexico's many edible flowers and insects.

Several of Goldman's published works are retellings of folk tales and draw on her interest in the folklore of Mexico. Many of these stories, such as *Muyal,* a Maya folk tale that is illustrated by Mónica Padilla, and *Sapo y Yuku,* a Yaqui tale illustrated by Arno Avilés, she heard from storytellers or discovered in musty libraries, in the pages of books that are falling apart. Goldman has also written academic articles about children's books and participates in congresses and conferences. The regional advisor of Mexico for the Society of Children's Book Writers and Illustrators, she is also coeditor of *La cometa,* a Spanish-language electronic bulletin with news about the field of children's books including contests, conferences, and book fairs.

In her first English-language picture book *Uncle Monarch and the Day of the Dead,* Goldman explores the fall holiday when many Mexicans honor relatives who have passed away. Little Lupita is enchanted when her uncle, tío Urbano, tells her that the monarch butterflies that return to Mexico each fall carry the souls of their family's loved ones. When the man dies a few days before the Day of the Dead, Lupita's grief is eased by the holiday's rituals. "Multicultural customs and monarch butterflies are favorite subjects in classrooms, and this offering nicely combines the two," a *Kirkus Review* critic noted in appraising *Uncle Monarch and the Day of the Dead.* Kirsten Cutler remarked of the same work in *School Library Journal* that Goldman's "lovely picture book effectively blends a poignant story about losing a beloved relative with a lucid description" of the holiday.

Biographical and Critical Sources

PERIODICALS

Kirkus Reviews, July 15, 2008, review of *Uncle Monarch and the Day of the Dead.*

School Library Journal, August, 2008, Kirsten Cutler, review of *Uncle Monarch and the Day of the Dead,* p. 90.

ONLINE

Society of Children's Book Writers and Illustrators Web site, http://www.scbwi.org/ (January 18, 2010), "Judy Goldman."

*   *   *

GRATZ, Alan 1972-

Personal

Born January 27, 1972, in Knoxville, TN; married; wife's name Wendi; children: Jo (daughter). *Education:*

Alan Gratz (Reproduced by permission.)

University of Tennessee, B.A. (creative writing), 1993, M.S. (education), 1998. *Hobbies and other interests:* Eating pizza, reading kids' and young-adult books, soccer, science fiction, mysteries, action figures, video games, robots, manga, travel, and watching baseball.

Addresses

Home and office—P.O. Box 35, Penland, NC 28765. *E-mail*—bigcheese@alangratz.com.

Career

Writer. Has also worked as a bookseller, librarian, eighth-grade English teacher, and writer for television and radio.

Awards, Honors

Kimberly Colen memorial grant (co-recipient), Society of Children's Book Writers and Illustrators, 2003; *Washington Post* Top Ten Books for Children designation, 2006, and Bank Street College of Education Best Books of the Year designation, Young Adult Library Services Association Top Ten Best Books for Young Adults designation, and Cooperative Children's Book Center Choices selection, all 2007, all for *Samurai Shortstop;* American Library Association Quick Pick for Reluctant Young-Adult Readers designation, 2008, for *Something Rotten;* Top Ten Sports Books for Youth designation, *Booklist,* and Editor's Choice designation, *Library Media Connection,* both 2009, both for *The Brooklyn Nine.*

Writings

YOUNG-ADULT NOVELS

Samurai Shortstop, Dial Books (New York, NY), 2006.

Something Rotten: A Horatio Wilkes Mystery, Dial Books (New York, NY), 2007.

Something Wicked: A Horatio Wilkes Mystery, Dial Books (New York, NY), 2008.

The Brooklyn Nine: A Novel in Nine Innings, Dial Books (New York, NY), 2009.

PLAYS

Sweet Sixteen, produced at Knoxville Actors Co-op, TN, 1998.

Indian Myths and Legends, produced at Knoxville Actors Co-op, TN, 1998.

Young Hickory, produced at Knoxville Actors Co-op, TN, 1999.

The Gift of the Magi (adapted from the story by O. Henry), produced at Knoxville Actors Co-op, TN, 1999.

Measured in Labor: The Coal Creek Project, produced at Knoxville Actors Co-op, TN, 2004.

The Legend of Sleepy Hollow (adapted from the story by Washington Irving), produced at Knoxville Actors Co-op, TN, 2004.

Cover of Gratz's young-adult novel Samurai Shortstop, *featuring photography by Tony Sahara.* (Cover image © 2006 by Tony Sahara. Reproduced by permission of Speak, a division of Penguin Putnam Books for Young Readers.)

OTHER

Also contributor of articles to periodicals. Writer for *City Confidential* (television series), Arts and Entertainment Network.

Sidelights

Although Alan Gratz boasts a writing resumé that includes plays, television scripts, a popular Web log, and radio advertising, he is best known to teen readers for his novels *Samurai Shortstop, The Brooklyn Nine: A Novel in Nine Innings,* and his "Horatio Wilkes" mysteries.

Gratz was born in 1972, in Knoxville, into a football-mad family that included players, referees, cheerleaders, and coaches. Breaking with tradition, Gratz loved baseball, even though he was not an accomplished baseball player. As he recalled to an *ALAN Online* interview, "My greatest Little League moment: I misplayed a long drive to left field, then absolutely launched the ball, trying to throw a runner out at the plate. The ball sailed up the first base line, over the fence, and into the bleachers, where it hit my little brother in the arm. All the runners scored. After the inning was over, the coach told me I had a good arm. He also told me not to come back."

Fortunately, Gratz had more success in pursuing his second love: writing. He contributed stories and articles to school newspapers and then studied writing in college. After graduation, while working at a bookstore, he began his writing career in earnest. His first published young-adult novel, *Samurai Shortstop,* reflects his interest in Japan and the country's long-time involvement with baseball. Set in 1890, a time when Japan had begun to modernize, the novel follows sixteen-year-old Toyo Shimada. As the story opens, Japan's emperor has recently put an end to the legion of roving warrior known as samurai, and Toyo's uncle Koji now kills himself in the ritualistic way of the samurai, aided by both Toyo and Toyo's father, Sotaro. Sotaro also plans to kill himself rather than face life in a modernized world, but he decides to wait until he has finished training Toyo in bushido. As Toyo trains, he also faces the traditional hazing period at his new high school. In a review for *School Library Journal,* Marilyn Taniguchi stated that Gratz's "well-written tale offers plenty of fascinating detail, a fast-paced story, and a fresh perspective on 'America's pastime.'" A *Kirkus Reviews* contributor dubbed *Samurai Shortstop* "an unusual take on the American (and Japanese) pastime," and in *Publishers Weekly,* a reviewer described Gratz's debut as "an intense read about a fascinating time and place in world history."

Gratz returns to baseball in *The Brooklyn Nine,* a middle-grade novel that follows several generations of an immigrant family beginning in the early 1800s. In nine interlocking tales, Gratz focuses on a different generation of the Schneider family as they establish themselves in Brooklyn, New York. Shortly after arriving from Germany, young Felix Schneider discovers baseball when he watches the Knickerbockers play an early version of the game. Moving forward in time, Walter Snider plays baseball at the turn of the twentieth century while also dealing with anti-Semitism. Another Snider generation is represented by Kat Flint, who plays in the first professional women's league during World War II. Other chapters follow the family history to the present day in what *Horn Book* critic Jonathan Hunt described as a "wonderful baseball book that is more than the sum of its parts." A *Kirkus Reviews* contributor also had praise for *The Brooklyn Nine,* terming it "an entertaining and compelling look at the deep roots of our national pastime," while *Booklist* critic Ian Chipman lauded Gratz for producing what the critic described as a "sweeping diaspora of Americana."

Something Rotten: A Horatio Wilkes Mystery begins Gratz's Shakespeare-themed "Horatio Wilkes" mystery series. The protagonist, Horatio Wilkes, accompanies his friend Hamilton Prince to Hamilton's home in Denmark, Tennessee, during a school break, to find that the boy's Uncle Claude has married Hamilton's mother only two months after the death of Hamilton's father. The marriage puts Claude in charge of the family business, a successful paper plant that has been steadily polluting the Copenhagen River. Disheartened by his mother's callousness, Hamilton begins drinking heavily, leaving Horatio to investigate the situation with the help of Olivia, an environmental protester. Noting the similarities to William Shakespeare's *Hamlet,* a *Kirkus Reviews* contributor remarked of *Something Rotten* that Gratz's "well-crafted mystery has appeal for readers familiar with both Raymond Chandler's novels and Shakespeare's masterpiece," and *Kliatt* critic Myrna Marler deemed the novel "good fun."

Horatio returns in *Something Wicked,* which takes Shakespeare's *Macbeth* as its inspiration. Here Horatio is attending a Scottish festival in rural Tennessee when he discovers the body of local landowner Duncan MacRae. Realizing that MacRae has been murdered, Horatio attempts to find the killer, even as suspicion falls on his friend Mac, son of the murdered man. Mac and Mac's girlfriend, Beth, appear to have a motive: they hoped to take over MacRae's land and open a ski resort. In *Kliatt* Paula Rohrlick predicted that Gratz's "suspenseful mystery will work even for those unfamiliar with the Shakespeare play," and a *Kirkus Reviews* contributor called *Something Wicked* "a satisfying remake of one of the Bard's most familiar works."

"I'm greatly influenced by other storytellers, both classic and contemporary," Gratz once explained. "I enjoy reading something and asking, 'What would I have done with that idea?' or looking for new ideas out of old ones. At the same time, I enjoy charting new territory in fiction, and discovering historical events that haven't been written about and finding the story in them.

Cover of Gratz's Shakespeare-themed teen novel Something Wicked, *featuring artwork by Greg Stadnyk.* (Jacket art © 2008 by Greg Stadnyk. Reproduced by permission of Dial Books, a division of Penguin Putnam Books for Young Readers.)

"I begin with a loose idea and let it percolate—sometimes months and years at a time—and then begin to do research, if there is any to be done. I let the story develop from my notes, and when I feel as though I have the makings of a good story I begin to outline it. I go back and work on those places where the story lags or doesn't work, then finalize the outline, moving any relevant notes I'll need into my detailed plan for the novel. When that work is done, I can usually sit down and write a chapter a day until I have a first draft, at which point I bring in other readers and begin the long work of revision. When I'm satisfied that the novel is the best I can make it, I hand it over to my editor, and then the revision process begins all over again." "I hope first and always to entertain," Gratz concluded.

Biographical and Critical Sources

PERIODICALS

Booklist, April 15, 2006, Carolyn Phelan, review of *Samurai Shortstop,* p. 58; November 15, 2006, Hazel Rochman, "Top Ten First Novels for Youth," p. 60; November 1, 2008, Carolyn Phelan, review of *Something Wicked: A Horatio Wilkes Mystery,* p. 36; February 1, 2009, Ian Chipman, review of *The Brooklyn Nine: A Novel in Nine Innings,* p. 40.

Horn Book, March-April, 2009, Jonathan Hunt, review of *The Brooklyn Nine,* p. 194.

Kirkus Reviews, April 15, 2006, review of *Samurai Shortstop,* p. 406; September 1, 2007, review of *Something Rotten: A Horatio Wilkes Mystery;* October 1, 2008, review of *Something Wicked;* January 15, 2009, review of *The Brooklyn Nine.*

Kliatt, September, 2007, Myrna Marler, review of *Something Rotten,* p. 13; September, 2008, Paula Rohrlick, review of *Something Wicked,* p. 11.

Publishers Weekly, May 22, 2006, review of *Samurai Shortstop,* p. 53.

School Library Journal, May, 2006, Marilyn Taniguchi, review of *Samurai Shortstop,* p. 62; January, 2008, John Leighton, review of *Something Rotten,* p. 118; January, 2009, Jake Pettit, review of *Something Wicked,* p. 102.

Voice of Youth Advocates, December, 2007, Angelica Delgado, review of *Something Rotten,* p. 427.

Washington Post, December 10, 2006, Elizabeth Ward, review of *Samurai Shortstop,* p. T7.

ONLINE

Alan Gratz Home Page, http://www.alangratz.com (January 10, 2010).

Alan Gratz Web log, http://gratzindustries.blogspot.com/ (January 10, 2010).

ALAN Online, http://www.alan-ya.org/ (January 4, 2007), interview with Gratz.

Cynsations Web log, http://cynthialeitichsmith.blogspot.com/ (March 31, 2009), Cynthia Leitich Smith, interview with Gratz.

PaperTigers.org, http://www.papertigers.org/ (March 31, 2009), Aline Pereira, interview with Gratz.

*   *   *

GREENE, Jacqueline Dembar 1946-

Personal

Born May 21, 1946, in Hartford, CT; married Malcolm R. Greene (an optometrist), 1967; children: Matthew, Kenneth. *Education:* University of Connecticut, B.A. (with honors), 1967; Central Missouri University, M.A. (with special distinction), 1970. *Hobbies and other interests:* Gardening, cross-country skiing, hiking, biking, travel, photography.

Addresses

Home and office—21 Sunnyside Ave., Wellesley, MA 02482.

Career

French teacher in and near Boston, MA, 1967-71; worked variously as a reporter, columnist, and feature writer for newspapers, including *Middlesex News,* Framingham, MA, and *Wellesley Townsman,* Wellesley, MA, 1971-80; writer, beginning 1980.

Member

Society of Children's Book Writers and Illustrators.

Awards, Honors

Pick of the List citation, *American Bookseller,* 1984, for *The Leveller;* National Jewish Book Award finalist, 1984, for *Butchers and Bakers, Rabbis and Kings;* Sidney Taylor Honor Book citation, Association of Jewish Libraries, and Books for the Teen Age citation, New York Public Library, both 1988, both for *Out of Many Waters;* Sidney Taylor Honor Book designation, 1994, for *One Foot Ashore.*

Writings

FOR CHILDREN

A Classroom Hanukah, illustrated by Debra G. Butler, Pascal Publishers, 1980.

The Hanukah Tooth, illustrated by Pauline A. Ouellet, Pascal Publishers, 1980.

Butchers and Bakers, Rabbis and Kings, Kar-Ben Copies (Rockville, MD), 1984.

The Leveller, Walker (New York, NY), 1984.

Nathan's Hanukah Bargain, illustrated by Steffi Karen Rubin, Kar-Ben Copies (Rockville, MD), 1986.

Out of Many Waters, Walker (New York, NY), 1988.

The Maya (nonfiction), edited by Iris Rosoff, Franklin Watts (New York, NY), 1992.

What His Father Did, illustrated by John O'Brien, Houghton Mifflin (Boston, MA), 1992.

The Chippewa (nonfiction), edited by Russell Primm, Franklin Watts (New York, NY), 1993.

One Foot Ashore, Walker (New York, NY), 1994.

Manabozho's Gifts: Three Chippewa Tales, Houghton Mifflin (Boston, MA), 1994.

Marie: Mystery at the Paris Ballet, Paris, 1775 ("Girlhood Journeys" series), illustrated by Lyn Durham, Aladdin (New York, NY), 1997.

Marie: Summer in the Country, France, 1775 ("Girlhood Journeys" series), illustrated by Lyn Durham, Aladdin (New York, NY), 1997.

The Tohono O'Odham (nonfiction), Franklin Watts (New York, NY), 1998.

(And photographer) *Powwow: A Good Day to Dance* (nonfiction), Franklin Watts (New York, NY), 1998.

Slavery in Greece and Rome (nonfiction), Franklin Watts (New York, NY), 1999.

Slavery in Egypt and Mesopotamia (nonfiction), Franklin Watts (New York, NY), 2000.

The Emperor's Teacup, and Other Tales from Near and Far, Rigby (Crystal Lake, IL), 2002.

The 2001 World Trade Center Attack, Bearport Pub. (New York, NY), 2007.

The Triangle Shirtwaist Factory Fire, Bearport (New York, NY), 2007.

Grizzly Bears: Saving the Silvertip, Bearport Pub. (New York, NY), 2008.

Nathan's Hanukkah Bargain, illustrated by Judith Hierstein, Pelican Pub. (Gretna, LA), 2008.

The Secret Shofar of Barcelona, illustrated by Doug Chayka, Kar-Ben (Minneapolis, MN), 2009.

Contributor to periodicals, including *Boston Globe, Day Care, Highlights for Children, Lollipops, Ladybugs and Lucky Stars, Nitty Gritty City, Parenting, Parents' Choice, Small Talk,* and *Wellesley.*

"REBECCA" SERIES; FOR CHILDREN

Meet Rebecca: An American Girl, illustrated by Robert Hunt, American Girl Pub. (Middleton, WI), 2009.

Candlelight for Rebecca, illustrated by Robert Hunt, American Girl Pub. (Middleton, WI), 2009.

Changes for Rebecca, illustrated by Robert Hunt, American Girl Pub. (Middleton, WI), 2009.

Rebecca to the Rescue, illustrated by Robert Hunt, American Girl Pub. (Middleton, WI), 2009.

Rebecca and Ana, illustrated by Robert Hunt, American Girl Pub. (Middleton, WI), 2009.

Rebecca and the Movies, illustrated by Robert Hunt, American Girl Pub. (Middleton, WI), 2009.

Sidelights

Jacqueline Dembar Greene came to writing for children as a result of a college course in children's literature. After changing careers from teaching French to journalism, she published her first book, *A Classroom Hanukah,* and left "the bustle of the news office for the quiet of my own imagination," as she once remarked. "I have continued to use the research skills from my former career to find the facts and history that I feel make a story relevant and alive." Among Greene's books are the historical novel *Out of Many Waters* and its sequel, *One Foot Ashore,* the six-volume "Rebecca" series for the popular "American Girl" collection, as well as a number of books on the history and customs of Native American tribes.

Historical facts are woven into many of Greene's books for children. *Butchers and Bakers, Rabbis and Kings* tells of the seemingly all-powerful King Alfonson the Warrior, who strides into Tudela, Spain, in 1114 thinking he needs no help from anyone in establishing his rule. Concerned about their safety in the new kingdom, the Jews of the city devise a plan to convince the king that without his subjects he is just an ordinary man. Tom Cook, the real-life protagonist of *The Leveller,* was shunned by his eighteenth-century Massachusetts neighbors because they thought he was in league with the

devil. Using the people's superstition to avoid capture, Tom set out to secretly "level" the fortunes of the poor farmers with those who had an abundance of food and wealth, all the while trying to outwit the devil, who coveted his soul. In *Marie: Mystery at the Paris Ballet, Paris, 1775* and *Marie: Summer in the Country, France, 1775*—two installments in the "Girlhood Journeys" series—Greene opens a window for modern readers onto the daily life, clothes, and living situation of girls growing up in pre-Revolutionary France.

Greene's historical novels *Out of Many Waters* and *One Foot Ashore* relate the story of sisters Isobel and Maria Ben Lazar, who, during the Inquisition, are taken from their parents in Portugal and shipped as slaves to a monastery in Brazil. Escaping in 1654, they attempt to rejoin their parents, but become separated during their flight. *Out of Many Waters* is twelve-year-old Isobel's story. Forced to stow away on a ship, Isobel is rescued by a small group of Jewish colonists who eventually founded the first Jewish settlement in America. Storms, pirates, kidnaping, first love, landing in New Amsterdam, and Isobel's hopes of finding her family move the plot along. Susan Levine, writing for the *Voice of Youth Advocates,* noted that Greene's characterization of Isobel helps the reader "sympathize with her and be inter-

Jacqueline Dembar Greene captures the drama of a Native American day of ceremony in her self-illustrated **Powwow.** (Photographs © 1998 by Jacqueline Dembar Greene. Reproduced by permission of Scholastic, Inc.)

ested in her success." Praising *Out of Many Waters* as "a good story with a memorable character," Levine added that the book is "an easy way to learn a little history." Eli N. Evans noted in the *New York Times Book Review* that Greene "has done a relatively smooth job of weaving history, drama and narrative into an arresting story."

In the companion volume, *One Foot Ashore,* Isobel's sister, sixteen-year-old Maria, also stows away on a ship headed for the Netherlands and survives the brutal voyage. In Amsterdam, she meets the artist Rembrandt van Rijn, gets a job working as Rembrandt's housemaid, and is aided in her search for her parents by a series of helpful people. While noting that "there is much that is contrived" in the plot, *School Library Journal* contributor Renee Steinberg praised *One Foot Ashore* as "an absorbing read." In *Booklist,* Carolyn Phelan called it an "intriguing historical novel that will lead to requests for sequels," and praised Greene for creating a "concrete, convincing sense of . . . time and place."

In her books for the popular "American Girl" series, Greene focuses on nine-year-old New Yorker Rebecca Rubin, one of five children in her Russian Jewish immigrant family. When readers meet Rebecca, it is 1914 and Rebecca dreams of being an actress and starring on stage like her cousin Max. *Candlelight for Rebecca* finds the Jewish girl in a quandary when a class assignment requires her to create a Christmas decoration for her family, because her family celebrates Hanukkah. A trip to New York's Coney Island with her cousins turns into a day of adventure and daring do in *Rebecca to the Rescue,* while in *Changes for Rebecca* the girl learns first hand about the labor strife that is affecting both workers and factory owners in her New York home town. Discussing the "Rebecca" novels on her home page, Greene remarked: "I hope the books give [readers] . . . an idea of what it is like to be an immigrant in America, whether they are thinking about their great-grandparents, or their next door neighbor. I also hope that Rebecca shows readers that one person can make a difference in the world, as long as she has the courage to try."

Greene's picture book *What His Father Did* is a humorous story of Herschel, a trickster who figures prominently in Jewish folklore. Traveling on a long journey with little money, Herschel stops at an isolated inn and tricks the innkeeper into giving him supper by vaguely threatening to "do what his father did" if he is left hungry. The frightened innkeeper gathers food from nearby merchants, imagining all manner of horrible things the father could have done, and gets a surprise when Herschel reveals what his father REALLY did. A *Kirkus Reviews* contributor noted that Greene's "lively and economical" writing is "fine for sharing aloud," while a *Publishers Weekly* critic dubbed *What His Father Did* "dexterously written [and] exquisitely illustrated."

Greene weaves elements of several cultures in her picture book **The Secret Shofar of Barcelona,** *featuring artwork by Doug Chayka.* (Illustration copyright © 2009 by Lerner Publishing Group. Reprinted with permission of Kar-Ben, a division of Lerner Publishing Group. All rights reserved. No part of this excerpt may be used or reproduced in any manner whatsoever without the prior written permission of Lerner Publishing Group, Inc.)

Greene also focuses on Jewish culture in the picture books *Nathan's Hanukkah Bargain,* illustrated by Judith Hierstein, and *The Secret Shofar of Barcelona,* illustrated by Doug Chayka. In *Nathan's Hanukkah Bargain* a boy goes shopping with his grandfather, hoping to purchase his own menorah. Although the new menorahs are either too expensive or use candles or electricity rather than the preferred oil, his grandfather shares some wisdom from the old country that helps the boy achieve his goal and also share a family tradition. Citing the "straightforward appeal" of Greene's story, *School Library Journal* contributor Eva Mitnick recommended *Nathan's Hanukkah Bargain* as "a good intergenerational" choice for storyhour, and a *Kirkus Reviews* writer noted that Hierstein's "realistic gouache paintings . . . bring a vivid authenticity" to Greene's family-centered tale.

In addition to fiction, Greene has authored several works of nonfiction for young students. The realities of slavery in the ancient world are brought to light in both *Slavery in Ancient Egypt and Mesopotamia* and *Slavery in Ancient Greece and Rome.* Including a discussion of the daily life of slaves in northern Africa, the first volume moves forward in time to the beginnings of slave trading with Europeans, and then with merchants in the

Americas. In Greene's second book, the role slaves played in allowing for the flowering of Greek culture is discussed; both books feature what *School Library Journal* contributor Eunice Weech characterized as a "straightforward, factual text [that] does not gloss over the brutality of this institution."

The Chippewa or Ojibway people are the focus of two books by Greene. *The Chippewa* presents an overview of tribal culture, history, and religion through to modern times, while shape-shifter legends are collected in *Manabozho's Gifts: Three Chippewa Tales,* which includes the story of how the tribe first harvested wild rice to help its members survive the winter, how Manabozho gave his people the gift of fire by stealing the substance from an aged sorcerer, and a third tale, "How Manabozho Saved the Rose," which focuses on native ecology. Praising Greene's retellings for their "quiet dignity," *School Library Journal* contributor Jacqueline Elsner also commented on the inclusion of a foreword by Greene that grounds "readers in the Manabozho archetype," a tradition that also is known under the names Nanabozho, Hiawatha, and Manabush. Noting the environmental underpinnings of the collection, Elizabeth Bush commented in the *Bulletin of the Center for Children's Books* on the "deep respect for nature [that] emerges from the Manabozho legend."

In *Powwow: A Good Day to Dance,* Greene follows a ten-year-old Abenaki boy to a twentieth-century tribal gathering, providing a history and background of the day of dance. Focusing on one boy's experiences at a Wampanoag powwow in eastern Massachusetts, Greene "is able to relate many details and describe the event in a personal way," noted Darcy Schild in *School Library Journal.* In addition to a discussion of the boy and his activities, Greene includes sidebars that focus on clothing, music, dance, food, drumming, and powwow "etiquette."

Other series nonfiction includes *The 2001 World Trade Center Attack, The Triangle Shirtwaist Factory Fire,* and *Grizzly Bears: Saving the Silvertip,* the last a book in the "America's Animal Comebacks" series that pairs color photographs with what *School Library Journal* contributor Nancy Call described as a "well organized" and "accessible" text. Reviewing *The Triangle Shirtwaist Factory Fire,* which focuses on a fire in New York City's garment district in which 146 young garment workers were killed in March of 1911, Kay Weisman wrote in *Booklist* that Greene follows the fire from its start through its tragic death toll and the protests that erupted in its aftermath. The author's detailed history will be "an enticing" choice for history buffs attracted "by the dramatic subject," Weisman added.

"I always remember that we are never far from childhood," Greene once commented to *SATA* in reflecting on her role as a writer. "All the things we have done, the friends we have made, the embarrassments and successes we felt, are part of us and make us the people

we are. When I write a book, it is not just written with children in mind. It reflects my feelings and should strike a responsive chord in every reader, regardless of age. I hope my characters speak to everyone expressing the ageless and human emotions we all share, and making readers feel as if they have met someone they never knew before, and will remember for a long time."

Biographical and Critical Sources

PERIODICALS

Booklist, March 15, 1992, Hazel Rochman, review of *What His Father Did,* p. 1282; June 15, 1992, Karen Hutt, review of *The Maya,* pp. 1829-1830; February 15, 1994, Ilene Cooper, review of *The Chippewa,* p. 1078; April 1, 1994, Carolyn Phelan, review of *One Foot Ashore,* p. 1446; March 15, 1995, Linda Ward-Callaghan, review of *Manabozho's Gifts: Three Chippewa Tales,* p. 1324; April, 1998, Denia Hester, review of *Marie: Summer in the Country, France, 1775,* p. 1319; January, 1999, Karen Hutt, review of *Powwow: A Good Day to Dance,* p. 865; April 1, 2007, Kay Weisman, review of *The Triangle Shirtwaist Factory Fire,* p. 74.

Bulletin of the Center for Children's Books, February, 1995, Elizabeth Bush, review of *Manabozho's Gifts,* p. 198.

Horn Book, August, 1984, Mary M. Burns, review of *The Leveller,* p. 474; May-June, 1992, Hanna B. Zeiger, review of *What His Father Did,* p. 346; July-August, 1994, Elizabeth S. Watson, review of *One Foot Ashore,* p. 451.

Kirkus Reviews, February 1, 1992, review of *What His Father Did,* p. 183.

New York Times Book Review, March 19, 1989, Eli N. Evans, review of *Out of Many Waters,* p. 24.

Publishers Weekly, February 10, 1992, review of *What His Father Did,* p. 81.

School Library Journal, April, 1984, Deborah M. Locke, review of *The Leveller,* pp. 114-115; November, 1984, Micki S. Nevett, review of *Butchers and Bakers, Rabbis and Kings,* p. 108; August, 1992, Marcia Posner, review of *What His Father Did,* pp. 151-152, 164; June, 1994, Renee Steinberg, review of *One Foot Ashore,* p. 128; January, 1995, Jacqueline Elsner, review of *Manabozho's Gifts,* p. 118; August, 1997, Nancy Menaldi-Scanlan, review of *Marie: Mystery at the Paris Ballet, Paris, 1775,* p. 135; April, 1998, Anne Knickerbocker, review of *Marie: Summer in the Country, France, 1775,* p. 131; February, 1999, Darcy Schild, review of *Powwow,* p. 97; March, 2001, Eunice Weech, review of *Slavery in Ancient Egypt and Mesopotamia,* and Ann Welton, *Slavery in Ancient Greece and Rome,* both p. 266; July, 2007, Grace Oliff, review of *The Triangle Shirtwaist Factory Fire,* p. 88; August, 2007, Jennifer Cogan, review of *The 2001 World Trade Center Attack* p. 96; December, 2007, Nancy Call, review of *Grizzly Bears: Saving the Silvertip,* p. 106; October, 2008, Eva Mitnick, review of *Nathan's Hanukkah Bargain,* p. 94.

ONLINE

Jacqueline Greene Web site, http://www.jdgbooks.com (January 10, 2010).*

*   *   *

GREGORY, Kristiana 1951-

Personal

Born June 12, 1951, in Los Angeles, CA; daughter of Harold (an inventor) and Jeanne (a recreation supervisor) Gregory; married 1982; children: two sons. *Religion:* Christian. *Hobbies and other interests:* Swimming, walking, reading, doing crossword puzzles, spending time with family and friends.

Addresses

Home—Boise, ID. *Agent*—Elizabeth Harding, Curtis Brown, Ltd., Ten Astor Pl., New York, NY 10003. *E-mail*—kgregorybooks@yahoo.com.

Career

Journalist and author. *Gardena Valley News,* Gardena, CA, freelance feature writer, 1977-79, freelance reporter, 1978; *Southern California Business,* Los Angeles, CA, associate editor, 1978; *Los Angeles Times,* book reviewer and columnist, 1978-91; *San Luis Obispo County Telegram-Tribune,* San Luis Obispo, CA, reporter, 1980-81; homemaker and writer, 1982—.

Member

Society of Children's Book Writers and Illustrators, L'Alliance Française, Young Woman's Christian Association.

Awards, Honors

Golden Kite Award for Fiction, Society of Children's Book Writers and Illustrators, Notable Children's Trade Book in Social Studies citation, National Council for the Social Studies/Children's Book Council (NCSS/CBC), and Book for the Teen Age citation, New York Public Library, all 1989, all for *Jenny of the Tetons;* Best Book for Young Adults citation, American Library Association, and Notable Children's Trade Book in Social Studies citation, NCSS/CBC, both 1992, and Best Children's Book about California citation, California Commonwealth Club, 1993, all for *Earthquake at Dawn;* Notable Children's Trade Book in the Field of Social Studies designation, NCSS/CBC, for 1996, *The Winter of Red Snow;* Oppenheim Toy Portfolio award, 2001, for *Seeds of Hope.*

Writings

HISTORICAL FICTION

Jenny of the Tetons, Harcourt (San Diego, CA), 1989.

The Legend of Jimmy Spoon, Harcourt (San Diego, CA), 1990.
Earthquake at Dawn, Harcourt (San Diego, CA), 1992.
Jimmy Spoon and the Pony Express, Scholastic, Inc. (New York, NY), 1994.
The Stowaway: A Tale of California Pirates, Scholastic, Inc. (New York, NY), 1995.
Orphan Runaways, Scholastic, Inc. (New York, NY), 1998.
My Darlin' Clementine, Holiday House (New York, NY), 2009.

"DEAR AMERICA" SERIES

The Winter of Red Snow: The Revolutionary War Diary of Abigail Jane Stewart, Valley Forge, Pennsylvania, 1777, Scholastic, Inc. (New York, NY), 1996.
Across the Wide and Lonesome Prairie: The Oregon Trail Diary of Hattie Campbell, 1847, Scholastic, Inc. (New York, NY), 1997.
The Great Railroad Race: The Diary of Libby West, Utah Territory, 1868, Scholastic, Inc. (New York, NY), 1999.
Seeds of Hope: The Gold Rush Diary of Susanna, California Territory, 1849, Scholastic, Inc. (New York, NY), 2001.
Cannons at Dawn (sequel to *The Winter of Red Snow*), Scholastic, Inc. (New York, NY), 2011.

"MY AMERICA" SERIES

Five Smooth Stones: Hope's Revolutionary War Diary, Scholastic, Inc. (New York, NY), 2001.
We Are Patriots: Hope's Revolutionary War Diary, Scholastic, Inc. (New York, NY), 2002.
When Freedom Comes: Hope's Revolutionary War Diary, Scholastic, Inc. (New York, NY), 2004.

"ROYAL DIARIES" SERIES

Cleopatra VII: Daughter of the Nile, Egypt, 57 B.C., Scholastic, Inc. (New York, NY), 1999.
Eleanor: Crown Jewel of Aquitaine, France, 1136, Scholastic, Inc. (New York, NY), 2002.
Catherine: The Great Journey, Russia, 1743, Scholastic, Inc. (New York, NY), 2005.

"PRAIRIE RIVER" SERIES

A Journey of Faith, Scholastic, Inc. (New York, NY), 2003.
A Grateful Harvest, Scholastic, Inc. (New York, NY), 2003.
Winter Tidings, Scholastic, Inc. (New York, NY), 2004.

"CABIN CREEK MYSTERIES"

The Secret of Robber's Cave, Scholastic, Inc. (New York, NY), 2008.
The Clue at the Bottom of the Lake, Scholastic, Inc. (New York, NY), 2008.

The Legend of Skull Cliff, Scholastic, Inc. (New York, NY), 2008.

The Haunting of Hillside School, Scholastic, Inc. (New York, NY), 2008.

The Blizzard on Blue Mountain, Scholastic, Inc. (New York, NY), 2008.

The Secret of the Junkyard Shadow, Scholastic, Inc. (New York, NY), 2009.

OTHER

Bronte's Book Club (novel), Holiday House (New York, NY), 2008.

Contributor of short fiction to *Moody Monthly.*

Adaptations

The Winter of Red Snow and *Cleopatra VII* were both adapted as television films by the HBO Family Channel.

Sidelights

Kristiana Gregory is the author of numerous works of historical fiction for children and young adults. In novels such as *Jenny of the Tetons, A Journey of Faith,* and

Cover of Kristiana Gregory's middle-grade mystery novel **The Legend of Skull Cliff,** *featuring artwork by Patrick Faricy.* (Jacket art copyright © 2008 by Patrick Faricy. Reproduced by permission of Scholastic, Inc.)

My Darlin' Clementine, Gregory transforms historical documents into full-fledged stories of eighteenth-, nineteenth-, and early-twentieth-century American life. Central to her works are the adventures of young people who, like their modern counterparts, face emotional crises and hard choices. Careful research, convincing characters, and historical accuracy distinguish her books, which have received a host of honors.

Books were always an important part of Gregory's life. As she once told *SATA:* "We had books everywhere, and my parents read to me a lot. If we had questions, my father would say, 'Let's look it up in the encyclopedia.' Then we'd get in this long, involved, fun adventure going through an encyclopedia, and I think that's where I got my love for research. All the historical things I write remind me of my childhood and the excitement of exploring something and finding out about it."

One subject Gregory chose to write about as an adult, Native-American history and culture, was also part of her upbringing. "When we moved to New Mexico we were very close to the Mescalero Apache Indian reservation," she recalled. "My parents were interested in the Native Americans, and they would take us around to the different powwows and pueblos. They had almost a reverent respect for them, and they passed that on to us. Anything that had to do with Native Americans they were interested in. We would go to museums, and we had Navajo rugs in our home and trinkets and that sort of thing."

During the 1970s Gregory worked as a freelance writer for newspapers. "I went to the editor of the *Gardena Valley News* and said, 'I don't have any writing experience but I love to write—will you hire me?' I can't believe I did this, because I had no experience. He hired me to write feature stories for ten dollars each, plus they would give me a byline. Eventually that editor, Charles Ferrell, became editor of the Los Angeles Chamber of Commerce's weekly tabloid, *Southern California Business,* and asked me to come along. Later I met *Los Angeles Times* editor Art Seidenbaum through a college course on writing and he offered me a job there."

Children's books became an increasingly important part of Gregory's life after she married and started a family in Pocatello, Idaho. "I was invited to write a children's book column for the *Los Angeles Times Book Review,*" she explained. "I was in the middle of nowhere, in very cold weather—it was below zero for weeks at a time, which was difficult for a native Californian, plus I had a toddler and an infant—and the United Parcel Service would deliver these huge boxes of books, brand-new children's books. It was quite a thrill, because the editor said, 'Just write a column, pick eight or so books per column.' The column appeared every other week and I had all these wonderful books to choose from.

"When my children were a little older I started tutoring at the Pocatello High School. I got to know a lot of the Native Americans from Fort Hall, which was seven miles north of Pocatello. That was the real spark of the desire to write, when I saw how hungry these teenagers were to know about their culture. We would try to find books to interest them in reading, and very little is written about their ancestors. That was my main motivation for writing *Jenny of the Tetons.* I found a real Shoshone woman with nothing written about her, and I wanted to honor her and honor the culture."

In *Jenny of the Tetons* Gregory tells of Jenny and Beaver Dick's lives from the point of view of fictional immigrant orphan Carrie Hill, who has been adopted by the Leighs. Grieving for her parents, who were killed in an Indian raid, fifteen-year-old Carrie agrees to help Beaver Dick's wife tend their many children, unaware that this woman is herself Native American. Once Carrie arrives at the Leighs' rustic home, she struggles to reconcile her own prejudices with Jenny's kindness. Gradually the family's love eases the girl's grief, and when tragedy strikes the Leighs, Carrie fully shares their emotional pain. According to Richard Peck, assessing *Jenny of the Tetons* for the *Los Angeles Times Book Review,* "the strength of the writing lies in its research and the underplayed description of unqualified sorrow."

Gregory also focuses on Native-American themes in *The Legend of Jimmy Spoon,* the tale of a young white boy who goes to live among the Shoshone. In a story based on the memoirs of a nineteenth-century pony express rider, twelve-year-old Jimmy is frustrated with both his father's refusal to give him a horse and the boredom of working at the family store. After meeting two Indian boys outside of town, Jimmy decides to accept their gift of a horse in return for a visit to their camp. The tribe wants him to stay permanently, however, and for the next three years Jimmy works to learn and understand Shoshone ways as the adopted son of the chief's mother. Eventually Jimmy's father discovers his son's whereabouts and threatens war if Jimmy does not return; to preserve the peace, the young man leaves the tribe. Although *Los Angeles Times Book Review* writer Eileen Heyes praised *The Legend of Jimmy Spoon* as "rich in its portrait of Indian philosophy and daily life." Paula J. Lacey, reviewing the same novel in the *Voice of Youth Advocates,* described Gregory's story as "well researched" and "exciting."

Gregory's readers were the inspiration behind *Jimmy Spoon and the Pony Express.* "I got so many letters from children all over the country asking for a sequel to *The Legend of Jimmy Spoon* that I said okay. . . . I spent months researching the pony express. Because I couldn't get to Nevada, I called bookstores and museums all along the pony express trail and asked them to tell me what titles they had. I had bookstores send me things about Nevada flowers and the terrain and immigrant diaries from that era. One man sent me a video-

tape of the pony express trail that he had done all the way from Missouri to California so I could see what the terrain was like in Nevada."

In *Jimmy Spoon and the Pony Express* Jimmy is seventeen year old and itching for adventure after working in his father's store. He liked his time with the Shoshone far better than his staid life in Salt Lake City. When he comes across an advertisement for riders for the Pony Express, he sees it as a way out of his boring life and as an opportunity to travel once again through Shoshone territory. However, the teen soon learns that delivering the U.S. mail, despite some small adventures, is not quite as exciting as he hoped it would be. Reviewing *Jimmy Spoon and the Pony Express* for *Booklist,* Chris Sherman noted that "Gregory packs her short chapters with enough action, drama, and humor to please even hard-core reluctant readers."

In *Earthquake at Dawn* Gregory chronicles the experiences of photographer Edith Irvine and her traveling companion, the fictional Daisy Valentine, who were visiting San Francisco when the great earthquake hit on April 18, 1906. The two young women come to the city early that morning, planning to board a ship bound for Australia and, ultimately, Paris, where Edith has been invited to exhibit her photographs. The earthquake shatters their plans, however. They spend the next several days trying to find Edith's father, from whom they have been separated, and sharing the trials of several residents who become like family to the young women. One of their new friends is Mary Exa, whose 1906 letter describing the earthquake provides revealing quotes for the beginning of each chapter. Despite thirst, hunger, exhaustion, fires, rats, and additional earth tremors, Edith manages to photograph the devastation. This itself endangers the women, for city authorities hoping to conceal the extent of the catastrophe have been confiscating and destroying cameras and photographic plates. Mary Hedge, assessing *Earthquake at Dawn* in the *Voice of Youth Advocates,* wrote that "the emotional impact . . . blends well with the adventure plot, making it an excellent choice for the rare teenage historical fiction lover." *Earthquake at Dawn* was honored as the best children's book about California by the California Commonwealth Club in 1993.

In *The Stowaway: A Tale of California Pirates* Gregory takes middle-grade readers from the West coast out to sea with eleven-year-old Carlito, who stows away on a pirate ship to seek revenge for the killing of his father. Partially set in Monterey, California, in the nineteenth century, the book is based on the adventures of a real pirate named Hipolyte de Bouchard. Barbara Chatton praised *The Stowaway* in a *School Library Journal* review, calling it "exciting" and further noting that Gregory "brings to life events and perspectives not often found in the standard history texts."

In addition to her standalone novels, Gregory has also penned many titles in the "Dear America" series, in which aspects of American history are illuminated by the fictional diaries of young people of the time. She takes a look at America's Revolutionary War experience in *The Winter of Red Snow: The Revolutionary War Diary of Abigail Jane Stewart, Valley Forge, Pennsylvania, 1777* and *Five Smooth Stones: Hope's Revolutionary War Diary*. In *The Winter of the Red Snow*, Gregory relates the hardships of the Revolutionary Army during the bitter winter of 1777-78 at Valley Forge through the eyes of eleven-year old Abby, whose family lives nearby. "Although Gregory's overall tone is positive," noted Ann W. Moore in *School Library Journal*, "she doesn't neglect . . . the horrors of war." A sequel, *Cannons at Dawn*, finds Abigail joining the camp followers all the way to the final battle in Yorktown, Virginia, in 1782. By the time of battle, Abigail has married her sweetheart, soldier Willie Campbell, and is expecting their first child.

Gregory returns to the topic of the American Revolution in two companion volumes. With *Five Smooth Stones,* readers follow the events of 1776 through the eyes of nine-year-old Hope Potter—"one brave, young girl," according to Mary Laub in *Childhood Education*—who records daily life and her brushes with famous patriots in and around Philadelphia at the beginning of the war. Denise Wilms had positive words for the novel in *Booklist,* remarking that Gregory does "an effective job of evoking the times." Elizabeth Bush reached a similar conclusion in her review of *Five Smooth Stones* for the *Bulletin of the Center for Children's Books.* Noting the inclusion of "kid-pleasing, authentic details of everyday life abound," Bush also cited details ranging from the humorous "to the severe discomforts of life without electricity and central heating."

Hope's story is continued in *We Are Patriots,* which finds the Potter fleeing to the country, but still unable to find peace. Hope's brother, gone off to fight with the British, has been arrested as a spy, and her father is fighting with the colonists. Meanwhile, there is a new baby to care for, and concern for the safety of the family forces Hope's mother to return the family to Philadelphia, where they must deal with the invading British troops. Trying to regain normalcy, they reopen their bakery, but when Mr. Potter returns from the battlefield he has fearful stories to relate. A contributor for *Kirkus Reviews* noted that "strong imagery and well-researched details make this an engrossing as well as educational selection." In *When Freedom Comes: Hope's Revolutionary War Diary, Book Three* the year is 1777 and Hope now awaits the safe return of her father and brother.

A journey west on the Oregon Trail is the subject of *Across the Wide and Lonesome Prairie: The Oregon Trail Diary of Hattie Campbell, 1847.* Set in 1847, this journal-novel chronicles the hardships of thirteen-year-old Hattie and her family as they travel from Missouri west along the Oregon Trail. Although disaster strikes the group on more than one occasion—including when Hattie herself makes a fatal mistake—the youngster also makes friends and has her horizons broadened. Noting Gregory's ability to tell a story "rich with details of pioneer life," *Booklist* contributor Carolyn Phelan added that the fictional diary "has a good deal of truth in it." The "details of life on the trail will be fascinating to young readers," concluded *School Library Journal* critic Connie Parker in a review of *Across the Wide and Lonesome Prairie.*

Another trek west is at the heart of *The Great Railroad Race: The Diary of Libby West, Utah Territory, 1868,* which chronicles the construction of the transcontinental railroad in 1868 as seen through the eyes of the fourteen-year-old daughter of a newspaper reporter in Utah Territory. Building the railway connected the West with the East coast, reducing the arduous six-month stagecoach or wagon-train journey to a mere week by rail. To research the work, Gregory and her family traveled to the Golden Spike Historical Site, a national park in Utah. "When I heard the shriek of a train whistle and saw the replica of Engine 119 chugging toward the summit, I felt a thrill," she told Richard F. Abrahamson and Linda M. Pavonetti in a *Scholastic Canada* online interview. "I could imagine what it must have been like to watch the actual event." A contributor for *Kirkus Reviews* commented of *The Great Railroad Race* that "history is brought to life through Libby's candid narration."

Gregory deals with the California Gold Rush of 1849 in both *Seeds of Hope: The Gold Rush Diary of Susanna, California Territory, 1849* and *Orphan Runaways. Seeds of Hope* focuses on the journals of fourteen-year-old Susanna, who has traveled with her parents from New York to the West by ship. The family intended to head for the Oregon territory, but their goal changed after Susanna's mother was lost at sea on the journey. Landing in San Francisco on New Year's Day, 1849, Susanna's distraught father is struck with gold fever and takes his children off into the wilds of California in search of the elusive yellow metal. Life in the mining camps is "richly detailed in Susanna's vivid entries," wrote Ellen Mandel in a *Booklist* review of *Seeds of Hope,* the critic calling Gregory's novel a "gripping, realistic fictional glimpse of history."

Orphan Runaways provides a look at the Gold Rush through the eyes of twelve-year-old Danny and Danny's younger brother, Judd. Both boys run away from a San Francisco orphanage in search of an uncle residing in one of the California boom towns. Upon finding Uncle Hank, Danny decides to stay with a kindly hotel operator because he is prejudiced against his uncle's new wife, a Chinese woman. Finally, however, the young boy comes around, learning to accept his new aunt. Although *School Library Journal* critic Faith Brautigam complained that Gregory's "characters don't come to life," *Booklist* reviewer Kay Weisman maintained that *Orphan Runaways* serves as an effective "exploration of racial prejudice of the time."

Gregory's "Prairie River" series, which is set in Missouri at the end of the U.S. Civil War, focuses on Vanessa Clemens, a strong-willed, independent fourteen year old. In *A Journey of Faith* Vanessa flees the orphanage where she was raised after learning that the cruel headmaster has arranged for her to marry an older preacher. With the help of a kindly educator and her best friend, Vanessa boards a stagecoach and heads to Kansas, relying on her strong Christian beliefs as she begins a new life as a prairie schoolteacher. *A Journey of Faith* "is rich in description and historical detail," Heather E. Miller wrote in *School Library Journal,* and *Kliatt* reviewer Ann Hart called the work "an enjoyable coming-of-age story full of conflict and strength of character." In the sequel, *A Grateful Harvest,* Vanessa must protect her students from a host of dangers, including a deadly prairie fire. In *Kliatt* Maureen Griffin observed that "young readers will learn much as they identify with a nicely human and brave Nessa." Gregory concluded the series with *Winter Tidings.*

Inspired by a traditional folksong, *My Darlin' Clementine* explores life in a rugged Idaho mining town through the eyes of a spunky sixteen year old. Set in the 1860s, the work follows Clementine as she deals with the disappearance of her mother, helps raise her younger sisters, and confronts a corrupt judge who has jailed her father. "Gregory provides plenty of cliff-hangers and historical background to keep avid fans of the author, or the genre, reading," Wendy Scalfaro remarked in *School Library Journal,* and Phelan commented that the "resourceful and down-to-earth Clementine makes an appealing heroine."

Cleopatra VII: Daughter of the Nile, Egypt, 57 B.C. takes the reader far from Gregory's usual fictional and historical territory. Part of the "Royal Diaries" series, the novel transports readers to ancient Egypt and Rome, following twelve-year-old Cleopatra as she meets such luminaries as the soldier and statesman Mark Antony (who, many years later, will become her lover), the famous Roman orator Cicero, and Octavian, the man who will become Augustus Caesar and defeat Cleopatra and Mark Antony to win control of the Roman empire. Discussing her research efforts for these books, Gregory remarked in her *Scholastic Canada* interview with Abrahamson and Pavonetti that "digging into history of 2,000 years was a great challenge, and a frustrating one. Because some well-respected scholars disagree on what is true—from important events to dates to spellings of names—I was glad Cleopatra was to be fiction, not biography."

"The attention to detail draws readers headlong into Egypt," wrote a contributor for *Kirkus Reviews* in a review of *Cleopatra VII,* while in *Booklist,* Susan Dove Lempke praised Gregory's narrative style, noting that she "writes evocatively" and "has clearly done her research." Cynthia M. Sturgis, writing in *School Library Journal,* called the book an "enjoyable story," and further remarked that characters "are well drawn . . . and

historical background is well integrated into the text." Deborah Stevenson further lauded *Cleopatra VII* in her *Bulletin of the Center for Children's Books* review, writing that Gregory "paints an exciting picture of riches, heritage, and conspiracy," as the youthful Cleopatra tries to navigate treacherous diplomatic waters in Rome in an attempt to shore up her father's Egyptian reign.

Gregory continues her "Royal Diaries" series with *Eleanor: Crown Jewel of Aquitaine, France, 1136* and *Catherine: The Great Journey, Russia, 1743.* In the former, she examines a momentous year in the life of the historic figure, one of the most powerful women in Europe during the Middle Ages who became the queen consort of France in 1137 at the tender age of fifteen. According to Phelan, Gregory "does her subject justice": her portrayal of the main characters "are all convincing within their time and place." In *Catherine,* Gregory presents the diary of the eighteenth-century German princess who marries Peter, the grand duke of Russia, and eventually wrests power from her husband, reigning as the empress of Russia. Lynn K. Vanca, writing in *School Library Journal,* observed that the author's "strong characterizations bring the historically grounded figures to life."

In a departure from historical fiction, Gregory's suspense-filled "Cabin Creek Mysteries" feature the adventures of a pair of intrepid brothers, Jeff and David, as they investigate the strange occurrences on Lost Island with the help of their cousin, Claire. In *The Secret of Robber's Cave* the trio stumbles upon a skeleton while looking for buried treasure that is reputedly tied to a century-old stagecoach heist. Writing in *School Library Journal,* Krista Tokarz observed that Gregory's story "is well paced and has likable, engaging characters."

The Clue at the Bottom of the Lake finds Jeff, David, and Claire investigating a large bundle the size of a dead body that they saw dumped in the lake, while *The Legend of Skull Cliff* focuses on the disappearance of a camper from the dangerous lookout at Skull Cliff. In *The Haunting of Hillside School* a girl's face appears, then disappears, outside a window of the cousins' old schoolhouse. Other strange clues to be explored in the novel include piano music lilting through empty halls and the discovery of a secret passageway. *The Blizzard on Blue Mountain* finds the kids snowed-in and left behind in an unheated ski chalet, while in *The Secret of the Junkyard Shadow* after a mysterious stranger is spotted in the local dump. Soon bikes, toasters and items disappear all over town, only to reappear, fixed and freshly painted.

"The "Cabin Creek Mysteries" are based on stories I told my sons when they were little and restless and didn't want to go to bed," Gregory told *SATA.* "It began when our family vacationed in the Tetons, in a little log cabin on a beautiful lake. When the boys asked about a canoe going out to a small island, my imagination went wild. The setting is similar to many mountainous lakes in the West, where children have adventures camping, fishing, and floating the rivers."

Bronte's Book Club, a contemporary novel for middle-grade readers, centers on twelve-year-old Bronte, who has just moved with her family from New Mexico to a small, seaside town in California. To overcome her loneliness, Bronte decides to form a book discussion group that soon grows to include four other girls with wildly different personalities: secretive and pretty Willow; her humorous best friend, Lupe; free-wheeling Nan; and brooding Jessie. As the summer passes, the girls use Bronte's book choice—Scott O'Dell's *Island of the Blue Dolphins*—as a vehicle to share their thoughts and feelings with each other, and they begin to connect on a personal level. Gregory's "subtle message that an atmosphere of trust and understanding enhances friendship is presented effectively," a contributor in *Kirkus Reviews* observed.

In all her writing, Gregory tries to convey the need for love and hope. "Part of my motivation is I'm hoping that kids . . . see that there is hope, there is always hope, and there is always somebody to love, and there is always someone who will love you." Love is paramount in her books, Gregory asserted: "Love for your fellow human being regardless of color or circumstances, taking time to try to understand another person and not make snap judgments."

Biographical and Critical Sources

PERIODICALS

Booklist, November 15, 1994, Chris Sherman, review of *Jimmy Spoon and the Pony Express,* p. 590; September 15, 1995, Linda Perkins, review of *The Stowaway: A Tale of California Pirates,* pp. 162-163; April 15, 1997, Carolyn Phelan, review of *Across the Wide and Lonesome Prairie: The Oregon Trail Diary of Hattie Campbell, 1847,* p. 1428; February 15, 1998, Kay Weisman, review of *Orphan Runaways,* p. 1011; April 1, 1999, GraceAnne A. DeCandido, review of *The Great Railroad Race: The Diary of Libby West, Utah Territory, 1868,* p. 1426; January 1, 2000, Susan Dove Lempke, review of *Cleopatra VII: Daughter of the Nile, Egypt, 57 B.C.,* p. 922; March 1, 2000, Sally Estes, review of *Orphan Runaways,* p. 1212; January 1, 2001, Denise Wilms, review of *Five Smooth Stones: Hope's Revolutionary War Diary, Book One* p. 960; September 1, 2001, Ellen Mandel, review of *Seeds of Hope: The Gold Rush Diary of Susanna, California Territory, 1849,* p. 104; February 1, 2003, Carolyn Phelan, review of *Eleanor: Crown Jewel of Aquitaine, France, 1136,* p. 994; April 1, 2008, Hazel Rochman, review of *Bronte's Book Club,* p. 44; April 15, 2009, Carolyn Phelan, review of *My Darlin' Clementine,* p. 54.

Book Report, May-June, 1997, Jo Clarke, review of *Orphan Runaways,* p. 34.

Bulletin of the Center for Children's Books, October, 1995, Elizabeth Bush, review of *The Stowaway,* p. 55; October, 1996, Elizabeth Bush, review of *The Winter of Red Snow: The Revolutionary War Diary of Abigail Jane Stewart, Valley Forge, Pennsylvania, 1777,* pp. 55-56; December, 1999, Deborah Stevenson, review of *Cleopatra VII,* p. 130; April, 2001, Elizabeth Bush, review of *Five Smooth Stones,* p. 303.

Childhood Education, winter, 2001, Mary Laub, review of *Five Smooth Stones,* p. 110.

Children's Book Review Service, June, 1998, Kristi Steele, review of *Orphan Runaways,* p. 130.

English Journal, December, 1992, review of *Earthquake at Dawn,* p. 77.

Kirkus Reviews, April 1, 1999, review of *The Great Railroad Race,* p. 534; July 15, 1999, review of *Cleopatra VII,* p. 1133; May 1, 2002, review of *We Are Patriots: Hope's Revolutionary War Diary,* p. 654; April 1, 2008, review of *Bronte's Book Club.*

Kliatt, May, 2003, Maureen K. Griffin, review of *A Journey of Faith,* p. 16; November, 2003, Ann Hart, review of *A Journey of Faith,* p. 14; March, 2004, Maureen Griffin, review of *A Grateful Harvest,* p. 19.

Cover of Gregory's middle-grade novel Bronte's Book Club, *featuring artwork by Yolanda Gonzalez.* (Cover art copyright © 2008 by Yolanda Gonzalez. Reproduced by permission of Holiday House, Inc.)

Los Angeles Times Book Review, May 28, 1989, Richard Peck, "A Blending of Two Cultures," p. 8; October 28, 1990, Eileen Heyes, review of *The Legend of Jimmy Spoon,* p. 12.

Publishers Weekly, September 2, 1996, review of *The Winter of Red Snow,* p. 131; August 4, 2003, review of *A Journey of Faith,* p. 76.

School Library Journal, November, 1994, Sally Bates Goodroe, review of *Jimmy Spoon and the Pony Express,* p. 102; September, 1995, Barbara Chatton, review of *The Stowaway,* p. 200; September, 1996, Ann W. Moore, review of *The Winter of Red Snow,* p. 202; March, 1997, Connie Parker, review of *Across the Wide and Lonesome Prairie,* p. 187; March, 1998, Faith Brautigam, review of *Orphan Runaways,* p. 212; August, 1999, Cathy Coffman, review of *The Great Railroad Race,* p. 158; October, 1999, Cynthia M. Sturgis, review of *Cleopatra VII,* p. 150; July, 2001, Janet Gillen, review of *Seeds of Hope,* p. 108; November, 2003, Heather E. Miller, review of *A Journey of Faith,* p. 140; May, 2006, Lynn K. Vanca, review of *Catherine: The Great Journey, Russia, 1743,* p. 125; March, 2008, Krista Tokarz, review of *The Secret of Robber's Cave,* p. 164; May, 2009, Wendy Scalfaro, review of *My Darlin' Clementine,* p. 106.

Tribune Books (Chicago, IL), May 4, 1997, Katherine Seigenthaler, "Dear Diarists," pp. 1, 9.

Voice of Youth Advocates, December, 1990, Paula J. Lacey, review of *The Legend of Jimmy Spoon,* p. 281; June, 1992, Mary Hedge, review of *Earthquake at Dawn,* p. 94; April, 1995, Darlene Kelm, review of *Jimmy Spoon and the Pony Express,* p. 23.

ONLINE

KidsReads.com, http://www.kidsreads.com/ (July 2, 2002), Shannon Maughan, interview with Gregory.

Kristiana Gregory Home Page, http://kgregorybooks.com (January 1, 2010).

Scholastic Canada Web Site, http://www2.scholastic.ca/ (January 1, 2010), Richard F. Abrahamson and Linda M. Pavonetti, interview with Gregory.

*   *   *

GUDEON, Karla

Personal

Married; husband's name Kevin; children: Sam, Max. *Education:* Parsons School of Design, degree, 1982.

Addresses

Home—Long Island, NY. *Office*—Gudeon Family Press, 3 Milleridge La., Smithtown, NY 11787. *E-mail*—karla@karlagudeon.com.

Career

Artist, educator, and illustrator. Gudeon Family Press, Smithtown, NY, owner, 1998—; teacher of elementary school for fourteen years. *Exhibitions:* Work has been

Karla Gudeon (Reproduced by permission.)

shown in solo and group exhibitions in galleries and museums throughout the United States, including R. Michelson Galleries, Northampton, MA, and Cove Gallery, Wellfleet, MA.

Awards, Honors

National Jewish Book Award finalist, 2008, and Sydney Taylor Notable Books selection, Association of Jewish Libraries, 2009, both for *Hanukkah Haiku* by Harriet Ziefert.

Writings

Family Prayerbook for the High Holy Days, Chicago Sinai Congregation (Chicago, IL), 2004.

Harriet Ziefert, *Hanukkah Haiku,* Blue Apple Books (Maplewood, NJ), 2008.

Harriet Ziefert, *One Red Apple,* Blue Apple Books (Maplewood, NJ), 2009.

Sidelights

Combining watercolor painting with dry-point engraving, a method of hand-pulled printmaking, Karla Gudeon creates brightly colored works of folk art that have gained praise for their warmth and beauty. Gudeon's paintings often feature representations of joyous family experiences, cultural celebrations, and nature. A former elementary school teacher, Gudeon has also contributed illustrations to a number of children's books, including *Hanukkah Haiku,* a poetry collection by prolific writer Harriet Ziefert. "In creating art, I strive to conjure my most joyous experiences and bring them to a visual format," the artist told *SATA.* "I love knowing that through my artwork viewers garner a sense of shared humanity and purchasers delight in coming home to my paintings."

Before she was born, Gudeon's parents searched for a name for their new daughter that began with the letter "K." Upon discovering children's books by Karla Kuskin, they decided upon the name "Karla." As Gudeon notes, she loves the serendipity of having entered the field of her namesake.

In *Hanukkah Haiku,* Ziefert offers eight simple verses that celebrate the Jewish holiday. The haiku, one for each night of Hanukkah, describe such familiar activities as lighting the candles, spinning a dreidel, and enjoying latkes and applesauce. Gudeon's "vibrant, folksy paintings" of the family's traditions "create a feeling of tapestry," observed *Horn Book* critic Shoshana Flax. Comparing Gudeon's paintings to the works of Marc Chagall, a contributor in *Kirkus Reviews* stated that the artist's "intensely bright, detailed illustrations float and soar through the pages." Teri Markson, writing in *School Library Journal,* complimented the "lovely folkloric quality" of Gudeon's art, further noting the "gorgeous patterned edges" of the pages.

Biographical and Critical Sources

PERIODICALS

Horn Book, November-December, 2008, Shoshana Flax, review of *Hanukkah Haiku,* p. 655.

Gudeon's illustration projects include creating the intricate artwork for **Harriet Ziefert's** Hanukkah Haiku. (Blue Apple Books, 2008. Illustration copyright © 2008 by Karla Gudeon. Reproduced by permission.)

Kirkus Reviews, November 1, 2008, review of *Hanukkah Haiku.*
School Library Journal, October, 2008, Teri Markson, review of *Hanukkah Haiku,* p. 99.

ONLINE

Karla Gudeon Home Page, http://www.karlagudeon.com (January 1, 2010).

H

HEARN, Julie 1958-

Personal

Born 1958, in Abingdon, England; children: Tilly. *Education:* Earned B.A. (English); Oxford University, M.St. (women's studies). *Hobbies and other interests:* Gardening.

Addresses

Home and office—Oxfordshire, England. *Agent*—Felicity Bryan Literary Agency, 2A N. Parade, Oxford OX2 6LX, England; agency@felicitybryan.com.

Career

Writer, editor, and journalist. Worked as a journalist in Australia, Spain, and England. Presenter at workshops for children.

Awards, Honors

Carnegie Medal nomination, and Branford Boase Award shortlist, both for *Follow Me Down;* London *Guardian* Children's Fiction Prize shortlist, and Carnegie Medal nomination, both for *The Merrybegot;* Best Book for Young Adults selection, American Library Association, 2006, and Aesop Accolades citation, American Folklore Society, both for *The Minister's Daughter.*

Writings

NOVELS

Follow Me Down, Oxford University Press (Oxford, England), 2003, published as *Sign of the Raven,* Atheneum Books for Young Readers, 2005.
The Merrybegot, Oxford University Press (Oxford, England), 2005, published as *The Minister's Daughter,* Atheneum Books for Young Readers (New York, NY), 2005.

Julie Hearn (Photograph by Simon Duncan. Reproduced by permission.)

Ivy, Oxford University Press (Oxford, England), 2006, Atheneum Books for Young Readers (New York, NY), 2008.
Hazel, Oxford University Press (Oxford, England), 2007, Atheneum Books for Young Readers (New York, NY), 2009.

Rowan the Strange, Oxford University Press (Oxford, England), 2009.

Sidelights

Julie Hearn's debut novel, *Follow Me Down,* was nominated for both the Carnegie Medal and the Branford Boase Award, and her follow-up work, *The Merrybegot,* earned a second Carnegie nomination and was short-listed for London's *Guardian* Children's Fiction Prize. One of the joys of entering the field of children's literature, Hearn remarked on her home page, "was it made me feel a bit like a child again myself—getting all excited about what might happen next and truly believing, for hours at a time, in the magic of pink drinks, time travel and being invisible."

Hearn, a former journalist who studied women's studies at Oxford University, became inspired to write *Follow Me Down* while trying to decide on a topic for her thesis. While she was researching a potential area of focus, she became absorbed with a handbill for the Bartholomew Fair, urging the public to visit "The Changeling Child." "I kept thinking about this tiny person who, according to the handbill, never spoke and had no teeth but was 'the most voracious and hungry creature in the world.' I kept wondering who she had been and what had happened to her. So as soon as I'd finished studying for my master's degree I decided to write her story," Hearn stated on her home page.

Follow Me Down—published in the United States as *Sign of the Raven*—intertwines the past and the present as readers follow Tom while he seeks to recover the corpse of an eighteenth-century giant who was one of the named "freaks" in the Bartholomew Fair. While the premise is definitely out of the ordinary, this particular story has a much deeper and promising message: finding one's inner strengths and beauties, and overcoming superficial obstacles. Tom's quest originates when he discovers a portal in his grandmother's basement that takes him into the eighteenth century. After arriving on the other side of this fantastical intersect, he finds himself among the freaks who were kept in this very same basement during the Bartholomew Fair. At first Tom cannot touch these individuals without inflicting pain, but he eventually breaks through this barrier. When asked to aid them in recovering the corpse of their friend the giant, Tom agrees, hoping to give the deformed man a proper burial.

Follow Me Down delves into the darker aspects of human nature, and Hearn's portrayal of the abuse suffered by many of her characters made an impression on reviewers and readers alike. Jan Mark, reviewing the novel for the *Guardian,* called Hearn's writing both "vital and evocative," while noting that the supernatural aspects of the novel are somewhat underdeveloped. Praising the work for introducing teen readers to the grittier aspects of eighteenth-century life, Kit Spring stated in the London *Observer* that *Follow Me Down* is "a corker of a novel, original and rambunctious."

Set in seventeenth-century England, *The Merrybegot* centers on Nell, an apprentice village healer and granddaughter of the local cunning woman, and Nell's relationship with a Puritan minister's two daughters. When Grace, the minister's older, more beautiful daughter, becomes pregnant, she comes to Nell for an abortion. Nell refuses to terminate the pregnancy, however, because Grace's baby is a "merrybegot," a child conceived on May morning and believed to have special powers. Outraged, Grace convinces her simple-minded sister, Patience, to help her conspire against Nell and her grandmother by blaming her pregnancy on witchcraft. Published in the United States as *The Minister's Daughter,* Hearn's second novel earned strong reviews. "Hearn writes with great brio and style," observed *Guardian* critic Adèle Geras, who added that "the life of the village, its customs, inhabitants and especially the conflict between the old religion of paganism and a puritan Christianity is wonderfully evoked" in the work. Writing in *Horn Book,* Anita L. Burkam commented that Hearn "creates a richly magical ambiance, straddling the line between the supernatural and the concrete realm of human passions and weaknesses."

In *Ivy,* a Dickensian novel set in Victorian England, an orphan girl rises from the London slums after learning to take control of her life. Kidnapped at age five by a gang of thieves, the strikingly beautiful Ivy is trained as a "skinner," a thief who literally steals the clothes from her victims' backs. After she becomes addicted to laudanum, Ivy is returned to her predatory aunt and uncle, who force her to model for a wealthy but incompetent painter with an insanely jealous mother, until a chance meeting with PreRaphaelite artist Dante Gabriel Rossetti changes the course of Ivy's life. *Booklist* critic Francisca Goldsmith remarked that in *Ivy* Hearn "combines authentic nineteenth-century period detail with well-developed, credible characters," and Myrna Marler stated in *Kliatt* that "Ivy is likable, if naive, in a sordid world, and her story is compelling."

Hazel is a sequel of sorts to *Ivy* and focuses on twelve-year-old Hazel Mull-Dare, Ivy's daughter. Enrolled at an elite school for girls, Hazel comes under the spell of an American classmate who sparks her interest in the women's suffrage movement. After an ill-fated protest at Madame Tussaud's gallery in London, Hazel is sent to the Caribbean to live with her grandparents, where she learns about her family's slave-owning past. "There's a rich vein of social and political material to be found here," Kate Agnew wrote in her *Guardian* review of *Hazel.* Linda Newbery complimented the work in the same publication, writing of *Hazel* that "it's the quality of Julie Hearn's writing—assured, flexible, bringing every scene vividly to life—that makes [the book] . . . such a pleasure to read. From the larkiness of the school scenes to the drama of a Caribbean hurricane, she takes us on an exciting and memorable journey."

In *Rowan the Strange* Hearn continues the story of Ivy's lineage. At the onset of World War II, Rowan, the teen-

Cover of Hearn's young-adult historical novel Ivy, *featuring artwork by* **Michael Frost.** (2009. Reproduced by permission of Atheneum Books for Young Readers, an imprint of Simon & Schuster Macmillan.)

aged son of Hazel, is diagnosed as a schizophrenic and committed to a lunatic asylum. Placed under the care of a German doctor, a proponent of the controversial electro-convulsive therapy, Rowan forms an unlikely friendship with rebellious Dorothea, a fellow patient who sees angels. Noting Hearn's skill at creating memorable settings, Nicolette Jones observed in London's *Sunday Times* that "it is in the detail of human interactions that her novel is particularly remarkable." Philip Ardagh, writing in the *Guardian,* remarked that *Rowan the Strange* "works perfectly as a strangely beautiful stand-alone story. It is nothing short of extraordinary."

Biographical and Critical Sources

PERIODICALS

Booklist, May 15, 2005, Jennifer Mattson, review of *The Minister's Daughter,* p. 1669; June 1, 2008, Francisca Goldsmith, review of *Ivy,* p. 66.

Guardian (London, England), September 6, 2003, Jan Mark, review of *Follow Me Down,* p. 32; February 12, 2005, Adèle Geras, "Piskies and Puritans," review

of *The Merrybegot,* p. 33; June 24, 2006, Marcus Sedgwick, "Destiny's Child," review of *Ivy,* p. 20; September 18, 2007, Kate Agnew, review of *Hazel,* p. 7; November 3, 2007, Linda Newbery, "Girl Power," review of *Hazel,* p. 20; July 4, 2009, Philip Ardagh, "Shock and War," review of *Rowan the Strange,* p. 14.

Horn Book, September-October, 2005, Anita L. Burkam, review of *The Minister's Daughter,* p. 579; January-February, 2006, Deirdre F. Baker, review of *Sign of the Raven,* p. 79.

Independent (London, England), February 22, 2005, Julie Hearn, "I See Life in a Whole New Light," p. 6.

Kirkus Reviews, September 1, 2005, review of *Sign of the Raven,* p. 973.

Kliatt, September, 2005, Janis Flint-Ferguson, review of *Sign of the Raven,* p. 8; July, 2008, Myrna Marler, review of *Ivy,* p. 14.

Observer (London, England), August 3, 2003, Kit Spring, review of *Follow Me Down,* p. 17.

Publishers Weekly, October 31, 2005, review of *Sign of the Raven,* p. 58; June 9, 2008, review of *Ivy,* p. 51.

School Library Journal, June, 2005, Margaret A. Chang, review of *The Minister's Daughter,* p. 160; November, 2005, Beth Wright, review of *Sign of the Raven,* p. 136; July, 2008, Denise Moore, review of *Ivy,* p. 99.

Sunday Times (London, England), February 6, 2005, Nicolette Jones, review of *The Merrybegot,* p. 54; May 10, 2009, Nicolette Jones, review of *Rowan the Strange.*

Times (London, England), February 5, 2005, Celia Dodd, "On the Bright Side," p. 14; February 26, 2005, review of *The Merrybegot,* p. 13.

ONLINE

Julie Hearn Home Page, http://www.julie-hearn.com (January 1, 2010).*

*   *   *

HEMINGWAY, Edward 1969(?)-

Personal

Born c. 1969; son of Gregory (a doctor and writer) and Valerie (a journalist and writer) Hemingway. *Education:* Rhode Island School of Design, B.A.; School of Visual Arts, M.F.A.

Addresses

Home—Brooklyn, NY.

Career

Illustrator and writer.

Writings

(Illustrator) Mark Bailey, *Hemingway and Bailey's Bartending Guide to Great American Writers,* Algonquin Books of Chapel Hill (Chapel Hill, NC), 2006.

(Self-illustrated) *Bump in the Night,* G.P. Putnam's Sons (New York, NY), 2008.

Contributor of articles and illustrations to periodicals, including *Nickelodeon Magazine, Gentleman's Quarterly, Gourmet,* and the *New York Times.*

Sidelights

Illustrator and author Edward Hemingway comes from a long line of writers. His grandfather, Ernest Hemingway, was the Nobel Prize-wining author of works like *The Sun Also Rises,* and both his parents were writers as well. Nevertheless, as the younger Hemingway explained in an article for the London *Times Online,* having a famous last name "opens a lot of doors, but it doesn't prevent them being slammed in your face if people don't like what they see when you step through." A writer and artist, Hemingway has made his career by contributing both artwork and articles to various periodicals.

The idea for Hemingway's first children's book came to him after he was frightened by a leftover Halloween mask left in a closet. "I realized it's kind of fun to get scared," he told Jodi Hausen in the *Bozeman Daily Chronicle.* "But it's funny because, after you realize it, it's not as scary as you thought." In his self-illustrated picture book *Bump in the Night,* young Billy is initially scared by the monster in his closet, until the two become friends and share adventures. "Hemingway's

Edward Hemingway pairs a simple story with his stylized artwork in his debut picture book **Bump in the Night.** (Copyright © 2008 by Edward Hemingway. All rights reserved. Reproduced by permission of G.P. Putnam's Sons, a division of Penguin Putnam Books for Young Readers.)

tongue-in-cheek text keeps the action moving along and adds a touch of humor," a *Kirkus Reviews* critic observed of the work. In *School Library Journal* Carolyn Janssen remarked of *Bump in the Night* that Hemingway's "acrylic-on-wood illustrations create the perfect mood for this appealing bedtime story" and his text explores bedtime fears with the "right mix of silliness and reassurance."

Biographical and Critical Sources

PERIODICALS

Bozeman Daily Chronicle, August 23, 2008, Jodi Hausen, "Book Festival Brings in Authors, Illustrators."
Kirkus Reviews, May 15, 2008, review of *Bump in the Night.*
School Library Journal, August, 2008, Carolyn Janssen, review of *Bump in the Night,* p. 92.

ONLINE

Edward Hemingway Home Page, http://www.edwardhemingway.com (January 15, 2010).
Times Online (London, England), http://www.timesonline.co.uk/ (June 3, 2007), Edward Hemingway, "My Hols."*

*   *   *

HIERSTEIN, Judith (Judy Hierstein)

Personal

Female. *Education:* University of Iowa, B.A. (art education).

Addresses

Home—Tucson, AZ.

Career

Teacher and illustrator. Former elementary-school teacher; Ironwood Ridge High School, Oro Valley, AZ, graphic and media-arts teacher.

Writings

(Self-illustrated) *Multicultural Bulletin Boards,* F. Schaffer Publications (Torrance, CA), 1995.

ILLUSTRATOR

Gloria Teles Pushker, *Toby Belfer Never Had a Christmas Tree,* Pelican Publishing (Gretna, LA), 1991.

Judith Hierstein creates the engaging illustrations in Gloria Teles Pushker's holiday-themed picture book **Toby Belfer and the High Holy Days.** (Pelican Publishing Company, 2001. Judith Hierstein, illustrator. Reproduced by permission.)

Gloria Teles Pushker, *Toby Belfer's Seder: A Passover Story Retold,* Pelican Publishing (Gretna, LA), 1994.

Gloria Teles Pushker, *A Belfer Bar Mitzvah,* Pelican Publishing (Gretna, LA), 1995.

Gloria Teles Pushker, *Toby Belfer and the High Holy Days,* Pelican Publishing (Gretna, LA), 2001.

(As Judy Hierstein) Douglas M. Rife, *Research and Writing: Activities That Explore Family History,* Teaching & Learning Co. (Carthage, IL), 2002.

(As Judy Hierstein) Mary Tucker, *Washington Crossing the Delaware: A Hands-on-History Look at George Washington Crossing the Delaware River, a Pivotal Event in the American Revolution,* Teaching & Learning Co. (Carthage, IL), 2002.

(As Judy Hierstein) Robynne Eagan, *Cattle Drive: A Hands-on-History Look at the Cowboy of the 1800s West,* Teaching & Learning Co. (Carthage, IL), 2002.

(As Judy Hierstein) Elaine Hansen Cleary, *Mayflower: A Hands-on-History Look at the Pilgrims' Journey to the New World,* Teaching & Learning Co. (Carthage, IL), 2003.

Gloria Teles Pushker, *Toby Belfer Visits Ellis Island,* Pelican Publishing (Gretna, LA), 2003.

Laura Crawford, *The Pilgrims' Thanksgiving from A to Z,* Pelican Publishing (Gretna, LA), 2005.

Rickey Pittman, *Jim Limber Davis: A Black Orphan in the Confederate White House,* Pelican Publishing (Gretna, LA), 2007.

Jacqueline Dembar Greene, *Nathan's Hanukkah Bargain,* Pelican Publishing (Gretna, LA), 2008.

Sherry Garland, *Voices of Gettysburg,* Pelican Publishing (Gretna, LA), 2009.

Laura Crawford, *The American Revolution from A to Z,* Pelican Publishing (Gretna, LA), 2009.

Sidelights

Art teacher and illustrator Judith Hierstein enjoys exploring other cultures and times through her work. Many of the books she has illustrated help illuminate Jewish culture and traditions, among them several volumes in Gloria Teles Pushker's "Toby Belfer" series. Similar themes are the focus of Jacqueline Dembar Greene's picture book *Nathan's Hanukkah Bargain,* and here Hierstein's artwork helps tell the story of young boy who wants to buy his own old-fashioned menorah and only finds the right one with the help of his grandfather. "The full-spread illustrations do a good job of complementing the text," Eva Mitnick remarked in her *School Library Journal* review of *Nathan's Hanukkah Bargain,* while a *Kirkus Reviews* critic observed that Hierstein's illustrations "bring a vivid authenticity to this intergenerational story of traditional values, respect and understanding."

Hierstein has also lent her artistic talents to books with historical themes that cover U.S. history from the ar-

Hierstein's many illustration projects includes creating detailed images for Jacqueline Dembar Greene's picture book **Nathan's Hanukkah Bargain.** (Pelican Publishing, 2008. Illustration copyright © 2008 by Judith Hierstein. Reproduced by permission.)

rival of the pilgrims to the American Revolution and the U.S. Civil War. Rickey Pittman's *Jim Limber Davis: A Black Orphan in the Confederate White House* is based on the true story of a former slave boy who is rescued and freed by the family of Confederate president Jefferson Davis only to be lost after Union troops capture and imprison Davis. A *Children's Bookwatch* reviewer found that Hierstein's "earthy illustrations" for this book "add a complementary touch" to a little-known subject.

Biographical and Critical Sources

PERIODICALS

Booklist, October 1, 2001, Ilene Cooper, review of *Toby Belfer and the High Holy Days,* p. 338.

Children's Bookwatch, September, 2007, review of *Jim Limber Davis: A Black Orphan in the Confederate White House.*

Kirkus Reviews, November 1, 2008, review of *Nathan's Hanukkah Bargain.*

School Library Journal, September, 2007, Anne Chapman Callaghan, review of *Jim Limber Davis,* pp. 185-186; October, 2008, Eva Mitnick, review of *Nathan's Hanukkah Bargain,* p. 94.

ONLINE

Pelican Publishing Web site, http://pelicanpub.com/ (January 19, 2010), "Judith Hierstein."*

*   *   *

HIERSTEIN, Judy
   ## See HIERSTEIN, Judith

*   *   *

HOWARD, Arthur 1948-
   ## (Arthur Charles Howard)

Personal

Born January 26, 1948, in New York, NY; son of Bernard (an executive engineer and inventor) and Cora (an artist) Howard. *Education:* Reed College, B.A., 1970.

Addresses

Home—New York, NY. *E-mail*—arthurhoward@earthlink.net.

Career

Writer and illustrator. Professional actor, performing in stage productions on Broadway, off-Broadway, and in regional theater and in television commercials and for seven seasons on *Square One* (television series), Public Broadcasting Service.

Awards, Honors

ABC Children's Bestsellers Choice designation, for *Mr. Putter and Tabby Bake the Cake* by Cynthia Rylant; American Book Award (ABA) Pick of the Lists designation, ABC Children's Bestsellers Choice designation, and American Library Association (ALA) Notable Book designation, 1996, all for *Mr. Putter and Tabby Pick the Pears* by Rylant; ABA Pick of the Lists designation, Oppenheim Toy Portfolio Best Book Award, Crayola Kids Best Book of the Year choice, International Reading Association/Children's Book Council (IRA/CBC) Children's Choice designation, and Charlotte Award, New York State Reading Association, all 1998, all for *When I Was Five;* Reading Magic Award, *Parenting* magazine, for *Mr. Putter and Tabby Toot the Horn* by Rylant; Best Book of the Year citation, *School Library Journal,* 2001, Nevada Young Readers Award, and Kentucky Bluegrass Award, both 2003, and Best of the Best citation, Bank Street College, and IRA/CBC Children's Choice designation, all for *Hoodwinked;* IRA Teacher's Choice selection, 2001, for *100th Day Worries* by Margery Cuyler; Irma and James Black Award, Bank Street College, 2002, for *Bubba and Beau, Best Friends* by Kathie Appelt; ABA Pick of the Lists designation, IRA/CBC Children's Choice designation, Washington State Children's Choice Picture Book Award, 2002, and Tennessee Volunteer State Book Award, 2003, all for *Cosmos Zooms;* ABA Pick of the Lists designation, and Oppenheim Toy Portfolio Platinum Award, both 2001, both for *Mr. Putter and Tabby Paint the Porch* by Rylant; Oppenheim Toy Portfolio Gold Award, and Top-Ten Easy Readers citation, *Booklist,* both 2004, both for *Mr. Putter and Tabby Stir the Soup* by Rylant; Oppenheim Toy Portfolio Platinum Award, 2005, for *Mr. Putter and Tabby Write the Book* by Rylant.

Writings

SELF-ILLUSTRATED

When I Was Five, Harcourt (San Diego, CA), 1996, published as *Now I Am Six,* Hazar (London, England), 1998.

Cosmos Zooms, Harcourt (San Diego, CA), 1999.

Hoodwinked, Harcourt (San Diego, CA), 2001.

Serious Trouble, Harcourt (San Diego, CA), 2003.

The Hubbub Above, Harcourt (Orlando, FL), 2005.

Co-author, with Julie Logan, of "The World according to He & She" (humor column) for *Glamour* magazine, 1992-95, and a book of the same title.

Howard's work has been translated into several languages, including Chinese, Italian, French, German, Norwegian, Brazilian, Portuguese, and Korean.

ILLUSTRATOR, "MR. PUTTER AND TABBY" SERIES

Cynthia Rylant, *Mr. Putter and Tabby Pour the Tea,* Harcourt (San Diego, CA), 1994.

Cynthia Rylant, *Mr. Putter and Tabby Walk the Dog,* Harcourt (San Diego, CA), 1994.

Cynthia Rylant, *Mr. Putter and Tabby Bake a Cake,* Harcourt (San Diego, CA), 1994.

Cynthia Rylant, *Mr. Putter and Tabby Pick the Pears,* Harcourt (San Diego, CA), 1995.

Cynthia Rylant, *Mr. Putter and Tabby Fly the Plane,* Harcourt (San Diego, CA), 1997.

Cynthia Rylant, *Mr. Putter and Tabby Row the Boat,* Harcourt (San Diego, CA), 1997.

Cynthia Rylant, *Mr. Putter and Tabby Toot the Horn,* Harcourt (San Diego, CA), 1998.

Cynthia Rylant, *Mr. Putter and Tabby Take the Train,* Harcourt (San Diego, CA), 1998.

Cynthia Rylant, *Mr. Putter and Tabby Paint the Porch,* Harcourt (San Diego, CA), 2000.

Cynthia Rylant, *Mr. Putter and Tabby Feed the Fish,* Harcourt (San Diego, CA), 2001.

Cynthia Rylant, *Mr. Putter and Tabby Catch the Cold,* Harcourt (San Diego, CA), 2002.

Cynthia Rylant, *Mr. Putter and Tabby Stir the Soup,* Harcourt (San Diego, CA), 2003.

Cynthia Rylant, *Mr. Putter and Tabby Write the Book,* Harcourt (Orlando, FL), 2004.

Cynthia Rylant, *Mr. Putter and Tabby Make a Wish,* Harcourt (Orlando, FL), 2005.

Cynthia Rylant, *Mr. Putter and Tabby Spin the Yarn,* Harcourt (Orlando, FL), 2006.

Cynthia Rylant, *Mr. Putter and Tabby See the Stars,* Harcourt (Orlando, FL), 2007.

Cynthia Rylant, *Mr. Putter and Tabby Run the Race,* Harcourt (Orlando, FL), 2008.

Cynthia Rylant, *Mr. Putter and Tabby Spill the Beans,* Harcourt (Orlando, FL), 2009.

ILLUSTRATOR

Cynthia Rylant, *Gooseberry Park,* Harcourt (San Diego, CA), 1995.

Margery Cuyler, *The Battlefield Ghost,* Scholastic, Inc. (New York, NY), 1999.

Margery Cuyler, *100th Day Worries,* Simon & Schuster (New York, NY), 2000.

Margery Cuyler, *Stop, Drop, and Roll,* Simon & Schuster (New York, NY), 2001.

Kathi Appelt, *Bubba and Beau, Best Friends,* Harcourt (San Diego, CA), 2002.

Kathi Appelt, *Bubba and Beau Go Night-Night,* Harcourt (San Diego, CA), 2003.

Kathi Appelt, *Bubba and Beau Meet the Relatives,* Harcourt (Orlando, FL), 2004.

Betsy Byars, Betsy Duffey, and Laurie Myers, *The SOS File,* Holt (New York, NY), 2004.

Margery Cuyler, *Hooray for Reading Day!,* Simon & Schuster Books for Young Readers (New York, NY), 2008.

Margery Cuyler, *Bullies Never Win,* Simon & Schuster Books for Young Readers (New York, NY), 2009.

Margery Cuyler, *I Repeat, Don't Cheat!,* Simon & Schuster Books for Young Readers (New York, NY), 2010.

Sidelights

Illustrator Arthur Howard began his career as an actor, working on stage and screen in everything from television commercials and Broadway and off-Broadway productions to the Public Broadcasting Service television series *Square One.* After twenty years in theater, Howard began illustrating Cynthia Rylant's "Mr. Putter and Tabby" picture-book series, creating characters that enliven Rylant's adventures of an old man and his cat. In 1996 he also began creating original, self-illustrated stories such as *When I Was Five, Serious Trouble,* and *The Hubbub Above.* Covering themes such as friendship, laughter, being a good neighbor, and judging people for their qualities not for their looks, Howard's books have been published around the world, including in the United Kingdom, France, and Korea.

"People ask me, which comes first, the story or the pictures?," Howard once told *SATA,* "and I've always been quick to explain that definitely it's the story. . . . I do try to have a complete text finished before I work on the illustrations. But before I start writing a story, I have to have an idea—and my initial ideas for a story are always visual images."

Howard's first independent title, *When I Was Five,* tells the story of a six-year-old boy who remembers what it was like to be five years old by describing the things that were important to him a year ago. Noting that while many of his favorite things have changed with advancing age, the boy's best friend is still the same. "Few books this short and up beat are as involving and ultimately moving as this one," Carolyn Phelan stated in her *Booklist* review of *When I Was Five.* Writing in *Horn Book,* Lolly Robinson praised Howard for his ability to capture and sustain the perspective of a six year old, writing that "both text and art demonstrate the self-assurance acquired at this age, ringing true in every detail."

In his self-illustrated *Cosmos Zooms,* Howard introduces a small black-and-white schnauzer that does not feel as though it is especially good at anything. All of the other pets in the story have unique abilities, and it is not until Cosmo falls asleep on a skateboard that it discovers its own talent. "The six canine characters (and single Siamese cat) exude personality," a reviewer wrote in praising Howard's illustrations for *Publishers Weekly.* Kay Weisman, writing for *Booklist,* commented that "young children are sure to identify with Cosmo's insecurities and eventual success."

Hoodwinked tells a story of beauty, but not in a typical way. As Howard once told *SATA, Hoodwinked* "began with a simple visual image. One day my nieces asked me to tell them a story. At the time they each had at least two Barbie dolls with them. I don't have anything against Barbie dolls, but I decided to tell them the most un-Barbie story I could think of; nothing about pretty clothes, or pretty hair, or pretty anything. So I began, 'Mitzi the witch liked creepy things. Creepy bedroom slippers. Creepy breakfast cereal.' The third line, 'Creepy relatives,' occurred to me later—right after Thanksgiving." Mitzi's dilemma in the story is a search for a pet. She wants a truly creepy pet, but the toad is boring and the bats do not pay attention to her. One night, a kitten appears at her door, and Mitzi allows it to stay, but just for one night, because she is not interested in a pet that is cute. The kitten has other ideas, however, and it accompanies Mitzi on all of her witchy activities. Finally Mitzi realizes that the kitten is the perfect pet for her, in spite of its non-creepy outward appearance. In *Booklist* Shelley Townsend-Hudson commented that "children will enjoy the preposterous fun and hilarious illustrations" in *Hoodwinked*, while a *Publishers Weekly* critic noted the "cute-fierce characters and cobwebby settings" highlighting Howard's art in the book. "A satisfying story," *Hoodwinked* is "illustrated with effective humorous line drawings" in "ghastly greens and putrid purples," commented Martha V. Parravano in a *Horn Book* review, while Ruth Semrau concluded in *School Library Journal* that "every page is a delight."

Another self-illustrated book by Howard, *Serious Trouble*, introduces Ernest, a young prince who wants to be a jester but now has to outsmart a dragon. Ernest makes a deal with the dragon: if he can get the creature to laugh, it will not eat him. "Children will giggle right up to the fitting conclusion of this lighthearted romp," predicted Marilyn Taniguchi in her *School Library Journal* review, while a *Kirkus Reviews* contributor noted that Howard tucks "plenty of wordplay into the brief text to complement his playful, loosely drawn illustrations." Recommending *Serious Trouble* for storytime groups, *Horn Book* contributor Kitty Flynn asserted that Howard's "crowd pleaser will tickle even a heckler's funny bone."

Reflecting on his self-illustrated picture book *The Hubbub Above*, Howard told *SATA:* "I had a friend who often complained about her upstairs neighbors. One day she referred to them as 'the elephants upstairs.' I was immediately struck by the image of elephants dwelling in a small New York apartment. What would their home look like?, I wondered. What kind of friends would they have? And the kitchen. I suppose it would be extremely well stocked . . . with peanuts. A book was born."

Sydney, the star of *The Hubbub Above*, is a resident of the fifty-second floor of the Ivory Towers. She does not know that her upstairs neighbors are actually elephants. What she does know is that they are noisy, especially on Saturday nights when they host parties for their many friends. When Sydney confronts her neighbors during one such party, she discovers the reason for all the noise: her neighbors and their guests are all wild animals! When the elephants realize they have caused Sydney aggravation, they promise they will try to be more quiet, and they invite the girl to all their future parties. "Howard's sherbet-colored, highly atmospheric art

serves as the perfect setting" for the tale, according to a *Kirkus Reviews* contributor. Mary Elam, writing in *School Library Journal,* deemed *The Hubbub Above* "a humorous tale with a subtle message of tolerance and cooperation," while Kitty Flynn wrote in *Horn Book* that Howard's "friendly conflict-resolution [is] . . . accompanied by boisterous cartoon illustrations."

Although Howard's self-illustrated picture books have been popular with readers, the bulk of his work has been as an illustrator. Howard's long-running collaboration with Rylant on the "Mr. Putter and Tabby" series begins when elderly Mr. Putter decides that his loneliness can be cured if he gets a cat. When a trip to the pet store produces only kittens, Mr. Putter makes his way to the animal shelter and meets Tabby, a cat in just as much need of a friend as Mr. Putter. Tabby proves to be a good companion, and the pair accomplishes tasks from travel to baking to recovering from illness. Linda Perkins, writing in *Booklist,* noted of the series that Howard's illustrations "add character and sly humor" to Rylant's text. Diane Janoff commented that the "clearly rendered illustrations" in *Mr. Putter and Tabby Paint the Porch* make the book "a perfect choice for any weather," while Anne Knickerbocker considered the illustrations in *Mr. Putter and Tabby Feed the Fish* to be "expressive." Stephanie Zvirin complimented Howard's "cozy, freewheeling artwork" in her *Booklist* review of *Mr. Putter and Tabby Stir the Soup,* and *Mr. Putter and Tabby Spin the Yarn* was described by *School Library Journal* critic Kathleen Pavin as a "successful addition" to Rylant's series. Howard's "funny . . . drawings catch the emotional presences of each character," Pavin added of the book.

Howard's illustrations have also appeared in books by Margery Cuyler and Betsy Byars, as well as in Kathi Appelt's "Bubba and Beau" chapter-book series. Writing in *Booklist,* Kathy Broderick considered Howard's watercolors for *Bubba and Beau, Best Friends* to be "familiar and comforting." A *Kirkus Reviews* critic wrote of *Bubba and Beau Go Night-Night* that "snappy pencil-and-watercolor illustrations feature the amusing cast of characters, providing honest down-home fun."

Collaborations between Howard and Cuyler include *Stop, Drop, and Roll, Hooray for Reading Day!, Bullies Never Win,* and *I Repeat, Don't Cheat!* All part of the "Jessica Worries" series, these books focus on a first grader who worries about absolutely everything, from her clothes to her grades to what her friends are up to. In a review of *Stop, Drop, and Roll,* Annie Ayers commented in *Booklist* that "Howard's quavering caricatures . . . are a hoot, adding to the general hilarity" of the story. Noting Cuyler's use of "simple" language in *Bullies Never Win, Booklist* contributor Hazel Rochman added that the artist's "cartoon-style illustrations" depict "the drama and familiar feelings . . . that come with facing up to bullies, while in *School Library Journal* Maryann H. Owen observed that Howard's "pen-and-ink and watercolor illustrations . . . deftly reveal . . .

the characters' variety of emotions." Howard's colorful cartoons for *Horray for Reading Day!* "add to the humor and exaggerate Jessica's expressions of angst, anguish, and ultimate achievement," concluded Mattern in another *School Library Journal* review.

Biographical and Critical Sources

PERIODICALS

Booklist, January 1, 1996, Linda Perkins, review of *Mr. Putter and Tabby Pick the Pears,* p. 850; November 1, 1999, Kay Weisman, review of *Cosmo Zooms,* p. 538; September 1, 2001, Shelly Townsend-Hudson, review of *Hoodwinked,* p. 120; September 15, 2001, Annie Ayers, review of *Stop, Drop, and Roll,* p. 230; April 1, 2002, Kathy Broderick, review of *Bubba and Beau, Best Friends,* p. 1331; November 1, 2002, Ilene Cooper, review of *Mr. Putter and Tabby Catch the Cold,* p. 509; July, 2003, Stephanie Zvirin, review of *Mr. Putter and Tabby Stir the Soup,* p. 1903; April 1, 2008, Carolyn Phelan, review of *Mr. Putter and Tabby Run the Race,* p. 58; August 1, 2008, Carolyn Phelan, review of *Hooray for Reading Day!,* p. 78; July 1, 2009, Hazel Rochman, review of *Bullies Never Win,* p. 65.

Bulletin of the Center for Children's Books, September, 2001, review of *Hoodwinked,* p. 19.

Childhood Education, spring, 2004, Gina Hoagland, review of *Serious Trouble,* p. 161.

Horn Book, September-October, 1996, Lolly Robinson, review of *When I Was Five,* p. 579; January-February, 2002, Martha V. Parravano, review of *Hoodwinked,* p. 68; November-December, 2003, Kitty Flynn, review of *Serious Trouble,* p. 730; May-June, 2005, Kitty Flynn, review of *The Hubbub Above,* p. 309.

Instructor, April, 1998, review of *When I Was Five,* p. 26; May, 2000, review of *Cosmo Zooms,* p. 14.

Kirkus Reviews, October 15, 2002, review of *Mr. Putter and Tabby Catch the Cold,* p. 1538; March 1, 2003, review of *Bubba and Beau Go Night-Night,* p. 378; October 1, 2003, review of *Serious Trouble,* p. 1225; May 1, 2005, review of *The Hubbub Above,* p. 539; June 15, 2008, review of *Hooray for Reading Day!*

Publishers Weekly, July 12, 1999, review of *Cosmo Zooms,* p. 93; August 16, 1999, review of *When I Was Five,* p. 87; September 24, 2001, review of *Hoodwinked,* p. 42; October 6, 2003, review of *Cosmos Zooms,* p. 87; November 3, 2003, review of *Serious Trouble,* p. 72.

Reading Teacher, October, 1997, review of *When I Was Five,* p. 132; October, 2000, review of *Cosmo Zooms,* p. 195.

School Librarian, spring, 2002, review of *Cosmo Zooms,* p. 19.

School Library Journal, May, 1996, Marianne Saccardi, review of *When I Was Five,* p. 92; September, 1999, Pat Leach, review of *Cosmo Zooms,* p. 184; July, 2000, Diane Janoff, review of *Mr. Putter and Tabby Paint the Porch,* p. 86; May, 2001, Anne Knickerbocker, review of *Mr. Putter and Tabby Feed the Fish,* p. 134; September, 2001, Ruth Semaru, review of *Hoodwinked,* p. 190; October, 2001, Roxanne Burg, review of *Stop, Drop, and Roll,* p. 46; November, 2003, Marilyn Taniguchi, review of *Serious Trouble,* p. 96; May, 2005, Mary Elam, review of *The Hubbub Above,* p. 86; October, 2005, Sandra Welzenbach, review of *Mr. Putter and Tabby Make a Wish,* p. 127; October, 2006, Kathleen Pavin, review of *Mr. Putter and Tabby Spin the Yarn,* p. 126; September, 2007, Erika Qualls, review of *Mr. Putter and Tabby See the Stars,* p. 175; February, 2008, Kelly Roth, review of *Mr. Putter and Tabby Run the Race,* p. 96; August, 2008, Lynne Mattern, review of *Horray for Reading Day!,* p. 86; June, 2009, Maryann H. Owen, review of *Bullies Never Win,* p. 82.

ONLINE

Simon & Schuster Web site, http://authors.simonand schuster.net/ (January 15, 2010), "Arthur Howard."*

*   *   *

HOWARD, Arthur Charles
See HOWARD, Arthur

I-J

INNS, Chris

Personal
Born in England; married; children: two.

Addresses
Home—Sevenoaks, Kent, England. *Agent*—Philippa Milnes-Smith, Lucas Alexander Whitley Agency, 14 Vernon St., London W14 0RJ, England.

Career
Author and illustrator. Art director and illustrator for English publishers, including Octopus, Hamlyn, Penguin, and Pan Macmillan, c. 1988-2008.

Writings

SELF-ILLUSTRATED

Next! Please, Tricycle Press (Berkeley, CA), 2001.
The Jokers, Frances Lincoln (London, England), 2005.
Cuddle Me, Kingfisher (Boston, MA), 2005.
What Will I Be?, Kingfisher (Boston, MA), 2005.
Peekaboo Panda and Other Animals: A Lift-the-flap Book, Kingfisher (Boston, MA), 2006.
Peekaboo Puppy and Other Pets: A Lift-the-flap Book, Kingfisher (Boston, MA), 2006.

ILLUSTRATOR

Samantha Hay, *Purr-Fect Pete,* Kingfisher (London, England), 2008.

Biographical and Critical Sources

PERIODICALS

School Library Journal, August, 2008, Laura Scott, review of *Purr-Fect Pete,* p. 92.

ONLINE

Lucas Alexander Whitley Agency Web site, http://www.lawagency.co.uk/ (January 15, 2010).*

*   *   *

JAMES, B.J.
See JAMES, Brian

*   *   *

JAMES, Brian 1976-
(B.J. James)

Personal
Born January 7, 1976, in Portsmouth, VA; son of Nicholas Masino and Anita Uhl; married Sarah Vischer (a photographer), March 16, 2002. *Education:* New York University, B.A. *Hobbies and other interests:* Reading, drawing, listening to music, watching cartoons, movies, and sci-fi television.

Addresses
Home and office—Phoenicia, NY. *E-mail*—brianjamespush@hotmail.com.

Career
Writer.

Awards, Honors
Quick Pick for Reluctant Young-Adult Readers selection, American Library Association, for *Thief.*

Writings

NOVELS

Pure Sunshine, Push Books (New York, NY), 2002.
Tomorrow, Maybe, Push Books (New York, NY), 2003.

Perfect World, Push Books (New York, NY), 2005.
Dirty Liar, Push Books (New York, NY), 2006.
Thief, Push Books (New York, NY), 2008.
Zombie Blondes, Feiwel & Friends (New York, NY), 2008.
The Heights, Feiwel & Friends (New York, NY), 2009.

PICTURE BOOKS

The Shark Who Was Afraid of Everything, illustrated by
    Bruce McNally, Scholastic, Inc. (New York, NY),
    2002.
Spooky Hayride, illustrated by Bryan Langdo, Scholastic,
    Inc. (New York, NY), 2003.
Easter Bunny's on His Way!, illustrated by Dara Goldman,
    Scholastic, Inc. (New York, NY), 2005.

"PIRATE SCHOOL" SERIES

The Curse of Snake Island, illustrated by Jennifer Zivoin,
    Grosset & Dunlap (New York, NY), 2007.
Ahoy! Ghost Ship Ahead, illustrated by Jennifer Zivoin,
    Grosset & Dunlap (New York, NY), 2007.
Attack on the High Seas!, illustrated by Jennifer Zivoin,
    Grosset & Dunlap (New York, NY), 2007.
Port of Spies, illustrated by Jennifer Zivoin, Grosset &
    Dunlap (New York, NY), 2007.
Treasure Trouble, illustrated by Jennifer Zivoin, Grosset &
    Dunlap (New York, NY), 2008.
Camp Buccaneer, illustrated by Jennifer Zivoin, Grosset &
    Dunlap (New York, NY), 2008.
Yo-ho-ho!, illustrated by Jennifer Zivoin, Grosset & Dun-
    lap (New York, NY), 2008.
Shiver Me, Shipwreck!, illustrated by Jennifer Zivoin,
    Grosset & Dunlap (New York, NY), 2009.

"CATKID" SERIES

I'm No Fraidy Cat, illustrated by Ned Woodman, Scholas-
    tic, Inc. (New York, NY), 2007.
A Purrfect Princess, illustrated by Ned Woodman, Scho-
    lastic, Inc. (New York, NY), 2007.
The Fishy Field Trip, illustrated by Ned Woodman, Scho-
    lastic, Inc. (New York, NY), 2007.
Three's a Crowd, illustrated by Ned Woodman, Scholastic,
    Inc. (New York, NY), 2008.

"SUPERTWINS" SERIES

(As B.J. James) *Supertwins Meet the Bad Dogs from Space,*
    illustrated by Chris Demarest, Scholastic, Inc. (New
    York, NY), 2003.
(As B.J. James) *Supertwins and Tooth Trouble,* illustrated
    by Chris Demarest, Scholastic, Inc. (New York, NY),
    2003.
(As B.J. James) *Supertwins Meet the Dangerous Dinobots,*
    illustrated by Chris Demarest, Scholastic, Inc. (New
    York, NY), 2003.
(As B.J. James) *Supertwins and the Sneaky, Slimy Book-
    worms,* illustrated by Chris Demarest, Scholastic, Inc.
    (New York, NY), 2004.

Sidelights

Brian James, the author of more than a dozen picture
books for young readers, including the works in the
"Pirate School" and "Catkid" series, is perhaps best
known for his critically acclaimed young-adult novels.
In works such as *Pure Sunshine, Dirty Liar,* and *The
Heights,* James examines prejudice, drug use, alien-
ation, and other emotionally charged subjects. In a *Cynsations* online interview, James told Cynthia Leitich
Smith that writing for a teen audience holds great
appeal. "They're really open to understanding different
points of view," he remarked. "I also think they respond
to a work of fiction on a much more personal level
sometimes, and as a writer, it's great to know your
work has real meaning to its readers."

In *Pure Sunshine,* James's debut title for young adults,
readers are introduced to a shy teenaged drug user
named Brendon, as he realizes that his habit is beginning to take over his life. During the two days covered
in James's novel, Brendon drifts through a typical
school day, his free time spent tripping on LSD, going
clubbing with his burnout friends Will and Kevin, and
wandering the streets of Philadelphia. Noting that
James' "language is raw and gritty," *School Library
Journal* contributor Debbie Stewart maintained that
Brendon's character rings true. "The conclusion may
not be grounded in reality, but sustains the mood and
plot," Stewart added. Dubbing *Pure Sunshine* a literary
"acid trip," a *Publishers Weekly* reviewer cited James
for his "airy, hallucinogenic imagery and nonjudgmental portraits of teen behavior," but cautioned that the
novel contains "no clear anti-drug message."

Inspired by the author's own memories of arriving alone
in New York City, *Tomorrow, Maybe* focuses on Chan,
a teenaged squatter who befriends Elizabeth, a homeless eleven year old, and tries to steer her away from
the streets. "With a conclusion both sorrowful and satisfying," Deborah Kaplan stated in *Kliatt,* "Chan's story
is truly worthwhile." Elizabeth makes a return appearance in *Thief,* a companion title. Now living with a ma-
nipulative foster mother, Elizabeth earns her keep by
working as a pickpocket. When she learns that her abusive father may be released from prison soon, the preteen flees her home with Dune, another foster child.
"Elizabeth's story is a bleak, often hopeless, one," remarked Amanda MacGregor in a *Kliatt* review of *Thief,*
the critic adding that "her fast-paced, unpredictable
days keep the story moving."

A young woman struggles with haunting memories following her father's suicide in *Perfect World,* James'
third novel for teen readers. Unable to confide in Jenna,
her increasingly shallow best friend, Lacie tries to hide
her pain by maintaining appearances in public. Lacie finally relaxes her guard after meeting Benji, a quiet and
sensitive boy with difficult family circumstances of his
own. The stream-of-consciousness narrative "brings a
very real sense of being inside Lacie's head," Cindy
Welch commented in *Booklist,* and Ronni Krasnow,

Cover of Brian James' young-adult novel The Heights, *featuring artwork by Rich Deas.* (Feiwel and Friends, 2009. Rich Deas, illustrator. Cover art and design copyright © 2009 by Rich Deas. Reproduced by permission.)

writing in *Kliatt,* observed that "James clearly understands how debilitating depression can be for adolescents." Benji serves as the protagonist of *Dirty Liar,* a "heartbreaking and believable" tale, in the words of *School Library Journal* contributor Johanna Lewis. In the work, the troubled teen must move in with his neglectful father to escape abuse at the hands of his mother's sadistic boyfriend. Ultimately, Benji finds hope and solace in Rianna, a popular classmate, in a novel deemed "powerful, compelling, and, in the end, almost sweet" by GraceAnne A. DeCandido in *Booklist.*

Zombie Blondes is a departure from James' adolescent novels. This horror tale centers on fifteen-year-old Hannah, who relocates to a small Vermont town with her father to escape his creditors. Upon meeting the school's cheerleaders, a squad of beautiful and deathly pale blondes, Hannah senses that something is not quite right. Despite the dire warnings of her nerdy schoolmate Lukas, however, she joins the team when its members begin to woo her with promises of instant popularity. According to Cara von Wrangel Kinsey in *School Library Journal,* in *Zombie Blondes* "James has created a believable novel about starting over, making friends, bullying, and ostracism, while adding a dash of the supernatural."

Based on *Wuthering Heights,* Emily Brontë's classic romance novel, *The Heights* concerns an ill-fated love affair. "The relationship between [Heathcliff and Catherine] in *Wuthering Heights* was very much a teenage romance, or least, how most of my teenage romances were . . . meaning, unfulfilled," James remarked in an *Edge of Seventeen* online interview. "I was really drawn to the aspect of fate and bad timing and missed chances that always managed to spoil their love for each other." *The Heights* explores the relationship between wealthy Catherine and her stepbrother, Henry, a Mexican orphan who was adopted by Catherine's father. When her father dies, Catherine's tyrannical older brother, Hindley, drives a wedge between the two teens, infuriating Henry and leading him to commit a series of destructive acts. According to Elissa Gershowitz in *Horn Book,* James "succeeds at creating a modern-day story of doomed love with convincing depths of emotion."

James' books span a host of genres, and he noted in a Macmillan Web site interview that his ideas come from a variety of sources. "I get inspiration from other art, be it music, literature, film, or visual art," he stated. "I also find inspiration in the world around me. Any little thing can be inspiring if you take the time to look at. I like to keep a notebook on me at all times and write down ideas because I never know when a passing stranger or a bit of conversation will spark my imagination."

Biographical and Critical Sources

PERIODICALS

Booklist, January 1, 2005, Cindy Welch, review of *Perfect World,* p. 845; February 1, 2006, GraceAnn A. De-Candido, review of *Dirty Liar,* p. 45; May 1, 2009, Gillian Engberg, review of *The Heights,* p. 72.

Horn Book, May-June, 2009, Elissa Gershowitz, review of *The Heights,* p. 297.

Kirkus Reviews, January 1, 2006, review of *Dirty Liar,* p. 42; June 1, 2008, review of *Zombie Blondes.*

Kliatt, May, 2003, Deborah Kaplan, review of *Maybe, Tomorrow,* p. 18; July, 2008, Myrna Marler, review of *Zombie Blondes,* p. 14; September, 2008, Amanda MacGregor, review of *Thief,* p. 26.

New York Times Book Review, July 13, 2008, Regina Marler, review of *Zombie Blondes,* p. 15.

Publishers Weekly, December 10, 2001, review of *Pure Sunshine,* p. 71; June 9, 2008, review of *Zombie Blondes,* p. 51.

School Library Journal, July, 2002, Debbie Stewart, review of *Pure Sunshine,* p. 120; January, 2005, Ronni Krasnow, review of *Perfect World,* p. 132; March, 2006, Johanna Lewis, review of *Dirty Liar,* p. 223; September, 2008, Cara von Wrangel Kinsey, review of *Zombie Blondes,* p. 186; July, 2009, Leah J. Sparks, review of *The Heights,* p. 85.

ONLINE

Brian James Web log, http://brianjamestheauthor.blogspot.com/ (January 1, 2010).

Cynsations Web log, http://cynthialeitichsmith.blogspot.
   com/ (June 19, 2008), Cynthia Leitich Smith, interview with James.
Edge of Seventeen Web log, http://eoseventeen.blogspot.
   com/ (November 9, 2009), interview with James.
Macmillan Web site, http://us.macmillan.com/ (January 1,
   2010), interview with James.
Push Web site, http://www.thisispush.com/ (January 1,
   2010), David Levithan, interview with James.
Scholastic Web site, http://www2.scholastic.com/ (January
   1, 2010), "Brian James."

*   *   *

JAVINS, Marie 1966-

Personal

Born 1966, in VA. *Education:* Antioch College, B.A.
(communications), 1988. *Hobbies and other interests:*
Traveling the world by public transportation.

Addresses

Home—New York, NY. *E-mail*—marie@mariejavins.
com.

Career

Author and travel writer. Marvel Comics, New York,
NY, editor and colorist, c. 1990s; Teshkeel Comics, Kuwait City, Kuwait, editor-in-chief, 2006—. School of
Visual Arts, New York, NY, member of adjunct faculty
in illustration/cartooning, beginning 2008.

Awards, Honors

Solas Award, 2009, for "Bragging Rights: Antarctica"
(article in *Perceptive Travel*).

Writings

(Coauthor) Randy Porter, *The Best in Tent Camping: Virginia,* second edition, Menasha Ridge Press/Globe Pequot Press (Birmingham, AL), 2004.
The Best in Tent Camping: New Jersey, Menasha Ridge
   Press/Globe Pequot Press (Birmingham, AL), 2005.
*Stalking the Wild Dik-Dik: One Woman's Solo Misadven-
   tures across Africa,* Seal Press (Emeryville, CA),
   2006.
3-D World Atlas and Tour, Chronicle Books (San Francisco, CA), 2008.

Contributor to *Rough Guides: Make the Most of Your
Time on Earth,* 2007, and *National Geographic: Journeys of a Lifetime,* 2007. Contributor to online periodicals, including *Amtrak Whistle-stop, Perceptive Travel,*
and *GoNOMAD.com,* 1999—. Contributor to *Comicul-
ture* (comics anthology).

Marie Javins (Reproduced by permission.)

Author's works have been translated into several languages, including Korean.

Biographical and Critical Sources

PERIODICALS

Atlantica, November-December, 2006, review of *Stalking
   the Wild Dik-Dik: One Woman's Solo Misadventures
   across Africa.*
Bookwatch, November, 2004, review of *The Best in Tent
   Camping Virginia.*
Kirkus Reviews, November 1, 2008, review of *3-D World
   Atlas and Tour.*
Transitions Abroad, January-February, 2007, review of
   Stalking the Wild Dik-Dik.
Travelgirl, May-June, 2007, review of *Stalking the Wild
   Dik-Dik.*

ONLINE

Marie Javins Home Page, http://www.mariejavins.com
   (January 10, 2010).
Marie Javins Web log, http://mariejavins.blogspot.com
   (January 10, 2010).
Marie's World Tour 2001 Web site, http://mariesworldtour.
   com (January 10, 2010).

*   *   *

JORDAN, Chris
See PHILBRICK, Rodman

K

KAJIKAWA, Kimiko
(Evelyn Clarke Mott)

Personal

Married; children: Christopher.

Addresses

Home and office—New Hope, PA.

Career

Writer and photographer.

Awards, Honors

Children's Books of Distinction designation, *Riverbank Review,* Teacher's Choice citation, International Reading Association, Red Clover Award, and Charlotte Zolotow Award, all 2001, all for *Yoshi's Feast*; Gold Award, Oppenheim Toy Portfolio, 2000, Best Children's Book of the Year designation, Bank Street College of Education, and nominations for Missouri Building Block Picture Book Award and Florida Reading Association Children's Book Award, both 2001, all for *Sweet Dreams*; Gold Award, Oppenheim Toy Portfolio, Kansas State Reading Circle selection, and Christopher Award, all 2009, all for *Close to You;* Noteworthy Books for Children selection, Capitol Choices, 2009, for *Tsunami!*

Writings

Sweet Dreams: How Animals Sleep, Henry Holt (New York, NY), 1999.
Yoshi's Feast, illustrated by Yumi Heo, DK (New York, NY), 2000.
Close to You: How Animals Bond, Henry Holt (New York, NY), 2008.
Tsunami!, illustrated by Ed Young, Philomel (New York, NY), 2009.

AND PHOTOGRAPHER, AS EVELYN CLARKE MOTT

Steam Train Ride, Walker (New York, NY), 1991.
Balloon Ride, Walker (New York, NY), 1991.
A Day at the Races with Austin and Kyle Petty, Random House (New York, NY), 1993.
(With Gwynne L. Isaacs) *Baby Face,* Random House (New York, NY), 1994.
Cool Cat, Random House (New York, NY), 1996.
Hot Dog, Random House (New York, NY), 1996.
(And photographer) *Dancing Rainbows: A Pueblo Boy's Story,* Cobblehill Books (New York, NY), 1996.

Adaptations

Sweet Dreams: How Animals Sleep was adapted as a sound recording.

Sidelights

Author Kimiko Kajikawa began writing as a child after her local librarian recommended that she read the novel *Harriet the Spy*. Like the main character in that novel, Kajikawa began keeping a journal and watching the people in her life. "I think *Harriet the Spy* . . . got me to write because I really started to look at the world and put down what I saw on paper," Kajikawa wrote on her home page.

As early as fifth grade, Kajikawa began winning writing contests, and her work was published in the *Philadelphia Inquirer,* the *Bucks County Courier Times,* and *Seventeen*. Led by her success, she worked as an assistant editor and columnist on the school newspaper when she was in high school, but she did not did not take up writing again until she began raising her family. Kajikawa's first picture book, *Steam Train Ride,* was inspired by her son, Chris. Like those she would produce after it, the work was published under the name Evelyn Clarke Mott and features photographs accompanied by a rhyming text. Kajikawa spent over a year writing and photographing *Steam Train Ride,* which was published in 1991.

Again as Mott, Kajikawa presents a photo-essay about Tewa Indian traditions in *Dancing Rainbows: A Pueblo Boy's Story.* Centering on the Feast Day as celebrated in San Juan Pueblo, New Mexico, she introduces Curt, a Tewa boy, as well as Kurt's grandfather and several other members of the Tewa Community as they bake the bread and dress for Feast Day celebrations. Karen Hutt, writing in *Booklist,* considered *Dancing Rainbows* to be "a nice addition" for libraries wanting to enhance their collections about Pueblo Indians, and a *Publishers Weekly* contributor felt that in the book, Kajikawa "has gone beyond preserving the pageantry of a single occasion to pay homage to the Tewa and their way of life."

Kajikawa has written two nonfiction picture books that include text and photography under her own name. *Sweet Dreams: How Animals Sleep* features creatures from all parts of the animal kingdom as they rest. A *Publishers Weekly* critic commented on the "unobtrusively rhyming captions" in this work, noting that, with the inclusion of endnotes that give facts about the sleeping habits of the featured animals, *Sweet Dreams* "goes beyond standard bedtime fare." Ilene Cooper, writing in *Booklist,* concluded that text and images are placed together in such a way that the pairing is "enough to introduce the concept of how animals sleep to young children."

Kajikawa's Christopher Award-winning *Close to You: How Animals Bond* uses the same technique as *Sweet Dreams* but shows animals cuddling with their young. The title "pairs beautiful, close-up, color photos . . . with a very simple, rhyming text," explained Hazel Rochman in her *Booklist* review. Ellen Heath, writing

of the same work in *School Library Journal,* complimented the "precise and engaging verbs" in Kajikawa's captions for *Close to You.*

Collaborating with Gwynne L. Isaacs to produce the photographs for *Baby Face* helped Kajikawa come to terms with her Japanese-American identity and take pride in her ethnic background. She has channeled that newfound pride into several books adapting traditional Japanese folk tales for an American audience. Her first title in this vein, *Yoshi's Feast,* is the story of a fan maker who saves money by smelling his neighbor Sabu's hibachi eel, rather than paying to eat it. When Sabu demands payment for the aroma Yoshi has stolen from him, the clever man clanks coins in his coin box, paying with the sound of their jingle. The disagreement escalates, and Sabu cooks incredibly foul-smelling fish to get even. Eventually, Yoshi offers to bring in customers to Sabu's grill by dancing, and Sabu, pleased with the outcome, offers to share his eel with Yoshi. Sue Sherif, reviewing *Yoshi's Feast* for *School Library Journal,* called the book "a striking adaptation," and *Horn Book* reviewer Joanna Rudge Long noted that while Kajikawa's story "resonates on several levels" as the pair grow from antagonists to allies, "the primary focus of this perfectly paced tale is on the fun." Gillian Engberg commented in her *Booklist* review on the "lively dialogue and rich text" in *Yoshi's Feast,* predicting that "this one will get a great response on the story-hour circuit."

A tale originally written by Lafcadio Hearn is the framework for Kajikawa's story in *Tsunami!* When the villagers all go to celebrate the upcoming harvest along the

Kimiko Kajikawa tells an exciting story in Tsunami!, *a picture book featuring artwork by award-winning illustrator Ed Young.* (Illustration copyright © 2009 by Ed Young. Reproduced by permission of Philomel Books, a division of Penguin Putnam Books for Young Readers.)

shore, wise and rich Ojiisan stays behind, sensing that something bad is about to happen. After feeling the tremors of an earthquake, Ojiisan remembers a tale his grandfather once told him about how tsunamis begin. He realizes that the villagers do not understand the danger coming in the form of a giant tidal wave, so he lights his rice fields on fire to draw their attention and cause them to rush back onto higher, safer ground to help him put out the fire. Kathy Krasniewicz, writing in *School Library Journal,* called *Tsunami!* "a simple story of the power of a simple act," and Long wrote in *Horn Book* that "the dramatic events carry the narrative gracefully."

Biographical and Critical Sources

PERIODICALS

Booklist, April 1, 1996, Karen Hutt, review of *Dancing Rainbows: A Pueblo Boy's Story,* p. 1368; April 1, 1999, Ilene Cooper, review of *Sweet Dreams: How Animals Sleep,* p. 1416; March 1, 2000, Gillian Engberg, review of *Yoshi's Feast,* p. 1242; May 1, 2008, Hazel Rochman, review of *Close to You: How Animals Bond,* p. 92.

Horn Book, May, 2000, Joanna Rudge Long, review of *Yoshi's Feast,* p. 325; March-April, 2009, Joanna Rudge Long, review of *Tsunami!* p. 182.

Kirkus Reviews, December 1, 2008, review of *Tsunami!*

Publishers Weekly, May 27, 1996, reviews of *Cool Cat* and *Hot Dog,* p. 77; March 4, 1996, review of *Dancing Rainbows,* p. 66; May 10, 1999, review of *Sweet Dreams,* p. 67.

School Library Journal, May, 2000, review of *Yoshi's Feast,* p. 146; May, 2008, Ellen Heath, review of *Close to You,* p. 115; January, 2009, Kathy Krasniewicz, review of *Tsunami!* p. 76.

ONLINE

Kimiko Kajikawa Home Page, http://www.author4kids.com (January 18, 2010).*

*   *   *

KARR, Kathleen 1946-

Personal

Born April 21, 1946, in Allentown, PA; daughter of Stephen (a mechanical engineer) and Elizabeth (a homemaker) Csere; married Lawrence F. Karr (a physicist and computer consultant), July 13, 1968 (died, 2007); children: Suzanne, Daniel. *Education:* Catholic University of America, B.A., 1968; Providence College, M.A., 1971; further study at Corcoran School of Art, 1972.

Addresses

Home—Washington, DC. *Agent*—Adams Literary, 7845 Colony Rd., Ste. 215, Charlotte, NC 28226. *E-mail*—karr@bellatlantic.net.

Kathleen Karr (Photograph by James Goodwin Smith. Reproduced by permission.)

Career

Novel and screenplay writer. Barrington High School, Barrington, RI, English and speech teacher, 1968-69; Rhode Island Historical Society Film Archives, curator, 1970-71; American Film Institute, Washington, DC, archives assistant, 1971-72, member of catalog staff, 1972; Washington Circle Theater Corporation, Washington, DC, general manager, 1973-78; Circle/Showcase Theaters, Washington, DC, advertising director, 1979-83, director of public relations, 1984-88; Circle Management Company/Circle Releasing, Washington, DC, member of public relations staff, 1988-93. Assistant professor at George Washington University, summer, 1979, and 1980-81. Lecturer or instructor in film and communications at various institutions, including Providence College, 1969-70, University of Rhode Island, 1971, University of Maryland, 1972, Catholic University of America, 1973-77, New Line Presentations Lecture Bureau, 1974-76, American Film Institute, 1979-80, and Trinity College, 1985-86, 1995; lecturer at film and writing conferences, 1973-89. Juror, American Film Festival, 1971, and Rosebud Awards, 1991.

Member

Washington Romance Writers (member of board of directors, 1985-86; president, 1986-87), Children's Book

Guild of Washington, DC (member of board of directors, 1998-2002; president, 2000-01), Society of Children's Book Writers and Illustrators.

Awards, Honors

Golden Medallion Award for best inspirational novel, Romance Writers of America, 1986, for *From This Day Forward;* Outstanding Emerging Artist Award finalist, Washington, DC, Mayor's Arts Awards, 1986; 100 Books for Reading and Sharing citation, New York Public Library, 1990, for *It Ain't Always Easy;* Parents' Choice Story Book citation, 1992, for *Oh, Those Harper Girls!;* Books for the Teen Age selection, New York Public Library, for *The Cave;* Notable Children's Trade Book in the Field of Social Studies designation, National Council for the Social Studies/Children's Book Council (NCSS/CBC), 1999, Notable Children's Book in the Language Arts, National Council of Teachers of English, 1999, and Prix de Bernard Verselo (Brussels, Belgium), 2000-01, all for *The Great Turkey Walk;* Best Book for Young Adults selection, American Library Association (ALA), 2000, for *Man of the Family;* Golden Kite Award, Society of Children's Book Writers and Illustrators, Notable Children's Trade Book in the Field of Social Studies, NCSS/CBC, Books for the Teen Age selection, New York Public Library, and Best Book for Young Adults selection, ALA, all 2001, all for *The Boxer;* Books for the Teen Age selection, New York Public Library, 2002, for *Playing with Fire,* 2003, for *Bone Dry;* Agatha Award for Best Children's Novel, 2003, and Anthony Award nomination, and Books for the Teen Age selection, New York Public Library, both 2004, all for *The 7th Knot;* Amelia Bloomer Project listee, ALA, Bank Street College of Education Best Children's Book designation, CCBC Choice designation, and Children's Literature Choice selection, all 2004, all for *Gilbert and Sullivan Set Me Free;* NCSS/CBC Notable Social Studies Trade Book designation, Children's Literature Choice designation, and Books for the Teen Age designation, New York Public Library, all 2005, all for *Exiled;* Bank Street College Best Children's Book designation, 2005, and NCSS/CBC Notable Social Studies Trade Book designation, 2006, both for *Worlds Apart;* Amelia Bloomer Project listee, 2006, for *Mama Went to Jail for the Vote;* Books for the Teen Age designation, New York Public Library, and Bank Street College Best Children's Book designation, both 2008, both for *Born for Adventure.*

Writings

FOR CHILDREN

It Ain't Always Easy, Farrar, Straus & Giroux (New York, NY), 1990.

Oh, Those Harper Girls!; or, Young and Dangerous, Farrar, Straus & Giroux (New York, NY), 1992.

Gideon and the Mummy Professor, Farrar, Straus & Giroux (New York, NY), 1993.

The Cave, Farrar, Straus (New York, NY), 1994.

In the Kaiser's Clutch, Farrar, Straus & Giroux (New York, NY), 1995.

Spy in the Sky, illustrated by Thomas F. Yezerski, Hyperion (New York, NY), 1997.

The Great Turkey Walk, Farrar, Straus & Giroux (New York, NY), 1998.

The Lighthouse Mermaid, illustrated by Karen Lee Schmidt, Hyperion (New York, NY), 1998.

Man of the Family, Farrar, Straus & Giroux (New York, NY) 1999.

Skullduggery, Hyperion (New York, NY), 2000.

The Boxer, Farrar, Straus & Giroux (New York, NY), 2000.

It Happened in the White House: Extraordinary Tales from America's Most Famous Home, illustrated by Paul Meisel, Hyperion (New York, NY), 2000.

Playing with Fire, Farrar, Straus & Giroux (New York, NY), 2001.

Bone Dry, Hyperion (New York, NY), 2002.

Gilbert and Sullivan Set Me Free, Hyperion Books for Children (New York, NY), 2003.

The 7th Knot, Marshall Cavendish (New York, NY), 2003.

Exiled: Memoirs of a Camel, Marshall Cavendish (New York, NY), 2004.

Mama Went to Jail for the Vote, illustrated by Malene Laugesen, Hyperion Books for Children (New York, NY), 2005.

Worlds Apart, Marshall Cavendish (New York, NY), 2005.

Born for Adventure, Marshall Cavendish (New York, NY), 2007.

Fortune's Fool, Alfred A. Knopf (New York, NY), 2008.

Author's work has been translated into Burmese, Catalan, French, Danish, and Italian.

"PETTICOAT PARTY" SERIES; FICTION; FOR CHILDREN

Go West, Young Women!, HarperCollins (New York, NY), 1996.

Phoebe's Folly, HarperCollins (New York, NY), 1996.

Oregon, Sweet Oregon, HarperCollins (New York, NY), 1998.

Gold-Rush Phoebe, HarperCollins (New York, NY), 1998.

ROMANCE NOVELS; FOR ADULTS

Light of My Heart, Zondervan (Grand Rapids, MI), 1984.

From This Day Forward, Zondervan (Grand Rapids, MI), 1985.

Chessie's King, Zondervan (Grand Rapids, MI), 1986.

Destiny's Dreamers Book I: Gone West, Barbour (Uhrichsville, OH), 1993.

Destiny's Dreamers Book II: The Promised Land, Barbour (Uhrichsville, OH), 1993.

OTHER

(Editor) *The American Film Heritage: Views from the American Film Institute Collection,* Acropolis Press (Washington, DC), 1972.

Also author of screenplays for short films, including *The Elegant Mr. Brown and I* (and director), 1969; *Mayor Tom Bradley,* 1973; *Profile: Tom Bradley,* 1974; and *No Smoking, Spitting, or Molesting,* 1976.

Contributor to anthology *Shelf Life: Stories by the Book,* edited by Gary Paulsen, Simon & Schuster (New York, NY), 2004; and to reference books *Cartoon: A Celebration of American Comic Art,* 1975, and *Magill's Survey of Cinema,* annual editions. Contributor to periodicals, including *Film Society Review, Film News, Journal of Popular Film, Providence Journal,* and *Rhode Island History.* Contributing editor, *Media and Methods,* 1970-72; editor, *ASFE News,* March, 1976. Member of advisory board, *Children's Literature,* beginning 1994.

Adaptations

The Great Turkey Walk was recorded as an audiobook, Recorded Books, 1999. *Gilbert and Sullivan Set Me Free* was recorded as an audiobook, Full Cast Audio, 2004.

Sidelights

Kathleen Karr's award-winning historical novels for young teens are noted for their humorous and suspenseful plots and boldly drawn characters. Besides their settings, which range from the streets of New York City to the "Wild West" of the late 1800s to even-more-exotic locales around the world, Karr's works also feature compelling portrayals of young people confronting adult-sized challenges, their efforts to deal with these challenges rendered in an upbeat prose that many critics have found engaging. Among Karr's books are the historical novels *The Cave, In the Kaiser's Clutch, Playing with Fire, The 7th Knot,* and *Bone Dry,* as well as the "Petticoat Party" series about women moving westward along the Oregon Trail during the early 1800s. Praising *The 7th Knot,* which finds two brothers drawn into the machinations of a secret society while touring Europe with their robber-baron uncle in the late 1880s, Beth L. Meister observed in *School Library Journal* that Karr's signature mix of "well-crafted plot and nonstop action will catch readers' attention from the first chapter."

Born in 1946 in Allentown, Pennsylvania, Karr began writing fiction "on a dare from my husband," as she once told *SATA.* "Tired of hearing me complain about not being able to find a 'good read,' he suggested I write a book myself." In 1984 she sold her third attempt, the romance novel *Light of My Heart,* and, as Karr described it, "entered the world of women's fiction." It was her two children who convinced her to switch genres, however; "They asked me to write a book for them." Karr agreed, penning *It Ain't Always Easy,* which, in 1990, would become her first published children's novel. Along the way she discovered a new vocation as an author of children's historical novels.

It Ain't Always Easy follows the efforts of two New York City orphans—eleven-year-old Jack and eight-year-old Mandy—who move out West in the hopes of

Cover of Karr's young-adult novel **Playing with Fire,** *featuring cover art by Steve Cieslawski.* (Jacket art © 2000 by Steve Cieslawski. Used by permission of Farrar, Straus & Giroux, LLC.)

finding a family to take care of them. Despite the odds, they stay together and, after many adventures, manage to find a home and family. While acknowledging the entertaining aspect of the children's adventures, some critics found the events and dialogue in *It Ain't Always Easy* unrealistic; Gail Richmond pointed out in *School Library Journal* that Jack's character is "too good to be true, and loses some credibility as a result." Describing Karr's book as "powerful," a *Publishers Weekly* writer concluded that "the spirit and perseverance of the protagonists are uplifting." Other critics cited authentic period details and well-rounded characterizations in praising *It Ain't Always Easy;* as *Horn Book* writer Elizabeth S. Watson observed, even "lesser characters are three-dimensional," making for "an extremely appealing" story.

Karr uses the setting of the nineteenth-century American West to a more comic effect in *Oh, Those Harper Girls!; or, Young and Dangerous.* In this novel, the six daughters of a hapless rancher engage in a number of foolhardy and illegal schemes to attempt to save their West Texas homestead from bankruptcy. Eventually, they land on the New York stage, reenacting their famous escapades. Centered on the youngest daughter,

Lily, the brains behind the girls' schemes, *Oh, Those Harper Girls!* also comments on the restricted roles available to women in the nineteenth century. *Booklist* contributor Mary Romano Marks commented favorably on this aspect of Karr's work, also writing that "the girls' hilarious escapades and good-natured sibling rivalry make the novel an enjoyable read." "Characterization is quite strong," Rita Soltan remarked in a *School Library Journal* review of the book, dubbing *Oh, Those Harper Girls!* "fast paced and satisfying," and a *Kirkus Reviews* critic called Karr's novel "a happy, rip-roaring adventure, capped by a whirlwind of marriages, family reunions, and wishes fulfilled."

The world of the American West is also the focus of Karr's "Petticoat Party" series, which features a group of pioneers on its way west in 1846. In *Go West, Young Women!* twelve-year-old Phoebe Brown finds herself part of a wagon train led solely by women after the men in their party are killed or seriously disabled during a buffalo stampede. Despite numerous hardships, the determined women take their wagon train nearly 1,400 miles by novel's end. Elizabeth Mellett found *Go West, Young Women!* to be a "light, entertaining tale of adventure on the trail to Oregon," in her *School Library*

Cover of Karr's The Great Turkey Walk, *featuring artwork by David Small.* (Jacket copyright © 1998 by David Small. Used by permission of Farrar, Straus & Giroux, LLC.)

Journal assessment of the book, while in *Kirkus Reviews,* a critic praised the novel as a "good adventure tale . . . and a real consciousness-raiser to boot."

In the second "Petticoat Party" novel, *Phoebe's Folly,* Phoebe learns how to pull her weight on the journey by becoming knowledgeable about firearms, her perky, positive attitude prompting *Booklist* contributor Lauren Peterson to call her a "likeable, spunky heroine who will attract a loyal following." *Oregon, Sweet Oregon* finds Phoebe reaching her destination, only to discover disappointment when she is expected to retire to an appropriately subservient "woman's place" in the growing society. The lure of riches prompts her to continue her travels, and in *Gold-Rush Phoebe,* Karr's protagonist joins with fellow teen Robbie Robson to make the trek to California, where they encounter further adventures and develop a romantic relationship. Calling Phoebe's saga in *Oregon, Sweet Oregon* "more entertainment than history," *Booklist* contributor Peterson praised the series as "a nice alternative to lengthier and more challenging historical fiction" about America's westward expansion.

Moving closer to the present, Karr sets *The Boxer* in 1885. Johnny Woods is a fifteen year old who boxes at a local saloon as a way to make some extra money to supplement the small wage he earns for working grueling hours at a New York City sweatshop in order to support his fatherless family. Unfortunately, boxing is illegal in New York, and Johnny is arrested and sent to prison for six months. There he is aided by a fellow inmate, a former pro boxer named Michael O'Shaunnessey, who teaches Johnny not only the finer points of boxing, but also how to turn his life around after his release from prison and start his climb to the top of the professional prizefighting circuit. Praising Karr's "clarity of purpose" in writing *The Boxer, Booklist* critic Carolyn Phelan cited the novel as unique due to its "focus on a lower-class character during peace time." In *Horn Book,* a contributor commended the inclusion of actual people of the period and described the novel's tenacious, determined protagonist as "a highly sympathetic, ultimately admirable character. . . . In or out of the ring, this kid is a fighter." Edward Sullivan praised *The Boxer* as a "wonderful blend of fascinating history and compelling drama," adding in his *School Library Journal* review that Karr succeeds admirably in "creating a vivid sense of time and place." The novel's "one-two-punch pacing and warmhearted resolutions will keep the pages turning," promised a *Publishers Weekly* reviewer.

Karr draws readers into the dustbowl era with *The Cave,* which is set in drought-burdened South Dakota during the Great Depression of the 1930s. The lack of rain poses many difficulties for a preteen named Christine: it threatens the livelihood of her family's farm and also aggravates her younger brother Michael's asthma. Her father is considering moving the family to California when Christine unearths a cave in the foothills near the

Cover of Karr's hard-hitting young-adult historical novel The Boxer, *featuring artwork by Ridrigs Corral.* (Jacket design copyright © 2000 by Rodrigs Corral. Used by permission of Farrar, Straus & Giroux, LLC.)

farm, complete with crystals, stalactites—and water. Although she wants to stay on the farm, Christine tries to keep her discovery from her father, afraid that in rescuing the farm he will destroy the cave's beauty. With numerous period details, "Karr excels in re-creating time and place," Cindy Darling Codell noted in *School Library Journal.* In addition, the critic wrote, the ecological conflict in *The Cave* enhances Karr's "sweet, well-crafted story of a family forced to be tough by the extremities of nature." Comparing the book to the children's classic *Caddie Woodlawn, Booklist* critic Mary Harris Veeder observed that "Karr creates an active and believable girl in the throes of both physical and emotional change" and praised the author's child's-eye view of the era. A *Kirkus Reviews* writer concluded of *The Cave* that "fine period detail and masterful writing grace Karr's story of quiet courage during hard times."

Another young girl is the focus of *Mama Went to Jail for the Vote,* a book illustrated by Malene Laugesen. In this picture book for older children, Karr introduces the struggles faced by women attempting to gain the right to participate in electoral politics. Susan Elizabeth accompanies her mother to suffragist rallies, and even pickets at the White House. When Mama is arrested, she is gone for several months, but Susan watches as civil disobedience ultimately wins out when the Nineteenth Amendment is passed by the U.S. Congress. In *Booklist* Ilene Cooper wrote that *Mama Went to Jail for the Vote* effectively captures "the momentum of the movement and its importance for a young audience," while Wendy Lukehart described Karr's story as "infuse[d] . . . with humor, spunk, and drama."

While many of Karr's books are set in the United States, some of her middle-grade stories stray into exotic cultures. For example, *Born for Adventure* takes readers into the jungles of Africa, *Skullduggery* and its sequel, *Bone Dry,* trek from the United States to Paris to Egypt, and *Fortune's Fool* goes back in time to fourteenth-century Germany. When sixteen-year-old Londoner Tom Ormsby, the hero of *Born for Adventure,* signs on to accompany explorer Henry Morton Stanley on Stanley's 1887 rescue mission to the Belgian Congo, he has no idea of the experiences he will have in the African jungle. In Karr's mix of fact and fiction, readers learn about the many cultures Stanley encountered, and also watch Tom's world view change as he matures and begins to see Stanley's quest in a new light. Writing that *Born for Adventure* is enriched by "a wealth of historical detail and a steady stream of action," a *Publishers Weekly* contributor predicted that Karr's novel will "captivate readers . . . [with] their own dreams of adventure." Kimberly Monaghan had a similar assessment, calling Karr's research "impressive" and praising the novel as "a truly informative and eye-opening read."

Skullduggery is set in 1839, a time when medicine still has many advances left to make, and quacks and unsound medical practices abound. For twelve-year-old Matthew Morrissey, orphaned after a cholera epidemic, getting a job with a doctor seems like a way of helping others avoid his family's terrible fate. However, Dr. Asa B. Cornwall is no ordinary doctor: he is a phrenologist who determines people's personalities by feeling the lumps and bumps on their head. Cornwall's efforts to develop his "science" requires skulls, and Matthew finds that his job description includes sneaking into cemeteries and digging up graves in order to provide them. This grave robbing eventually takes the pair to Europe, in search of the skulls of great men such as French philosopher Voltaire and former emperor Napoleon Bonaparte. Praising the novel's plot as "fast-paced," *School Library Journal* contributor Steven Engelfried added that the discussion of phrenology and the creepiness of grave robbing combine to make *Skullduggery* attractive to "curious readers not ordinarily drawn to historical fiction." A *Kirkus Reviews* critic called the novel "rich in period color and good old-fashioned derring do."

Matthew and Dr. Cornwall return in *Bone Dry,* and this time they leave Paris and go to the Sahara Desert in search of the skull of Alexander the Great. Travels by camel lead them through sandstorms and into the

Cover of Karr's middle-grade novel Fortune's Fool, *featuring cover art by Lars Hokanson.* (Jacket illustration copyright © 2008 by Lars Hokanson. Used by permission of Alfred A. Knopf, an imprint of Random House Children's Books, a division of Random House, Inc.)

clutches of a caravan of slavers, although the fourteen year old's budding skills as an illusionist win the duo's freedom and also the attentions of Nathalie, the beautiful daughter of a wealthy Egyptian. While noting that the good luck of Matthew and his friends sometimes strains credulity, a *Kirkus Reviews* writer wrote that "Karr's nearly perfect comic timing keeps the plot" of *Bone Dry* "dancing along," resulting in a "swashbuckling, occasionally bloody, and frequently hilarious adventure." In *School Library Journal* Bruce Ann Shook described the sequel to *Skullduggery* as "a terrific adventure" featuring "a larger-than-life hero and a great supporting cast."

Karr goes back in time four centuries to tell *Fortune's Fool*. Set in what is now Germany, the novel finds fifteen-year-old Conrad the Good working as a fool for Otto the Witless. A crude master, Otto punishes Conrad once too often for stating the truth, prompting Conrad to escape his service and find a master of greater wisdom. During his search for a place to call home, the jester learns that the medieval world beyond the court is one filled with dangers ranging from wild animals to

the Black Death. Surviving by entertaining the wealthy individuals he meets along his way, Conrad also gathers several traveling companions, including a boy rescued from the gallows and a love interest in Christa the Fair, who disguises herself as a young man in order not to attract unwanted attention. Noting that the story's "ornate" prose evokes the dialogue of a past epoch, Michael Cart added in *Booklist* that *Fortune's Fool* realistically depicts "all the challenges and hardships" of life as a medieval entertainer. Fans of the period "will be captivated by Conrad's cleverness," Cart added, while Caitlin August stated in *School Library Journal* that "it is hard to deny Conrad's Robin Hood charm or the gallows cheat's wit." Describing the book's "enchanting containers," August dubbed *Fortune's Fool* "consistently entertaining."

"After a number of years working in the 'real' worlds of motion pictures and education, I find it a pleasure to be able to create my own worlds in fiction," Karr once commented regarding her developing career as a novelist. "To watch a character come alive—become real flesh and blood and take the reins of a story in hand—is an exhilarating experience. It's also hard work.

"As for my penchant for historical settings, well, I've discovered that I feel quite comfortable in the nineteenth century. It's a challenge to try to recreate a specific time and place, with its specific language patterns. Short of inventing a time machine, this is my way of reentering the past and attempting to show my readers that while events may change, the nature of human beings is fairly constant. Courage and common decency against difficult odds have always existed."

Biographical and Critical Sources

PERIODICALS

Booklist, April 15, 1992, Mary Romano Marks, review of *Oh, Those Harper Girls!; or, Young and Dangerous,* p. 1523; September 15, 1994, review of *The Cave,* p. 92; December 1, 1996, Lauren Peterson, review of *Phoebe's Folly,* p. 654; June 1, 1998, Chris Sherman, review of *The Great Turkey Walk,* p. 1748, and Ilene Cooper, review of *The Lighthouse Mermaid,* p. 1767; July, 1998, Lauren Peterson, review of *Oregon, Sweet Oregon,* p. 1881; September 15, 1999, Hazel Rochman, review of *Man of the Family,* p. 257; April 1, 2000, John Peters, review of *Skullduggery,* p. 1477; September 1, 2000, Carolyn Phelan, review of *The Boxer,* p. 116; April 1, 2001, Ilene Cooper, review of *Playing with Fire,* p. 1483; July, 2003, GraceAnne A. DeCandido, review of *The 7th Knot,* p. 1881; May 1, 2005, Ilene Cooper, review of *Mama Went to Jail for the Vote,* p. 1591; March 1, 2008, Michael Cart, review of *Fortune's Fool,* p. 60.
Children's Book Review Service, review of *In the Kaiser's Clutch,* p. 33.

Horn Book, March, 1991, Elizabeth S. Watson, review of *It Ain't Always Easy,* pp. 199-200; May-June, 1992, Maeve Visser Knoth, review of *Oh, Those Harper Girls!,* p. 341; September-October, 1993, Elizabeth S. Watson, review of *Gideon and the Mummy Professor,* p. 599; November, 1999, Mary M. Burns, review of *Man of the Family,* p. 742; May, 2000, review of *Skullduggery,* p. 315; September, 2000, review of *The Boxer,* p. 573; July-August, 2003, Lolly Robinson, review of *Gilbert and Sullivan Set Me Free,* p. 460.

Journal of Adolescent & Adult Literacy, September, 2001, Rosie Kerin, review of *The Boxer,* p. 84.

Kirkus Reviews, April 15, 1992, review of *Oh, Those Harper Girls!,* p. 539; July 15, 1994, review of *The Cave,* p. 987; October, 1, 1995, review of *In the Kaiser's Clutch,* p. 1430; December 1, 1995, review of *Go West, Young Women!,* p. 1703; March 15, 1997, review of *Spy in the Sky,* pp. 463-464; December 15, 1999, review of *Skullduggery,* pp. 1958-1959.

Kliatt, September, 1995, Barbara Shepp, review of *Oh, Those Harper Girls!,* pp. 10-11.

New York Times Book Review, November 13, 2005, Gail Collins, review of *Mama Went to Jail for the Vote,* p. 27.

Publishers Weekly, September 28, 1990, review of *It Ain't Always Easy,* p. 103; March 23, 1992, review of *Oh, Those Harper Girls!,* p. 73; May 24, 1993, review of *Gideon and the Mummy Professor,* p. 89; September 12, 1994, review of *The Cave,* p. 92; February 12, 1996, review of *Go West, Young Women!,* p. 78; April 20, 1998, review of *The Great Turkey Walk,* p. 67; October 4, 1999, review of *Man of the Family,* p. 76; February 7, 2000, review of *Skullduggery,* p. 86; October 30, 2000, review of *The Boxer,* p. 76; January 22, 2001, review of *Playing with Fire,* p. 325; June 23, 2003, review of *Gilbert and Sullivan Set Me Free,* p. 68; April 19, 2004, review of *Exiled: Memoirs of a Camel,* p. 61; March 19, 2007, review of *Born for Adventure,* p. 65.

School Library Journal, December, 1990, Gail Richmond, review of *It Ain't Always Easy,* p. 104; May, 1992, Rita Soltan, review of *Oh, Those Harper Girls!,* p. 133; June, 1993, Beth Tegart, review of *Gideon and the Mummy Professor,* p. 107; September, 1994, Cindy Darling Codell, review of *The Cave,* p. 218; January, 1996, Kelly Dillery, review of *In the Kaiser's Clutch,* p. 128; May, 1996, Elizabeth Mellett, review of *Go West, Young Women!,* p. 114; August, 1997, Linda L. Plevak, review of *Spy in the Sky,* p. 136; March, 1998, Coop Renner, review of *The Great Turkey Walk,* p. 214; August, 1998, Elaine Lesh Morgan, review of *The Lighthouse Mermaid,* p. 141; January, 1999, Shawn Brommer, review of *Gold Rush Phoebe,* p. 128; March, 2000, Steven Engelfried, review of *Skullduggery,* p. 239; November, 2000, Edward Sullivan, review of *The Boxer,* p. 157; May, 2001, Patricia B. McGee, review of *Playing with Fire,* p. 154; August, 2002, Bruce Anne Shook, review of *Bone Dry,* p. 190; July, 2003, Ronni Krasnow, review of *Gilbert and Sullivan Set Me Free,* p. 131; August, 2003, Beth L. Meister, review of *The 7th Knot,* p. 161; May, 2005, Wendy Lukehart, review of *Mama Went to Jail for the Vote,* p. 86, Renee Steinberg, review of *Worlds Apart,* p. 130; May, 2007, Coop Rener, review of *Exiled,* p. 150; July, 2007, Kimberly Monaghan, review of *Born for Adventure,* p. 104; July, 2008, Caitlin Augusta, review of *Fortune's Fool,* p. 102.

ONLINE

Children's Book Guild of Washington, DC, Web site, http://www.childrensbookguild.org/ (January 10, 2010), "Kathleen Karr."

Hyperion Web site, http://www.hyperionbooksforchildren.com/ (January 15, 2010), "Kathleen Karr."

Macmillan Web site, http://us.macmillan.com/ (January 10, 2010), "Kathleen Karr."

Reading Is Fundamental Web site, http://www.rif.org/ (January 15, 2010), interview with Karr.

* * *

KEHRET, Peg 1936-

Personal

Surname pronounced "carrot"; born November 11, 1936, in LaCrosse, WI; daughter of Arthur R. (an executive of Geo. A. Hormel Co.) and Elizabeth M. (a homemaker) Schulze; married Carl E. Kehret (a player-piano restorer), July 2, 1955 (deceased, April 28, 2004); children: Bob C., Anne M. *Education:* Attended University of Minnesota, 1954-55. *Hobbies and other interests:* Reading, foster care for rescued cats.

Addresses

Home—Wilkeson, WA. *Agent*—Emilie Jacobson, Curtis Brown Ltd., 10 Astor Place, New York, NY 10003. *E-mail*—pegkehre@tx3.net.

Career

Writer, 1973—. Volunteer for animal welfare causes and public libraries.

Member

Authors Guild, Authors League, Society of Children's Book Writers and Illustrators, Mystery Writers of America.

Awards, Honors

Forest Roberts Playwriting Award, Northern Michigan University, 1978, Best New Play of 1979 designation, Pioneer Drama Service, and Best Plays for Senior Adults designation, American Theatre Association, 1981, all for *Spirit!;* Children's Choice Award, International Reading Association/Children's Book Council (IRA/CBC), 1988, for *Deadly Stranger;* Service Award, American Humane Association, 1989; Recommended Books for Reluctant Young-Adult Readers designation,

Peg Kehret (Photograph by Vicki Taylor. Reproduced by permission.)

American Library Association (ALA), 1989, for *The Winner;* Books for the Teen Age selection, New York Public Library, for *Winning Monologs for Young Actors;* Young Hoosier Book Award, Association for Indiana Media Educators, 1992, Golden Sower Award, Nebraska Library Association, 1993, and Maud Hart Lovelace Award, Minnesota Youth Reading Awards, 1995 all for *Nightmare Mountain;* Young Adult's Choice Award, IRA, 1992, for *Sisters, Long Ago;* Recommended Books for Reluctant Young-Adult Readers, ALA, Books for the Teen Age designation, New York Public Library, IRA Young Adult's Choice designation, and Maud Hart Lovelace Award, all 1992, all for *Cages;* Pacific Northwest Writers' Conference Achievement Award, 1992; IRA Young Adult's Choice designation, Land of Enchantment Book Award, New Mexico Library Association, Pacific Northwest Young Reader's Choice selection, Pacific Northwest Library Association, and Utah Children's Book Award, all for *Terror at the Zoo;* Sequoyah Book Award, Oklahoma Library Association, Young Hoosier Book Award, Association for Indiana Media Educators, and Honor Book designation, West Virginia Children's Book Award, all for *Horror at the Haunted House;* Quick Picks for Reluctant Young-Adult Readers selection, ALA, and Children's Choice selection, IRA, both for *Danger at the Fair;* Children's Books of the Year Award, Child Study Children's Book Committee, 1995, for *The Richest Kids in Town;* IRA

Children's Choice Award, and ALA Recommended Books for Reluctant Young-Adult Readers selection, both 1995, both for *Danger at the Fair;* Golden Kite Award, Society of Children's Book Writers and Illustrators, 1996, Recommended Books for Reluctant Young-Adult Readers selection and Notable Books for Children designation, both ALA, and PEN Center USA West Award for Children's Literature, both 1997, Dorothy Canfield Fisher Award, 1998, Mark Twain Readers Award, Missouri Association of School Librarians, 1999, and Young Hoosier Book Award, and IRA Children's Choice Award, all for *Small Steps;* IRA Children's Choice Award, 1997, for *Searching for Candlestick Park;* Recommended Books for Reluctant Young-Adult Readers selection, ALA, and IRA Children's Choice Award, Children's Crown Award, and National Christian Schools Association, all 1998, all for *Earthquake Terror;* Sunshine State Young Reader's Award, 1998, for *The Volcano Disaster;* IRA Children's Choice Award, Recommended Books for Reluctant Young-Adult Readers, ALA, Lamplighter Award, National Christian School Association, and International Honor Book designation, Society of School Librarians, all for *I'm Not Who You Think I Am;* IRA Children's Choice Award, and Young Hoosier Book Award, both for *Don't Tell Anyone;* Henry Bergh Award, American Society for the Prevention of Cruelty to Animals (ASPCA), 2001, and Children's Crown award nominee, both for *Saving Lilly;* Recommended Books for Reluctant Young-Adult Readers, ALA, 1999, for *Shelter Dogs;* Kansas State Reading Circle Award, and Disney Adventures Award nominee, both 2002, both for *Five Pages a Day;* IRA Children's Choice Award, Nevada Young Reader's Award, Sequoyah Book Award, and Missouri Young Reader Award, all 2002, all for *The Stranger Next Door;* IRA Children's Choice Award, and Prairie Pasque Book Award, South Dakota Library Association, both for *Spy Cat;* Sunshine State Young Reader's Award, Maud Hart Lovelace Award, Golden Sower Award, Nevada Young Reader's Award, and Young Hoosier Book Award, all for *Escaping the Giant Wave;* Prairie Pasque Book Award, Mark Twain Readers Award, Young Hoosier Book Award, and Edgar Allen Poe Award nominee, Mystery Writers of America, all for *Abduction!;* Prairie Pasque Book Award, Sasquatch Award, Washington Library Media Association, Volunteer State Book Award, Great Stone Face Award, Children's Librarians of New Hampshire, Nevada Young Reader's Award, and Young Hoosier Book Award, all 2005, all for *The Ghost's Grave;* IRA Children's Choice Award, 2008, for *Stolen Children;* IRA Celebrate Literacy Award; numerous child-selected awards and state master-list inclusions.

Writings

JUVENILE FICTION

Deadly Stranger, Dodd, Mead (New York, NY), 1987.
The Winner, Turman (Seattle, WA), 1988.

Nightmare Mountain, Cobblehill Books (New York, NY), 1989.

Sisters, Long Ago, Cobblehill Books (New York, NY), 1990.

Cages, Cobblehill Books (New York, NY), 1991.

Terror at the Zoo, Cobblehill Books (New York, NY), 1992.

Horror at the Haunted House, Cobblehill Books (New York, NY), 1992.

Night of Fear, Cobblehill Books (New York, NY), 1994.

The Richest Kids in Town, Cobblehill Books (New York, NY), 1994.

Danger at the Fair, Cobblehill Books (New York, NY), 1995.

Earthquake Terror, Cobblehill Books (New York, NY), 1996.

Searching for Candlestick Park, Cobblehill Books (New York, NY), 1997.

The Volcano Disaster, Pocket Books (New York, NY), 1998.

The Blizzard Disaster, Pocket Books (New York, NY), 1998.

The Secret Journey, Pocet Books (New York, NY), 1999.

I'm Not Who You Think I Am, Dutton Children's Books (New York, NY), 1999.

The Flood Disaster, Pocket Books (New York, NY), 1999.

My Brother Made Me Do It, Pocket Books (New York, NY), 2000.

Don't Tell Anyone, Dutton Children's Books (New York, NY), 2000.

The Hideout, Pocket Books (New York, NY), 2001.

Saving Lilly, Pocket Books (New York, NY), 2001.

(With Pete the Cat) *The Stranger Next Door,* Dutton Children's Books (New York, NY), 2002.

Escaping the Giant Wave, Simon & Schuster Books for Young Readers (New York, NY), 2003.

(With Pete the Cat) *Spy Cat,* Dutton Children's Books (New York, NY), 2003.

Abduction!, Dutton Children's Books (New York, NY), 2004.

The Ghost's Grave, Dutton Children's Books (New York, NY), 2005.

(With Pete the Cat) *Trapped,* Dutton Children's Books (New York, NY), 2006.

Stolen Children, Dutton Children's Books (New York, NY), 2008.

Runaway Twin, Dutton Children's Books (New York, NY), 2009.

"FRIGHTMARES" SERIES

Don't Go Near Mrs. Tallie, Pocket Books (New York, NY), 1995.

Desert Danger, Pocket Books (New York, NY), 1995.

Cat Burglar on the Prowl, Pocket Books (New York, NY), 1995.

Bone Breath and the Vandals, Pocket Books (New York, NY), 1995.

Backstage Fright, Pocket Books (New York, NY), 1996.

Screaming Eagles, Pocket Books (New York, NY), 1996.

Race to Disaster, Pocket Books (New York, NY), 1996.

The Ghost Followed Us Home, Minstrel (New York, NY), 1996.

The Secret Journey, Pocket Books (New York, NY), 1999.

JUVENILE NONFICTION

Winning Monologs for Young Actors: Sixty-five Honest-to-Life Characterizations to Delight Young Actors and Audiences of All Ages, Meriwether Publishing (Colorado Springs, CO), 1986.

Encore!: More Winning Monologs for Young Actors, Meriwether Publishing (Colorado Springs, CO), 1988.

Acting Natural: Monologs, Dialogs, and Playlets for Teens, Meriwether Publishing (Colorado Springs, CO), 1991.

Small Steps: The Year I Got Polio, (autobiography) Albert Whitman (Morton Grove, IL), 1996, tenth anniversary edition, 2006.

Shelter Dogs: Amazing Stories of Adopted Strays, Albert Whitman (Morton Grove, IL), 1999.

Five Pages a Day: A Writer's Journey (autobiography), Albert Whitman (Morton Grove, IL), 2002.

Tell It like It Is: Fifty Monologs for Talented Teens, Meriwether Publishing (Colorado Springs, CO), 2007.

PLAYS

Cemeteries Are a Grave Matter, Dramatic Publishing (Woodstock, IL), 1975.

Let Him Sleep 'till It's Time for His Funeral, Contemporary Drama Service (Colorado Springs, CO), 1977.

Spirit!, Pioneer Drama Service (Englewood, CO), 1979.

Dracula, Darling, Contemporary Drama Service (Colorado Springs, CO), 1979.

Charming Billy, Contemporary Drama Service (Colorado Springs, CO), 1983.

Bicycles Built for Two (musical), Contemporary Drama Service (Colorado Springs, CO), 1985.

FOR ADULTS

Wedding Vows: How to Express Your Love in Your Own Words, Meriwether Publishing (Colorado Spring, CO), 1979, second edition, 1989.

Refinishing and Restoring Your Piano, Tab Books (Blue Ridge Summit, PA), 1985.

Also contributor to periodicals.

Adaptations

Some of Kehret's works have been adapted as audiobooks.

Sidelights

Peg Kehret is the author of dozens of children's novels, many of them, such as award-winners *Terror at the Zoo, Abduction!,* and *The Ghost's Grave,* serving up generous doses of suspense and danger. Winner of the Dorothy Canfield Fisher Award, Kehret's *Small Steps:*

The Year I Got Polio documents the author's own fight with childhood polio, a battle that left her temporarily paralyzed. "I try to be a good role model for the children who love my books," Kehret stated in an interview with Mary Berry for *Teacher Librarian.* "My polio experience left me with a strong belief in the sanctity of all life and the ability to appreciate each moment. I believe that love is stronger than hate, and I try to create stories with protagonists who are compassionate, smart and brave."

Kehret writes nonfiction for adults as well as for children. Her *Winning Monologs for Young Actors: Sixty-five Honest-to-Life Characterizations to Delight Young Actors and Audiences of All Ages* and *Acting Natural: Monologs, Dialogs, and Playlets for Teens* both reflect her own commitment to theater; the multi-talented Kehret has also penned a number of plays. Her prose works have won a host of honors, including the PEN Center USA West Award for Children's Literature, a Golden Kite award from the Society of Children's Book Writers and Illustrators, and a Henry Bergh award from the American Society for the Prevention of Cruelty to Animals.

Small Steps:

THE YEAR I GOT POLIO

Peg Kehret

Born in LaCrosse, Wisconsin, in 1936, Kehret developed an early passion for words and writing. Paid three cents a story by her grandfather, she wrote, published, and sold her own newspaper about the dogs in her neighborhood. Her youthful broadsheet soon went out of business, though, because she continually featured her own dog on the front page. The experience still proved worthwhile, as Kehret once remarked to *SATA:* "I learned that if I expect other people to read what I wrote, I must make it interesting to them."

Kehret's idyllic childhood was shattered when she contracted polio in the seventh grade and became paralyzed from the neck down. Although she was told that she would never walk again, after spending more than nine months in the hospital she gradually regained the use of her muscles and made a full recovery. The episode had a profound influence on her life, Kehret recalled in an autobiographical essay for *SATA:* "Polio not only affected my body, it also shaped my personality. I had to deal with pain, disability, and loneliness while my friends back home were concerned only with spelling tests and weenie roasts. I had been a sheltered daughter in a small Midwestern town; in the hospital I learned to get along with people of all ages and backgrounds." The experience also taught her perseverance, "an attribute that I needed when I began submitting my early writing to potential publishers."

As a teen, Kehret dreamed of being either a veterinarian or a writer, finally opting for the latter. "I'm glad I chose writing," she later reflected, "but two of the main characters in my books want to be veterinarians. Dogs, cats, llamas, and elephants have played important parts in my books." With high school came a new direction for Kehret's interest in words: theater. Cast as a hillbilly in a one-act play as a freshman, Kehret was seriously bitten by the theater bug, working backstage or in acting roles in every production she could. She briefly attended the University of Minnesota before marrying in 1955. Children soon followed and she lived the busy life of mother and homemaker while also volunteering for her local Humane Society branch.

Kehret began writing in the early 1970s, spurred on by her work in community theater as well as by her interest in research of various sorts. She began selling magazine stories, eventually logging over 300 of them before turning her hand to lengthier works. There followed one-act and full-length plays, including the award-winning *Spirit!,* as well as by two adult-nonfiction titles, before she began writing books for young people. Kehret's initial juvenile title, *Winning Monologs for Young Actors,* appeared in 1986 and was followed by her first novel for young people, *Deadly Stranger.* The story of a kidnapping, *Deadly Stranger* was dubbed a "cliffhanger" by a *Kirkus Reviews* contributor. "As soon as I tried writing from a youthful point of view," Kehret later explained to *SATA,* "I knew I had found my place in the writing world."

Cover of Kheret's **The Secret Journey,** *featuring artwork by C. Michael Dudash.* (Minstrel, 1999. C. Michael Dudash, illustrator. Reproduced by permission.)

Another popular early title, *Nightmare Mountain,* is a thriller involving young Molly and her visit to her aunt's ranch at the foot of Mt. Baker. The fun visit turns into a nightmare when Molly's Aunt Karen falls into a coma and the woman's three valuable llamas are stolen. *Booklist* critic Denise Wilms observed that in *Nightmare Mountain* Kehret delivers "a fast-paced mystery-adventure tale with a heroine who, when forced to deal with disaster, shows courage and resourcefulness." Jeanette Larson concluded in *School Library Journal* that the book is a "satisfying novel that will keep readers guessing until the end."

One of Kehret's personal favorites, *Cages,* allowed her to write about the Humane Society, for which she has a special passion. When young Kit—who has an alcoholic stepfather and a mother in denial—gives in to a momentary urge and shoplifts a bracelet, she sets off a chain of events that has lasting repercussions in her life. Caught, Kit is sentenced to community service at the Humane Society. There she falls in love with the homeless dogs and learns lessons about personal responsibility and facing her problems. As Andrea Davidson noted in *Voice of Youth Advocates, Cages* "will appeal to young teen readers interested in getting out of the 'cages' represented by their [own] problems." *School*

Library Journal reviewer Sylvia V. Meisner concluded that Kit's determination to set herself free from "the cages of alcohol enablement, jealousy, and, ultimately, the secret of her crime make her an appealing protagonist."

Kehret's best-selling *Terror at the Zoo* is the story of two siblings and an overnight campout at the zoo that goes very wrong. *Horror at the Haunted House,* continues the adventures of Ellen and Corey from *Terror at the Zoo.* This time around, they help with a Halloween haunted-house project at the local historical museum, only to discover that the house really is haunted. Overcoming her fear of ghosts, Ellen helps discover who is stealing from the museum's collection. Donna Houser noted in a *Voice of Youth Advocates* review of *Terror at the Zoo* that this "fun, fast-paced novel can be read in an evening." In *Booklist* Chris Sherman concluded that readers "will be waiting in line for this action-packed novel, which combines a good mystery with an exciting ghost story, a little danger, and a satisfying ending that ties everything up neatly."

Ellen and Corey return in *Danger at the Fair,* "this time sharing a thrill-a-minute adventure set at a county fair," according to Zvirin. Atop the Ferris wheel, Corey spies a pickpocket at work, but when Corey subsequently trails the thief, he is trapped inside the "River of Fear" ride. Zvirin concluded that the mystery-suspense components of the story, plus "a pair of enthusiastic, heroic, quite likable" protagonists, all added up to a book "that won't stay on the shelf for long."

Two other personal favorites by Kehret are *The Richest Kids in Town* and *Searching for Candlestick Park.* The former title is a comic novel that finds Peter's money-making ventures gone awry. New in town, Peter desperately wants to save up enough money to buy a plane ticket that will let him go back and visit his best friend. Peter enlists the help of some other kids, including Wishbone Wyoming, in some of his crazy money-making schemes. Their plans range from an alternative health club to a rubber-duck race, and all fail miserably and rather humorously. Finally Peter comes to see that he no longer needs to make money for a ticket; he has a new best friend in Wishbone. A critic for *Kirkus Reviews* concluded that there are "clever antics in this fun book."

In *Searching for Candlestick Park* twelve-year-old Spencer is trying to find the father who left him and his mom three years before. Sure that his dad works for the San Francisco Giants, Spencer sets off on his bicycle from Seattle, accompanied by his cat, Foxey. Lauren Peterson noted in *Booklist* that Spencer's "honesty and integrity are repeatedly tested" in this "fast-paced, exciting adventure." A *Kirkus Reviews* contributor commented of *Searching for Candlestick Park* that "Spencer's impulsive escapade may give readers infatuated with the notion of running way some second thoughts."

Cover of Kehret's chapter book My Brother Made Me Do It, *featuring artwork by C. Michael Dudash.* (Pocket Books, 2001. Cover art copyright © 2000 by C. Michael Dudash. Reproduced by permission.)

With *Earthquake Terror* Kehret returns to her typical thriller format. When an earthquake destroys the only bridge to the mainland from the tiny island where Jonathan and his disabled sister Abby are staying, the young boy finds himself pitted against nature. With no food or supplies, and unable to find help, Jonathan must single-handedly save Abby, his dog, and himself. With displaced waters from the quake beginning to flood the island, the clock is ticking on Jonathan's efforts. "It will be a rare thriller fan who won't want to see what happens," Stephanie Zvirin commented in her *Booklist* review of *Earthquake Terror*. Roger Sutton, writing in the *Bulletin of the Center for Children's Books,* noted that Kehret's "focus on the action is tight and involving," while Elaine E. Knight concluded in *School Library Journal* that "Jonathan is a sympathetic and realistic character," and that this "exciting tale is a fine choice for most collections."

My Brother Made Me Do It, the story of eleven-year-old Julie Walsh and her eighty-nine-year-old pen pal, Mrs. Kaplan, unfolds through Julie's letters. As part of a school project, Julie begins a correspondence with Mrs. Kaplan, who lives in Kansas. The preteen shares stories with her pen pal about everything from her younger brother's pranks to her run for student council.

When Julie is diagnosed with juvenile arthritis, Mrs. Kaplan is the first friend she tells. It turn out that Mrs. Kaplan also suffers from arthritis, and through the pen pals continued exchanges readers can follow their triumphs and struggles with a physical challenge at two different stages of life. A reviewer for *School Library Journal* noted that "the incidents are treated with humor and sensitivity." Susan Allen, writing for *Voice of Youth Advocates,* called *My Brother Made Me Do It* "an unexpected gem" that tackles "many topics, such as the challenges of chronic illness and the payoff for perseverance."

Kehret has also authored several titles in the "Frightmares" series, a competitor to the popular "Goosebumps" books by R.L. Stine. Her books feature friends Rosie and Kayo, who get involved in all manner of adventures and mysteries, from solving a kidnapping in Arizona in *Desert Danger* to solving a possible poisoning in *Don't Go Near Mrs. Tallie* to discovering vandals in the school with the help of a pet in *Bone Breath and the Vandals.* In *Booklist* Peterson, reviewing *Bone Breath and the Vandals,* noted that "Kehret delivers some likable characters and a thrilling plot that won't disappoint suspense fans."

Nonfiction for children has also received the Kehret touch. Among her books of monologues for young actors, one of the most popular is *Acting Natural.* "A wide range of topics is addressed in this sourcebook of sixty original scenes and monologues," noted Dianne G. Mahoney in *School Library Journal.* Donna Houser commented in *Voice of Youth Advocates* that "all sections have their own merit because they deal with problems that are relevant to today's youth."

In another nonfiction work, *Shelter Dogs: Amazing Stories of Adopted Strays,* Kehret shared a collection of stories about dogs that found a second life after being taken from Humane Society shelters. A *Kirkus Reviews* critic called the book "an amiable collection of short anecdotes," concluding that there was "a ready audience to cry over and gasp at the tale behind every dog." Kehret donates ten percent of her royalties to animal welfare groups.

Several of Kehret's fictional works also reflect her commitment to animal welfare. In *Don't Tell Anyone* a spunky twelve year old rescues a group of feral cats after she learns that the field the animals live in will soon be bulldozed as part of a construction project. In the process, Megan uncovers a worker's criminal enterprise scheme that involves kidnapping and arson. According to *Booklist* contributor Debbie Carton, "a strong sense of justice is part of the happy, satisfying ending" of the middle-grade novel. A youngster stumbles upon a group of bear poachers, putting his life at risk, in *The Hideout,* "a suspenseful and quick-reading adventure story," remarked *School Library Journal* critic Toni D. Moore. A group of sixth graders hopes to raise enough funds to send a mistreated circus elephant to an animal sanctuary in *Saving Lilly,* a work that "entertains and informs as it highlights the darker side of animal entertainment," according to a *Kirkus Reviews* contributor.

Kehret's coauthor for the animal-centered novels *The Stranger Next Door, Spy Cat,* and *Trapped* is Pete the Cat, whose contributions to the stories appear in italics. Pete, the pet of twelve-year-old Alex Kendrill, makes his first appearance in *Stranger.* Alex has moved to a new neighborhood where his life is threatened by an arsonist and where the unfriendly boy with whom he tries to establish a friendship is in a witness-protection program. "Readers will be caught up in the action even as they are amused by Pete's astute observations and adroit detective work," commented a *Kirkus Reviews* contributor.

In *Spy Cat,* Alex's younger brother, Benjie, is kidnaped by thieves when he learns too much about them for his own good. Pete, whose mewlings are not understood by humans, nonetheless aids in Benjie's rescue and discovering the solution to the crimes. *Spy Cat* "is a fast-moving mystery adventure," concluded Terry Dorio in a *School Library Journal* review of the book. In *Trapped* Pete the cat is kidnaped after Alex investigates a suspicious game trap he finds hidden in the woods. According to *School Library Journal* reviewer Kristen Oravec, in a review of *Trapped*, "animal lovers will get a kick out of this intriguing mystery."

Abduction!, another thriller by Kehret, centers on the efforts of thirteen-year-old Bonnie to locate her young half-brother after he is abducted by his biological father. Kehret "demonstrates a deft touch in maintaining suspense," noted a *Kirkus Reviews* critic. Kidnaping is also the focus of *Stolen Children,* a novel filled with "ample suspense and drama," in the words of *Booklist* contributor Andrew Medlar. When Amy and the toddler she baby-sits for are taken captive by a pair of small-time crooks, the teen manages to send coded messages to her parents in a series of DVDs recorded by her abductors. "The story is fast-paced, plot-driven and involving," observed a contributor in *Kirkus Reviews.* In *The Ghost's Grave,* a youngster expecting to spend a dull summer with his elderly great-aunt instead finds mystery and excitement when he meets the spirit of an old miner and discovers buried treasure. "Kehret shares her extensive knowledge of turn-of-the-[twentieth-]century mining towns in a warm-hearted novel of the relationship between a boy an old woman, and a ghost," Michele Winship wrote in a *Kliatt* review of *The Ghost's Grave.*

Kehret details her own battle with the paralyzing aftereffects of polio in her award-winning *Small Steps.* "This heartfelt memoir takes readers back to 1949 when the author, at age twelve, contracted polio," noted Zvirin. Kehret describes the progress of the illness, the paralysis, and her slow recovery. Christine A. Moesch concluded in *School Library Journal* that Kehret's memoir is an "honest and well-done book." In her autobiographical essay, Kehret mentioned her "increased difficulties with post-polio syndrome," which has caused her to retire from making school visits. "The muscle pain and weakness are similar to what I experienced when I was twelve," she wrote. "Fatigue is also a symptom. It is hard for me to acknowledge that the disease I thought I'd conquered is once more giving me trouble. However, I can still walk (I have a cane that has cat faces all over it) and do the activities I love most: read, write, enjoy visits from my children and grandchildren, and play with my animals."

In a second memoir, *Five Pages a Day: A Writer's Journey,* Kehret recalls her beginnings as a writer, including her prize of a trip to Hawaii and a new car for her twenty-five-word entry on why she liked Kraft Macaroni and Cheese Dinner. "Like her novels, this memoir is written in spare, lively prose with plenty of interesting details, anecdotes, and insights," said a *Kirkus Reviews* critic.

Over her writing career, Kehret has amassed a large body of work and a legion of loyal fans—both girls and boys—for her middle-grade thrillers. Blending exciting action, likable characters, and hi-lo language, she writes books that lead her readers on to more difficult fiction

Keheret captivates readers with her middle-grade thriller **Trapped,** *featuring artwork by Brandon Dorman.* (Puffin Books, 2008. Reproduced by permission of Puffin Books, a division of Penguin Putnam Books for Young Readers.)

and nonfiction. As Kehret once noted in an autobiographical essay for *SATA*, "I hope my books will continue to help young people know the joy of reading, the satisfaction of volunteering for a worthy cause, and the importance of leading an honorable life."

Biographical and Critical Sources

BOOKS

Kehret, Peg, *Small Steps: The Year I Got Polio*, Albert Whitman (Morton Grove, IL), 1996, tenth anniversary edition, 2006.

Kehret, Peg, *Five Pages a Day: A Writer's Journey*, Albert Whitman (Morton Grove, IL), 2002.

PERIODICALS

Booklist, September 15, 1989, Denise Wilms, review of *Nightmare Mountain*, p. 184; February 15, 1990, review of *Sisters, Long Ago*, p. 1166; May 15, 1992, Karen Hutt, review of *Acting Natural: Monologs, Dialogs, and Playlets for Teens*, p. 1672; September 1, 1992, Chris Sherman, review of *Horror at the Haunted House*, pp. 56, 60; September 1, 1994, Mary Harris Veeder, review of *The Richest Kids in Town*, p. 41; December 1, 1994, Stephanie Zvirin, review of *Danger at the Fair*, p. 664; May 1, 1995, Lauren Peterson, review of *Bone Breath and the Vandals*, p. 1573; October 1, 1995, Lauren Peterson, review of *Don't Go Near Miss Tallie*, p. 314; January 1, 1996, Stephanie Zvirin, review of *Earthquake Terror*, p. 834; November 1, 1996, Stephanie Zvirin, review of *Small Steps*, pp. 492-493; August, 1997, Lauren Peterson, review of *Searching for Candlestick Park*, p. 1901; August, 1998, Carolyn Phelan, review of *The Volcano Disaster*, p. 2005; August, 2000, Debbie Carton, review of *Don't Tell Anyone*, p. 2140; May 1, 2001, Stephanie Zvirin, review of *The Hideout*, p. 1612; January 1, 2003, Catherine Andronik, review of *Spy Cat*, p. 890; December 1, 2006, John Peters, review of *Trapped*, p. 47; December 15, 2008, Andrew Medlar, review of *Stolen Children*, p. 44.

Bulletin of the Center for Children's Books, February, 1995, review of *Danger at the Fair*, pp. 202-203; March, 1996, Roger Sutton, review of *Earthquake Terror*, p. 231; November, 1996, review of *Small Steps*, pp. 100-101; November, 1997, review of *Searching for Candlestick Park*, pp. 88-89.

Kirkus Reviews, March 1, 1987, review of *Deadly Stranger*, p. 373; August 15, 1994, review of *The Richest Kids in Town*, p. 1131; June 1, 1997, review of *Searching for Candlestick Park*, p. 874; April 1, 1999, review of *Shelter Dogs: Amazing Stories of Adopted Strays*, p. 535; October 15, 2001, review of *Saving Lilly*, p. 1486; March 15, 2002, review of *The Stranger Next Door*, p. 415; September 15, 2002, review of *Five Pages a Day*, p. 1393; February 1, 2003, review of *Spy Cat*, p. 233; November 15, 2004, review of *Abduction!*, p. 1090; July 1, 2005, review of *The Ghost's Grave*, p. 737; September 15, 2008, review of *Stolen Children*.

Kliatt, July, 1993, review of *Cages*, p. 10; March, 1997, review of *Bone Breath and the Vandals*, p. 40; November, 2004, Janis Flint-Ferguson, review of *Abduction!*, p. 8; July, 2005, Michele Winship, review of *The Ghost's Grave*, p. 12.

School Library Journal, October, 1989, Jeanette Larson, review of *Nightmare Mountain*, p. 120; March, 1990, Bruce Ann Shook, review of *Sisters, Long Ago*, pp. 218-219; June, 1991, Sylvia V. Meisner, review of *Cages*, p. 126; August, 1992, Dianne G. Mahoney, review of *Acting Natural*, p. 182; September, 1994, Suzanne Hawley, review of *The Richest Kids in Town*, p. 218; May, 1995, Christina Dorr, review of *Cat Burglar on the Job*, p. 108; December, 1995, Carrie A. Guarria, review of *Don't Go Near Mrs. Tallie*, p. 104; February, 1996, Elaine E. Knight, review of *Earthquake Terror*, and Anne Connor, review of *Desert Danger*, both p. 100; November, 1996, Christine A. Moesch, review of *Small Steps*, p. 114; July, 1998, Edith Ching, review of *The Volcano Disaster*, p. 96; April, 2000, Julie Ventura, review of *Don't Tell Anyone*, p. 138; September, 2000, Sharon McNeil, review of *My Brother Made Me Do It*, p. 232; August, 2001, Toni D. Moore, review of *The Hideout*, p. 185; November, 2001, Jean Gaffney, review of *Saving Lilly*, p. 159; March, 2002, Heather Dieffenbach, review of *The Stranger Next Door*, p. 232; January, 2003, Terrie Dorio, review of *Spy Cat*, p. 140; December, 2004, Diana Pierce, review of *Abduction!*, p. 149; October, 2005, Alison Grant, review of *The Ghost's Grave*, p. 163; November, 2006, Kristen Oravec, review of *Trapped!*, p. 138; March, 2008, Terrilyn Fleming, review of *Tell It like It Is: Fifty Monologs for Talented Teens*, p. 221; December, 2008, Jessica Miller, review of *Stolen Children*, p. 128.

Teacher Librarian, April, 2002, Mary Berry, interview with Kehret, p. 50.

Voice of Youth Advocates, June, 1991, Andrea Davidson, review of *Cages*, pp. 97-98; June, 1992, Donna Houser, review of *Acting Natural*, pp. 126-127; October, 1992, Donna Houser, review of *Horror at the Haunted House*, p. 224; February, 1996, review of *Don't Go Near Mrs. Tallie*, p. 373; December, 2000, Susan Allen, review of *My Brother Made Me Do It*, p. 350.

ONLINE

Peg Kehret Home Page, http://www.pegkehret.com (January 1, 2010).

Peg Kehret Web log, http://www.pegkehret.com/wordpress (January 1, 2010).

*   *   *

KROLL, Steven 1941-

Personal

Born August 11, 1941, in New York, NY; son of Julius (a diamond merchant) and Anita (a business executive) Kroll; married Edite Niedringhaus (a children's book

Steven Kroll (Photograph by Harry Heleotis. Reproduced by permission.)

editor), April 18, 1964 (divorced, 1978); married Abigail Aldridge (a milliner), June 3, 1989 (divorced, 1994); married Kathleen Beckett (a journalist), October 4, 1997. *Education:* Harvard University, B.A. (American history and literature), 1962. *Religion:* Jewish. *Hobbies and other interests:* Walking, traveling, playing tennis.

Addresses

Home—New York, NY; Bucks County, PA. *Office*—64 W. 11th St., Apt. 3R, New York, NY 10011. *E-mail*—stevenkroll2005@msn.com.

Career

Author and editor. *Transatlantic Review,* London, England, associate editor, 1962-65; Chatto & Windus, London, reader and editor, 1962-65; Holt, Rinehart & Winston, New York, NY, acquiring editor, adult trade department, 1965-69; freelance writer, beginning 1969. Instructor in English, University of Maine at Augusta, 1970-71. Speaker at schools.

Member

PEN American Center (former chairman of children's book authors' committee and former member of execu-

tive board), Authors Guild, Authors League of America, Society of Children's Book Writers and Illustrators, Harvard Club (New York, NY).

Writings

FOR CHILDREN

Is Milton Missing?, illustrated by Dick Gackenbach, Holiday House (New York, NY), 1975.

That Makes Me Mad!, illustrated by Hilary Knight, Pantheon (New York, NY), 1976, illustrated by Christine Davenier, SeaStar Books (New York, NY), 2002.

The Tyrannosaurus Game, illustrated by Tomie de Paola, Holiday House (New York, NY), 1976.

Gobbledygook, illustrated by Kelly Oechsli, Holiday House (New York, NY), 1977.

If I Could Be My Grandmother, illustrated by Lady Mc-Crady, Pantheon (New York, NY), 1977.

Sleepy Ida and Other Nonsense Poems, illustrated by Seymour Chwast, Pantheon (New York, NY), 1977.

Santa's Crash-Bang Christmas, illustrated by Tomie de Paola, Holiday House (New York, NY), 1977.

T.J. Folger, Thief, illustrated by Bill Morrison, Holiday House (New York, NY), 1978.

Fat Magic, illustrated by Tomie de Paola, Holiday House (New York, NY), 1979.

The Candy Witch, illustrated by Marylin Hafner, Holiday House (New York, NY), 1979.

Space Cats, illustrated by Friso Henstra, Holiday House (New York, NY), 1979.

Amanda and the Giggling Ghost, illustrated by Dick Gackenbach, Holiday House (New York, NY), 1980.

Dirty Feet, illustrated by Toni Hormann, Parents Magazine Press (New York, NY), 1980.

Monster Birthday, illustrated by Dennis Kendrick, Holiday House (New York, NY), 1980.

Friday the Thirteenth, illustrated by Dick Gackenbach, Holiday House (New York, NY), 1981.

Giant Journey, illustrated by Kay Chorao, Holiday House (New York, NY), 1981.

Are You Pirates?, illustrated by Marylin Hafner, Pantheon (New York, NY), 1982.

Banana Bits, illustrated by Maxie Chambliss, Avon (New York, NY), 1982.

Bathrooms, illustrated by Maxie Chambliss, Avon (New York, NY), 1982.

The Big Bunny and the Easter Eggs, illustrated by Janet Stevens, Holiday House (New York, NY), 1982.

The Goat Parade, illustrated by Tim Kirk, Parents Magazine Press (New York, NY), 1982.

One Tough Turkey, illustrated by John Wallner, Holiday House (New York, NY), 1982.

The Hand-me-down Doll, illustrated by Evaline Ness, Holiday House (New York, NY), 1983.

Otto, illustrated by Ned Delaney, Parents Magazine Press (New York, NY), 1983.

Pigs in the House, illustrated by Tim Kirk, Parents Magazine Press (New York, NY), 1983.

Toot! Toot!, illustrated by Anne Rockwell, Holiday House (New York, NY), 1983.

Woof, Woof!, illustrated by Nicole Rubel, Dial (New York, NY), 1983.

The Biggest Pumpkin Ever, illustrated by Jeni Bassett, Holiday House (New York, NY), 1984.

Loose Tooth, illustrated by Tricia Tusa, Holiday House (New York, NY), 1984.

Happy Mother's Day, illustrated by Marylin Hafner, Holiday House (New York, NY), 1985.

Mrs. Claus's Crazy Christmas, illustrated by John Wallner, Holiday House (New York, NY), 1985.

Annie's Four Grannies, illustrated by Eileen Christelow, Holiday House (New York, NY), 1986.

The Big Bunny and the Magic Show, illustrated by Janet Stevens, Holiday House (New York, NY), 1986.

I'd Like to Be, illustrated by Ellen Appleby, Parents Magazine Press (New York, NY), 1987.

I Love Spring, illustrated by Kathryn E. Shoemaker, Holiday House (New York, NY), 1987.

It's Groundhog Day!, illustrated by Jeni Bassett, Holiday House (New York, NY), 1987.

Don't Get Me in Trouble!, illustrated by Marvin Glass, Crown (New York, NY), 1988.

Happy Father's Day, illustrated by Marylin Hafner, Holiday House (New York, NY), 1988.

Looking for Daniela: A Romantic Adventure, illustrated by Anita Lobel, Holiday House (New York, NY), 1988.

Newsman Ned Meets the New Family, illustrated by Denise Brunkus, Scholastic, Inc. (New York, NY), 1988.

Oh, What a Thanksgiving!, illustrated by S.D. Schindler, Scholastic, Inc. (New York, NY), 1988.

Big Jeremy, illustrated by Donald Carrick, Holiday House (New York, NY), 1989.

The Hokey-Pokey Man, illustrated by Deborah Kogan Ray, Holiday House (New York, NY), 1989.

Newsman Ned and the Broken Rules, illustrated by Denise Brunkus, Scholastic, Inc. (New York, NY), 1989.

Branigan's Cat and the Halloween Ghost, illustrated by Carolyn Ewing, Holiday House (New York, NY), 1990.

Gone Fishing, illustrated by Harvey Stevenson, Crown (New York, NY), 1990.

It's April Fools' Day!, illustrated by Jeni Bassett, Holiday House (New York, NY), 1990.

Annabelle's Un-Birthday, illustrated by Gail Owens, Macmillan (New York, NY), 1991.

Howard and Gracie's Luncheonette, illustrated by Michael Sours, Holt (New York, NY), 1991.

Mary McLean and the St. Patrick's Day Parade, illustrated by Michael Dooling, Scholastic, Inc. (New York, NY), 1991.

Princess Abigail and the Wonderful Hat, illustrated by Patience Brewster, Holiday House (New York, NY), 1991.

The Squirrels' Thanksgiving, illustrated by Jeni Bassett, Holiday House (New York, NY), 1991.

The Magic Rocket, illustrated by Will Hillenbrand, Holiday House (New York, NY), 1992.

Andrew Wants a Dog, illustrated by Molly Delaney, Hyperion Books (New York, NY), 1992.

The Hit and Run Gang, volumes 1-4, illustrated by Meredith Johnson, Avon (New York, NY), 1992.

The Pigrates Clean Up, illustrated by Jeni Bassett, Henry Holt (New York, NY), 1993.

Queen of the May, illustrated by Patience Brewster, Holiday House (New York, NY), 1993.

Will You Be My Valentine?, illustrated by Lillian Hoban, Holiday House (New York, NY), 1993.

I'm George Washington and You're Not!, illustrated by Betsy Lewin, Hyperion Books (New York, NY), 1994.

By the Dawn's Early Light: The Story of the Star-spangled Banner, illustrated by Dan Andreasen, Scholastic, Inc. (New York, NY), 1994.

Patrick's Tree House, illustrated by Roberta Wilson, Macmillan (New York, NY), 1994.

The Hit and Run Gang, volumes 5-8, illustrated by Meredith Johnson, Avon (New York, NY), 1994.

Lewis and Clark: Explorers of the American West, illustrated by Richard Williams, Holiday House (New York, NY), 1994.

Doctor on an Elephant, illustrated by Michael Chesworth, Henry Holt (New York, NY), 1994.

Eat!, illustrated by Diane Palmisciano, Hyperion Books (New York, NY), 1995.

Ellis Island: Doorway to Freedom, illustrated by Karen Ritz, Holiday House (New York, NY), 1995.

Pony Express!, illustrated by Dan Andreasen, Scholastic, Inc. (New York, NY), 1996.

The Boston Tea Party, illustrated by Peter Fiore, Holiday House (New York, NY), 1998.

Oh, Tucker!, illustrated by Scott Nash, Candlewick Press (Cambridge, MA), 1998.

Robert Fulton: From Submarine to Steamboat, illustrated by Bill Farnsworth, Holiday House (New York, NY), 1999.

William Penn: Founder of Pennsylvania, illustrated by Ronald Himler, Holiday House (New York, NY), 2000.

Patches Lost and Found, illustrated by Barry Gott, Winslow Press, 2001.

That Makes Me Mad!, illustrated by Christine Davenier, SeaStar Books (New York, NY), 2002.

A Tale of Two Dogs, illustrated by Mike Reed, Marshall Cavendish (New York, NY), 2004.

Patches Lost and Found, illustrated by Barry Gott, Marshall Cavendish (New York, NY), 2005.

Pooch on the Loose: A Christmas Adventure, illustrated by Michael Garland, Marshall Cavendish Children (New York, NY), 2005.

The Biggest Snowman Ever, illustrated by Jeni Bassett, Scholastic, Inc. (New York, NY), 2005.

Jungle Bullies, illustrated by Vincent Nguyen, Marshall Cavendish (New York, NY), 2006.

The Biggest Valentine Ever, illustrated by Jeni Bassett, Scholastic, Inc. (New York, NY), 2006.

The Biggest Easter Basket Ever, illustrated by Jeni Bassett, Scholastic, Inc. (New York, NY), 2008.

The Hanukkah Mice, illustrated by Michelle Shapiro, Marshall Cavendish Children (New York, NY), 2008.

Barbarians!, illustrated by Robert Byrd, Dutton Children's Books (New York, NY), 2009.

Stuff!: Reduce, Reuse, Recycle, illustrated by Steve Cox, Marshall Cavendish Children (Tarrytown, NY), 2009.

The Biggest Christmas Tree Ever, illustrated by Jeni Bassett, Cartwheel Books (New York, NY), 2009.

The Tyrannosaurus Game, illustrated by S.D. Schindler, Marshall Cavendish Children (New York, NY), 2010.

YOUNG-ADULT BOOKS

Take It Easy, Four Winds (Bristol, FL), 1983.

Breaking Camp, Macmillan (New York, NY), 1985.

Multiple Choice, Macmillan (New York, NY), 1987.

Sweet America, Jamestown Publishers (Chicago, IL), 2000.

When I Dream of Heaven, Jamestown Publishers (Chicago, IL), 2000.

Dear Mr. President: John Quincey Adams' Letters from a Southern Planter's Son, Winslow Press, 2001.

OTHER

Contributor of book reviews to *Book World, Commonweal, Village Voice, Listener, New York Times Book Review, Spectator, Times Literary Supplement,* and *London Magazine.* Contributor to poetry anthologies.

Kroll's works have been translated into French, Spanish, Dutch, Danish, Italian, and Japanese.

Adaptations

The Biggest Pumpkin Ever and Other Stories (includes *The Biggest Pumpkin Ever; Sleepy Ida and Other Nonsense Poems; T.J. Folger, Thief;* and *Woof, Woof!*) was recorded on audiocassette, Caedmon, 1986. *The Biggest Pumpkin Ever, The Big Bunny and the Easter Eggs, Will You Be My Valentine?,* and *Oh, Tucker!* were recorded on audiocassette, Scholastic, Inc.

Sidelights

Living and working in New York City, Steven Kroll is a prolific writer whose many picture books include *The Biggest Pumpkin Ever, Oh, Tucker!, Stuff!: Reduce, Reuse, Recycle,* and *The Hanukkah Mice.* Turning to older readers, Kroll has also produced chapter books and has drawn on his interest in history in writing nonfiction books for middle graders and historical fiction for young adults. Praising *Stuff,* which features artwork by Steve Cox, a *Kirkus Reviews* writer recommended Kroll's book as "an admirable introduction to beginning environmentalism for a young audience," while *Booklist* critic Karin Snelson dubbed *A Tale of Two Dogs* as a "tail-wagging, happy-ending picture book." "For me, writing is not just about writing," Kroll noted on his home page. "It's about travel." In addition to researching real-world locations for his many books, Kroll also travels in order to meet and connect with his readers.

As a child growing up in New York City, Kroll entertained himself with imaginative games, baseball, and trips to the local candy store. When he was older, he

The fanciful story in Kroll's Queen of the May *is brought to life in Patience Brewster's detailed art.* (Holiday House, 1993. Illustration © 1993 by Patience Brewster. Reproduced by permission of Patience Brewster.)

visited the Museum of Modern Art on Tuesday afternoons to study sculpture. Naturally, people thought that he would become a sculptor, but his career took a surprising turn. Appointed editor of *Panorama,* his secondary-school literary journal, Kroll discovered that "there wasn't much to publish. Someone had to fill the gap. I sat down and wrote two stories and I've been hooked on writing ever since."

Following his graduation from Harvard University in 1962, Kroll worked as an editor of adult trade books in both London, England, and in New York City. In 1969 he moved to Maine so he could write full time. He contributed book reviews to magazines and wrote adult fiction during the early 1970s, until his then wife, a children's book editor, echoed the advice of several other friends in children's publishing by suggesting that Kroll try writing for children. When he got an idea for a children's story, he gave it a try and found that writing for young readers was enjoyable.

Kroll spent a few years writing unsuccessful children's picture-book texts, and then returned to New York City, where he met writer and editor Margery Cuyler. Cuyler became his editor at Holiday House and published his first book, *Is Milton Missing?* Since the mid-1970s Kroll has produced at least two books per year—and often more—first for Holiday House and eventually expanding to write for other publishers.

For his story ideas and settings Kroll sometimes recalls places and instances from his own childhood. "When I write about a child's room, that room is often my own—the one in the Manhattan apartment house where I grew up," he once commented. "When I write about an urban street or an urban school, it is often my street or my school, taken out of time into a situation I have invented. And sometimes," the author continued, "if I'm writing about a suburb or a small town, that place will resemble the home of a summer camp friend I visited once, and longed to see again."

Several of Kroll's books help bring to life stories from U.S. history, the subject he majored in during college. Including *The Boston Tea Party* and *Pony Express!*, Kroll's colorful volumes are designed for older elementary-grade history buffs. *The Boston Tea Party*, for example, uses vivid impressionistic illustrations by Peter Fiore to chronicle the events leading up to the famous uprising of December 16, 1773. Setting the protest in its historical context, Kroll's text for *The Boston*

Tea Party opens with an explanation of how the Seven Years' War placed England in debt, and how that country planned to raise money to pay these debts by taxing its American colonies. Carolyn Phelan noted in a *Booklist* review of *The Boston Tea Party* that, although the lack of a central character gives the narrative unnecessary complexity, Kroll does a "credible job of summarizing history."

Another colonial-era story is recounted in *William Penn: Founder of Pennsylvania*. Aimed at a slightly older audience, Kroll's picture-book biography focuses on the rebellious William Penn, a man who, while born to privilege, dedicated his life to spreading religious and political freedom. Phelan again expressed concern that the subject matter may be too advanced for Kroll's young readership, citing Penn's background of civil disobedience and debt problems. Still, she recommended *William Penn* to school libraries as "a useful and certainly handsome addition" to history collections. In *Kirkus Reviews* a critic singled out Kroll's "highly

The battle between the Roman Legion and an army of Goths is covered in Kroll's text for Barbarians!, a book featuring artwork by Robert Byrd.
(Holiday House, 1993. Illustration © 1993 by Patience Brewster. Reproduced by permission of Patience Brewster.)

event-oriented and [information-]packed" text for the book. Reviewing another biography by Kroll, *Robert Fulton: From Submarine to Steamboat,* another *Kirkus Reviews* writer praised the work as a "handsomely illustrated" biography that "will make readers yearn for more information" on the visionary marine designer.

Kroll invites youngsters in grades three and older to saddle up in the pages of his book *Pony Express!* Oil paintings by Dan Andreasen underline his text, which follows the hunt for "young skinny wiry fellows not over eighteen, orphans preferred" and brought scores of riders to the fledgling mail delivery system between 1860 and 1861. *Pony Express!* earned high marks from critics, many of which cited its mix of depth of information (detailed route maps are provided), sharp graphic detail, and a compelling narrative that Kroll gears for his intended audience. In *Publishers Weekly* a contributor dubbed *Pony Express!* "an absorbing and enlightening dose of history and adventure."

Barbarians!, illustrated by Robert Byrd, takes a step back in time and across the seas, as Kroll focuses on the history of the Viking, Goth, Hun, and Mongol invaders that laid siege to sections of the vast Roman Empire until the fifteenth century, when European states began their own expansion and colonization. Focusing on each invading tribe's leaders, religion, culture, and technology, the author pairs his informative text with Byrd's vivid art to produce what *School Library Journal* contributor Lucinda Snyder Whitehurst described as "a thought-provoking, action-packed glimpse into a less-familiar part of history." According to Phelan, *Barbarians!* will treat "warrior-loving browsers" to "an informative and brightly illustrated" overview of a culture led by figures with names like Attila and Ghengis Khan.

More history for older readers is served up in two of Kroll's novel-length titles for young adults: *Sweet America* and *When I Dream of Heaven.* In the former, Kroll presents an immigrant's story by focusing on fourteen-year-old Tonio, an Italian immigrant who is gradually transformed into the American Tony in late nineteenth-century New York City. Gina Petrosino tries to balance her familial duties with her own wishes to continue her education in *When I Dream of Heaven.* In Kroll's story for this novel, "the appalling conditions of the New York City sweatshops at the turn of the 20th century and the plight of young immigrant girls come to life," according to Linda Bindner in *School Library Journal.*

Kroll takes a lighter tone in picture books such as *Patches Lost and Found,* "a masterful blend of text and illustration," according to Barbara Buckley in *School Library Journal.* In the story, Jenny would much rather draw than write stories, so when her beloved guinea pig, Patches, goes missing, she designs "missing" posters for the pet and distributes them all over town, with happy results. Meanwhile, in school Jenny has been un-

Kroll opens a window onto U.S. civil-war history in **By the Dawn's Early Light,** *featuring artwork by Dan Andreasen.* (Illustration copyright © 2000 by Dan Andreasen. Reproduced by permission of Scholastic, Inc.)

able to come up with a writing assignment for her teacher, but has been drawing pictures of what might have happened to Patches. Now her mother points out that Jenny's pictures tell a story; all she needs to do is add some words to complete her assignment. Buckley found *Patches Lost and Found* to be "a suspenseful, kid-friendly picture book that works on several levels," and in *Booklist* Phelan noted that the book is written "with a sure sense of narrative and an understanding of the concerns and the learning styles of children." Phelan deemed *Patches Lost and Found* "a fresh, fine offering," and in *Instructor* Judy Freeman commented that, "for many [young] . . . artists . . . this story will be a godsend."

For still younger readers, Kroll has published such whimsical stories as *The Biggest Pumpkin Ever, The Squirrel's Thanksgiving Oh, Tucker!,* and *Jungle Bullies.* In *Oh, Tucker!* he introduces readers to a playful, over-sized pup whose ability to generate household havoc is matched only by his loving personality. Noting that the pup "creates a trail of disaster," a *Publishers Weekly* critic went on to predict that early readers will "get swept up in the momentum" of Tucker's well-meaning rampages, and *Booklist* critic Ellen Mandel predicted that Tucker's "slapstick race through the house" will lead straight "into readers' hearts." Illustrated by Vincent Nguyen, *Jungle Bullies* follows a succession of animals as each one bullies its way into a favorite space by forcing another animal to do the same. Citing Kroll's use of a "rhythmic refrain" and Nguyen's "inviting and simple" charcoal and watercolor art, Kristine M. Casper added in *School Library Journal* that *Jungle Bullies* "makes . . . a good read-aloud and a helpful way to introduce the topic [of bullying] to children."

"I really love writing for children," Kroll once remarked to *SATA*. "I love starting the fireworks, love that explosion of emotion, of excitement, terror, and enthusiasm that comes with putting those words on paper and sometimes, if the mood is right, doing a draft of a whole picture-book story in one sitting." Writing for children also grants him a special connection with his own youth, something that he values greatly. "What is most important is the feeling that I am somehow in touch with my own childhood," Kroll explained. "To be in touch with your own childhood is to be, in some way, touched with wonder, and when I write for children, that is what I feel."

Biographical and Critical Sources

BOOKS

Behind the Covers: Interviews with Authors and Illustrators of Books for Children and Young Adults, Libraries Unlimited (Littleton, CO), 1985.

PERIODICALS

Booklist, March 1, 1996, review of *Pony Express!,* p. 177; May 1, 1998, Ellen Mandel, review of *Oh, Tucker!,* p. 521; September 15, 1998, Carolyn Phelan, review of *The Boston Tea Party,* p. 222; February 15, 2000, Carolyn Phelan, review of *William Penn: Founder of Pennsylvania,* p. 1108; March 1, 2001, Carolyn Phelan, review of *Patches Lost and Found,* p. 1277; January 1, 2002, Todd Morning, review of *Dear Mr. President: John Quincy Adams, Letters from a Southern Planter's Son,* p. 858; April 15, 2004, Karin Snelson, review of *A Tale of Two Dogs,* p. 1446; Septem-

Kroll's picture books for young children include **Patches Lost and Found,** *a story featuring colorful art by Barry Gott.* (Winslow Press, 2001. Illustration copyright © 2001 by Barry Gott. Reproduced by permission.)

Cover of Kroll's The Boston Tea Party, *a history of a resonant moment in American history that features artwork by Peter Fiore.* (Illustration copyright © 1998 by Peter Fiore. Reproduced by permission of Holiday House, Inc.)

ber 1, 2005, Ilene Cooper, review of *Pooch on the Loose: A Christmas Adventure,* p. 144; February 15, 2009, Gillian Engberg, review of *Stuff!: Reduce, Reuse, Recycle,* p. 94; May 1, 2009, Carolyn Phelan, review of *Barbarians!,* p. 76.

Horn Book, September-October, 1996, review of *Pony Express!,* p. 616; July-December, 2001, review of *Dear Mr. President.*

Instructor, April, 2002, Judy Freeman, review of *Patches Lost and Found,* p. 17.

Junior Literary Guild, September, 1975, review of *Is Milton Missing?,* p. 7.

Kirkus Reviews, February 1, 1999, review of *Robert Fulton: From Submarine to Steamboat;* January 1, 2000, review of *William Penn,* p. 60; June 15, 2002, review of *That Makes Me Mad!,* p. 883; November 1, 2005, review of *Pooch on the Loose,* p. 1194; November 1, 2008, review of *The Hanukkah Mice;* February 15, 2009, review of *Stuff!*

Publishers Weekly, February 5, 1996, review of *Pony Express!,* p. 90; May 4, 1998, review of *Oh, Tucker!,* p. 212; June 10, 2002, review of *That Makes Me Mad!,* p. 60; September 26, 2005, review of *Pooch on the Loose,* p. 86.

School Library Journal, September, 2000, Linda Bindner, review of *When I Dream of Heaven,* p. 233; May, 2001, Barbara Buckley, review of *Patches Lost and Found,* p. 126; August, 2002, Wanda Meyers-Hines, review of *That Makes Me Mad!,* p. 160; July, 2004,

Teri Markson, review of *A Tale of Two Dogs,* p. 80; November, 2006, Kristine M. Casper, review of *Jungle Bullies,* p. 98; October, 2008, Teri Markson, review of *The Hanukkah Mice,* p. 95; March, 2009, Sandra Welzenbach, review of *Stuff!,* p. 120; August, 2009, Lucinda Snyder Whitehurst, review of *Barbarians!,* p. 123.

ONLINE

Steven Kroll Home Page, http://www.stevenkrollauthor. com (January 15, 2010).

*   *   *

KUBICK, Dana

Personal

Born in NJ; moved to England, 1972; married Mark Leffler. *Education:* B.A. (art education; with honors); attended School of Visual Arts (New York, NY).

Addresses

Home—London, England. *E-mail*—dana@danakubick. co.uk.

Career

Illustrator and designer. Designer of greeting cards, ice cream wafers and cones, textiles, pottery, and everything from tea pots to tin boxes. *Exhibitions:* Work has been shown at Anna-Mei Chadwick Gallery, London, England, Victoria and Albert Museum, London, Somerset House, London, London Design Centre, Illustration Cupboard, London, and Marwell Zoo, Winchester, England.

Awards, Honors

Gold Award for Best in Metal, Metal Packaging Manufacturers Association, 1988, 1991, both for tin-box designs; Red House Children's Book Award shortlist, Federation of Children's Book Groups, 2003, for *To Mum with Love;* Platinum Award, Oppenheim Toy Portfolio, 2003, and Best Children's Books of the Year selection, Bank Street College of Education, 2004, both for *A Present for Mom.*

Writings

SELF-ILLUSTRATED

Little Teddies on a Picnic (board book), Walker Books (London, England), 1987.

Little Teddies at a Party (board book), Walker Books (London, England), 1987.

Little Teddies at the Playground (board book), Walker Books (London, England), 1987.

Dana Kubick (Photograph by Michele Greenstein. Reproduced by permission.)

Little Teddies at the Beach (board book), Walker Books (London, England), 1987.

Midnight Teddies, Walker Books (London, England), 1989, miniature edition, 2004.

My Pop-up Ballerina Bear, Campbell (London, England), 1993.

My Pop-up Ballerina Cat, Campbell (London, England), 1994.

Cinderella Cat's Press-out Book, Campbell (London, England), 1995.

Ballerina Bear's Press-out Book, Campbell (London, England), 1995.

Cats, Cats, and More Cats, Barrons (Hauppauge, NY), 2000.

Tabby the Wild Cat, Piccadilly (London, England), 2003.

Author's books have been published in Germany, Australia, France, Japan, and other nations.

ILLUSTRATOR

Richard Edwards, *Something's Coming!,* Candlewick Press (Cambridge, MA), 1995.

Edward Lear, *The Owl and the Pussycat,* new edition, Walker Books (London, England), 1996.

Richard Edwards, *Kitty Kit,* Oxford University Press (Oxford, England), 1998.

Richard Edwards, *Raggybear's Rescue,* Walker Books (London, England), 1999.

Vivian French, *To Mum, with Love,* Walker Books (London, England), 2002, published as *A Present for Mom,* Candlewick Press (Cambridge, MA), 2002.

Vivian French, *I Love You, Grandpa,* Candlewick Press (Cambridge, MA), 2004.

David Wood, *A Present for Father Christmas: A Magical 3-D Adventure,* Walker Books (London, England), 2008, published as *A Present for Santa Claus: A Magical 3-D Adventure,* Candlewick Press (Cambridge, MA), 2008.

Books featuring Kubick's illustrations have been translated in eight foreign-language editions.

Sidelights

Dana Kubick, an American-born artist and designer now living in England, is the author and illustrator of *Midnight Teddies, Tabby the Wild Cat,* and other books for young readers. Kubick has also provided the artwork for several stories by other authors, including *Something's Coming!,* a work by Richard Edwards, and Vivian French's *To Mum with Love* and *I Love You, Grandpa.* In *A Present for Father Christmas: A Magical 3-D Adventure* she even designed an innovative pop-up cottage-shaped 3-D viewer as part of author David Wood's narrative. In an essay on the National Literacy Trust Web site, Kubick stated: "Reading allows you to . . . be brave and experience perilous adventures, to be in love, to be anything you want, just by opening a book."

In *Something's Coming!,* a toy elephant startles its companions with a series of incredibly loud sneezes. Kubick's artwork for Edwards' story drew compliments from a *Publishers Weekly* critic, who remarked that the "effectively grainy pastel crayon art gives these stuffed animal characters a fetching, cuddly quality." French's *To Mum, with Love*—published in the United States as *A Present for Mom*—focuses on Stanley the kitten's efforts to find the perfect Mother's Day present. Here

Kubick's humorous self-illustrated picture books include Cats, Cats, and More Cats. (Courtesy of Dana Kubick.)

***Kubick's illustration projects include creating the cartoon art for Vivian French's picture book* A Present for Mom.** (Illustration copyright © 2002 by Dana Kubick. Reproduced by permission of the publisher Candlewick Press, Inc., Cambridge, MA.)

"Kubick's . . . watercolor and gouache illustrations are precisely drawn and vividly hued, filled with pattern and detail," observed a *Kirkus Reviews* contributor, and a *Publishers Weekly* reviewer noted that the book's art "evokes the sweetness of an earlier era."

In a companion volume, *I Love You, Grandpa,* Stanley comforts his grandfather at the end of a busy day. "The action tumbles across spreads," Ilene Cooper explained in her *Booklist* review of the picture book, and Andrea Tarr, writing in *School Library Journal,* noted of *I Love You, Grandpa* that Kubick's "exuberant cartoon illustrations work perfectly with the endearing text."

Biographical and Critical Sources

PERIODICALS

Booklist, November 1, 2004, Ilene Cooper, review of *I Love You, Grandpa,* p. 488.

Kirkus Reviews, March 1, 2002, review of *A Present for Mom,* p. 334; November 1, 2004, Ilene Cooper, review of *I Love You, Grandpa,* p. 864.

Publishers Weekly, July 24, 1995, review of *Something's Coming!,* p. 63; March 11, 2002, review of *A Present for Mom,* p. 71.

School Library Journal, May, 2002, Heather E. Miller, review of *A Present for Mom,* p. 114; October, 2004, Andrea Tarr, review of *I Love You, Grandpa,* p. 113.

ONLINE

Dana Kubick Home Page, http://www.danakubick.co.uk (January 1, 2010).

National Literacy Trust Web site, http://www.literacytrust.org.uk/ (January 1, 2010), "Dana Kubick."

L

LEON, Carol Boyd

Personal

Born in NY; married; children: one son, two other children. *Education:* Brown University, degree. *Religion:* Jewish.

Addresses

Home—Burke, VA. *E-mail*—cbleon@hotmail.com.

Career

Songwriter/composer, performer, and author. Musician, beginning 1991; founder of Chai Notes Publications (music publisher), Burke, VA, 2000. Recording artist; music specialist and choir director. Cantor or soloist at synagogues in Alexandria, Arlington, Fairfax, and Springfield, VA, as well as at libraries, hospitals, and folk festivals. Encore Summer Performance Camp, Burke, founder and instructor. Formerly worked as a government economist; freelance writer and editor.

Member

American Society of Composers, Authors, and Publishers, Women Cantors' Network, National Association for the Education of Young Children.

Awards, Honors

Parents' Choice Award, 2004, and Best Jewish Album nomination, Just Plain Folks, 2008, both for *Gan Shirim*.

Writings

Songs from the Heart: Family Shabbat (with CD), Tara Publications (Owings Mills, MD), 2000.
Jewish Life Cycle (songbook), Chai Notes Publications (Burke, VA), 2002.
Gan Shirim: A Garden of Songs for Schools and Families (songbook; with CD), KTAV Pub. House (Jersey City, NJ), 2004.
Voices in Prayer: Fifty Liturgical Songs for Congregational Singing (songbook; with CD), Chai Notes Publications (Burke, VA), 2008.
Dayenu!: A Passover Haggadah for Families and Children (with CD), KTAV Pub. House (Jersey City, NJ), 2008.

Biographical and Critical Sources

PERIODICALS

Kirkus Reviews, December 1, 2008, review of *Dayenu!: A Passover Haggadah for Families and Children.*
School Library Journal, March, 2009, Heidi Estrin, review of *Dayenu!,* p. 136.

ONLINE

Carol Boyd Leon Home Page, http://www.carolboydleon.com (January 10, 2010).*

* * *

LEVINE, Anna

Personal

Born in Montréal, Québec, Canada; immigrated to Israel, c. 1982; married; husband a university professor; children: two sons. *Education:* McGill University, B.A.; Hebrew University of Jerusalem, M.A. (English literature). *Religion:* Jewish. *Hobbies and other interests:* Biking and running in the hills of Jerusalem, reading poetry, exploring archaeological sites, travel.

Addresses

Home—Israel. *E-mail*—annalevine.il@gmail.com.

Anna Levine (Reproduced by permission.)

Career

Writer and educator. Teaches middle school in Mevasseret Zion, Israel, and at Reuben Academy for Music and Dance, Jerusalem, Israel.

Member

Society of Children's Book Writers and Illustrators, Authors Guild, Authors League of America.

Awards, Honors

Books for the Teen Age citation, New York Public Library, 2000, for *Running on Eggs;* Magazine Merit Award Competition second place award, Society of Children's Book Writers and Illustrators (SCBWI), 2006, for short story "The Wednesday Club"; Magazine Merit Award Competition first place award, SCBWI, 2006, for poem "Saxophone Summer"; Sydney Taylor Honor Award for Teen Readers, Association of Jewish Libraries, 2009, for *Freefall;* Sydney Taylor Notable Books for Younger Readers selection, 2009, for *Jodie's Hanukkah Dig;* Magazine Merit Award Competition honor award, SCBWI, 2009, for short story "Live Wires."

Writings

Running on Eggs (novel), Front Street/Cricket Books (Chicago, IL), 1999.

Freefall (novel), Greenwillow Books (New York, NY), 2008.

Jodie's Hanukkah Dig, illustrated by Ksenia Topaz, Kar-Ben Publishing (Minneapolis, MN), 2008.

Contributor of short stories and poems to periodicals, including *Cicada, Cricket, Spider,* and *Highlights for Children.*

Sidelights

A Canadian-born writer and educator who now makes her home in Israel, Anna Levine is the author of *Running on Eggs* and *Freefall,* a pair of award-winning young adult novels, as well as of the picture book *Jodie's Hanukkah Dig.* "I am a strong believer of the power that literature can have as a way of crossing cultural and linguistic borders," Levine told Amy Bowllan in a *School Library Journal* online interview. "As writers, if we can envision and create worlds in which people co-exist then we can plant the seeds of change."

Levine immigrated to Israel at the age of twenty, just before the 1982 Lebanon War, and quickly realized how radically her life was changed. In an interview on the HarperCollins Web site, she recalled that the kibbutz where she lived "was so close to the border with Lebanon, if we hit a home run, we couldn't retrieve the ball. My husband, boyfriend then, was called for military duty soon after we met. While he spent the month of August in Lebanon as a medic, I worked with the children on the kibbutz, trying to keep them entertained inside the bomb shelters."

By the time of the Second Lebanon War in 2006, Levine was living in Jerusalem with her husband and two grown sons, both of whom were also required to serve their country. Discussing the inspiration for her works in a *Through the Wardrobe* online conversation with Janet Fox, Levine remarked: "I guess for me writing is a reflection of my personal life. I have two boys in the army. My husband is a professor at the Hebrew University. My experiences, my life and my family all find their way into my books."

Running on Eggs, Levine's debut novel, concerns the relationship between a Jewish girl and her Arab schoolmate. Living on a kibbutz, thirteen-year-old Karen has been raised to distrust the Palestinians who live in a nearby village. Then Karen forms a strong bond with Yasmine, a member of her school track team. When the Palestinian Yasmine is forced to leave the squad, the two friends secretly continue to train together in a "no man's land" until they are spotted by Yasmine's suspicious brother. Hazel Rochman, writing in *Booklist,* offered praise for *Running on Eggs,* stating that "Levine knows the place, and she dramatizes the arguments with complexity through Karen's personal experience." A *Publishers Weekly* contributor wrote that the "realistic story offers a peaceful resolution of its potentially volatile conflicts; a timely and sympathetic treatment."

In *Freefall,* a coming-of-age tale, Levine examines a young woman's entry into the Israel Defense Forces. Determined to serve in an elite women's combat unit, eighteen-year-old Abigail Jacobs finds herself challenged physically and mentally by an arduous boot camp experience in the desert. She then turns to Noah, a fellow soldier and the older brother of her best friend, for support and comfort. A number of critics noted the absence of politics in *Freefall, Horn Book* contributor Elissa Gershowitz writing that "the characters spend most of their time away from the battlefield." Rachel Kamin maintained in *School Library Journal* that Levine's novel "could easily take place in any war-torn country where military service is a way of life for young people."

A budding archaeologist is the focus of *Jodie's Hanukkah Dig.* When Jodie's father gives her the opportunity to join him on an excursion to Modi'in, where Judah Maccabee fought against the Syrians, the youngster makes a surprising discovery while investigating a small cave. "Levine provides an intriguing alternative to conventional retellings of the Hanukkah tale," wrote a contributor in *Kirkus Reviews,* reviewing the picture book.

Biographical and Critical Sources

PERIODICALS

Booklist, January 1, 2000, Hazel Rochman, review of *Running on Eggs,* p. 906; November 1, 2008, Kay Weisman, review of *Jodie's Hanukkah Dig,* p. 46.

Horn Book, January-February, 2009, Elissa Gershowitz, review of *Freefall,* p. 95.

Kirkus Reviews, November 1, 2008, review of *Jodie's Hanukkah Dig.*

Kliatt, November, 2008, Claire Rosser, review of *Freefall,* p. 14.

Publishers Weekly, December 20, 1999, review of *Running on Eggs,* p. 81.

School Library Journal, October, 2008, Teri Markson, review of *Jodie's Hanukkah Dig,* p. 95; January, 2009, Rachel Kamin, review of *Freefall,* p. 108.

ONLINE

Anna Levine Home Page, http://www.annalevine.org (January 1, 2010).

HarperCollins Children's Books Web site, http://www.harpercollinschildrens.com/ (January 1, 2010), interview with Levine.

School Library Journal Online, http://www.schoollibraryjournal.com/ (September 29, 2009), Amy Bowllan, "Writers against Racism: Anna Levine."

Through the Wardrobe Web log, http://kidswriterjfox.blogspot.com/ (November 9, 2009), Janet Fox, interview with Levine.

LUEBS, Robin 1949-

Personal

Born 1949; has children. *Education:* University of Illinois, B.A.

Addresses

Home and office—Urbana, IL.

Career

Author and illustrator. Previously worked as a fine artist, a staff artist at a local library, and a display artist for Border's Bookstore.

Writings

SELF-ILLUSTRATED

Please Pick Me Up, Mama!, Atheneum (New York, NY), 2009.

ILLUSTRATOR

Raina Moore, *How Do You Say Goodnight?,* HarperCollins (New York, NY), 2008.

Deborah Ruddell, *Who Said Coo?,* Beach Lane Books (New York, NY), 2010.

Sidelights

Robin Luebs began her career as a fine artist before she delved into the world of picture books. That career decision was at least in part inspired by her twin sister, author Deborah Ruddell, who was then working on a children's book. During off-hours from her job as a bookstore display artist, Luebs helped her sister by drawing mock-up images for Ruddell's current picture-book text. When Ruddell presented her manuscript to her agent, Steven Malk, she also included Luebs' images and Malk immediately agreed to represent Luebs as well. "That's how I got an agent without even writing a letter," Luebs explained in an article for the *Prairie Wind* Web site. The sisters' first picture-book collaboration was published as *Who Said Coo?*

Luebs' illustrations also appear in *How Do You Say Goodnight?,* a story by Raina Moore that features anthropomorphized animal children saying good night to their parents. "Luebs' soft, pastel-shaded artwork meshes nicely with Moore's verses," wrote Kay Weisman in a *Booklist* review of the work. Commenting on the "medley of tranquil hues" in the book's art, a *Kirkus Reviews* writer observed that Luebs "indulges in a bit of whimsy" by hiding a robin on each page for readers to find. Blair Christolon noted that the "painterly" illustrations in the book incorporate both "curving lines and deep-hued tones."

***Robin Luebs' illustration assignments include the engaging picture book* Please Pick Me Up, Mama!** (Copyright © 2009 by Robin Luebs. Reproduced by permission of Atheneum Books for Young Readers, an imprint of Simon & Schuster Macmillan.)

Luebs takes a turn as both writer and illustrator in her picture book *Please Pick Me Up, Mama!* In the story, a young raccoon asks its mother to pick it up and put it down throughout the day, so that the youngster can accomplish all the things it wants to do, from having its hat put on to whirling around to dressing up the cat. Noting that the book has "both sweetness and spunk," a contributor to *Kirkus Reviews* commented on Luebs' decision to incorporate text witnin the illustrations for *Pick Me Up, Mama!,* creating "spiraling words drift across the spacious background like a cloud" in one image. Maryann H. Owen, writing for *School Library Journal,* called Luebs' original picture book "a loving tribute" to the relationship between mother and child.

Biographical and Critical Sources

PERIODICALS

Booklist, October 15, 2008, Kay Weisman, review of *How Do You Say Goodnight?,* p. 45.
Herald & Review (Decatur, IL), October 13, 2008, "Twins Find Perfect Fit in Publishing."
Kirkus Reviews, May 15, 2008, review of *How Do You Say Goodnight?*; February 15, 2009, review of *Please Pick Me Up, Mama!*
School Library Journal, August, 2008, Blair Christolon, review of *How Do You Say Goodnight?,* p. 99; April, 2009, Maryann H. Owen, review of *Please Pick Me Up, Mama!,* p. 112.

ONLINE

Prairie Wind Web site, http://www.intelligentlight.com/ PrairieWind/ (January 18, 2010), "Robin Luebs."

Robin Luebs Home Page, http://www.robinluebs.com (January 18, 2010).*

*   *   *

LYON, Lea 1945-

Personal

Born 1945. *Education:* Earned B.A.; M.B.A. (marketing).

Addresses

Home and office—Richmond CA. *E-mail*—lea_lyon@ pacbell.net.

Career

Illustrator. Formerly worked as a puppet and doll maker; worked in the greeting-card industry and as a product manager for high-tech companies. Teacher of watercolor paintings and children's book illustration at senior residences, community centers, and other venues.

Member

Society of Children's Book Writers and Illustrators (illustration coordinator for San Francisco region).

Awards, Honors

Two Society of Children's Book Writers and Illustrators awards; Teachers' Choice designation, *Learning* magazine, and Notable Social Studies Book designation, Na-

Lea Lyon (Reproduced by permission.)

tional Council for the Socials Studies, both 2005, both for *Say Something* by Peggy Moss; 25 Best Multicultural Picture Books inclusion, *Stepping Stones* magazine, 2006, for *Playing War* by Kathy Beckwith; Moonbeam Award, 2008, for *Keep Your Ear on the Ball* by Genevieve Petrillo.

Illustrator

Peggy Moss, *Say Something,* Tilbury (Gardiner, ME), 2004.

Kathy Beckwith, *Playing War,* Tilbury (Gardiner, ME), 2005.

Genevieve Petrillo, *Keep Your Ear on the Ball,* Tilbury (Gardiner, ME), 2007.

Audrey Penn, *The Miracle Jar: A Hanukkah Story,* Tanglewood (Terre Haute, IN), 2008.

Sidelights

Lea Lyon took a circuitous route to becoming a children's book illustrator. Beginning art lessons as a child, she graduated from watercolors to oils at age eleven, and continued her training during college. After spending several years balancing her time raising her family with creating and selling handmade dolls and puppets, Lyon began working in the greeting-card industry. This experience led her to return to school, earn her M.B.A., and find work in a high-tech field. In 1991 she started painting again, and a class at the University of California's Berkeley extension inspired Lyon to focus her creative talents on illustrating books for children. As a child, Lyon had wanted to be a children's book illustrator when she grew up, and now she has fulfilled that dream.

Lyon's first illustration project was creating the art for *Say Something* by Peggy Moss. Her research for the book's artwork included sitting in on student classes, describing how picture books are made, having students act out the story, and taking digital photographs which she later printed and brought in for students to see. Lyon then used these photos as the basis for her paintings for the pages of the book. Corina Austin, writing for *School Library Journal,* commented that Lyon's "realistic watercolor illustrations depict busy school life and represent a diverse population." Hazel Rochman, a *Booklist* critic, called the illustrations for *Say Something* both "realistic" and "lively," while a *Publishers Weekly* reviewer noted that Lyon's "impressionistic watercolors . . . successfully capture the . . . expressions and moods" of the story's central character.

Reviewing Kathy Beckwith's *Playing War* Rebecca Sheridan wrote in *School Library Journal* that the author's anti-war message is lightened by Lyon's art. Another illustration project, Genevieve Petrillo's *Keep Your Ear on the Ball,* tells the story of a blind boy and how he cultivates friends in a new class. Mary Hazelton, reviewing *Keep Your Ear on the Ball* for *School Library Journal,* wrote that "Lyon's engaging pencil-and-watercolor illustrations invite readers into this picture book." Reviewing the artist's work for *The Miracle Jar: A Hanukkah Story* by Audrey Penn, Teri Markson commented in *School Library Journal* that Lyon's "watercolor spreads depict the family in muted colors and simple patterns," while a *Kirkus Reviews* critic deemed them both "cheerful and energetic."

Lyon's evocative art is a feature of Audrey Penn's holiday-themed story **The Miracle Jar: A Hanukkah Story.** (Tanglewood Pres, 2008. Illustration © 2008 by Lea Lyon. Reproduced by permission.)

Biographical and Critical Sources

PERIODICALS

Booklist, September 1, 2004, Hazel Rochman, review of *Say Something,* p. 134.

Kirkus Reviews, November 1, 2008, review of *The Miracle Jar: A Hanukkah Story.*

Publishers Weekly, May 31, 2004, review of *Say Something,* p. 74.

School Library Journal, September, 2004, Corina Austin, review of *Say Something,* p. 176; November, 2005, Rebecca Sheridan, review of *Playing War,* p. 83; January, 2008, Mary Hazelton, review of *Keep Your Ear on the Ball,* p. 94; October, 2008, Teri Markson, review of *The Miracle Jar,* p. 97.

ONLINE

Lea Lyon Home Page, http://www.lealyon.com (January 17, 2010).

Society of Children's Book Writers and Illustrators—North California Chapter Web site, http://www.scbwinorthca.org/ (January 17, 2010), "Lea Lyon."

M

MACKENZIE, Anna 1963-

Personal
Born 1963, in New Zealand; married; children: two children. *Education:* Earned college degree.

Addresses
Home—Hawkes Bay, New Zealand. *E-mail*—amack@ airnet.net.nz.

Career
Writer. Formerly worked in publishing and public relations. Teacher of creative writing to teenagers; participant in New Zealand Book Council Writers-in-Schools program.

Awards, Honors
Notable Book designation, Children's Literature Foundation of New Zealand, 2003, for *High Tide; New Zealand Post* Book Award Honor Book award, Sir Julius Vogel Award for Fantasy and Science Fiction, White Raven listee, International Youth Library (Germany), and LIANZA Esther Glen Medal shortlist and Notable Book designation, all 2008, all for *The Sea-wreck Stranger;* Notable Book designation, Children's Literature Foundation of New Zealand, 2008, for *Shadow of the Mountain.*

Writings

YOUNG-ADULT NOVELS

High Tide, Scholastic New Zealand (Auckland, New Zealand), 2003.
Out on the Edge, Longacre (Dunedin, New Zealand), 2005.
The Sea-wreck Stranger, Longacre (Dunedin, New Zealand), 2007.

Anna Mackenzie (Photograph by David Evans. Reproduced by permission.)

Shadow of the Mountain, Longacre (Dunedin, New Zealand), 2008.
Ebony Hill, Random House (Auckland, New Zealand), 2010.

Also author of educational materials.

Adaptations
Out on the Edge was optioned for film.

Biographical and Critical Sources

PERIODICALS

Magpies, March, 2009, Trevor Agnew, interview with MacKenzie, p. S1.

ONLINE

New Zealand Book Council Web site, http://www. bookcouncil.org.nz/ (January 15, 2010), "Anna Mackenzie."
Storylines Web site, http://www.storylines.org.nz/ (January 15, 2010), "Anna Mackenzie."

*   *   *

MARSDEN, Carolyn 1950-

Personal

Born August 14, 1950, in Mexico City, Mexico; daughter of Wesley Matzigkeit (a minister) and Winifred (a teacher) Marsden; married Panratt Manoorasada (an electrician), August 8, 1987; children: Maleeka, Preeya. *Education:* Attended University of Arizona; University of Colorado, B.A. (philosophy), 1972; Prescott College, teaching credential; Vermont College, M.F.A., 2000. *Religion:* Buddhist. *Hobbies and other interests:* Watercolor painting, hiking, traveling, boogie boarding.

Addresses

Home—San Diego, CA. *E-mail*—carolynmarsden@gmail.com.

Career

Children's book author and educator. Former bilingual (Spanish-English) elementary and preschool teacher in Tucson, AZ, Chula Vista, CA, and National City, CA; worked variously as a maid, paralegal, bartender, and care provider. Arizona Commission on the Arts, writer-in-residence, 1978-85.

Member

Society of Children's Book Writers and Illustrators.

Awards, Honors

Candlewick scholarship to Vermont College, 2000.

Writings

The Gold-threaded Dress, Candlewick (Cambridge, MA), 2002.
Mama Had to Work on Christmas, illustrated by Robert Casilla, Viking (New York, NY), 2003.

Carolyn Marsden (Reproduced by permission.)

Silk Umbrellas, Candlewick (Cambridge, MA), 2004.
Moon Runner, Candlewick (Cambridge, MA), 2005.
The Quail Club, Candlewick (Cambridge, MA), 2006.
(With Virginia Shin-Mui Loh) *The Jade Dragon,* Candlewick (Cambridge, MA), 2006.
When Heaven Fell, Candlewick (Cambridge, MA), 2007.
Bird Springs, Candlewick (Cambridge, MA), 2007.
(With Thay Phap Niem) *The Buddha's Diamonds,* Candlewick (Cambridge, MA), 2008.
(With Philip Merlin Matzigkeit) *Sahwira: An African Friendship,* Candlewick (Cambridge, MA), 2009.
Take Me with You, Candlewick (Cambridge, MA), 2010.

Adaptations

Sidelights

While poet, short-story writer, and novelist Carolyn Marsden began publishing multicultural children's books in 2002, as a teacher of bilingual students she had been active in helping children appreciate the wonders of language for many years. More importantly, Marsden's own life had presented her with the hurdles faced by children attempting to adapt to a new culture: born in Mexico, she eventually married a Thai immigrant and has raised Thai-American daughters. Her first novel, *The Gold-threaded Dress,* which introduces readers to Thai culture, is geared for readers in the upper-elementary grades, as are its sequel, *The Quail Club,* and the novels *Silk Umbrellas* and *Moon Runner.* Marsden also introduces younger readers to different cultures in her chapter books *Mama Had to Work on Christmas* and, with coauthor Virginia Shin-Mui Loh, *The Jade Dragon.* Reviewing *The Jade Dragon* for *School Library Journal,* Terrie Dorio commented that, in their story about second-grader Ginny Liao and her attempts to befriend an adopted Chinese classmate, Marsden effectively highlights "the push/pull between American and ethnic culture . . . that many children of immigrants feel."

After earning her bachelor's degree in philosophy at the University of Colorado, Marsden went on to study with poet Steve Orlen in the M.F.A. program at the University of Arizona. With the support of the Arizona Arts Commission, she taught poetry writing in classes ranging from kindergarten through high school. The author also studied poetry at the University of Arizona. For Marsden, these were fulfilling activities; as she once explained to *SATA,* "I gain inspiration and courage from the children with whom I spend my days." Her poetry took on a new form when she began inventing stories for the oldest of her two daughters. As Marsden remembered, "I made up bedtime stories about a family of rabbits. My little girl always giggled when the baby rabbit drove the green car very fast! Picture books seemed like another form of poetry and my interest in writing for children grew."

Returning to school, Marsden studied writing for children at Vermont College, earning her M.F.A. in 2000. While there, she "got to study with the giants of contemporary children's literature," as she recalled. "I also made many close writer friends. We call ourselves 'The Hive' because we are always buzzing with ideas!" Marsden's hard work paid off in several ways. In 2000 she won Vermont College's Candlewick scholarship, and Candlewick Press bought the rights to her first novel, *The Gold-threaded Dress.*

The Gold-threaded Dress tells the story of Oy, a shy fourth grader whose family has emigrated from Thailand, as she attempts to find acceptance from the students in her predominately Mexican-American school. In *Booklist,* Carolyn Phelan praised Marsden for her "keen observation" and understanding of school children, and a *Publishers Weekly* reviewer noted that the author deals with the subject matter "squarely and truthfully." Deborah Stevenson wrote in the *Bulletin of the Center for Children's Books* that, while the topic is common, Marsden's focus on a Thai family is "unusual" in preteen fiction. Several reviewers also complimented Marsden's narrative style, Alison Follos describing it in *School Library Journal* as representing a "natural voice" while Stevenson praised its "straightforward sweetness." Remarking on the "forceful message" contained in *The Gold-threaded Dress,* a *Kirkus Reviews* critic maintained that readers can learn important lessons about friendship from its pages, and a *New York Times* reviewer deemed it "a fine novel for newly independent readers."

In writing *The Gold-threaded Dress,* Marsden borrowed from her personal experiences as well as those of several other people she knew. The novel "was inspired when my younger daughter was teased about being Chinese at school," rather than her peers recognizing her Thai heritage, the author once explained to *SATA.* "I mulled over her situation in my mind. I combined her story with experiences that I had had with a Vietnamese immigrant family when I taught preschool. Also, my husband's brother was considering coming over to the United States to work as a cook." Marsden put her experiences as a classroom teacher to use as well; as she explained, "the making and breaking of friendships, bullying and teasing, and an increasingly diverse United States are all an integral part of school experience."

The characters from *The Gold-threaded Dress* reappear in *The Quail Club,* which was also inspired by school events involving Marsden's daughter. Marsden once explained of the novel to *SATA* that, like her daughter's friends at the time, Oy's "friends want her to dance a rock-and-roll song with them in the talent show, but Oy longs to perform her Thai dance instead. Once again, she is faced with the difficult decision of choosing between friendship and culture." Oy's ability to share her culture with Liliandra, the bossy leader of a group of fifth graders known as the Quail Club because they have been charged with monitoring quail eggs until they hatch, provides readers with a solution to what a *Kirkus Reviews* writer called "classic school dilemma, enriched by . . . cross-cultural notes." Alexa Sandman, writing for *School Library Journal,* noted that "Thai words add much to the cultural authenticity" of the novel, and in *The Quail Club* a common predicament among multicultural students is "handled with poignancy and grace."

"In 1994, while visiting Thailand, I learned of the electronic factories located in the northern part of the country," Marsden once recalled to *SATA.* "These factories operate without regulations for the protection of the environment or worker safety. On returning home, I began *Silk Umbrellas.* This book is about a young girl, Noi, whose older sister works in a radio factory. Noi must work against time to fulfill her dream of becoming an umbrella painter, like her grandmother, instead of joining her sister as a factory worker." Praising the work as a "graceful, compact novel" that "captures the exotic smells, tastes and sounds" of a different culture, a *Publishers Weekly* reviewer observed that, in the story of eleven-year-old Noi, Marsden also presents readers with an "affecting portrait of a family coping with the changes thrust upon it." The author's "gentle and exotic story" about a young artist features "language [that] is soft and clear as rainwater," according to a *Kirkus Reviews* contributor. In *School Library Journal,* Susan Oliver praised *Silk Umbrellas* as "a simple but inspiring story of a child with talent, desire, and belief in herself."

The act of enjoying brunch at a fancy hotel restaurant on Christmas Day sparked the idea for Marsden's short, illustrated chapter book *Mama Had to Work on Christmas.* "I became uncomfortable thinking of the families of the people who were working," she later recalled. "Drawing upon my knowledge of California Latino culture, I wrote a book from the point of view of a little girl whose mother works in the ladies' restroom of a sumptuous hotel." The story, which focuses on nine-year-old Gloria as she experiences the condescension of a more affluent child while serving the well-dressed guests in the hotel dining room, "will be an eye-opener for many youngsters," according to a *Publishers Weekly* reviewer. Praising the black-and-white illustrations by Robert Casilla, Hazel Rochman wrote in *Booklist* that Marsden's short chapter book "bring[s] home the painful truth about class differences, a subject seldom addressed in children's books."

Another personal experience led to *Moon Runner,* a sports book. "When my daughter was in fifth grade, she suddenly began to excel in the long jump and fifty-meter sprint," noted Marsden. "Yet my daughter wasn't a competitor at heart and [she] worried that by jumping too high or running too fast, she would make her athletic friends jealous and lose their friendship." When she combined her daughter's story in journal form with a plot about a sibling conflict, the result was *Moon Runner,* a chapter book for seven-to-nine year olds. *Moon Runner* focuses on the close friendship of the "Fellow Friends": four fourth graders who have a special handshake and a close bond. Each of the four girls excels at a different skill, but when Mina realizes that she shares a talent for running with Fellow Friend Ruth, problems result. "With its combination of cozy and prickly elements," *Moon Runner* serves as "accessible and rewarding reading," wrote *Booklist* contributor Carolyn Phelan, while in *School Library Journal* Caroline Ward described *Moon Runner* as "a quiet, lyrical story that sensitively explores issues of friendship and being true to oneself."

Although her children have since grown up, Marsden still gains inspiration from young people through her teaching. "I watch and listen closely in the classroom. Sometimes I carry a notebook with me to jot down a description, an interesting thing that a person says, or a conflict I see unfolding. I then use my imagination to shape these bits and pieces into stories." As the well-traveled writer noted on her home page, "through writing, I have the chance to live many lives."

Marsden's students were the inspiration for *Bird Springs,* a story about ten-year-old Gregory, who has to move from the Arizona Navajo reservation to a shelter in Tucson when hard times hit his family. Gregory relies on an imaginary friend to help him cope with feeling out of place, but he begins to form a real friendship with Matt, who vacillates between offering friendship and teasing Gregory. Although she felt that one of the classes in the novel comes across as too "messagey,"

Hazel Rochman wrote in *Booklist* that "the terse narrative remains true to the boy's viewpoint" and the novel features a "moving final scene." A *Publishers Weekly* critic also felt that "Marsden creates some decidedly poignant moments" in *Bird Springs,* while Kim Dare noted in *School Library Journal* that "Marsden packs a lot into a small package."

Sometimes Marsden's travels and the stories she hears on her journeys spark the idea for a novel. *When Heaven Fell,* which is set in Vietnam, draws on the true stories of the many half-American/half-Vietnamese children who were sent from Vietnam to the United States during the Vietnam War. Typically these children were the sons and daughters of soldiers, but they were treated as orphans and adopted by families in the United States. In the novel, nine-year-old Binh is delighted that her American aunt, Di, one of the adopted children, is coming to visit, to reconnect with her birth mother. Di is utterly lost in Vietnamese culture, and Binh helps the American woman navigate life in Vietnam, while at the same time feeling ashamed that her family is too poor to send her to school. According to Faith Brautigam, writing in *School Library Journal,* "the story of Binh and her family shines through the spare text, creating a welcome chance to experience another culture." Writing in *Booklist,* Carolyn Phelan called *When Heaven Fell* "an unusually accessible introduction to the culture of modern Vietnam."

Marsden gains inspiration from cowriters in *The Jade Dragon, The Buddha's Diamonds,* and *Sawhira: An African Friendship.* Coauthored with Virginia Shin-Mui Loh, *The Jade Dragon* tells of two girls, one adopted Chinese and one Chinese American, as they build an awkward friendship. Ginny, who was born in the United States but grew up with the strong influence of her family's Chinese heritage, is excited when Stephanie comes to her school, because Stephanie is Chinese. Stephanie was adopted into a white American family, however, and she is thoroughly Americanized. Noting the complex issues confronted by both first-generation children and immigrants, a *Publishers Weekly* critic noted that "the authors tackle it all with a light touch."

The Buddha's Diamonds, a collaboration between Marsden and Thay Phap Niem, draws on the childhood of Niem, a Buddhist monk who grew up in postwar Vietnam. Young Tinh is poor, but he dreams of owning the same kind of electronic toys that his friends have. When he saves a toy car during a storm, but fails to save the family's boat or keep his sister from being injured, Tinh has to face the consequences and learn to balance what he wants and what is good for his family and community. "Cultural references are beautifully integrated into this lovely coming-of-age story," wrote Ernie Bond in a review of *The Buddha's Diamonds* for *School Library Journal.* A *Publishers Weekly* critic considered the story to be "most rewarding for its graceful unfolding of differences" by providing the opportunity for readers "to spend time in a community guided by

Buddhist values." Gillian Engberg, writing in *Booklist,* complimented Marsden and Niem's "detailed descriptions" for offering "a strong sense of Tinh's culture," and predicted that readers will identify with the main character's "poignant struggles to please his parents and use good judgment."

Coauthor Philip Matzigkeit, like Blessing, the main character of *Sahwira: An African Friendship,* grew up in Rhodesia (now Zimbabwe) in the 1960s. Although Blessing's father, a minister, and the missionary father of Blessing's best friend, Evan, both preach peace and advocate change for Rhodesia via the examples set by Reverend Martin Luther King, Jr., and Gandhi, Blessing finds himself drawn to the militant groups who seek freedom from colonial rule. At his segregated school, Evan hears racist comments from students who support the unjust white government that is currently in power. *Booklist* reviewer Hazel Rochman noted that, although *Sahwira* "will hold readers" who will notice "the connections with the civil-rights struggle in the U.S." Kathleen Isaacs, writing in *School Library Journal,* found the opening of the story to be slow, but explained that soon, "the action takes over and the suspense will carry readers to the hoped-for conclusion."

A full-time writer, Marsden has several books in process at any one time. Every day she spends several hours in her writer's studio, a silver Airstream trailer permanently parked just outside her California home. "I love the form of the middle-grade chapter book," she once enthused in *SATA,* discussing her intended audience. "It isn't as lengthy as a full novel and doesn't have the constraints of a picture book. I write intuitively, without much of an outline. I draw upon my past experience and training in poetry for imagery and musicality of language."

Biographical and Critical Sources

PERIODICALS

Booklist, May 1, 2002, Carolyn Phelan, review of *The Gold-threaded Dress,* p. 1521; September 1, 2003, Hazel Rochman, review of *Mama Had to Work on Christmas,* p. 133; February 1, 2004, Carolyn Phelan, review of *Silk Umbrellas,* p. 975; March 1, 2005, Carolyn Phelan, review of *Moon Runner,* p. 1198; March 1, 2006, Carolyn Phelan, review of *The Quail Club,* p. 88; November 1, 2006, Ilene Cooper, review of *The Jade Dragon,* p. 61; March 1, 2007, Carolyn Phelan, review of *When Heaven Fell,* p. 83; May 15, 2007, review of *Bird Springs,* p. 45; March 15, 2008, Gillian Engberg, review of *The Buddha's Diamonds,* p. 50; April 15, 2009, Hazel Rochman, review of *Sahwira: An African Friendship,* p. 54.

Bulletin of the Center for Children's Books, June, 2002, Deborah Stevenson, review of *The Gold-threaded Dress;* December, 2003, Karen Coats, review of *Mama Had to Work on Christmas,* p. 158; March, 2005, Hope Morrison, review of *Moon Runner,* p. 301; May, 2006, Hope Morrison, review of *The Quail Club,* p. 413.

Kirkus Reviews, February 15, 2002, review of *The Gold-threaded Dress,* p. 262; November 1, 2003, review of *Mama Had to Work on Christmas,* p. 1318; February 1, 2004, review of *Silk Umbrellas,* p. 136; March 1, 2005, review of *Moon Runner,* p. 291; March 15, 2006, review of *The Quail Club,* p. 295; November 15, 2006, review of *The Jade Dragon,* p. 1176.

New York Times Book Review, July 14, 2002, Lawrence Downes, review of *The Gold-threaded Dress,* p. 18.

Publishers Weekly, March 4, 2002, review of *The Gold-threaded Dress,* pp. 79-80; September 22, 2003, review of *Mama Had to Work on Christmas,* p. 72; March 22, 2004, review of *Silk Umbrellas,* p. 86; May 15, 2006, "And Then What Happened?" p. 74; November, 2006, Terrie Dorio, review of *The Jade Dragon,* p. 106; February 19, 2007, review of *When Heaven Fell,* p. 169; May 14, 2007, review of *Bird Springs,* p. 53; September 10, 2007, review of *Silk Umbrellas,* p. 63; February 18, 2008, review of *The Buddha's Diamonds,* p. 153.

School Library Journal, April, 2002, Alison Follos, review of *The Gold-threaded Dress,* p. 117; October, 2003, Eva Mitnick, review of *Mama Had to Work on Christmas,* p. 66; March, 2004, Kathleen T. Isaacs, review of *The Gold-threaded Dress,* p. 68, and Susan Oliver, review of *Silk Umbrellas,* p. 216; June, 2005, Caroline Ward, review of *Moon Runner,* p. 122; April, 2006, Alexa Sandmann, review of *The Quail Club,* p. 144; November, 2006, Terrie Dorio, review of *The Jade Dragon,* p. 106; March, 2007, Faith Brautigam, review of *When Heaven Fell,* p. 180; May, 2007, Kim Dare, review of *Bird Springs,* p. 104; June, 2008, Ernie Bond, review of *The Buddha's Diamonds,* p. 146; May, 2009, Kathleen Isaacs, review of *Sahwira,* p. 114.

ONLINE

Carolyn Marsden Home Page, http://www.carolynmarsden.com (November 21, 2009).

Autobiography Feature

Carolyn Marsden

Carolyn Marsden contributed the following autobiographical essay to *SATA* in 2009:

Entry

I entered the world alone. In the maternity ward of the American-British Hospital of Mexico City, my mother lay knocked out by scopolamine, adrift in twilight sleep. This was common in 1950, when doctors assumed that women were better off unconscious during the painful and messy process of bearing their children. Dads were not allowed into the birthing rooms, but stayed outside in the halls until the doctor announced, "It's a girl!" or "It's a boy!"

When I was born, my parents had been working in Mexico as Methodist missionaries for five years. They'd graduated from living in a small apartment with orange-crate furniture to a real house. My mother had hoped to design the house of her dreams—a Moorish-style palace with a turquoise tile dome and a courtyard with a fountain and singing birds. Instead, a fledgling architect, eager to try out modern architecture, had fashioned for us a plain, cold prison.

It was a pumpkin-colored, blocky house with a water tank on the roof and tile floors that stayed icy even in the summer. From the bathroom we could see the volcano, Popocatepetl, with its snow-capped crown. We also had a view of the rats scampering over mounds of garbage in the vacant lot next door.

The little hut out back housed Antonio, our gardener, and his wife, Guadalupe, who always seemed to be ironing our clothes. She doted on my blonde hair, lightening it further with applications of lime juice. When she tried to teach me how to make tortillas, patting the *masa* from one hand to the other, I got impatient, threw my fistful of masa to the floor and stamped on it.

My mom had traveled through Mexico in the early 1940s, a golden age when American tourists were treated like royalty. Mom, who grew up near Hollywood and even saw Shirley Temple in the grocery store, was in love with the new resorts like Acapulco with their movie-star guests. When she met my father and signed on to be a missionary, Mom thought she was in for a life of glamour.

At first my mother accompanied Daddy on his mission trips. Typically, he traveled on horseback to remote villages where he tried to rustle up enthusiasm for build-

"This is me at about a year old." (Reproduced by permission.)

ing latrines, growing better corn, and embracing not the Catholic, but the Methodist, Jesus. Soon my mother grew disenchanted with eating spicy food and sleeping on dirt floors, and she let my father travel for weeks at a time on his own.

Mom languished alone in Mexico. Whereas Daddy had a whole country of friends, she had none. She didn't know what to say to the other missionary wives. Plus, she'd found that she wasn't, after all, on the same wavelength as the Methodists.

Detour

When I was eighteen months old, my parents took a sabbatical from missionary life. We traveled to a Europe still recovering from World War II.

Although I was young, the trip made such an impression that I stored up little memories: screaming when

Daddy put me in the stateroom crib instead of in the bunk bed on the *Queen Mary;* receiving a green metal car from Father Christmas; lying feverish in a pea-green Italian hotel room; sitting in a high chair while my parents breakfasted on kippered herrings in England; and walking past cabins in a piney Swedish forest.

I went on a food protest. Nothing would pass my lips but oatmeal cooked on the camping stove by the side of the road. I went on a clothing protest, refusing to wear anything but my blue satin Thumbelina dress.

On that trip I first had a dream that would recur for years: I stood on a rooftop watching Daddy and Mommy walking down the street below; Mommy wore her brown-and-white hound's-tooth coat. Suddenly, either a body of water would shape itself into a huge tidal wave, or a single flame would burst into a conflagration. I flew down to my parents and struggled to put them in a burlap sack. Night after night, I strove to rescue them. But that wall of water, those sheets of fire, kept me from them.

Back to Mexico and the Main Story

Mom returned from Europe as lonely and disenchanted with Mexico as ever. When I was five my brother, Jamie, was born. So now my mom was marooned with not just one, but two screaming kids and Guadalupe endlessly starching the tablecloths.

The food in Mexico looked fine, but had no nutrients. Jamie coughed stuff out of his lungs, and I was thin as a rake.

"Just look at your children," my mother pleaded with Daddy. "They need to get out of Mexico."

"Mexico is as good a place as any," Daddy would reply. "There's plenty of good food here."

"Good food! I can't even give them milk! The cows have TB!"

"This is our house in Mexico City." (Reproduced by permission.)

"We visited Scotland while traveling." (Reproduced by permission.)

Evidently, I was the one who got us out of there. One day, I said to Mom and my grandmother, Nanny, who came down from Los Angeles on vacation breaks from being a music teacher, "Let's go. Let's just go." I was six and had graduated from counting my age on just one hand. Mom wore her starched orange dress, and I a matching one.

I wanted to head north to the U.S. border, to be welcomed by a friendly man in a white uniform. I wanted to go to the market where they had kid-size shopping carts with pastel-colored handles. I wanted to load up on the celery and other raw veggies we couldn't eat in Mexico.

Mom glanced at Nanny. Their eyes met and they exchanged a tiny nod. Before I knew it, they were hitching up the Aljo travel trailer to the two-tone 1956 Chevy station wagon.

They packed my smocked dresses that Mom had paid young Mexican women to stitch, the square black-and-green plates from the outdoor market, the hand-embroidered tablecloths, the chunky turquoise glasses. They packed my miniature pots and pans and glass animals.

We took off that very afternoon. If we were caught, we'd never get away. My dad's will to hold us there was too strong. So while Daddy was off riding a horse, we headed for the Golden State: two small children and two women pulling a trailer along the roads of 1950s Mexico.

California, Here I Come

We ended up in the blue-gray house in Laguna Beach where Nanny and my grandfather, Gong Gong, lived. After all that traveling, we wanted to land somewhere secure. But the house was built high on a steep hill, and tilted precariously toward the ocean.

When Daddy got home from his mission trip and found us gone, he rushed up to California to tell Mom how mad he was. He was a *missionary,* for heaven's sake. How did it look to have a *missionary's* family pick up and leave? We'd gone off with no discussion. None. What would the Church think?

I hoped Mom had forgotten it was my idea to leave.

For a while, Daddy went back and forth between Mexico City and Southern California. Finally, he gave up missionary life, gave up the horses and seeing real volcanoes blowing their tops, and came to live with us.

When things had calmed down, we all moved to Santa Barbara. Nanny and Gong Gong lived near us in a huge, old brown house. Our own nine-bedroom house was, I convinced myself, full of ghosts.

Daddy heartily disapproved of the way Mom had gone back to being an Episcopalian and was raising her children in the Anglican Church. They had fierce arguments that my mom always won. Although the refined pale pink building on Santa Barbara Street was a far cry from the huts of the mission field, and even though my father was the minister there, we never set foot in his church.

When my mother enrolled me in Catholic school, this was like pouring gasoline on a fire. Daddy had spent ten years trying to convert those Mexican Catholics!

Early on, I was learning a lot about conflict, character, and setting!

Sally, Dick, and Jane

I was not the kid who read under the covers with the flashlight. In fact, I hardly recall reading much at all. The 1950s was hardly the Golden Age of children's literature. Although both my parents had master's degrees, there were no books in the house. Once in school, I obediently suffered through the basal reader of *Fun with Dick and Jane.*

It was a miracle that with so little literary nurture, I became a writer.

I did read a *few* books. One was a series of adventure stories featuring two boys and their dad; the adventures took place in exotic locations, like inside volcanoes and atop icy mountain peaks. There were the Bobbsey Twins books and a British series based on a doll, Noddy, and his elf friend, Big Ears. I adored a book of Mom's from the 1920s called *Myths and Enchantment Tales,* especially the romantic story of Cupid and Psyche. I loved a book called *Mazli,* written by Johanna Spyri, author of *Heidi.* In *Mazli,* a group of kids explores the grounds of an ancient castle in the moonlight, happening upon a gigantic ghost walking beside a cypress. And finally, each month our local grocery store offered the next installment of an illustrated encyclopedia for children.

Mystery and Romance

When I was thirteen, I watched the movie *Twenty Thousand Leagues Under the Sea,* based on Jules Verne's book of the same title. My whole adolescent being resonated with the gloomy melodrama of Captain Nemo. I wanted to *be* him. Under the eaves of our quaintly sloping roof, I fashioned a submarine and hauled all of my mom's silverware, good china, and lace tablecloths to

"When we lived in Mexico, I took Spanish dancing." (Reproduced by permission.)

"Here is the house in Ojai with its sloping roof." (Reproduced by permission.)

my new lair. I wore my Catholic school uniform blazer and sat in my creation, in the dusty heat, mice *scritch-scratching* in the corners.

Yet somehow the magic was missing.

I decided that instead of *being* Captain Nemo, I needed to write about him. So I launched into my first piece of fiction. Instead of being set in a submarine, my story took place in a spaceship. Instead of underwater adventures, I wrote about outer space. In the privacy of the area under the eaves, I wrote in pencil on blue-lined paper, each sentence taking me further into a marvelous escape from being thirteen.

*

The day U.S. President John F. Kennedy died, the principal nun came into our classroom and whispered something to our teacher nun. Her face turned as white as her round collar. "Boys and girls," Sister Marie Angel turned to announce, leaning her knuckles into the desk, "The President has been shot."

There was no more appropriate place to mourn Kennedy than among the Catholics. No more appropriate age than thirteen to mourn a handsome dead president. We sat day after day in front of our black-and-white television sets, soaking up the mood of the stately funeral procession until our very hearts beat to the ponderous dirge. Our sadness felt *personal,* as if we'd actually known Jack.

Kennedy's death opened our hearts wide. It stretched us beyond our little lives, beyond all we knew. His death opened doors to emotions that were deeper, subtler,

more layered than we'd ever guessed. His death filled us with longing. We would never be the same.

*

And then the Beatles came along.

At first, in the same way I'd wanted to be Captain Nemo, I wanted to *be* a Beatle. I cut off my long hair. I again wore my school blazer. I strummed my ukulele in time to the songs. I sang along in my thin, girl voice, but began to get a strange, hungry feeling.

I woke up: I didn't want to *be* Paul McCartney; I wanted to *love* him. I clutched my transistor radio tight, waiting for my favorite songs, my heart trembling. I had posters of all four Beatles tacked to the inside of my closet door. Each night, I kissed Paul's paper lips until the paper was worn through.

But Paul was not here. Certainly not on my closet door. He was in England. Or in the Bahamas, making *Help!* Or onstage at the Hollywood Bowl, an unbridgeable distance away. Because there were no videos, no DVDs, and no Internet, I only got to see Paul on bubble-gum trading cards, in fan magazines, and in the movies when they came to town. The fan magazines teased us with suggestions of who Paul really was, who he really loved.

Once again, there remained only one solution. I penned lurid fantasies of meeting Paul and, sometimes, if I was in a brave mood, the wild and unpredictable George.

*

Even as I grew older, I read not real books, but only textbooks in my Catholic schools. These had black-and-white photographs, and very dry, dull text. They certainly didn't make me want to be a writer!

Not until I was a junior in high school was I lucky enough to run across a teacher passionate about literature. Miss Sheryl Owens so loved the romantic poets—Lord Byron and Shelley, Coleridge and Blake— that she transferred her love to me. We'd moved to Del Mar by that time, close to the cliffs that rose above the beach. My favorite pastime was walking along those cliffs, reciting romantic poems. The beautiful language sank into me. Something new was entering my soul: rhythm and musicality, vivid images, interesting words. Something within me started stirring.

Though Mary Stewart didn't write fine literature, she was popular during the 1960s; her mysteries and thrillers gave me a sense of setting and plot. The Brontë sisters delivered a large dose of passion, fueling my desire to write.

I joined Miss Owen's creative writing club, kept a journal, and carried a notebook to the romantic cliffs. I wrote my own stories, created my own worlds, and through my characters, lived other lives.

College and Beyond

At Pomona College, I planned to be an English major, concentrating on creative writing. However, when my professor called my writing self-indulgent, I was devastated and changed my major to philosophy.

By the late 1960s, young people were beginning to see the post-World War II values as stale, artificial, and lacking in meaning. The world was bursting with the fresh ideas of the counterculture. As new values developed, important movements were born: civil rights, Native American rights, feminism, pacifism. . . .

Suddenly, anything was possible. Anyone could be anyone. We marched to the rhythms of the new music—blues, Rock 'n' roll, the songs of the psychedelic bands.

My small, white liberal arts college east of Los Angeles lay far from the action. But thankfully, some of that action came to us. Famous old blues musicians visited the campus. People like Angela Davis and the diary writer, Anaïs Nin, spoke at a neighboring college.

The era also arrived in the mail: the boys I knew got their draft numbers. A low number meant you'd be sent to the war in Vietnam for sure. My friends made plans to become conscientious objectors. All of us protested the war through marches, rallies, and sit-ins.

"Here I am in my school uniform blazer." (Reproduced by permission.)

In my junior year I transferred to the University of Colorado at Boulder. There I got more interested in my philosophy studies. With the Christmas bombings of Hanoi, the war grew more serious, and our protests escalated. When we learned that our university was involved with the defense industry, we boycotted classes.

I wrote continuously during that time, concentrating on realistic short stories. These stories were usually based on people I knew, and I modified events that had actually happened.

*

After college, I lived in Berkeley, where I watched the *Beverly Hillbillies* every morning on television and worked in San Francisco microfilming checks. I thought of going to graduate school. But my philosophical interest had been in existentialism—asking heavy, meaningful questions about life—and grad schools only offered degrees in logical positivism, a branch of philosophy that was more like mathematics.

I returned to Santa Barbara where I took writing classes from a passionate, larger-than-life man with flashing green eyes. Having fought in the Pacific, Bill Richardson struggled to convey those awful, slow-motion battle scenes in his writing. Bill hunted wild boar in the rolling hills around Santa Maria. He dove without a tank, spearing halibut on the ocean floor. After his morning stint of writing at the downtown coffee shop, he jogged to his mountain home, ascending a thousand feet in a mile. Afternoons, he danced ballet in the South Coast studio, partnering ballerinas a fraction of his age.

"Writing makes us forget we're dying," said Bill in his class.

Studying with him, I learned to write short, honest pieces about ordinary life.

The Wild West

I spent the next few years in Philadelphia where I made lamps in a downtown factory; New York where I attended paralegal school and studied modern dance at the Martha Graham Studio; and San Diego where I lived in the house near the beach cliffs. I eventually ended up in Tucson, Arizona, where I worked as a bartender in a blue-collar men's club.

I studied improvisational dance with a pioneer named Barbara Mettler. The sessions in her round Frank Lloyd Wright studio were serious business. Wearing all black, we improvised dances using a natural, non-dance vocabulary. Mettler's specialty was the group body. Fifty or more of us would silently, without eye contact, create a group dance that hung together organically and artistically.

Outside the Mettler studio, I danced with ex-students of Mettler's. This was way more fun than dancing under Mettler's stern eye. We took our dancing to the desert, to wild canyons, to long hot afternoons in the downtown studio that had once been the Owl's Club.

*

At the University of Arizona, I sat in on poetry classes. Because I hadn't paid my student loans, I couldn't actually enroll in the Master of Fine Arts program. One day, the poet Steve Orlen slapped his hand on the desk, saying, "Imagine a train bumping over the tracks. *Ba hum, ba bum.*" After that, my poetry never clunked. From Steve I also learned the musicality of language and how to create visual, painterly imagery.

I became part of a wonderful community of writers. We enjoyed writing parties and writing potlucks. We read and critiqued each other's work, shared the latest books, and published poems in literary magazines.

With the sun streaming through the orange curtains of my desert house, and with Gila monsters parked in the shade of the house, I happily tapped away on my typewriter.

In those days, there were no computers. If I wanted to change something in my poem or story, I had to retype it. There weren't even copy machines. The only way to make a copy of my manuscript was to insert a carbon behind the white sheet in the typewriter. The carbon copy was fuzzy and often hard to read. I always thought very carefully about submitting my only good copy for publication!

*

In the mid-1970s, I got my first paying job as a writer, working for the Arizona Commission for the Arts as a poet-in-residence. Sometimes I taught in the local schools and traveled to far-flung towns.

I used to joke that I had about a minute to win the children over, convincing them that writing poetry could be fun.

The classroom teachers were always surprised that I hadn't written any poems for children. Although I taught children, the idea of writing for them had never crossed my mind. Perhaps this was because I still hadn't read any children's literature.

El Rancho de los Gatos

One bright, November day I walked into a complex of ancient adobes. There was a single palm, a salt cedar, an old fig tree, and stands of prickly pear cactus, their elderly leaves withered and spineless. Feral cats scattered at my approach, escaping though a fence made of rusted bedsprings.

The duplex in the middle of the property was stuffed to the ceiling with the owner's junk: old stoves, lamps, and furnaces with the auction tags still on. The paper-thin cement floor was badly cracked. Bare wires draped with spider webs hung from the ceilings.

Yet as I walked through the house, my soul bonded with those Pepto-Bismol-colored walls. I breathed deeply. In a flash I knew this place had to be mine.

There was also a big house in the front, a smaller one in the back, and two more tiny adobes—one with a peaked roof, and one that was long and low. The latter had a cave underneath.

With Mom's help, the place became mine.

I fed the feral cats. I trapped them and got them neutered, and named them after Greek and Egyptian mythological figures: Creon, Agamemnon, Isis, Persephone. . . .

*

One day when I was cleaning house—which meant removing adobe rubble with a wheelbarrow—an old man, dressed completely in white, danced into my living room. He told me his name was Apolino Morales, and that this had once been the Guadalupe Luna Bakery, named for a husband and wife both named Guadalupe Luna.

"The oven was here," he said, indicating my bathroom. He told me that the front house, with its wooden floors and double doors, had once been the store where the *pan dulce* was sold.

Later, I got in touch with the family who'd owned the property for one hundred years. The Valenzuelas told me that several people had reported seeing the ghost of a Chinese baker dressed in a tall white hat. Others confirmed that such a real life man *had* once lived and baked there. The descriptions of phantom and human being matched.

The Valenzuelas also told me that the cave underneath the tiny long building had been created when the adobe was dug out to build the houses. Later on, during the hot summers, the underground hideaway had come in handy for sleeping and storing bakery supplies.

*

My poetry friends left town, so I made friends with photographers who used my quaint adobe complex for photo shoots. For example, a group of us lay down on huge sheets of blueprint paper. As we held still, the paper became exposed in the sunshine. When we got up, the blue paper bloomed with our ghostly forms.

Once a photographer took a few of us women to the desert at night. We all wore blue organdy dresses from the thrift store. With tiny flashlights strapped underneath the dresses and the coyotes howling, we danced. The photographer captured the otherworldly scene with her pinhole camera.

I envied those visual artists because they were doing such crazy things. No matter how much I experimented with writing, it could never be as fun as what they were up to!

California Again

For the third time, I circled back to Santa Barbara. One day, getting into my car after I'd placed an ad to find a house to rent, I spotted the most exotic-looking man I'd ever seen. He wore a red Chairman Mao cap and was walking a dog. I knew he was Asian, but I'd never seen such a *dark* Asian before. He had lovely almond eyes, a wide nose, and full lips.

A week later, I attended an event called Dance Jam. Miraculously, that cute Asian guy was there and we danced together to "I'll Go South to Birmingham." After the dance, I wished I'd slipped him my phone number.

I got the cottage I'd advertised for. Right across from two parks, it was in a complex of cottages called "The Magnolia" after the tree that spread its branches, laden with huge waxy blooms, over the lawn. When the hot Santa Ana winds blew, miniature coconuts dropped from the palm trees.

The windows of my quaint cottage didn't close. When I asked the manager to get them fixed, she hired a repairman who left his tools all over the floor.

I'd just finished transferring the last load of stuff from my car to the house, when a knock came at the door. It was *the guy*.

We both started.

"I saw you. . ." he began.

"Me with two girlfriends at El Rancho de los Gatos." (Reproduced by permission.)

"I saw *you*. . . We danced. . . ."

I stood in the doorway, and he on the front porch, with the background of bamboo behind him. This man told me his name was Pal. He told me he came from Thailand. I'd never seen a Thai person before, had never eaten Thai food. I couldn't have located the place on a map. Later on, I made the connection between Thailand and Siamese cats and the kitchy musical, *Anna and the King of Siam*.

I watched Pal retrieve his tools. It was like a fairy tale: the magical three encounters. And yet this third one was passing and no magic was happening.

Pal went away again, hoisting his stepladder out the door. It seemed we'd had another fruitless chance encounter.

But moments later, he returned, saying, "I forgot to show you how to work the windows."

A few days later, Pal arrived for our first date carrying a casserole made with chayote squash and cheese. We spread a blanket under the magnolia tree and feasted.

A week into our romance, we decided to get married.

For our wedding, we chose a park up in the Santa Barbara hills. We splurged and spent a hundred dollars on a contra dance band. By noon, the sky was a perfect azure and the band's music wound energetically through the sycamore trees. Pal's many friends arrived, bearing dishes for the potluck.

During the Thai-style ceremony, people dipped a seashell into a bowl of scented water. Pouring the water over our hands, they offered us blessings.

Afterward, the band played and all of us danced a waltz, a simple mixer. Each blade of grass vibrated with green life. Hawks rode the updrafts. The sun and moon hung together in the afternoon sky.

A few people warned me that our marriage wouldn't work out because Pal was so "foreign." But as of this writing, our marriage has flourished for over twenty-three years.

South of the Border

Once Pal and I had gotten married, it was time to make a baby. I was thirty-seven and pushing the age envelope. But living in pricey Santa Barbara, we couldn't afford kids. I'd need to leave that beautiful city for a third time.

My thoughts turned to Mexico. Having been born there, I was a Mexican national, so we could start a business. We'd begin anew, clear our debts, and maybe do some traveling.

"Pal and me, happily married." (Reproduced by permission.)

In Mexico, I'd have time to write. Life would be freer, more relaxed. I couldn't help thinking of the stereotype of a Mexican napping against a cactus, a sombrero over his face.

At the consulate in Los Angeles, Pal filled out paperwork and submitted multiple copies of visa photos. As one of the few Thais to have visited Mexico, he was regarded with great suspicion. Finally, with a great show, the young woman lifted the stamp and pounded it briskly onto the ink pad. In the staccato rhythm of flamenco footwork, she issued the tourist visa.

We bought a twenty-three-foot vintage Airstream trailer and Mom made blue denim covers for the couches. At an auction, we acquired our mustard-colored 1972 Buick Estate Wagon for $350, thus completing our "outfit."

*

We ended up in Ensenada, at King's Court, a trailer park on the ocean where loud waves beat against the rocks of the coastline, and papery purple everlasting flowers grew over the cliffs.

Rusty, barnacled boats docked in the port. The air smelled of fish. Ensenada was also a tourist destination, with a multitude of cheap shops selling tequila with worms in the bottle, sunglasses from China, fake silver jewelry, and mermaids made out of seashells.

But *our* search was for the auto parts store. We needed to fix the trailer. The oven had broken; the heater too. Pal picked up the only Spanish he'd ever learn: *empaque* (seal); *destorniallador* (screwdriver); and *tornillo* (screw).

*

At King's Court, a little mutt wandered from one American's trailer to another. He had the size and temperament of a Chihuahua, but the fur and shape of a German shepherd. He was a spirited, opportunistic little dog. When word got out that Mrs. King was getting ready to do away with this mutt, we adopted him.

We named him *Jefe*, which means "boss" in Spanish. While Jefe was generally amiable, he also bit viciously when crossed.

Although we hadn't counted on getting pets in Mexico, we became dog magnets. When a blond puppy was being shoved by a woman wielding a broom, I glared and scooped the puppy up. We took her home to King's Court and christened her Sphinx.

In La Paz we also adopted a black puppy from the gutter and named her Pearl.

In the evenings, Pal built a campfire and cooked dinner for the dogs. They waited a safe distance from the hot fire while he turned squid with a long stick, then waited patiently while the squid cooled.

*

We eventually settled down on a ranch outside the border town of Tecate. The ranch was hundreds of acres in size, a limitless landscape of oaks and boulders. Even the owners didn't know where their land ended. In this place of no boundaries, our dogs enjoyed running after horses and cows.

There, in the oak grove with the cattle lowing outside the Airstream windows, I got pregnant. Pal grew teary-eyed when I told him the results of the at-home pregnancy test. We rushed to a doctor's tiny office in tiny downtown Tecate. The ultrasound revealed a tiny embryo the size of a pea. I placed my hand on my convex belly, sensing that grain of life already growing.

In the evenings, Pal and I climbed into our mustard-colored Buick for a trip to the plaza, about twenty kilometers away. Perched on the park's wrought iron benches, we ate coconut *paletas*, trying to figure out if we should keep on living in a travel trailer on a cattle ranch. Was a ranch a good place to raise a baby? If not, then where?

Pal had had a little job in Santa Barbara manufacturing utility straps out of neoprene nylon, and we planned to do a similar business in Mexico. At the picnic table, he struggled to fashion a prototype with his collection of tools, buckles, and black rolls of neoprene.

Once he'd made a workable strap, we went to a government office to investigate setting up a *maquiladora* to manufacture our product. Without my Mexican nationality this venture would have been impossible. With it, I expected the process to be a cinch.

A man in a brown uniform explained the grim facts, tapping his pencil for emphasis. The initial investment would be enormous. Workers had to be hired for life. The books would have to be audited monthly by the government.

What a bureaucratic nightmare! I felt confused— Mexico had always seemed so easy going, so laissez-faire. . .

*

Meanwhile, an encounter with an American in Tijuana seemed to solve all of our problems. In a huge concrete warehouse, the guy showed us the T-shirt printing machine he'd invented—it could print in a multitude of colors instead of the four of traditional silk screening. No one else in the world had this machine.

As Pal and I fingered the image of Mickey Mouse, we smiled at each other. The image looked just like a photograph. The possibilities were stunning. Compared with this, utility straps seemed like a pitiful venture. We could go to *Disney* with this idea! From a pay phone we called Mom with the news.

On impulse, Mom bought $10,000 worth of T-shirts from China.

While the shirts were en-route, we discovered that the T-shirt machine didn't work so well after all. The colors bled. The images were blurry. But we couldn't back out of the shipment.

When the T-shirts arrived, we transported them to a warehouse in Tecate and put them up for sale. We spread the word to people we knew: the owners of our ranch, an artist we'd met named Pablo, even the government bureaucrat in the brown shirt.

By then we fully understood that our trailer home *wasn't* the place for our baby. We wanted to get out of Mexico, and daydreamed of life in my ancient Tucson adobes.

In desperation, we sold the T-shirts at a huge loss, packed up camp, and headed north. Defeated in business and having borrowed every available penny on our many credit cards, we arrived in Tucson on Halloween with our Mexican mutts, just three months before our daughter would be born.

Home Again, Home Again

I gave birth to Maleeka in the room where the *pan dulce* oven had once stood. As a baby, she looked like Pal, but with lighter skin. I caressed her dark hair and her itsy-bitsy feet, stared into her Asian eyes.

Now that I had Maleeka, I began to read picture books. I also made up bedtime stories. When I told the one about a rabbit with a green car who liked to go *FAST!*, Maleeka giggled and snuggled against me.

The idea of writing for kids eased into me. I'd grown tired of writing poetry. Maybe I could transfer my skills to picture books.

I started to experiment, pecking away at my computer in the little long house with the cave underneath. In the brain-numbing heat of summer, my writing studio had no air conditioning. A small fan disturbed my papers. Mosquitoes gnawed at my ankles.

*

My most ambitious project was a manuscript that would eventually come to fruition as a published book. On my first visit to Thailand I'd met an activist friend of Pal's. Kanlaya Yaiprasan was dedicated to protecting young workers and the environment from the devastating effects of heavy-metal poisoning resulting from the Japanese and American electronics factories.

I promised Kanlaya that I'd go back to the United States and do something to help her. I envisioned contacting an agency like Greenpeace. Instead I began my first children's novel. Having no idea what I was doing, no clue about my new craft, my first attempt was grim. The story morphed from picture book to holiday book, from holiday book to chapter book, with several different plots. Yet I persisted. Ten years after conception, *Silk Umbrellas* became not my first, but my third published book.

*

I realized I was floundering, plus I missed being part of the kind of community of writers I'd known as a poet. So when my second daughter, Preeya, was five years old, I enrolled in the Master of Fine Arts low-residency program in writing for children at Vermont College.

When the list of recommended books arrived, I submerged myself in the exquisite pleasure of reading children's literature. I was in heaven! I couldn't believe I'd missed out on so much! I hadn't even read *Island of the Blue Dolphins*!

Montpelier, Vermont, is a Disney-cute little town with white clapboard houses, real seasons, and stores that aren't chains. Right away, I bonded with my classmates.

Here I encountered fellow writers as confoundedly sensitive as I was. Others called our class the Hive because we were like bees—always buzzing.

In my final semester, my mentor was Amy Ehrlich, a senior editor at Candlewick Press. She was interested in a manuscript I'd just begun which featured a Thai immigrant girl. The story had been inspired by events in Preeya's life. At a predominately Hispanic school in our Tucson barrio, she'd been called *china,* the way Pal had been called Chinese in Mexico. While helping her brainstorm ways to prove that she was Thai, I took notes. With Amy's guidance, I completed the manuscript. After a grueling decision process, Candlewick bought the manuscript that became *The Gold-Threaded Dress.*

Simultaneously, Viking editor Melanie Cecka pulled my picture-book manuscript out of the slush pile. One Christmas Day in a fancy hotel, I'd imagined what it might be like for a young girl whose mother worked as a bathroom maid on Christmas. Melanie wrote to say she liked the story, but felt the subject matter was more suitable for a young chapter book. I balked, saying I'd lived a long time among Arizona Hispanics, but didn't have an in-depth feeling for those in California, where my story was set. Nonetheless, Melanie encouraged me.

"Maleeka and Preeya in their Thai costumes." (Reproduced by permission.)

Reading *The Circuit,* Francisco Jimenez' autobiographical account of growing up as a son of migrant laborers, helped me to write *Mama Had to Work on Christmas.*

Teacher Woman

My mom, a classroom teacher, had always encouraged me to be one too. For about twenty-eight years I'd resisted the idea, not wanting to be locked into a schedule, boxed into a classroom. Yet I became a teacher of sorts, arriving at the profession through the back door—teaching poetry in the schools and dance in two mining towns north of Tucson. I supplemented that income by substitute-teaching, bouncing from one classroom to another.

Suddenly I wanted my own classroom. I wanted to spend a whole year with the same kids, bringing the arts to them in a more sustained, meaningful way.

To earn my teaching credentials, I attended Prescott College, an innovative school without traditional classrooms wherein students designed their own programs.

I first taught in a crazy charter school located in an old grocery store building. The state had funded the charter two weeks before school started. It opened with four hundred and fifty students but no furniture, books, or materials. Nor did it have any walls, so the noise level was tremendous. To escape, I took groups of students on field trips every day for six weeks straight. By Christmas, I had used up the school's entire bus budget!

A year later, I left the charter school to teach in a public preschool. I'd gotten interested in the world-renowned northern Italian schools of Reggio Emilia, and formed a team of five people committed to implementing those principles.

The Reggio Emilia schools were founded after World War II by Italian parents and educators who wanted to ensure that fascism would never again garner mass appeal in Italy. They created an educational system that emphasized critical-thinking skills.

Our Reggio-inspired classrooms were quite beautiful. We painted the brick walls white and added plants and natural objects like driftwood and shells. Alongside the children's art, we hung photographs of them engaged in play and project work.

Ironically, in this lavish environment, we served not the rich, but Tucson's poorest children.

In our first year as a "Reggio School," our classrooms were visited by over two hundred visitors from all over the United States and several foreign countries.

*

I eventually left preschool teaching for a third/fourth grade classroom in one of the poorest schools in Tucson. One of my students was an eight-year-old boy who'd come from the Navajo reservation and was taking refuge at the nearby homeless shelter. I learned all I could about Timothy's story while watching him develop an interesting friendship with another boy. I added fictional details and characters (including the teacher!) and wrote *Bird Springs*.

The Golden State Again

In 2001, our family moved from Tucson to La Jolla, California to live with my mom.

My first job there was in a charter school in Chula Vista. I'd eagerly been hired to teach a monolingual Spanish first grade class because I was "Out of the Box" and innovative. But the school was actually quite conservative, and I lasted only one year.

I moved on to National City to teach fifth grade. But right away I wasn't happy. Whereas my joy as a teacher was in bringing the arts to my students, the students were forbidden to sing or draw. I resigned myself to concentrating on the art of writing. When the administrators told me I could only teach creative writing once a month, I broke my contract and left, effectively ending my teaching career.

I planned to write full time. I had three books published and had heard that seven books could support an author. I got to work on both *Moon Runner*, inspired by Maleeka's brief stint as a track star, and *The Quail Club*, the sequel to *The Gold-threaded Dress*.

Deer Park

In the section of the newspaper that features the comics and *Dear Abby*, I opened to an article about Vietnamese Zen Master Thich Nhat Hanh. Although he usually lived in France, he'd recently established a monastery in the town of Escondido, just forty-five minutes from my house in La Jolla.

The newspaper article described how 400 acres of chaparral-covered land had been acquired for the monastery, and how Thich Nhat Hanh was there with all of his 200 monks and nuns for the traditional Buddhist three-month rainy season retreat. The article announced an upcoming retreat for writers and entertainers.

I studied the photo of rows of people sitting in meditation, a photo of Thich Nhat Hanh himself. He wore a wooly cap and was smiling widely, the skin around his eyes creased in playful wrinkles.

I dialed the number listed in the article, spoke to a woman with a heavy Vietnamese accent, and reserved my ride to heaven's door.

*

Three weeks later, with the handwritten directions on the seat beside me, I made my way north on the freeway. I passed through the boom town of Escondido, then turned toward the boulder-strewn mountainsides, the road growing rutty and potholed. Finally, at the base of the hillside, sheltered by a stand of eucalyptus, I came to a wooden sign in Vietnamese. Below, in small letters, the English words were printed: DEER PARK MONASTERY, THE GREAT HIDDEN MOUNTAIN.

The road led upward, through low chaparral, then dipped into a luscious oak grove. The March grass, deep under the trees, glowed bright green. On the oak in the middle of the road hung a sign written in flowing calligraphy: I HAVE ARRIVED. I AM HOME.

Men and women appeared, walking along the road wearing loose brown or gray robes and cone-shaped Vietnamese straw hats. With their shaven heads, these had to be the Buddhist monks and nuns.

As the road ascended, a tall Western monk directed me to a dirt lot shaded by oaks, bounded by a row of turquoise outhouses. I jumped out of my car, slamming the door on my old life.

*

After registration, I set up my tent under an oak tree, climbed in, stretched out, and began to read Thich Nhat Hanh's book, *Peace Is Every Step*. Overhead the oak leaves rustled, casting patterns of light and dark. I read and dozed. I'd become what the Buddha called a "Stream Enterer." I had reached the stream of life and had waded in.

Vietnam

Because of Thich Nhat Hanh's opposition to the Vietnam War, he'd been in exile from his country for thirty-nine years. But politics were about to change all that. In late 2004 the Communist government, seeking better trade relations with the United States, needed to appear to support religious freedom. They invited Thich Nhat Hanh to return.

The Zen Master negotiated a three-month tour, not only for himself, but for his *sangha* as well. He wanted to return to his homeland accompanied by his disciples, the fruits of his teaching. He wanted to demonstrate to the people of Vietnam that Buddhism was thriving in the West.

When an entourage of one hundred monastics and three consecutive groups of one hundred laypeople was approved, I knew I had to go.

Although I'd traveled to Thailand, I'd never imagined going to Vietnam. As an anti-war protester, I'd pictured the place thoroughly. Now I'd see that tropical country of bamboo huts and dense green jungles with my own eyes.

Of course, everything turned out differently than I'd imagined. For one thing, the weather in Hanoi was bitterly cold. Instead of bamboo huts, the landscape was populated by cartoonishly tall, skinny buildings painted colors like fuchsia, chartreuse, and Home Depot orange.

All of us, including Thich Nhat Hanh, got very sick. Recovering from my prolonged fever in a hotel lobby, a friend told me the story of the documentary called *Daughter from Danang*. During Operation Babylift in 1972, the United States had airlifted out about 2,000 Vietnamese orphans with mixed blood, fearing that the Communists would retaliate against those with American blood. Many weren't actually orphans, but rather children whose mothers hoped for a safer, better life for their offspring.

The subject of the documentary had been sent to a family in Kentucky who'd raised her Southern-style with no Asian influence. One day, this woman decided to go back to Vietnam to reconnect with her birth mother. The trip was a cultural shock. She hadn't expected such poverty, so many people clustering around her. When her half-brother asked her to send back money for their mother each month, the woman overreacted and left, never to contact her Vietnamese family again.

Lying there on the stained couch, I listened with growing interest. My mind began to click. I could write a children's book from this story. I could tell it from the point of view of a girl whose mother's half-sister was returning to Vietnam. I reached into my bag for a pen and notebook. I sat up straight and made some notes for what would become *When Heaven Fell*.

I was no longer a passive victim, clobbered by a mystery ailment. I was a writer again.

Partnerships

Whereas in writing about cultures other than my own I'd always worked with gatekeepers—people from the culture who could vet my work for accuracy—I began to *collaborate* with people. This meant that I shared the writing process with them to varying degrees, almost always shared the publishing contract, and always split the royalties fifty-fifty.

Collaboration was usually a positive experience. I enjoyed working with a friend. I enjoyed learning about other cultures. Plus, because my collaborators had all lived fascinating childhoods, I didn't have to use my imagination to invent the material.

On the downside, I was often seduced by that beautiful material. Often I thought I had a story when I only had a collection of anecdotes. Too many interesting anecdotes make it hard to develop a coherent plot, so I always had to give some up.

Often my collaborators didn't understand why I abandoned interesting material, or why I created fictional material in order to make a plot. They were very attached to their "real" stories. Once I had to cancel a contract when my collaborator wasn't willing to let go of the truth.

*

My first collaboration came about with a young Chinese woman named Virginia Loh, a fellow teacher at the Chula Vista charter school where I'd taught first grade. At a Christmas party, Virginia talked about her life growing up as the daughter of Chinese immigrants. I loved her material and suggested she write a children's book. After a bit, I offered to co-author the book.

When we met for marathon brainstorming sessions, Virginia told me everything she could recall about her childhood while I wrote it all down. Soon we had a huge notebook filled with fascinating material which we then worked to shape.

This collaboration went smoothly, since Virginia did the rough first draft writing—the part that terrifies me—and I did the polishing, which I love. She worked nights and e-mailed the material to me in time for my daytime work. Our book is called *The Jade Dragon* and deals not only with the issues of Chinese immigrants, but also with international adoption.

*

One Sunday at Deer Park, a Vietnamese monk named Phap Niem told the story of how a cyclone had hit his village when he was a child. In the morning, all was devastated—houses damaged, rice too wet to cook, fruit trees knocked down.

The temple roof had been blown off. Phap Niem found the statue of the Buddha inside, washed by the storm, fresher than ever. The Buddha even smiled.

Right away, this story resonated with me. I had to write it! As Phap Niem talked, I took notes furiously. I continued as he finished his tale and the children who had come for his talk left the meditation hall.

During silent lunch, I was bursting with excitement. How could I concentrate on my plate of brown rice and kombucha squash cut into neat chunks, or the cluster of purple basil from the vegetable garden? I needed to ask Phap Niem if we could write together!

Maybe he'd be excited. Maybe even honored, I thought smugly, to be approached by a writer like myself.

I watched Phap Niem eating with a group of Vietnamese laypeople. The kids called him "Nemo." He had eyebrows like black caterpillars. His family, all boat people, had settled in Canada.

Now would I be able to approach him gracefully? Could I contain my excitement?

A nun invited the bell, signaling the end of the twenty-minute period of silence. Abandoning my half-eaten lunch, I made my way to Phap Niem's table. I squatted down beside him and without preamble, dove in: "That story you told the children. It was just beautiful. I want to write it with you."

"We can," he said simply.

I went back to my table, exultant.

Over the course of weeks, Phap Niem dictated to me all he could remember of his village: the plants, the fishing boats, the storm, the ocean, the fish, the weather. While this monk swung in a hammock under a pine tree, answering my endless questions, I scribbled furiously.

The Buddha's Diamonds is a story about being happy, smiling no matter what.

*

Whereas my parents were Methodist missionaries in Mexico, my cousin Philip Matzigkeit grew up on a Methodist mission in Rhodesia, now called Zimbabwe. For years, I was reluctant to tackle his story because of the challenges of writing an individual child's story against a large political backdrop.

After I had a few more books under my belt, we began to work together. As with Virginia, we met for long sessions in cafes, where I wrote down all that Philip said.

After a while, I wrote the "story." While it had a good setting and characters, and a few choice anecdotes thrown in, it made both of us yawn. We needed more conflict. So we again went to the café, drank huge amounts of coffee, and came up with a clever plot. To address two sides of the complex subject of race, I told the story from two points of view.

While Philip didn't actually do any of the writing, he wrote wonderful, evocative e-mails and always came up with the perfect anecdote. Since Zimbabwe was too dangerous a place for me to visit, Philip had to make the setting come alive for me. Our book is called *Sahwira: An African Friendship.*

*

Meanwhile, Philip introduced me to Daniella Cinque, who'd grown up in an institute for girls in 1950s Naples. These girls had been abandoned by their mothers, usually because they'd been born as the result of rape by a soldier. I spent one Christmas Day with Daniella (there seems to be something particularly inspiring about Christmas for me!) and couldn't resist her story.

Daniella recounted everything in one sitting while I typed away on my computer. By the end of the afternoon, I had twenty pages.

One of the stories she told me was about Bambolina, a real baby so tiny she fit into the nun's pocket. The girls of the institute cared for her until she died at age fourteen, only about two feet tall. I had to let go of odd little nuggets like this because they distracted from the main plot and made it exceptionally hard to make *Take Me with You* into a story.

Alone Again

At present I'm working on a manuscript called *Starfields,* which is set in Chiapas, Mexico and involves the Mayan prophesy of 2012. In order to explore the prophesy, I'm layering the story with present time and antiquity, telling the story through the perspectives of a contemporary Mayan girl and an ancient boy shaman.

Working alone, I miss the company of a collaborator. I also miss the authenticity of the real stories a collaborator brings.

How I Do It

My first Candlewick editor, Amy Ehrlich, would always ask for huge revisions, requiring me to tear the story down to its very foundations a few weeks before copyediting. To meet these deadlines, I had to learn to write anywhere, anytime. I've worked on my manuscripts at red lights, while having my toe operated on, waiting in line at the Department of Motor Vehicles, on the deck of a cruise ship while seasick. . . .

I type up the manuscript on my computer in my 1959 Airstream trailer. I then three-hole punch the pages, put them in a binder, and take the binder into the world. Some favorite places to edit include the beach, the art library, or the Goldfish Point Café which overlooks the ocean. I get a large cup of mostly decaf coffee, seat myself at a tall table in the back—I like to be way up high since it gives me a feeling of power over the writing!—and work for an hour. If someone is having an annoying conversation nearby, I turn on my MP3 player and listen to bands like the Black-eyed Peas, Elvis Costello, Bob Dylan, the Rolling Stones, the Talking Heads. . . . One might think that loud, fast music would conflict with my rather measured and delicate writing, but I've trained my brain to hear the music as soothing white noise.

Once I've edited the manuscript by hand, I go back to the computer, clean the manuscript up, and repeat the process. I do this over and over. When I can't think of a way to improve the story, I send it to my agent or editor. After she makes suggestions, the process continues.

I'm known for writing about cultures other than my own. This is partly because my editors have encouraged it. Whenever I've written about a white kid in the United States, the manuscript has been rejected! I'm also naturally attracted to other cultures because of my own multicultural background, and because I live in California surrounded by people from many countries.

"Here is the Airstream trailer where I write." (Reproduced by permission.)

Of course I do lots of research: reading fiction and non-fiction, watching films, talking with people from the culture, and traveling. My learning curve is always steep.

Writing the first draft of a manuscript terrifies me. When I look at the blank computer screen, I know that this story can go in infinite directions and worry that I won't find the right one. Once I have a rough draft, I can relax and enjoy the revision because the scary work is done.

At some point, I realize that in spite of much hard work, the book is far from finished. Something is wrong with the story and I don't know how to fix it. I wonder why I ever undertook this project! But as a friend of mine says, he writes every day "against all doubts." Eventually, usually slowly, in a series of tiny *aha!* moments, the solution to the puzzle comes to me.

I never get writer's block. In fact, I sometimes feel panicky at the thought of all the books I want to write. I think of my projects as airplanes lined up on a runway, ready to take off. Sometimes I don't want to listen to someone's story, lest I feel captivated and compelled to write it!

While I seem to jump here, there, and everywhere, my books do follow patterns. Starting with *When Heaven Fell,* all of my stories have a backdrop of war. I didn't set out to address the issue of war, but unfortunately many countries—especially those of the Third World—are involved in armed conflict.

While my books take me all over the world and back and forth historically, each connects with my own life in at least a small way. For example, in the case of *Take Me with You,* I've had the experience of attending a Catholic girls' school run by nuns. Therefore, even though I'm not Italian nor have I lived in post-war Italy, in my writing I still have a link to the characters' lives. That link helped me to understand Susanna and Pina and the time and place of 1950s Naples.

I used to joke that I was going to cover every country in Asia, then later that my books would address every major world religion. I've almost done the latter. I also find that I like to write about places where bougainvillea grows. If you read closely, you'll find that tropical plant in almost all of my books! But joking aside, I write the stories that touch my heart.

My writing acts as a magnifying mirror, a way to learn about myself. It also serves as a window to the world, enabling me to see beyond my own life, to the lives of others. Similarly, I hope my books can become mirrors and windows for my readers.

MASSEY, Misty

Personal

Daughter of teachers; married; children: one son. *Hobbies and other interests:* Reading, belly dancing, Renaissance faires.

Addresses

Agent—Holly McClure/Sullivan Maxx Literary Agency, 210 N. Harrington St., St. Simons Island, GA 31522. *E-mail*—mistywrites@gmail.com.

Career

Writer and librarian. Currently a circulation librarian in a middle school; former preschool teacher.

Writings

Mad Kestrel, Tor (New York, NY), 2008.

Cover of Misty Massey's young-adult fantasy novel **Mad Kestrel,** *featuring artwork by Shelly Wan.* (Tom Doherty Associates, 2009. Shelly Wan, illustrator. Reproduced by permission.)

Sidelights

Misty Massey's first novel, *Mad Kestrel,* combines magic, intrigue, and pirates. "I have always been a voracious reader," Massey commented on her home page. "My parents encouraged my love of books, a gift more valuable to me than anything else they could have given me. It was no surprise to anyone when I began writing. I dabbled with short stories for years, even publishing a few in small press magazines, until I found and joined a writing critique group, and tried my hand at writing novels."

Mad Kestrel tells the story of Kestrel, a young woman struggling to deal with her magical abilities. Kestrel does not want to work for the Danisoban mages who control all magic on her world. To escape, she goes to sea, where her abilities are muted. Aboard ship, Kestrel eventually rises to become a quartermaster. After her captain is imprisoned, however, she must once again use her magic to help rescue him while avoiding capture herself.

Several reviewers found Massey's first novel to be an exciting adventure that will appeal to young adults. A "rollicking debut," *Mad Kestrel* combines swashbuckling sea adventure, fantasy and romance with great success," as a *Publishers Weekly* reviewer noted. In *Booklist* Frieda Murray remarked that, while the novel contains "loads of action and larger-than-life characters," Massey's story is "plausibly grounded in the realities of life at sea." Jackie Cassada also voiced praise in her *Library Journal* review, citing Massey's "swift pace" and "feisty, resourceful heroine," and Deirdre Root concluded in *Kliatt* that *Mad Kestrel* is "great swashbuckling fun with a bit of romance, in what one hopes will be the beginning of a series."

Biographical and Critical Sources

PERIODICALS

Booklist, March 1, 2008, Frieda Murray, review of *Mad Kestrel,* p. 57.

Kliatt, July, 2008, Deirdre Root, review of *Mad Kestrel,* p. 18.

Library Journal, March 15, 2008, Jackie Cassada, review of *Mad Kestrel,* p. 64.

Publishers Weekly, January 14, 2008, review of *Mad Kestrel,* p. 44.

ONLINE

Misty Massey Home Page, http://mistymassey.com (January 20, 2010).*

McCOY, Glenn 1965-

Personal

Born 1965, in St. Louis, MO; married; wife's name Laura; children: Molly, Jack. *Education:* Southern Illinois University, B.F.A. (graphic design), 1988.

Addresses

Home—Belleville, IL. *Office*—Belleville News-Democrat, 120 S. Illinois, P.O. Box 427, Belleville, IL 62220.

Career

Cartoonist, illustrator, and writer. *Belleville News-Democrat,* Belleville, IL, editorial cartoonist, c. 1988—. Universal Press Syndicate, creator of syndicated comic strip "The Duplex," 1993—; creator (with brother, Gary McCoy) of syndicated panel "The Flying McCoys," 2005—. Writer and designer for animation studios, including Dreamworks SKG, Film Roman, and Walt Disney TV and Feature Animation.

Member

National Cartoonists Society.

Glenn McCoy creates the cartoon art that brings to life his quirky story in the picture book **I See Santa Everywhere.** (Illustration © 2008 by Glenn McCoy. All rights reserved. Reproduced by permission of Disney-Hyperion, an imprint of Disney Books Group LLC. All rights reserved.)

Awards, Honors

National Cartoonists Society awards for gag cartoons, 1996, 2002, 2003, and 2005, award for editorial cartoons, 1997, awards for greeting cards, 2002, 2003, 2004, 2005, and award for newspaper strip, 2004, for "The Duplex."

Writings

FOR CHILDREN; SELF-ILLUSTRATED

Penny Lee and Her TV, Hyperion Books for Children (New York, NY), 2002.
I See Santa Everywhere, Hyperion Books for Children (New York, NY), 2008.

COMICS COLLECTIONS

The Duplex, foreword by Lynn Johnston, Andrews McMeel (Kansas City, MO), 1998.
Bad Habits: A Duplex Collection, Andrews McMeel (Kansas City, MO), 2006.
(With brother, Gary McCoy) *The Flying McCoys: Comics for a Bold New World,* Andrews McMeel (Kansas City, MO), 2006.
(With Gary McCoy) *Monkey Business: Another Cartoon Collection by the Flying McCoys,* Andrews McMeel (Kansas City, MO), 2007.

ILLUSTRATOR

Eoin Colfer, *The Legend of Spud Murphy,* Miramax Books/Hyperion Books for Children (New York, NY), 2004.
Eoin Colfer, *Legend of—Captain Crow's Teeth,* Hyperion Books for Children (New York, NY), 2005.
Eoin Colfer, *Legend of—the Worst Boy in the World,* Hyperion Books for Children (New York, NY), 2007.

Work has been anthologized in *Pot Shots* and *Pot Shots 2.* Contributor of cartoons to magazines.

Sidelights

The creator of the "Duplex" comic strip, versatile cartoonist Glenn McCoy also produces editorial cartoons for newspapers and gag cartoons for magazines and greeting cards. He is also the co-creator, with brother Gary McCoy, of the single-panel comic "The Flying McCoys," which has been collected in several book-length volumes. McCoy has also written and illustrated children's books, as well as created material for Disney and Dreamworks animation.

McCoy started cartooning at his grandfather's kitchen table, and he and older brother Gary "decided early on that cartooning was in our destiny," as McCoy told fellow cartoonist Scott Nickel on the *A Nickel's Worth* Web log. After serving as the resident cartoonist for his school newspapers from elementary school all the way through college, McCoy began drawing editorial cartoons for his hometown paper after graduation. He began drawing comic strips after entering a "Cartoonist of the '90s" contest sponsored by *USA Today* and cartooning syndicate King Features. He drew a few quick strips with the intention to qualify for the contest's early entrant prize and ending up winning the competition.

"I kind of backed into" the comic strip, McCoy later recalled to Frank Absher of the *St. Louis Journalism Review.* "Usually, a cartoonist will develop a comic strip to the point where they think, 'Now I want someone else to see it.' Then they'll send it off to the syndicate. I didn't have a comic strip, but I had all the syndicates waiting to see what I could do." McCoy came up with the idea of a macho guy named Eno and his dog sharing a duplex with a woman and her poodle, and "The Duplex" was born. He had such success with "The Duplex" that his syndicate suggested that he start a regular single-panel comic. The cartoonist shared the workload with his brother, Gary, and "The Flying McCoys" debuted in 2005.

As a sideline to cartooning, McCoy has also created several children's books. *Penny Lee and Her TV* introduces a young girl who is so devoted to her television set that she even sleeps on it. When the television breaks down, Penny Lee's dog shows her the wonders of the outside world on the way to the repair shop. A *Publishers Weekly* reviewer observed of *Penny Lee and Her TV* that "clever cartoons with a slapstick edge enliven newcomer McCoy's one-note tale." "It is McCoy's art that really pushes this [book] to the top," a *Kirkus Reviews* critic concluded, adding that "cartoon figures of big noses, big ears, goofy shapes perfectly capture the foolishness." *School Library Journal* contributor Sheilah Kosco similarly found McCoy's artwork to be "lively and engaging," calling *Penny Lee and Her TV* "a humorous and entertaining tale that kids and parents alike will enjoy."

Another original picture book, *I See Santa Everywhere,* presents a parody of "Santa Claus Is Coming to Town." A boy tells a psychiatrist that he feels stalked by the jolly old elf, who "sees me while I'm sleeping and knows when I'm awake," in the words of the popular holiday song. A *Kirkus Reviews* critic described *I See Santa Everywhere* as an "edgy holiday tale" that "offers something quite a bit different." "McCoy's wacky cartoons are sprinkled with visual jokes" that will interest older readers, Maureen Wade predicted in her *School Library Journal* review, the critic adding that McCoy's holiday story is a "fun read-aloud."

McCoy has also lent his cartooning talents to Eoin Colfer's humorous "Legend of" books. In installments like *Legend of—The Worst Boy in the World,* McCoy's "quirky cartoon illustrations add to the fun, creating a perfect selection for reluctant readers," according to *School Library Journal* contributor Jennifer Cogan.

Although he has been the recipient of numerous National Cartoonists Society awards for his oeuvre, McCoy has difficulty believing that his work is viewed as on par to that of cartooning greats such as *Peanuts* creator Charles Schulz. "Schulz is my number-one, all time greatest influence in my life," the cartoonist told Absher. "I was weaned on his little Snoopy paperbacks. I probably have rooms full of them. And the fact that now I can open up a comics page and see my stuff on the same page as Charles Schulz, it just seems to be too weird to even contemplate."

Biographical and Critical Sources

PERIODICALS

Editor & Publisher, July 1, 2005, Dave Astor, "McCoy Has Many 'Toons on His Plate."
Kirkus Reviews, March 15, 2002, review of *Penny Lee and Her TV,* p. 419; November 1, 2008, review of *I See Santa Everywhere.*
Publishers Weekly, February 25, 2002, review of *Penny Lee and Her TV,* p. 66.
School Library Journal, June, 2002, Sheilah Kosco, review of *Penny Lee and Her TV,* pp. 100-101; September, 2007, Jennifer Cogan, review of *Legend of—The Worst Boy in the World,* p. 161; October, 2008, Maureen Wade, review of *I See Santa Everywhere,* p. 96.
St. Louis Journalism Review, April, 1997, Frank Absher, "Local Cartoonist Hits Big Time," p. 9.

ONLINE

A Nickel's Worth Web log, http://scottnickel.blogspot.com/ (November 3, 2009), Scott Nickel, interview with Glenn McCoy.
Universal Press Syndicate Web site, http://www.amuniversal.com/ups/ (January 21, 2010), "Our Creators: Glenn McCoy."*

*   *   *

McCUE, Lisa 1959-

Personal

Born February 16, 1959, in New York, NY; daughter of Richard (a television director and producer) and Emiline (an artist) McCue; married Kenneth Stephen Karsten, Jr. (an electrical engineer), 1986; children: two sons. *Education:* Attended University of Hartford, 1978-79; University of Southeastern Massachusetts, B.A., 1981. *Hobbies and other interests:* Skiing, sailboat racing, reading, sewing.

Addresses

Home—Annapolis, MD. *Agent*—Herman Agency, 350 Central Park W., New York, NY 10025.

Career

Illustrator and author. Designer and creator of Fuzzytail Greetings (card line) and of artwork for fabrics, gift wrapping, greeting cards, and other objects.

Writings

SELF-ILLUSTRATED

(With father, Dick McCue) *Ducky's Seasons,* Simon & Schuster (New York, NY), 1983.
(With Dick McCue) *Froggie's Treasure,* Simon & Schuster (New York, NY), 1983.
(With Dick McCue) *Teddy Dresses,* Simon & Schuster (New York, NY), 1983.
(With Dick McCue) *Kitty's Colors,* Simon & Schuster (New York, NY), 1983.
(With Dick McCue) *Puppy's Day School,* Simon & Schuster (New York, NY), 1984.
(With Dick McCue) *Bunny's Numbers,* Simon & Schuster (New York, NY), 1984.
Fun and Games in Fraggle Rock, Holt (New York, NY), 1984.
(With Dick McCue) *Kitten's Christmas,* Simon & Schuster (New York, NY), 1985.
(With Dick McCue) *Baby Elephant's Bedtime,* Simon & Schuster (New York, NY), 1985.
(With Dick McCue) *Panda's Playtime,* Simon & Schuster (New York, NY), 1985.
(With Dick McCue) *Raccoon's Hide and Seek,* Simon & Schuster (New York, NY), 1985.
The Little Chick, Random House (New York, NY), 1986.
Ten Little Puppy Dogs, Random House (New York, NY), 1987.
Puppy Peek-a-Boo, Random House (New York, NY), 1989.
Kittens Love, Random House (New York, NY), 1990.
Puppies Love, Random House (New York, NY), 1990.
Whose Little Baby Says . . . ?, Random House (New York, NY), 1990.
Bunnies Love, Random House (New York, NY), 1991.
Ducklings Love, Random House (New York, NY), 1991.
Christmas Stories and Poems, Whistlestop (Mahwah, NJ), 1994.
Kitty's Carrier, Random House (New York, NY), 1995.
Little Fuzzytail, Random House (New York, NY), 1995.
Fuzzytail Farm, Random House (New York, NY), 1996.
Quick, Quack, Quick, Random House (New York, NY), 1996.
Fuzzytail Friends: Lift-and-Look Animal Book, Random House (New York, NY), 1997.
Jingle Bell Mice, Whistlestop (Mahwah, NJ), 1997.
Quiet Bunny, Sterling Pub. Co., Inc. (New York, NY), 2009.
The Animals' Christmas Countdown, Random (New York, NY), 2010.
Fuzzytails 123: A Touch-and-Feel Counting Book, Random House (New York, NY), 2010.
Fuzzytails ABC: A Foldout Counting Book, Random House (New York, NY), 2010.

ILLUSTRATOR

Marguerite Muntean Corsello, *Who Said That,* Western Publications, 1982.

Carol North, reteller, *The Three Bears,* Western Publications, 1983.

Michaela Muntean, *They Call Me Boober Fraggle,* Holt (New York, NY), 1983.

Michaela Muntean, *The Tale of the Traveling Matt,* Holt (New York, NY), 1984.

Louise Gikow, *Sprocket's Christmas Tale,* Holt (New York, NY), 1984.

M.C. Delaney, *Henry's Special Delivery,* Dutton (New York, NY), 1984.

Marilyn Elson, *Duffy on the Farm,* Western Publications, 1984.

Louise Gikow, *Wembley and the Soggy Map,* Holt (New York, NY), 1986.

Katharine Ross, *The Baby's Animal Party,* Random House (New York, NY), 1986.

Ben Cruise, reteller, *The Ugly Duckling,* Western Publications, 1987.

Katharine Ross, *Bear Island,* Random House (New York, NY), 1987.

Katharine Ross, *My Little Library of Fuzzy Tales: A Fuzzy Fussy Tale, A Fuzzy Sleepy Tale, A Fuzzy Wake-up Tale, A Fuzzy Friendly Tale,* Random House (New York, NY), 1987.

Katharine Ross, *Farm Fun,* Random House (New York, NY), 1987.

Stephanie Calmenson, *Spaghetti Manners,* Western Publications, 1987.

Stephanie Calmenson, *One Red Shoe,* Western Publications, 1987.

Jane Thayer, *The Puppy Who Wanted a Boy,* Morrow (New York, NY), 1988.

Katharine Ross, *Nighty-night, Little One,* Random House (New York, NY), 1988.

Jan Wahl, *Timothy Tiger's Terrible Toothache,* Western Publications, 1988.

Katharine Ross, *Animal Babies Book and Puzzle Set,* Random House (New York, NY), 1988.

Katharine Ross, *Sweetie and Petie,* Random House (New York, NY), 1988.

Judy Delton, *Hired Help for Rabbit,* Macmillan (New York, NY), 1988.

Katharine Ross, *The Fuzzytail Friends' Great Egg Hunt,* Random House (New York, NY), 1988.

Bill Wallace, *Snot Steb,* Holiday House (New York, NY), 1989, reprinted, Aladdin (New York, NY), 2008.

Diane Namm, *Little Bear,* Grolier, 1989.

Ann Turner, *Hedgehog for Breakfast,* Macmillan (New York, NY), 1989.

Jane Thayer, *The Popcorn Dragon,* new edition, Morrow (New York, NY), 1989.

Judy Delton, *My Mom Made Me Go to Camp,* Dell (New York, NY), 1990.

Ted Bailey, *Skunks! Go to Bed!,* Western Publications, 1990.

Judy Delton, *My Mom Made Me Go to School,* Dell (New York, NY), 1991.

Jim Latimer, *Fox under First Base,* Macmillan (New York, NY), 1991.

Judy Delton, *My Mom Made Me Take Piano Lessons,* Dell (New York, NY), 1994.

Ben Cruise, adaptor, *The Ugly Duckling* (based on the story by Hans Christian Andersen), Western Publishing (Racine, WI), 1995.

Marsha Arnold, *Quick, Quack, Quick!,* Random House (New York, NY), 1996.

Cynthia Alvarez, *Professor Pipsqueak's Guide to Birds*, Random House (New York, NY), 1997.

Cynthia Alvarez, *Professor Pipsqueak's Guide to Bugs*, Random House (New York, NY), 1997.

Herman Gall, *The Lion and the Mouse,* Random House (New York, NY), 1998.

Margaret Wise Brown, *Bunny's Noisy Book,* Hyperion (New York, NY), 2000.

Susan Ring, *Polar Babies,* Random House (New York, NY), 2001.

Annie Ingle, *Lift the Lid, Use the Potty!,* Random House (New York, NY), 2001.

Jane Thayer, *The Puppy Who Wanted a Boy,* HarperCollins (New York, NY), 2003.

Irving Berlin, *Easter Parade*, HarperCollins (New York, NY), 2003.

Gail Herman, *The Lion and the Mouse,* Random House (New York, NY), 2003.

Jane Thayer, *Part-Time Dog,* HarperCollins (New York, NY), 2004.

Eileen Spinelli, *Feathers: Poems about Birds,* Henry Holt (New York, NY), 2004.

Rick Walton, *The Remarkable Friendship of Mr. Cat and Mr. Rat,* Putnam (New York, NY), 2006.

Leslie Kimmelman, *How Do I Love You?,* HarperCollins (New York, NY), 2006.

Lola Schaefer, *Easter Surprises,* Little Simon (New York, NY), 2009.

Lisa Schroeder, *Little Chimp's Big Day,* Sterling Pub. Co. (New York, NY), 2010.

ILLUSTRATOR; "SEBASTIAN (SUPER SLEUTH)" SERIES

Mary Blount Christian, *Sebastian (Super Sleuth) and the Hair of the Dog Mystery,* Macmillan (New York, NY), 1982.

Mary Blount Christian, *Sebastian (Super Sleuth) and the Crummy Yummies Caper,* Macmillan (New York, NY), 1983.

Mary Blount Christian, *Sebastian (Super Sleuth) and the Bone to Pick Mystery,* Macmillan (New York, NY), 1983.

Mary Blount Christian, *Sebastian (Super Sleuth) and the Santa Claus Caper,* Macmillan (New York, NY), 1984.

Mary Blount Christian, *Sebastian (Super Sleuth) and the Secret of the Skewered Skier,* Macmillan (New York, NY), 1984.

Mary Blount Christian, *Sebastian (Super Sleuth) and the Clumsy Cowboy,* Macmillan (New York, NY), 1985.

Mary Blount Christian, *Sebastian (Super Sleuth) and the Purloined Sirloin,* Macmillan (New York, NY), 1986.

Mary Blount Christian, *Sebastian (Super Sleuth) and the Stars-in-His-Eyes Mystery,* Macmillan (New York, NY), 1987.

Mary Blount Christian, *Sebastian (Super Sleuth) and the Egyptian Connection,* Macmillan (New York, NY), 1988.

Mary Blount Christian, *Sebastian (Super Sleuth) and the Time Capsule Caper,* Macmillan (New York, NY), 1989.

Mary Blount Christian, *Sebastian (Super Sleuth) and the Baffling Bigfoot,* Macmillan (New York, NY), 1990.

Mary Blount Christian, *Sebastian (Super Sleuth) and the Mystery Patient,* Macmillan (New York, NY), 1991.

Mary Blount Christian, *Sebastian (Super Sleuth) and the Impossible Crime,* Macmillan (New York, NY), 1992.

Mary Blount Christian, *Sebastian (Super Sleuth) and the Flying Elephant,* Macmillan (New York, NY), 1994.

ILLUSTRATOR; "CORDUROY" SERIES; BASED ON THE CHARACTER BY DON FREEMAN

B.G. Hennessy, *Corduroy's Day,* Penguin (New York, NY), 1985.

B.G. Hennessy, *Corduroy's Party,* Penguin (New York, NY), 1985.

B.G. Hennessy, *Corduroy's Toys,* Penguin (New York, NY), 1985.

B.G. Hennessy, *Corduroy Goes to the Doctor,* Viking (New York, NY), 1987.

B.G. Hennessy, *Corduroy on the Go,* Viking (New York, NY), 1987.

B.G. Hennessy, *Corduroy's Busy Street,* Penguin (New York, NY), 1987.

B.G. Hennessy, *Corduroy's Christmas Surprise* (board-book adaptation), Grosset & Dunlap (New York, NY), 2000.

B.G. Hennessy, *Corduroy's Easter Party* (board-book adaptation), Grosset & Dunlap (New York, NY), 2000.

B.G. Hennessy, *Corduroy* (board-book adaptation), Viking Penguin (New York, NY), 2002.

B.G. Hennessy, *Rhymes and Riddles with Corduroy* (board-book adaptation), Viking Penguin (New York, NY), 2002.

B.G. Hennessy, *Happy Easter, Corduroy* (board-book adaptation), Viking Penguin (New York, NY), 2004.

B.G. Hennessy, *Corduroy's Snow Day* (board-book adaptation), Viking Penguin (New York, NY), 2005.

B.G. Hennessy, *Corduroy's Thanksgiving* (board-book adaptation), Viking Penguin (New York, NY), 2006.

B.G. Hennessy, *Corduroy's 4th of July,* Viking (New York, NY), 2007.

B.G. Hennessy, *Corduroy's Sleepover,* Viking (New York, NY), 2007.

B.G. Hennessy, *Corduroy Helps Out,* Viking (New York, NY), 2009.

B.G. Hennessy, *Play Ball, Corduroy,* Viking Children's Books (New York, NY), 2010.

ILLUSTRATOR; "CORK AND FUZZ" SERIES

Dori Chaconas, *Cork and Fuzz,* Viking (New York, NY), 2005.

Dori Chaconas, *Short and Tall,* Viking (New York, NY), 2006.

Dori Chaconas, *Good Sports,* Viking (New York, NY), 2007.

Dori Chaconas, *The Collectors,* Viking (New York, NY), 2008.

Dori Chaconas, *Finders Keepers,* Viking (New York, NY), 2009.

Dori Chaconas, *The Babysitters,* Viking (New York, NY), 2010.

Adaptations

McCue's illustrated version of *The Ugly Duckling* was adapted as both audio-and videocassettes, Western Publications, 1987.

Sidelights

Lisa McCue has illustrated dozens upon dozens of children's books, including the canine detective series "Sebastian (Super Sleuth)," several adaptations of Don Freeman's popular "Corduroy" series about a lovable bear, and stories by Leslie Kimmelman, Judy Delton, and Dori Chaconas, among others. According to a *Kirkus Reviews* contributor, in *How Do I Love You?,* Kimmelman's poetic paean to the love between a crocodile mother and child, McCue's "illustrations positively sing with the love and the joy the two bring to each

Lisa McCue's engaging illustrations team with Margaret Wise Brown's toddler-friendly tale in Bunny's Noisy Book. (Illustration © 2000 by Lisa McCue. Reprinted with permission of Disney-Hyperion, an imprint of Disney Book Group LLC. All rights reserved.)

other's lives." Rick Walton's *The Remarkable Friendship of Mr. Cat and Mr. Rat,* a humorous story, is brought to life in what *School Library Journal* contributor Catherine Callegari dubbed "detailed watercolor illustrations" by McCue in which the artist's effective use of "simple backgrounds keep the focus on the action." On occasion, McCue has created self-illustrated stories for very young children, several of which she coauthored with her father, Dick McCue.

Despite McCue's love of animals, she did not enjoy a rural upbringing; in fact, she experienced quite the opposite. Born in Brooklyn, New York, McCue was raised in a nearby suburb. "My mother was a big influence on me," she once recalled of her budding artistic career. "She is an artist. Ever since I can remember, she was painting and drawing and doing every kind of craft. I was always involved in crafts. In elementary school, every time there was a classroom party or art involved, everybody would turn and say, 'Oh, Lisa could do it.' So I was always zeroed in on as the artist of the class. The more you're told you're good at something, the more you head toward that area."

McCue enjoyed the benefits of a happy childhood spent near a major city. "My parents liked to go to museums, so I ended up going with them. I would always go to the Metropolitan Museum and go to their costume exhibit, that was my favorite place. I loved all the costumes and stepping back in history and seeing how the people dressed, just trying to imagine lifestyles."

Art was not her only interest, however; as McCue explained, "Music and dance were big interests of mine. I played a lot of sports. In school, I ran track and I played soccer, but my main sport is skiing."

Despite her competing hobbies, drawing and painting eventually won out, and after high school McCue studied art at Southeastern Massachusetts University. There she met Dutch author Loek Kessels, and it was at Kessels' suggestion that she sent a portfolio of her work to the editors of a children's book Kessels was then producing. The editors liked her work, and before she even graduated from college McCue had illustrated her first published book. "It was the best thing I ever did," the artist/author recalled: "I got right into children's books the summer after I graduated. I haven't had much time for anything else."

McCue's style has sometimes been compared to that of Garth Williams, the illustrator of E.B. White's beloved *Charlotte's Web* and the "Little House" series by Laura Ingalls Wilder. "When I started I was much more comfortable doing animals, and my portfolio had a lot of animal drawings," McCue explained. "As my agent showed my portfolio around, clients tended to give me a lot of animal books, and it snowballed from there." When asked to describe her drawing style, she explained that she concentrates on accuracy and finds that her everyday experiences are helpful sources, as are animal

McCue's artwork enlivens new editions of Don Freeman's classic stories in books such as **Corderoy Goes to the Beach.** (Illustration copyright © 2006 by Lisa McCue. Reproduced by permission of Viking, a division of Penguin Putnam Books for Young Readers.)

picture books. "I have an extensive library of animal encyclopedias, but if you go through my books, you'll see all the neighborhood animals and children. My own cat and dog have . . . starred in many books, and bits and pieces of my home and places around my neighborhood and places I travel to show up in all the books. I try and make everything very happy. I try to give as much life and personality as I can. And since I have so much fun when I'm drawing, I think that comes through in the art work.

Because fuzzy and fluffy animal characters are among the artist's favorite subjects, McCue's own story books not surprisingly feature titles such as *Jinglebell Mice, Little Fuzzytail,* and *Ten Little Puppy Dogs.* In her work for others, if there is a way to work animals into the plot, McCue will find it. Describing the artist's unique illustrated version of Irving Berlin's classic popular song for *Easter Parade,* Ilene Cooper wrote in *Booklist* that the illustrator's "stuffed animal-like characters are instantly appealing, and children will have fun singing the familiar refrain."

Other original picture books by McCue include *Quiet Bunny, The Animals' Christmas Countdown,* and the twin interactive concept books *Fuzzytails 123: A Touch-and-Feel Counting Book,* and *Fuzzytails ABC: A Fold-out Counting Book.* In *Quiet Bunny* she uses words and pictures to capture a young bunny's efforts to make his own special sound to add to the many animal noises that make up the music of the forest. After trying to mimic the sound of an owl, a cricket, a bat, and several other creatures, the bunny finally realizes that his special sound is one that he makes without even trying.

Citing McCue's "onomatopoeic" text, Laura Stanfield added in *School Library Journal* that *Quiet Bunny* features "a pleasing link between story and pictures." In *Publishers Weekly* a contributor concluded of the same book that the story's welcoming forest setting combines with the author/illustrator's "canny sense of story-time dynamics" to make *Quiet Bunny* a storyhour success.

Animals feature in much of the work McCue does as an illustrator for stories by other writers. When choosing an illustrating project, she sidesteps the tedious whenever possible. "I think in terms of what type of pictures I would enjoy doing," she once explained. "Sometimes I've gotten stories where I thought the story was just wonderful but it took place in the same room. The characters were doing something different but it all took place in the same background. I like books where there's a lot going on. The characters will be outdoors one time, indoors one time. On every page there's something new going on so that it doesn't all start to look alike. You just get tired of drawing if you're drawing an animal in a kitchen and the kitchen is the background for every page. You get tired of drawing that stove and

McCue's detailed animal-centered art adds to the popularity of Dori Chaconas's series picture book **Cork and Fuzz: The Collectors.** (Illustration copyright © 2008 by Lisa McCue. Reproduced by permission of Viking, a division of Penguin Putnam Books for Young Readers.)

all the little doo-dahs on top of that stove over a hundred times. So I look for books that I think I can make interesting pictures from. I like upbeat stories, funny, silly stories."

McCue's collaborations with other writers include the popular "Cork and Fuzz" beginning-reader books by Chaconas. In a review of *Cork and Fuzz*, which introduces readers to Cork the muskrat and Fuzz the possum in a simple story, Kathleen Meulen wrote in *School Library Journal* that "McCue's endearing drawings add personality and humor to the animals' faces." In *Good Sports* Cork feels bested by Fuzz's talent at playing team sports, but then is able to save friend Fuzz from an angry mother duck in *The Collectors,* the latter which features what *Booklist* contributor Hazel Rochman described as "clear, lovely" illustrations. In *School Library Journal* Lisa Egly Lehmuller praised the McCue's ability to retain an element of realism in her art, writing that the illustrator gives Chaconas's endearing characters "a variety of expressions and convincing body language while remaining true to their animal natures."

Discussing her approach to illustrating a text by another writer, McCue noted: "I start with a sketch just like any other illustrator. You get your story, you do sketches, and you send it to the publisher for an 'okay.' As I'm reading a story for the first time, I visualize. I see things in my mind and I don't really go too far from what my initial reaction to the story is—everything down to what I think characters should be wearing, what type of setting they should be in, and, if it's a rabbit, what kind of rabbit?

"I'll start with a very, very rough, scribbly sketch, put a piece of tracing paper over it, and start neatening it up—maybe changing action and motion a little bit to get more of the feeling that I want, or enlarge or make things smaller to fit in better. I think when I'm figuring out a book and I'm working at a very steady pace, I can average a page a day. But this average varies with the size of the book and the amount of background and characters on each page.

"I use acrylics a lot in a background because they won't bleed later. When I'm doing my animals, I like colored inks because I can get a nice fine line with them, and they're waterproof to an extent. If I'm doing a background with watercolors, a lot of times I get brighter colors. Luma dyes also get nice bright colors, and I'll use those for clothing or things that need to be brighter, more colorful than I might be able to get with some of the acrylics or colored inks."

To gauge the success of her work, McCue relies on the reactions of children who encounter her books. "I have good friends and relatives . . . and they'll always call and say, 'Oh, so and so loves this page and every time we open the book up she only wants to skip right to that because she loves the kitty popping his head out of the bag.' And they tell me what pictures and what books tend to go over big with their children and why. I keep that in mind for the next stories. It's funny. My favorite pictures are the ones that compositionally work perfectly, but those are not necessarily the ones the kids go for. They tend to like the ones where there's a character that's being a little naughty or hiding or searching for something where the child can get involved."

Biographical and Critical Sources

PERIODICALS

Booklist, June 1, 1993, Kay Weisman, review of *My Mom Made Me Take Piano Lessons,* p. 1836; December 1, 1994, Kay Weisman, review of *Sebastian (Super Sleuth) and the Flying Elephant,* p. 680; March 15, 2003, Ilene Cooper, review of *Easter Parade,* p. 1328; March 15, 2004, Carolyn Phelan, review of *Feathers: Poems about Birds,* p. 1308; August, 2004, Karen Hutt, review of *Part-Time Dog,* p. 1946; January 1, 2006, Hazel Rochman, review of *Short and Tall,* p. 109; January 1, 2007, Ilene Cooper, review of *The Remarkable Friendship of Mr. Cat and Mr. Rat,* p. 118.

Horn Book, May-June, 2006, Betty Carter, review of *Short and Tall,* p. 311.

Kirkus Reviews, February 15, 2004, review of *Feathers,* p. 185; March 1, 2005, review of *Cork and Fuzz,* p. 284; February 14, 2006, review of *Short and Tall,* p. 179.

Publishers Weekly, December 5, 2005, review of *How Do I Love You?,* p. 54.

School Library Journal, April, 2004, Susan Scheps, review of *Feathers,* p. 114; September, 2004, Andrea Tarr, review of *Part-Time Dog,* p. 182; May, 2005, Kathleen Meulen, review of *Cork and Fuzz,* p. 78; February, 2005, Kathy Piehl, review of *How Do I Love You?,* p. 104; April, 2006, Laura Scott, review of *Short and Tall,* p. 98; December, 2006, Catherine Callegari, review of *The Remarkable Friendship of Mr. Cat and Mr. Rat,* p. 118.

ONLINE

Lisa McCue Home Page, http://www.lisamccueillustrator. com (January 15, 2010).*

*   *   *

MEDINA, Meg 1963-

Personal

Born June 11, 1963, in Alexandria, VA; married. *Education:* Attended City University of New York.

Addresses

Home and office—Richmond, VA.

Career

Writer.

Writings

Milagros: Girl from Away, Henry Holt (New York, NY), 2008.

Sidelights

Although Meg Medina was born in the United States, she grew up with a strong sense of her family's Cuban heritage. She shares this cultural identity with readers in her first novel, *Milagros: Girl from Away.*

Medina's parents fled from Cuba during the Cuban Revolution of the 1950s, and as a child growing up in New York City, she loved to read and play outside. She began writing in the third grade and had a passion for it, but for many years was reluctant to call herself a writer. Medina worked as a writing teacher, a grant writer, and a freelance writer for periodicals before she finally decided, at the age of forty, to begin writing what she wanted to write: fiction.

Milagros—the title translates as "Miracle"—is an adventure story that meshes historical Caribbean culture with that of modern New England. Twelve-year-old Mi-

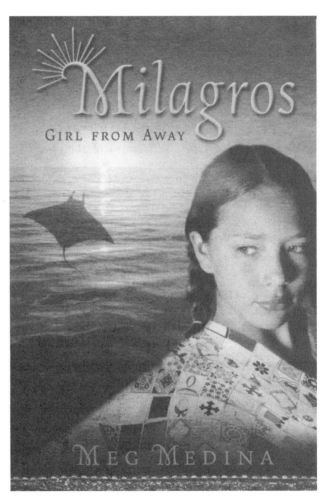

Cover of Meg Medina's evocative young-adult novel **Milagros: Girl from Away,** *which shares the author's Cuban culture.* (Christy Ottaviano Books, 2008. Jacket photographs (background) Tim Laman/Getty Images (girl)/Hola Images (shawl)/Spike Mafford/Getty Images.)

lagros has spent her life growing up fairly independently on the island paradise of Las Brisas. Her mother has an almost magical gift for making things grow, and she and Milagros are very close, in part because the girl's father abandoned them both to become a pirate. When Las Brisas is attacked, Milagros manages to escape and locate her father, whose help she refuses. Instead, she sets sail for a distant land, where she is taken in by a kind family of modern New Englanders. Full of magical realism, the story mixes cultures and customs through Milagros's eyes. "Medina has crafted a beautiful tale of a brave young girl," wrote Aimee Cole in a *Kliatt* review of *Milagros. School Library Journal* reviewer Carol A. Edwards maintained that the value of the novel is its language: "The book is written in accessible, but lively and lyrical language," Edwards noted, and "it is obvious that great care has been taken to choose every word."

On her home page, Medina explained the importance of representing bi-cultural characters in her fiction. "Writing for young people involves remembering the kid you once were. The girl's voice inside of me is bi-cultural—so I write from her point of view. . . . I like to name that bi-cultural experience for my readers so that they can be honest about it, make it a natural—and positive—part of themselves, and move on to a place of strength and pride."

Biographical and Critical Sources

PERIODICALS

Kirkus Reviews, October 1, 2008, review of *Milagros: Girl from Away.*
Kliatt, November, 2008, Aimee Cole, review of *Milagros,* p. 15.
School Library Journal, December, 2008, Carol A. Edwards, review of *Milagros,* p. 132.

ONLINE

Meg Medina Home Page, http://www.megmedina.com (January 18, 2010).*

*   *   *

MELMED, Laura Krauss

Personal

Born in New York, NY; married; husband's name Allan; children: Stephanie, Jonathan, Michael. *Education:* University of Buffalo, bachelor's degree; Tulane University, M.Ed. (early childhood education). *Religion:* Jewish.

Addresses

Home—Washington, DC. *E-mail*—laura@lauramelmed. com.

Laura Krauss Melmed (Reproduced by permission.)

Career

Writer and educator. Taught Head Start and kindergarten in New Orleans, LA.

Awards, Honors

Association of Booksellers for Children Award, for *The Rainbabies;* American Bookseller Pick of the Lists designation, Notable Children's Trade Book in the Field of Social Studies designation, National Council for the Social Studies/Children's Book Council (CBC), and Notable Books for Children selection, American Library Association, all *for Little Oh;* Gold Award, Oppenheim Toy Portfolio, National Jewish Book Award, and Sydney Taylor Notable Books for Younger Readers selection, Association of Jewish Libraries, all for *Moishe's Miracle;* Gold Award, Oppenheim Toy Portfolio, for *This First Thanksgiving Day;* Capitol Choices Noteworthy Book selection, 2003, for *Capital!;* Parents' Choice Award, 2002, for *A Hug Goes Around;* several International Reading Association/CBC Children's Choice selections and American Booksellers Book of the Year (ABBY) awards.

Writings

The Rainbabies, illustrated by Jim LaMarche, Lothrop, Lee & Shepard (New York, NY), 1992.
I Love You as Much . . ., illustrated by Henri Sorensen, Lothrop, Lee & Shepard (New York, NY), 1993.
The First Song Ever Sung, illustrated by Ed Young, Lothrop, Lee & Shepard (New York, NY), 1993.
Prince Nautilus, illustrated by Henri Sorensen, Lothrop, Lee & Shepard (New York, NY), 1994.
The Marvelous Market on Mermaid, illustrated by Maryann Kovalski, Lothrop, Lee & Shepard (New York, NY), 1995.

Little Oh, illustrated by Jim LaMarche, Lothrop, Lee & Shepard (New York, NY), 1997.

Jumbo's Lullaby, illustrated by Henri Sorensen, Lothrop, Lee & Shepard (New York, NY), 1999.

Moishe's Miracle: A Hanukkah Story, illustrated by David Slonim, HarperCollins (New York, NY), 2000.

This First Thanksgiving Day: A Counting Story, illustrated by Mark Buehner, HarperCollins (New York, NY), 2001.

A Hug Goes Around, illustrated by Betsy Lewin, Harper-Collins (New York, NY), 2002.

Fright Night Flight, illustrated by Henry Cole, HarperCollins (New York, NY), 2002.

Capital!: Washington, DC, from A to Z, illustrated by Frané Lessac, HarperCollins (New York, NY), 2003.

New York, New York!: The Big Apple from A to Z, illustrated by Frané Lessac, HarperCollins (New York, NY), 2005.

Hurry! Hurry! Have You Heard?, illustrated by Jane Dyer, Chronicle Books (San Francisco, CA), 2008.

Heart of Texas: A Lone Star ABC, illustrated by Frané Lessac, HarperCollins (New York, NY), 2009.

My Love Will Be with You, illustrated by Henri Sorensen, HarperCollins (New York, NY), 2009.

Eight Winter Nights: A Family Hanukkah Book, illustrated by Elisabeth Schlossberg, Chronicle Books (San Francisco, CA), 2010.

Adaptations

The Rainbabies was adapted as an audiobook, Weston Woods, 2007.

Sidelights

Laura Krauss Melmed is the author of more than a dozen books for young readers, including award winners such as *The Rainbabies* and *Capital!: Washington, DC, from A to Z.* A former kindergarten teacher, Melmed entered the field of children's literature after a bedtime conversation with one of her sons inspired her to begin writing. She noted in an essay on her home page that, "as with anything one strives to be good at, writing is hard work. But it is also terrific fun. One of the best things is to find a calling in life that makes you happy. I feel very fortunate to have been able to do just that."

The Rainbabies, Melmed's first published work, concerns a childless couple that discovers a dozen tiny babies after a magical "moonshower." When the new parents are visited by a mysterious figure, they must decide whether to continue caring for the rainbabies or accept a gift of a moonstone in exchange for them. A *Publishers Weekly* critic praised the originality of Melmed's fairytale, stating that "it's invigorating to find real creativity at work." *Prince Nautilus,* another fantastical story, focuses on a kindhearted young woman who helps a bewitched prince free himself from an evil spell. "Melmed's fluid, poetic style feels very much at home in the fairy-tale genre," a *Publishers Weekly* reviewer maintained of this book.

In *The First Song Ever Sung,* a work inspired by Melmed's talk with her inquisitive son, a youngster tries to find the answer to his musical query. The author's "words invite close attention," a *Publishers Weekly* reviewer observed, and Carolyn Phelan, writing in *Booklist,* described *The First Song Ever Sung* as "a poetic picture book with energy and depth." A mother elephant tries to lull her baby to sleep in *Jumbo's Lullaby,* another bedtime tale. Here "Melmed uses language that is lovely and lyrical," Donna Beales commented in *Booklist.*

Melmed has written several books appropriate for the holidays. She recounts the Pilgrim's feast with the Wampanoag tribe in *This First Thanksgiving Day: A Counting Story,* and by crafting a narrative told in rhyme, "the cheer is fairly irrepressible," as GraceAnne A. DeCandido stated in *Booklist.* A witch joins a group of ghoulish friends for an evening of trick or treating in *Fright Night Flight,* a book in which Melmed's narrative "builds suspense at just the right pace," according to *Booklist* critic Gillian Engberg. A nativity story, *Hurry! Hurry! Have You Heard?* follows a small bird as it flies across the countryside spreading the news of Jesus's birth. A *Kirkus Reviews* critic praised the tale's "bouncy rhythm and perfect rhyming pairs."

Melmed has enjoyed a successful collaboration with illustrator Frané Lessac on a number of alphabet books. In *Capital!,* the author introduces readers to such sights as the District of Columbia's Air and Space Museum and its National Zoo. "The illustrations work well with the prose explications," a contributor reported in *Kirkus Reviews.* Melmed and Lessac explore America's largest city in *New York, New York!: The Big Apple from A to Z,* another work told in verse in which "Melmed brilliantly touches on all the major sights of NYC," according to Elizabeth Bird in *School Library Journal.* In *Heart of Texas: A Lone Star ABC,* readers will learn about the Alamo, the Dallas Cowboys football team, and Zilker Metropolitan Park. Here Melmed's "jaunty rhymes entice readers to explore the many facts scattered across the pages" of the Texas-themed picture book, Patricia Austin concluded in *Booklist.*

Biographical and Critical Sources

PERIODICALS

Booklist, October 15, 1993, Carolyn Phelan, review of *The First Song Ever Sung,* p. 454; November 15, 1994, Lauren Peterson, review of *Prince Nautilus,* p. 613; September 1, 1997, Ilene Cooper, review of *Little Oh,* p. 134; October 1, 1999, Donna Beales, review of *Jumbo's Lullaby,* p. 362; September 1, 2000, Stephanie Zvirin, review of *Moishe's Miracle: A Hanukkah Story,* p. 134; September 1, 2001, GraceAnne A. DeCandido, review of *This First Thanksgiving Day: A Counting Story,* p. 121; June 1, 2002, Ilene Cooper, review of *A Hug Goes Around,* p. 1742; September 1, 2002, Gillian Engberg, review of *Fright Night Flight,* p. 140; February 1, 2003, Kathleen Odean, review of *Capital!: Washington, DC, from A to Z,* p. 998; May 1, 2009, Patricia Austin, review of *Heart of Texas: A Lone Star ABC,* p. 76.

Horn Book, March-April, 1993, Ellen Fader, review of *The Rainbabies* p. 200; September-October, 1997, Susan P. Bloom, review of *Little Oh,* p. 561.

Kirkus Reviews, August 15, 2001, review of *This First Thanksgiving Day,* p. 1218; August 15, 2002, review of *Fright Night Flight,* p. 1229; November 15, 2002, review of *Capital!,* p. 1698; June 1, 2005, review of *New York, New York!: The Big Apple from A to Z,* p. 640; November 1, 2008, review of *Hurry! Hurry! Have You Heard?;* April 1, 2009, review of *Heart of Texas.*

New York Times Book Review, January 19, 2003, review of *Capital!,* p. 16.

Publishers Weekly, August 17, 1992, review of *The Rainbabies,* p. 500; May 17, 1993, review of *The First Song Ever Sung,* p. 78; July 4, 1994, review of *Prince Nautilus,* p. 63; September 20, 1999, review of *Jumbo's Lullaby,* p. 86; September 25, 2000, Elizabeth Devereaux, review of *Moishe's Miracle,* p. 66.

School Library Journal, July, 2002, Martha Topol, review of *A Hug Goes Around,* p. 95; June, 2005, Elizabeth Bird, review of *New York, New York!,* p. 140; October, 2008, Eva Mitnick, review of *Hurry! Hurry! Have You Heard?,* p. 96; April, 2009, Mary Elam, review of *Heart of Texas,* p. 124.

ONLINE

Children's Book Guild Web site, http://www.childrensbookguild.org/ (January 1, 2010), "Laura Krauss Melmed."

Chronicle Books Web site, http://www.chroniclebooks.com/ (January 1, 2010), "A Conversation with Laura Krauss Melmed."

HarperCollins Web site, http://www.harpercollins.com/ (January 1, 2010), "Laura Krauss Melmed on *Capital!*"

Laura Krauss Melmed Home Page, http://www.laurakraussmelmed.com (January 1, 2010).*

*   *   *

MOORE, Raina 1970-

Personal

Born 1970, in Los Angeles, CA. *Education:* Attended college.

Addresses

Home—Brooklyn, NY.

Career

Author and editor. HarperCollins Publishers, New York, NY, editor of children's books.

Writings

(Adaptor with Kate Egan) *Good Boy!: Meet the Dogs* (novelization), HarperFestival (New York, NY), 2003.

(Adaptor) *The Three Bears,* illustrated by Thea Kliros, HarperFestival (New York, NY), 2003.

(Adaptor) Margery Williams, *The Velveteen Rabbit,* illustrated by Thea Kliros, HarperFestival (New York, NY), 2003.

(Adaptor) *Three Billy Goats Gruff,* illustrated by Thea Kliros, HarperFestival (New York, NY), 2003.

(Adaptor) *Three Little Pigs,* illustrated by Thea Kliros, HarperFestival (New York, NY), 2003.

(Adaptor) Jacob and Wilhelm Grimm, *The Elves and the Shoemaker,* illustrated by Thea Kliros, HarperFestival (New York, NY), 2004.

(Editor) *A Charming Princess Collection,* HarperFestival (New York, NY), 2005.

(Adaptor) *The Tall Book of Nursery Tales,* illustrated by Aleksey and Olga Ivanov, HarperFestival (New York, NY), 2006.

How Do You Say Goodnight?, illustrated by Robin Luebs, HarperCollins (New York, NY), 2008.

Biographical and Critical Sources

PERIODICALS

Booklist, October 15, 2008, Kay Weisman, review of *How Do You Say Goodnight?,* p. 45.

Kirkus Reviews, May 15, 2008, review of *How Do You Say Goodnight?*

School Library Journal, August, 2008, Blair Christolon, review of *How Do You Say Goodnight?,* p. 99.

ONLINE

HarperCollins Web site, http://www.harpercollins.com/ (January 15, 2010), "Raina Moore."*

*   *   *

MOTT, Evelyn Clarke
See KAJIKAWA, Kimiko

*   *   *

MOULTON, Mark Kimball

Personal

Born in Danbury, CT. *Education:* University of Connecticut, B.S. (horticulture), 1977. *Hobbies and other interests:* Kayaking, hiking, biking, cross-country skiing, photography, gardening.

Addresses

Home—Riverton, CT. *E-mail*—mark@markkimballmoulton.com.

Career

Writer, photographer, and literacy advocate. Worked variously as a store owner and restaurant manager. Speaker; presenter at schools.

Member

Society of Children's Book Writers and Illustrators, Riverton Merchants Association.

Writings

FOR CHILDREN

A Snowman Named Just Bob, illustrated by Karen Hillard Crouch, Ideals Children's Books (Nashville, TN), 2003.

The Visit, illustrated by Susan Winget, Ideals Children's Books (Nashville, TN), 2003.

A Cricket's Carol, illustrated by Lisa Blowers, Ideals Children's Books (Nashville, TN), 2004.

Everyday Angels, illustrated by Susan Winget, Ideals Childrens Books (Nashville, TN), 2004.

Miss Fiona's Stupendous Pumpkin Pies, illustrated by Karen Hillard Crouch, Ideals Children's Books (Nashville, TN), 2004.

One Enchanted Evening, illustrated by Karen Hillard Crouch, Ideals Children's Books (Nashville, TN), 2004.

A Snowgirl Named Just Sue, illustrated by Karen Hillard Good, Ideals Press (Nashville, TN), 2005.

Scarecrow Pete, illustrated by Karen Hillard Good, Ideals Press (Nashville, TN), 2005.

Miss Sadie McGee Who Lived in a Tree, illustrated by Karen Hillard Good, Ideals Children's Books (Nashville, TN), 2006.

Twisted Sistahs, illustrated by Karen Hillard Good, Riverton Press (Nashville, TN), 2006.

A Royal Wedding, Ideals Children's Books (Nashville, TN), 2007.

The Annual Snowman's Ball, illustrated by Karen Hillard Good, Ideals Children's Books, (Nashville, TN), 2007.

Reindeer Christmas, illustrated by Karen Hillard Good, Simon & Schuster Books for Young Readers (New York, NY), 2008.

The Very Best Pumpkin, illustrated by Karen Hillard Good, Simon & Schuster Books for Young Readers (New York, NY), 2010.

OTHER

A Fistful of Dandelions: Loving Thoughts for My Daughter on Her Wedding Day, illustrated by Marsha Winborn, Ideals Publications (Nashville, TN), 2006.

Chocolate Frosted Fingers: Loving Thoughts from Mom on Your Birthday, illustrated by Marsha Winborn, Ideals Publications (Nashville, TN), 2006.

Mark Kimball Moulton's holiday-themed picture book Reindeer Christmas *features folk-style paintings by Karen Hillard Good.* (Illustration copyright © 2008 by Karen Hillard Good. Reproduced by permission of Simon & Schuster Book for Young Readers, an imprint of Simon & Schuster Macmillan.)

Sidelights

Living and working in the rural northwestern corner of Connecticut, in a home he calls Sparrow Hill, Mark Kimball Moulton is the author of picture books that are known for their humorous rhyming stories and engaging art. Inspired by the oral storytelling tradition and featuring vivid descriptions and memorable characters, his stories include *A Snowman Named Just Bob, Miss Fiona's Stupendous Pumpkin Pies, Scarecrow Pete, Reindeer Christmas,* and *Everyday Angels.*

In creating his picture books, Moulton most often collaborates with his neighbor Karen Hillard Good, a Connecticut artist whose paintings echo Moulton's colonial/country aesthetic. *Reindeer Christmas,* which features Good's illustrations, tells the story of two children who rescue a wild deer on a snowy evening just before Christmas. While the deer—actually one of the famous sleigh-pulling reindeer—is gone come Christmas morning, the children's kindness is acknowledged by a special gift from Santa. Praising the book's watercolor illustrations for their "rich texture," *School Library Journal* critic Linda Israelson added that *Reindeer Christmas* is a "lyrical, rhyming [holiday] tale." In *Kirkus Reviews* a contributor cited the "old-fashioned flavor" of Moulton's "sweet-natured" story, and in *Booklist* Ilene Cooper praised *Reindeer Christmas* for "captur[ing] . . . the magic of Christmas" in its "sweet story" and "precise and lovely" art.

Biographical and Critical Sources

PERIODICALS

Booklist, December 15, 2005, Ilene Cooper, review of *Scarecrow Pete,* p. 51; September 1, 2008, Ilene Cooper, review of *Reindeer Christmas,* p. 107.
Kirkus Reviews, November 1, 2008, review of *Reindeer Christmas.*

School Library Journal, October, 2008, Linda Israelson, review of *Reindeer Christmas,* p. 97.

ONLINE

Mark Kimball Moulton Home Page, http://www.mark kimballmoulton.com (January 10, 2010).*

O-P

O'CONNELL, Rebecca 1968-
(Rebeccca Tova Ben-Zvi)

Personal

Born September 17, 1968, in Poughkeepsie, NY; daughter of Paul (an artist and professor of art and art history) and Linda (a teacher) Ben-Zvi; married John O'Connell (a social worker), June 16, 1991; children: Edgar. *Education:* Pennsylvania State University, B.A., 1990; University of Pittsburgh, M.L.S., 1992. *Politics:* "Leaning left." *Religion:* Jewish.

Addresses

Home—Pittsburgh, PA. *Agent*—BookStop Literary Agency, 67 Meadow View Rd., Orinda, CA 94563; info@0bookstopliterary.com. *E-mail*—rebecca@rebeccaoconnell.com.

Career

Librarian and author. Carnegie Library of Pittsburgh, Pittsburgh, PA, children's librarian, 1992—.

Member

Society of Children's Book Writers and Illustrators.

Awards, Honors

Best Books for Babies designation, and Charlotte Zolotow Award honor book designation, both 2004, both for *The Baby Goes Beep;* Notable Children's Books of Jewish Content for Older Readers designation, Association of Jewish Libraries, 2006, for *Four Sides, Eight Nights;* Sydney Taylor Notable Book for Older Readers, Association of Jewish Libraries, 2008, for *Penina Levine Is a Hard-boiled Egg.*

Writings

Myrtle of Willendorf (young-adult novel), Front Street Books (Asheville, NC), 2003.

Rebecca O'Connell (Reproduced by permission.)

The Baby Goes Beep, illustrated by Ken Wilson-Max, Roaring Brook Press (Brookfield, CT), 2003.

(As Rebecca Tova Ben-Zvi) *Four Sides, Eight Nights: A New Spin on Hannukah,* illustrated by Susanna Natti, Roaring Brook Press (Brookfield, CT), 2006.

Penina Levine Is a Hard-boiled Egg, illustrated by Majella Lue Sue, Roaring Brook Press (New Milford, CT), 2007.

Penina Levine Is a Potato Pancake, illustrated by Majella Lue Sue, Roaring Brook Press (New York, NY), 2008.

Danny Is Done with Diapers: A Potty ABC, illustrated by Amanda Gulliver, Albert Whitman (Chicago, IL), 2010.

Contributor to periodicals, including *Radiance, School Library Journal,* and *Pittsburgh Post-Gazette.*

Sidelights

Rebecca O'Connell, a children's librarian, is the author of several works for young readers, among them *The Baby Goes Beep* and *Penina Levine Is a Hard-boiled Egg.* In addition, O'Connell has authored *Myrtle of Willendorf,* a highly regarded young-adult novel. Discussing her literary ventures with Cynthia Leitich Smith on the *Cynsations* Web site, O'Connell remarked: "I love the idea of sharing something . . . with someone out there I've never even met. I know the intense pleasure I get from reading a good story, and I love the possibility that my story could bring that feeling to someone reading it."

Myrtle of Willendorf, O'Connell's debut work, traces its origins to the author's college days. As O'Connell once told *SATA:* "When I went to Pennsylvania State University in the mid-to-late 1980s, there was this thing called the Free U: non-credit courses in everything from archery to wine-tasting. I took a Free U course called 'Women's Mysteries.' The teacher was an undergraduate who knew a great deal about mythology and the history of women and religion. The course was mostly readings and discussion, but there were also meetings that featured candles, visualization, and pagan rituals. Even though I thought some parts of the 'Women's

Mysteries' course were goofy, it turned out to be a profound learning experience. That course was the inspiration for Margie's coven in *Myrtle of Willendorf.*

"I began writing *Myrtle of Willendorf* in 1996 as an exercise for another non-credit course, a class in writing for children taught by author Nancy Alberts. It began as a character sketch of Myrtle's friend, Margie. Once the class ended, I continued working on *Myrtle* in a writing group led by author Sally Alexander. I sent the manuscript to Front Street Books early in October, 1998. The day before Halloween, I got a call from Stephen Roxburgh, president and publisher of Front Street Books. I hyperventilated, I was so excited."

Myrtle of Willendorf centers on Myrtle Parcittadino, an obese young woman who is about to enter her sophomore year of college. Estranged from Margie, a high-school friend and practicing Wiccan, Myrtle shares an apartment with Jada, a beautiful and sexually uninhibited young woman who is obsessed with diet and exercise. An aspiring artist, Myrtle submits an erotic portrait of Jada's boyfriend to a local show, which earns her the derision of her roommate's friends. The painful experience also spurs Myrtle to action, however, and she creates a painting that recalls the Venus of Willendorf, a Rubenesque stone figure. "This powerful first novel is well written and thought-provoking," Susan Riley commented in *School Library Journal,* while *Booklist* critic Ilene Cooper remarked that in *Myrtle of Willendorf* O'Connell "offers a story that's sad and funny, in almost equal measure." In *Horn Book,* Lauren Adams noted that "the potent theme of the female deity, made suitably incarnate by the character of Myrtle, puts a fresh twist on the journey of self-discovery."

In *The Baby Goes Beep* O'Connell uses rhythmic verses and an onomatopoeic narrative to describe a toddler's busy day. Jennifer M. Brabander, reviewing the work in *Horn Book,* complimented the "catchy beat of O'Connell's simple text," and *Booklist* reviewer Jennifer Mattson noted that the author "plays on the delighted repetition and experimentation that are hallmarks of language development."

Penina Levine Is a Hard-boiled Egg centers on a sixth grader who causes a stir after she defies her teacher. When she is asked to complete a assignment about the Easter Bunny, Penina, who is Jewish, refuses to comply. Unable to confide in her parents, who are already upset with her behavior at home, Penina turns to her grandmother, who counsels the youngster as they prepare eggs for a Seder meal. "Penina is a feisty and thoroughly enjoyable heroine with whom readers will easily connect," Kim Dare predicted in *School Library Journal,* and a *Kirkus Reviews* critic praised the work as a "captivating, realistic middle-grade novel where conflicts are addressed, if not resolved, in pragmatic and convincing scenarios." In a sequel, *Penina Levine Is a Potato Pancake,* the protagonist finds it difficult to enjoy Hanukkah knowing that her favorite teacher is re-

O'Connell's middle-grade story **Penina Levine Is a Hard-boiled Egg** *features artwork by Sue Lue Majella.* (Illustration copyright © 2007 by Majella Lue Sue. Reprinted by permission of Henry Holt & Company, LLC.)

signing and her best friend is leaving on vacation. "This is a sweet and funny holiday tale," reported Kathleen Meulen in her *School Library Journal* review of *Penina Levine Is a Potato Pancake*. Writing in *Kirkus Reviews,* a contributor maintained that "O'Connell's feisty, endearing 'tween character allows readers a glimpse into a typical Jewish-American modern household."

Biographical and Critical Sources

PERIODICALS

ALAN Review, winter, 2008, Catherine S. Quick, review of *Myrtle of Willendorf.*

Booklist, October 15, 2000, Ilene Cooper, review of *Myrtle of Willendorf,* p. 432; November 1, 2003, Jennifer Mattson, review of *The Baby Goes Beep,* p. 505; March 15, 2007, Kay Weisman, review of *Penina Levine Is a Hard-boiled Egg,* p. 49.

Horn Book, September-October, 2000, Lauren Adams, review of *Myrtle of Willendorf,* pp. 578-579; January-February, 2004, Jennifer M. Brabander, review of *The Baby Goes Beep,* p. 72.

Kirkus Reviews, July 1, 2000, review of *Myrtle of Willendorf,* p. 963; February 1, 2007, review of *Penina Levine Is a Hard-boiled Egg,* p. 127; September 1, 2008, review of *Penina Levine Is a Potato Pancake.*

Kliatt, July, 2000, Paula Rohrlick, review of *Myrtle of Willendorf,* p. 11.

Publishers Weekly, July 17, 2000, review of *Myrtle of Willendorf,* p. 196; September 8, 2003, review of *The Baby Goes Beep,* p. 74.

School Library Journal, October, 2000, Susan Riley Farber, review of *Myrtle of Willendorf,* p. 168; March, 2007, Kim Dare, review of *Penina Levine Is a Hard-boiled Egg,* p. 216; December, 2008, Kathleen Meulen, review of *Penina Levine Is a Potato Pancake,* p. 134.

ONLINE

Boyds Mills Press Web site, http://www.boydsmillspress.com/ (January 1, 2010), "Rebecca O'Connell."

Cynsation, http://www.cynthialeitichsmith.com/ (October-November, 2000), Cynthia Leitich Smith, interview with O'Connell.

Ravenstone Press Web site, http://www.ravenstonepress.com/ (January 1, 2010), interview with O'Connell.

Rebecca O'Connell Home Page, http://www.rebeccaoconnell.com (January 1, 2010).

*   *   *

PAGLIARULO, Antonio 1977(?)-

Personal

Born c. 1977, in New York, NY. *Education:* State University of New York, Purchase College, B.A. *Hobbies and other interests:* Reading.

Addresses

Home—New York, NY.

Career

Writer. Formerly worked as a tutor for urban children.

Awards, Honors

Quick Picks for Reluctant Readers designation, American Library Association, and New York Public Library Books for the Teen Age selection, both 2006, both for *A Different Kind of Heat.*

Writings

A Different Kind of Heat, Delacorte (New York, NY), 2006.

"THE CELEBUTANTES" NOVEL SERIES

On the Avenue, Delacorte (New York, NY), 2007.
In the Club, Delacorte (New York, NY), 2008.
To the Penthouse, Delacorte (New York, NY), 2008.

Sidelights

Antonio Pagliarulo could be called a quintessential New Yorker. Born in the Bronx, he was raised in Manhattan and attended Fiorello H. LaGuardia High School of Music and Art and the Performing Arts. For higher education, Pagliarulo headed just out of the city to attend the State University of New York, Purchase College. He still resides in New York, where he has tutored inner-city children and enjoys window shopping on Fifth Avenue. The city also serves as the setting for his first four books, including the novels in his "The Celebutantes" series.

Pagliarulo's first novel, *A Different Kind of Heat,* is framed as the diary of main character Luz Cordero. The story follows her thoughts and troubles two years after the shooting of her brother Julio by a police officer. Luz ends up in a group home for troubled youths after starting a violent demonstration against police brutality, and there she finds friends who eventually help her soften her anger. Johanna Lewis, writing for *School Library Journal,* commented that Pagliarulo catches the rhythm of the street slang in *A Different Kind of Heat,* but that the depiction of Luz falls out of character and into social-work horror story. Regarding the teen's friends, Lewis said that "Luz seems the most real, and the novel least stilted or preachy when she interacts with them." Frances Radburn, a reviewer for *Booklist,* discussed the adolescent rage that Luz feels. Speaking of the girl's anger and her attempt to focus that emotion into a constructive outlet, Radburn wrote that "it is the challenge of redirecting that rage into 'a different kind of heat' . . . that Pagliarulo depicts so graphically."

Cover of To the Penthouse, *the third volume of Antonio Pagliarulo's "The Celebutantes" teen thriller series.* (Delacorte Press, 2008. Used by permission of Delacorte Press, an imprint of Random House Children's Books, a division of Random House, Inc.)

Pagliarulo's "The Celebutantes" series follows the Hamilton triplets, Lexington, Park, and Madison. Throughout the novels *On the Avenue, In the Club,* and *To the Penthouse,* the sisters—each named for a street in New York City—are called upon to use their crime-solving skills to solve mysteries involving New York society's upper crust. In a review of *On the Avenue* for *Booklist,* Ilene Cooper wrote that "the mystery element is good with plot turns that will string readers along."

Biographical and Critical Sources

PERIODICALS

Booklist, April 1, 2006, Frances Bradburn, review of *A Different Kind of Heat,* p. 37; May 1, 2007, Ilene Cooper, review of *On the Avenue,* p. 44.
School Library Journal, December, 2006, Johanna Lewis, review of *A Different Kind of Heat,* p.152; June, 2007, Anne Rouyer, review of *On the Avenue,* p. 156.

ONLINE

Teens@Random Web site, http://www.randomhouse.com/teens/ (January 20, 2010), "Antonio Pagliarulo."*

*   *   *

PARRY, Rosanne

Personal
Born in Oak Park, IL; married; children: four. *Hobbies and other interests:* Playing violin, juggling, bike riding, hiking, skiing, climbing trees, going to the beach, reading books, dancing tango.

Addresses
Home and office—Portland, OR.

Career
Author and educator.

Awards, Honors
Kay Snow Award Third Place, Willamette Writers, 2003, for short story "The Chess Men"; first place, Oregon Writers Colony Short Story Contest, 2007, for "The Man of the House"; ABC Best Books for Children selection, and *Kirkus Reviews* Best Books of the Year citation, both 2009, both for *Heart of a Shepherd.*

Writings

Daddy's Home!, illustrated by David Leonard, CandyCane (Nashville, TN), 2009.
Heart of a Shepherd, Random House (New York, NY), 2009.

Adaptations
Heart of a Shepherd was optioned for film by Tashtego Films.

Sidelights
A part-time writer and teacher of children ranging from elementary to middle grades, Rosanne Parry is also the author of the picture book *Daddy's Home!* as well as of the middle-grade novel *Heart of a Shepherd.*

Parry remembers her early efforts at writing as challenging. "I had terrible handwriting and was a terrible speller," she admitted to an interviewer in *Publishers Weekly.* On her home page, she explained: "I did not want to be an author when I was a child. Authors were quiet and studious and worked at desks. I was not quiet." Parry preferred activity, playing outdoors and honing her skills in order to achieve her dream of becoming a circus performer. Although she enjoys her dual career as a writer and teacher, Parry still prefers working outside to sitting at a desk. She has a tree house that serves as her primary work location.

Parry's first novel, *Heart of a Shepherd,* has its roots in a poem the author began ten years before it was published. Inspired by watching her father teach her son how to play chess, the book is an effort to capture the man and boy's unique personalities in words. *Heart of a Shepherd* tells the story of twelve-year-old Ignatius, called Brother, and Ignatius's grandfather, as the two assume on responsibility for the family's ranch after Brother's soldier father is sent to fight in Iraq. A story of family and of coming of age, *Heart of a Shepherd* was called "heartfelt and often heartwarming" by *Booklist* reviewer Michael Cart, and a *Kirkus Reviews* contributor dubbed the novel "an unassuming, transcendent joy." Brother has trouble imagining himself as either a soldier or a rancher; his year taking care of the family ranch brings him to a hope for his future career that Roger Sutton described in *Horn Book* as surprising "because we haven't seen anything like it in children's books in quite a long time."

During the ten years that *Heart of a Shepherd* was distilling from a poem to a novel, Parry wrote another novel, as well as short stories, newspaper and magazine articles, and two mysteries. One of these stories became the rhyming picture book *Daddy's Home!,* a bedtime story about the relationship between a father and child. On her home page, Parry explained that she wrote the

book "because I never want to forget the joy of seeing my children run to their dad every day when he came home from work."

Biographical and Critical Sources

PERIODICALS

Booklist, February 15, 2009, Michael Cart, review of *Heart of a Shepherd,* p. 82.
Horn Book, May-June, 2009, Roger Sutton, review of *Heart of a Shepherd,* p. 304.
Kirkus Reviews, December 1, 2008, review of *Heart of a Shepherd.*
Publishers Weekly, June 22, 2009, "Spring Flying Starts," pp. 22-25.
School Library Journal, March, 2009, Sara Paulson, review of *Heart of a Shepherd,* p. 150.

ONLINE

Rosanne Parry Home Page, http://www.rosanneparry.com (January 19, 2010).*

* * *

PENN, Audrey 1947-
(Audrey Penn Zellan)

Personal

Born May 4, 1947, in Tacoma Park, MD; daughter of Harry Joseph (a lawyer and business manager) and Rose Penn; married Lester Zellan (a lighting technician), December 19, 1970 (divorced); married Joel Koren (employed by the U.S. Postal Service), May 4, 1980: children: (first marriage) Garth L.; (second marriage) Jayme S., Stefanie R. *Education:* Attended Washington Ballet School, 1951-55, National Ballet School, 1955-65; attended University of Maryland, 1967-68, and New York City dance and acting schools, 1968-70. *Politics:* "Independent."

Addresses

Home—Olney, MD. *E-mail*—audrey@audreypenn.com.

Career

Author of books for children. Professional actress, 1958-76; professional ballet dancer, 1962-76; writer, beginning 1975. Dance coach for Olympic gymnasts and ice skaters, 1973-75; dance teacher at Carnegie-Melon Univeristy and Southern Illinois University, beginning 1975. Lecturer; presenter at schools; participant in programs sponsored by Reading Is Fundamental and Kennedy Center Very Special Arts Festival.

Rosanne Parry's picture book Daddy's Home! *features humor-filled cartoon art by David Leonard.* (Illustration copyright © 2009 by Ideals Publications. Reproduced by permission.)

Audrey Penn (Photograph by Ken Ashman. Reproduced by permission.)

Awards, Honors

Happy Apple Told Me was presented by the U.S. State Department to School 157 Proletarskya Dicturtura I, Leningrad, USSR (now Russia), as a gift from the children of the United States, 1976, and was awarded the Mid-State Children's Library Selection Award, 1979; named among Outstanding Young Women of America, 1975; Mid-State Library Association Award, 1984, for *Blue out of Season;* Distinguished Achievement Award for Excellence in Educational Journalism, Educational Press Association of America, 1994, for *The Kissing Hand;* Helen Keating Ott Award for Outstanding Contribution to Children's Literature, 2002; iParenting Media Award, 2006.

Writings

FOR CHILDREN

(As Audrey Penn Zellan) *Happy Apple Told Me,* Independence Press (Independence, MO), 1975.

Blue out of Season, illustrated by C.S. Ewing, Great Ocean Publishers (Arlington, VA), 1984.

No Bones about Driftiss, illustrated by Judy V. Loving and Pam Post, McDonald & Woodward Pub. Co. (Blacksburg, VA), 1989.

Sassafras, illustrated by Ruth E. Harper, Child & Family Press (Washington, DC), 1995.

Feathers and Fur, illustrated by Monica Dunsky Wyrick, Child & Family Press (Washington, DC), 2000.

The Whistling Tree, illustrated by Barbara Leonard Gibson, Child & Family Press (Washington, DC), 2003.

A.D.D. Not B.A.D., illustrated by Monica Dunsky Wyrick, Child & Family Press (Washington, DC), 2003.

Mystery at Blackbeard's Cove, illustrated by Joshua Miller and Philip Howard, Tanglewood Press (Terre Haute, IN), 2004.

Blackbeard and the Gift of Silence, illustrated by Philip Howard, Tanglewood Press (Terre Haute, IN), 2007.

Blackbeard and the Sandstone Pillar: When Lightning Strikes, illustrated by Philip Howard, Tanglewood Press (Terre Haute, IN), 2007.

The Miracle Jar: A Hanukkah Story, illustrated by Lea Lyon, Tanglewood Press (Terre Haute, IN), 2008.

Blackbeard's Legacy: Shared/Time, illustrated by Philip Howard, Tanglewood Press (Terre Haute, IN), 2010.

"KISSING HAND" SERIES; FOR CHILDREN

The Kissing Hand, Child Welfare League of America (Washington, DC), 1993.

A Pocket Full of Kisses, illustrated by Barbara Leonard Gibson, Child & Family Press (Washington, DC), 2004.

A Kiss Goodbye, illustrated by Barbara L. Gibson, Tanglewood Press (Terre Haute, IN), 2007.

Chester Raccoon and the Big Bad Bully, illustrated by Barbara L. Gibson, Tanglewood Press (Terre Haute, IN), 2008.

Chester Raccoon and the Acorn Full of Memories, illustrated by Barbara L. Gibson, Tanglewood Press (Terre Haute, IN), 2009.

A Bedtime Kiss for Chester Raccoon, illustrated by Barbara L. Gibson, Tanglewood Press (Terre Haute, IN), 2010.

Chester the Brave, illustrated by Barbara L. Gibson, Tanglewood Press (Terre Haute, IN), 2011.

OTHER

Contributor to *The New Private Practice,* edited by Lynn Grodzki, W.W. Norton (New York, NY), 2002.

Adaptations

The Kissing Hand was adapted as a picture-book-with CD narrated by Heather Koren, music by Garth Koren, Tanglewood Press, 2007. *Chester Raccoon and the Big Bad Bully* was adapted as a picture-book-with CD narrated by Koren, Tanglewood Press, 2009.

Sidelights

Although she trained to be a professional ballet dancer, Audrey Penn saw her chosen career came to a tragic end in her mid-twenties when she lost her twenty-year battle with juvenile rheumatoid arthritis. While coaching gymnasts in the central United States, Penn took ill and was transported to Washington, DC. She was bed-ridden during her eighteen-month recovery, and she needed many more months to regain her body's basic strength and mobility. During this time the former dancer refocused her creative energies on another interest, writing, producing *Blue out of Season,* one of her many published works for children. Penn's books *The Kissing Hand,* and its sequels are geared for younger readers and introduce an engaging raccoon character that shares the same feelings and experiences of most youngsters venturing out into the wide world. In *A.D.D. Not B.A.D.* Penn helps younger elementary graders understand and find compassion for children who sometimes disrupt classroom activities without intending to, and she entertains middle-grade mystery buffs with her adventure series that includes *Blackbeard and the Gift of Silence.*

Featuring illustrations by several artists, Penn's "Kissing Hand" books include *A Pocket of Kisses, A Kiss Goodbye, Chester Raccoon and the Big Bad Bully,* and *Chester Raccoon and the Acorn Full of Memories* and focus on Chester Raccoon and his adventures. The first day of school provides a challenge for Chester in *The Kissing Hand,* while the pesky antics of his toddler brother Ronny are the focus of *A Pocket Full of Kisses.* In *A Kiss Goodbye* the raccoon is less than enthusiastic about joining his family in a move to a new tree hollow, and Chester must learn to deal with a tough young badger in *Chester Raccoon and the Big Bad Bully.* In *Chester Raccoon and the Acorn Full of Memories* he is told that his friend Skiddel Squirrel has had "an accident" and will not be returning to school, so his mother helps him make a lasting memory of his friend. In each

story, Chester and his family members affirm their affection for each other with a kiss to the palm, an action that gives the "Kissing Hand" series its name. Writing that Gibson contributes "sharply focused art" to *A Kiss Goodbye,* a *Publishers Weekly* contributor added that Penn's gentle story for this book "should provide reassurance to kids facing a similar transition." "Penn understands the powerful pull of old-fashioned sentiment," concluded another *Publishers Weekly* critic, observing that in *A Pocket Full of Kisses* the "poignant" story and detailed illustrations "seem to spring straight from the heart." Reviewing the same book for *School Library Journal,* Gay Lynn Van Vleck cited Penn's ability to "clearly express" the emotions of her animal characters. In reviewing *Chester Raccoon and the Acorn Full of Memories* in *School Library Journal,* Margaret Tassia cited Penn's "simple, direct dialogue" and added that the story's "reassuring tone . . . provides an opening for a discussion on death and remembering loved ones."

Other books by Penn include *Feathers and Fur,* the story of a cat that caretakes a nest of duck eggs in anticipation of a tasty dinner until tragedy strikes and the cat's concern turns to caring. In her series beginning with *Mystery at Blackbeard's Cove* Penn turns to older readers. Using a mix of fiction and nonfiction, she crafts the series of quandaries that confront four young teens living on Ocracoke Island after they discover more than just a cache of hidden pirate treasure.

A tale about a poor family trying to make the cooking oil last long enough to prepare the eight days of traditional holiday treats, *The Miracle Jar: A Hanukkah Story* was praised as "a satisfying holiday tale with a nostalgic feel" by *School Library Journal* contributor Teri Markson, and a *Kirkus Reviews* writer concluded that "Penn's storytelling" accurately conveys "the holiday's significance through joyful . . . celebration."

"I hope all authors enjoy their research and writing as much as I do . . . ," Penn once told *SATA.* "In my mysteries, I do what I ask my characters to do and often get into trouble doing it. But what fun. Imitation is life itself, so why not enjoy it?"

Biographical and Critical Sources

BOOKS

Smith, Jean Kennedy and George Plimpton, *Chronicles of Courage: Very Special Artists,* 1993.

PERIODICALS

Booklist, October 15, 2004, Carolyn Phelan, review of *A Pocket Full of Kisses,* p. 411; January 1, 2005, Cindy Welch, review of *Mystery at Blackbeard's Cove,* p. 860.

Penn's "Kissing Hand" books include **Chester Raccoon and the Big Bad Bully,** *featuring artwork by Barbara L. Gibson.* (Tanglewood Press, 2008. Illustration © 2008 by Barbara L. Gibson. Reproduced by permission.)

Children's Bookwatch, January, 2005, review of *Mystery at Blackbeard's Cove.*

Kirkus Reviews, November 1, 2008, review of *The Miracle Jar: A Hanukkah Story;* July 1, 2009, review of *Chester Raccoon and the Big Bad Bully.*

Publishers Weekly, February 24, 1975, review of *Happy Apple Told Me;* June 21, 2004, review of *A Pocket Full of Kisses,* p. 62; May 28, 2007, review of *A Kiss Goodbye,* p. 60.

School Library Journal, October, 2000, Lisa Gangemi Kropp, review of *Feathers and Fur,* p. 133; April, 2003, Linda Beck, review of *A.D.D. Not B.A.D.,* p. 136; January, 2005, Gay Lynn Van Vleck, review of *A Pocket Full of Kisses,* p. 96; September, 2008, Grace Oliff, review of *Chester Raccoon and the Big Bad Bully,* p. 156; October, 2008, Teri Markson, review of *The Miracle Jar,* p. 97; January, 2010, Margaret R. Tassia, review of *Chester Raccoon and the Acorn Full of Memories.*

ONLINE

Audrey Penn Home Page, http://audreypenn.com (January 15, 2010).

*   *   *

PERKINS, Lynne Rae 1956-

Personal

Born July 31, 1956, in Pittsburgh, PA; married Bill Perkins; children: Lucy, Frank. *Education:* Pennsylvania State University, B.F.A., 1978 (printmaking); University of Wisconsin—Milwaukee, M.A., 1981.

Addresses

Home—Cedar, MI.

Career

Children's book writer and illustrator. Formerly worked as a graphic designer in Boston, MA.

Awards, Honors

Boston Globe/Horn Book Honor Book designation, 1995, for *Home Lovely,* and 2004, for *Snow Music;* 100 Titles for Reading and Sharing selection, New York Public Library, *Booklist* Best Books designation, Blue Ribbon for Fiction, *Bulletin of the Center for Children's Books,* and American Library Association Best Book designation, all 1999, all for *All Alone in the Universe;* Newbery Medal, 2006, for *Criss Cross.*

Writings

SELF-ILLUSTRATED PICTURE BOOKS

Home Lovely, Greenwillow Books (New York, NY), 1995.

Clouds for Dinner, Greenwillow Books (New York, NY), 1997.

The Broken Cat, Greenwillow Books (New York, NY), 2002.

Snow Music, Greenwillow (New York, NY), 2003.

Pictures from Our Vacation, Greenwillow Books (New York, NY), 2007.

The Cardboard Piano, Greenwillow Books (New York, NY), 2008.

YOUNG-ADULT NOVELS

All Alone in the Universe, Greenwillow Books (New York, NY), 1999.

Criss Cross, Greenwillow (New York, NY), 2005.

ILLUSTRATOR

Sharon Phillips Denslow, *Georgie Lee,* Greenwillow Books (New York, NY), 2002.

Sidelights

In her picture books and longer fiction, Lynne Rae Perkins creates worlds that "are individual yet palpable, with people who could walk right into the real world without any adjustment," observed Deborah Stevenson in the *Bulletin of the Center for Children's Books.* Perkins' work is unusual because she uses illustrations even in her novels for older readers, an audience that is typically targeted with text alone. This combination, which can be found in the Newbery Award-winning novel *Criss Cross* as well as in Perkins' picture books, creates what Stevenson called an "offhand verisimilitude of moments in text and image that catch readers, hooking them on for the ride to wherever Perkins wants to take them."

Perkins' picture book *Home Lovely* concerns Janelle and her young daughter Tiffany, a girl who combats her loneliness by planting a garden near the family's trailer home. As the plants grow, Tiffany imagines a garden full of trees and flowers, but she is devastated when their mailman, Bob, compliments her instead on the wonderful-looking tomatoes, melons, and other vegetables she has mistakenly planted. A *Publishers Weekly* reviewer called *Home Lovely* "a spacious story that allows ordinary loneliness and unexpected kindness to assume their proper proportions." *Horn Book* contributor Martha V. Parravano praised Perkins for her "rich" characterizations and her theme that "a home does not have to be a palace to feel like one."

Clouds for Dinner, which is also accompanied by Perkins' pen-and-ink drawings, tells the story of Janet and her unorthodox home life. The family home is eighty-seven steps up, in an observatory, and the girl's astronomy-loving parents spend more time gazing at the sky than they do preparing dinner. Janet longs for an ordinary life, and her wish comes true when she is invited to stay with her suburban, traditional, and totally practical aunt. At her aunt's house the girl immerses herself in the slow pace of everyday life, including regular dinner and even a car wash, until the first time she tries to describe the magic of nature to her aunt. In a "strong text" accompanied by pictures that "do justice to the beauty of the northern Michigan landscape," according to *Horn Book* contributor Parravano, Perkins "once again celebrates the nontraditional."

The picture book *The Broken Cat* tells two parallel stories: in one tale Andy's cat is at the veterinarian, while the other goes back in time to when Andy's mother was a child and broke her arm. Called a "quirky, effective slice-of-life memoir" by a *Publishers Weekly* contributor, *The Broken Cat* was dubbed a "charming book" and a "captivating family story" by Caroline Ward in *School Library Journal*. "The cat (and . . . an arm) may be broken, but the picture book itself is indisputably a whole, imaginatively conceived and emotionally satisfying," wrote Parravano.

A winter scene in which the young narrator searches for his dog is the setting for *Snow Music*. The self-illustrated title features hints of where the dog has gone as the boy walks through a winter wonderland to find it. "Perkins spectacularly recreates the music of a winter's day," declared a *Publishers Weekly* critic, while Joanna Rudge Long commented in *Horn Book* that "onomatopoeic language, offbeat details, and skillfully nuanced tones of earth and sky all convey the charms of quiet observation." Shelly A. Robinson, writing in *Childhood Education*, noted that Perkins' "beautiful illustrations give a peaceful glimpse into the snowy world," while *Horn Book* contributor Rudine Sims Bishop deemed the text of *Snow Music* "a delightful word song." According to Dennis Duffy in the *New York Times*, "*Snow Music* offers a sophisticated experience" that is "accessible to all."

A summer holiday with a disappointing start is commemorated in a series of poignantly melancholy watercolor images in *Pictures from Our Vacation,* a picture book containing "the insights, warm humor, and close observation [readers have] . . . come to expect" from Perkins, according to *Horn Book* contributor Martha V. Parravano. The young narrator of this vacation story looks forward to visiting the farm that has been in her family for generations, but rain, mud, and overgrown vegetation are not the stuff of holidays. Fortunately, the farmhouse is soon full of family members—cousins, aunts, uncles, and grandparents—and the weeds and bad weather cease to matter. "Perkins is exhilaratingly free in her approach to the picture book form," asserted Parravano in her review of *Pictures from Our Vacation,* while Catherine Threadgill wrote in *School Library Journal* that the "deceptively simple, thoroughly engaging story" is paired with Perkins' "colorful, line-intensive illustrations" to produce "a journey into family dynamics, shared experience, and memory that is well worth the trip." In *Booklist,* Cooper praised Per-

kins' skill as an illustrator, writing that her images for the book show "overhead perspectives and . . . an eye for small details."

Debbie and Tina, the stars of *The Cardboard Piano,* are neighbors as well as the best of friends, but they also have many differences. Debbie now wants to learn to play the piano, and to share her activity with Tina she constructs a pretend piano made out of cardboard. When Tina balks at the prospect of learning scales on a cardboard keyboard, her reaction causes Debbie to ponder what friendship really means, and what it looks like. Nina Lindsay noted that the book's "straightforward yet emotionally complex narrative" combines with comic-book-style word balloons and Perkins' "intricate pen-and-ink and watercolor" art to craft a multi-dimensional exploration of "the delicate nature of friendship." The author/illustrator's message about "the necessity of understanding differences between friends" will be conveyed effectively to story-hour audiences, asserted *School Library Journal* contributor Barbara Elleman, and a *Kirkus Reviews* critic deemed the conversations between Tina and Debbie in *The Cardboard Piano* "pitch-perfect."

Cover of Lynne Rae Perkins' middle-grade novel **All Alone in the Universe,** *which follows a girl on an unusual journey.* (HarperTrophy, 2001. Cover art © 2001 by Lynne Rae Perkins. Reproduced by permission.)

In addition to creating picture books, Perkins has written several award-winning novels for teen readers. Called "a quiet story about growing up" by Roxanne Burg in *School Library Journal, All Alone in the Universe* follows best friends Debbie and Maureen as they grow apart during a school year full of changes and growth. "The agony of change is depicted well" in this powerful telling of "the all-too-familiar experience," commented Deborah Stevenson in her review of the book for the *Bulletin for the Center of Children's Books.*

Debbie returns in *Criss Cross,* which is told through a series of vignettes featuring a variety of different perspectives and follows the relationship between Debbie and new best friend Hector. Photographs, drawings, haiku, and dialogue are all used by Perkins to move the story along. Her "writing sparkles with inventive, often dazzling metaphors," wrote a *Kirkus Reviews* contributor, who found the novel to be "a poignantly funny coming-of-age story." According to B. Allison Gray in *School Library Journal,* "young teens will certainly relate to the self-consciousness and uncertainty of all of the characters, each of whom is straining toward clarity and awareness." As Myrna Marler wrote in her *Kliatt* review, *Criss Cross* "is not a novel for those addicted to adrenaline, but rewards those who patiently explore the story's treasures."

Biographical and Critical Sources

PERIODICALS

Booklist, September 1, 1999, Hazel Rochman, review of *All Alone in the Universe,* p. 127; March 15, 2005, Ilene Cooper, review of *The Broken Cat,* p. 1264; September 1, 2003, Francisca Goldsmith, review of *Snow Music,* p. 130; October 15, 2005, Gillian Engberg, review of *Criss Cross,* p. 47; May 1, 2007, Ilene Cooper, review of *Pictures from Our Vacation,* p. 88; January 1, 2009, Hazel Rochman, review of *The Cardboard Piano,* p. 90.

Bulletin of the Center for Children's Books, October, 1999, Deborah Stevenson, review of *All Alone in the Universe,* pp. 65-66.

Childhood Education, spring, 2005, Shelly A. Robinson, review of *Snow Music,* p. 167.

Horn Book, November, 1995, Martha V. Parravano, review of *Home Lovely,* p. 736; September, 1997, Martha V. Parravano, review of *Clouds for Dinner,* pp. 562-563; May-June, 2002, Martha V. Parravano, review of *The Broken Cat,* p. 320; November-December, 2003, Joanna Rudge Long, review of *Snow Music,* p. 734; September-October, 2005, Christine M. Hepperman, review of *Criss Cross,* p. 585; July-August, 2006, Lynne Rae Perkins, transcript of Newbery Medal acceptance speech, p. 377, and Virginia Duncan, interview with Perkins, p. 385; May-June, 2007, Martha V. Parravano, review of *Pictures from Our Vacation,* p. 273; September-October, 2008, Nina Lindsay, review of *The Cardboard Piano,* p. 571.

Kirkus Reviews, June 15, 1997, review of *Clouds for Dinner,* p. 955; August 15, 2005, review of *Criss Cross,* p. 920; September 15, 2008, review of *The Cardboard Piano.*

Kliatt, September, 2005, Myrna Marler, review of *Criss Cross,* p. 12.

New York Times, January 18, 2004, Dennis Duffy, review of *Snow Music;* August 12, 2007, Julie Just, review of *Pictures from Our Vacation,* p. 17.

Publishers Weekly, October 9, 1995, review of *Home Lovely,* p. 86; October 18, 1999, review of *All Alone in the Universe,* p. 84; December 20, 1999, Kate Pavao, "Writing from Experience" (interview), p. 25; April 1, 2002, review of *The Broken Cat,* p. 81; October 27, 2003, review of *Snow Music,* p. 67; October 31, 2005, review of *Criss Cross,* p. 58; June 11, 2007, review of *Pictures from Our Vacation,* p. 59.

School Library Journal, October, 1999, Roxanne Burg, review of *All Alone in the Universe,* pp. 156-157; June, 2002, Caroline Ward, review of *The Broken Cat,* p. 107; November, 2003, Carolyn Janssen, review of *Snow Music,* p. 112; September, 2005, B. Allison Gray, review of *Criss Cross,* p. 210; March, 2006, Barb Barstow, "Private I," pp. 66-69; June, 2007, Catherine Threadgill, review of *Pictures from Our Vacation,* p. 119; November, 2008, Barbara Elleman, review of *The Cardboard Piano,* p. 98.

Washington Post, January 25, 2006, "Lynne Rae Perkins Wins Newbery Medal for *Criss Cross,*" p. C3.

ONLINE

Bulletin of the Center for Children's Books Online, http://bccb.lis.uiuc.edu/ (February 1, 2000), Deborah Stevenson, "Rising Star: Lynne Rae Perkins."

Lynne Rae Perkins Home Page, http://www.lynnerae perkins.com (January 15, 2010).*

*   *   *

PERRIMAN, Cole
See PERRIN, Pat

*   *   *

PERRIMAN, Cole
See COLEMAN, Wim

*   *   *

PERRIN, Pat
(Cole Perriman, a joint pseudonym)

Personal

Born in VA; married Wim Coleman (a writer); children: Monse. *Education:* Duke University, B.A. (English); Hollins College, degree (liberal studies); University of Georgia, degree (art theory and criticism).

Addresses

Home—San Miguel de Allende, Gto., Mexico. *E-mail*—wim-pat@playsonideas.com.

Career

Writer and visual artist. Formerly worked as an art teacher.

Member

PEN (San Miguel de Allende chapter).

Writings

FOR CHILDREN

(Adaptor with Wim Coleman) *Marilyn Ferguson's Book of Pragmagic: Pragmatic Magic for Everyday Living: Ten Years of Scientific Breakthroughs, Exciting Ideas, and Personal Experiments That Can Profoundly Change Your Life,* illustrated by Kristin Ferguson, Pocket Books (New York, NY), 1990.

(With Wim Coleman) *The Jamais Vu Papers; or, Misadventures in the Worlds of Science, Myth, and Magic,* Harmony Books (New York, NY), 1991.

(Reteller with Wim Coleman) Charles Dickens, *A Tale of Two Cities,* Perfection Learning (Logan, IA), 1994.

(With Wim Coleman) *Retold Classic Chillers,* illustrated by Sue Cornelison, Perfection Learning (Logan, IA), 1997.

(With Wim Coleman) *Crime and Punishment: The Colonial Period to the New Frontier,* Discovery Enterprises (Carlisle, MA), 1998.

(Editor and author of introduction) *Architecture: An Image for America,* Discovery Enterprises (Carlisle, MA), 1998.

(With Wim Coleman) *Aviation: Early Flight in America,* Discovery Enterprises (Carlisle, MA), 1999.

(With Wim Coleman) *Sister Anna,* Discovery Enterprises, Ltd. (Carlisle, MA), 2000.

(With Wim Coleman) *The Declaration of Independence,* Discovery Enterprises (Carlisle, MA), 2000.

(With Arden Bowers) *The Native Americans,* Discovery Enterprises (Carlisle, MA), 2000.

The Revolutionary War, Discovery Enterprises (Carlisle, MA), 2000.

(Editor and author of introduction) *Slavery,* Discovery Enterprises (Carlisle, MA), 2000.

(With Wim Coleman) *George Washington: Creating a Nation,* Enslow Publishers (Berkeley Heights, NJ), 2004.

(With Wim Coleman) *The Mystery of the Piltdown Skull,* Perfection Learning (Logan, IA), 2004.

(With Wim Coleman) *The Mystery of the Cardiff Giant,* Perfection Learning (Logan, IA), 2004.

(With Wim Coleman) *The Mystery of the Murdered Playwright,* Perfection Learning (Logan, IA), 2004.

Getting Started: America's Melting Pot, Discovery Enterprises (Carlisle, MA), 2004.

Getting Started: Our Fifty United States, Discovery Enterprises (Carlisle, MA), 2004.

(With Wim Coleman) *The Mystery of the Vanishing Slaves,* Perfection Learning (Logan, IA), 2004.

(With Wim Coleman) *Colonial Williamsburg,* MyReportLinks.com Books (Berkeley Heights, NJ), 2005.

(With Wim Coleman) *Martin Luther King, Jr., National Historic Site,* MyReportLinks.com Books (Berkeley Heights, NJ), 2005.

(With Wim Coleman) *The Alamo,* MyReportLinks.com Books (Berkeley Heights, NJ), 2005.

(With Pat Perrin) *The American Civil War,* Greenhaven Press (San Diego, CA), 2005.

(With Wim Coleman) *Iraq in the News: Past, Present, and Future,* MyReportLinks.com Books (Berkeley Heights, NJ), 2006.

(With Wim Coleman) *Osama Bin Laden,* Greenhaven Press (Farmington Hills, MI), 2006.

(With Wim Coleman) *The Amazing Erie Canal and How a Big Ditch Opened Up the West,* MyReportLinks.com Books (Berkeley Heights, NJ), 2006.

(With Wim Coleman) *The Rebellious Californians and the Brave Struggle to Join the Nation,* MyReportLinks. com Books (Berkeley Heights, NJ), 2006.

(With Wim Coleman) *The Transcontinental Railroad and the Great Race to Connect the Nation,* MyReportLinks.com Books (Berkeley Heights, NJ), 2006.

(With Wim Coleman) *What Made the Wild West Wild,* MyReportLinks.com Books (Berkeley Heights, NJ), 2006.

(Reteller with Wim Coleman) *Robert Louis Stevenson's Treasure Island,* illustrated by Greg Rebis, Stone Arch Books (Mankato, MN), 2007.

(With Pat Perrin) *Anna's World,* Chiron, 2008.

(With Wim Coleman) *Racism on Trial: From the Medgar Evers Murder Case to "Ghosts of Mississippi",* Enslow Publishers (Berkeley Heights, NJ), 2009.

Contributor to books, including *Retold Northern European Myths,* and *Retold World Myths,* Perfection Learning (Logan, IA), 1993; *Retold Edgar Allan Poe,* Perfection Learning, 2000; *Retold Jack London,* 2001; *Retold American Hauntings,* 2001; *Retold Classics: O. Henry,* 2002; and *World War II Chronicle,* Publications International (Lincolnwood, IL), 2007.

OTHER

(With Wim Coleman, under joint pseudonym Cole Perriman) *Terminal Games* (adult mystery novel), Bantam (New York, NY), 1994.

Biographical and Critical Sources

PERIODICALS

Booklist, August, 2005, Hazel Rochman, review of *The Alamo,* p. 2013; October, 2006, Roger Leslie, review of *The Amazing Erie Canal and How a Big Ditch Opened Up the West,* p. 66.

Kirkus Reviews, November 1, 2008, review of *Anna's World.*

School Library Journal, March, 2005, Andrew Medlar, review of *George Washington: Creating a Nation,* p. 226; May, 2005, Jody Kopple, review of *The Alamo,* p. 146; April, 2006, Ann W. Moore, review of *Osama bin Laden,* p. 152; December, 2006, Kathleen Gruver, review of *Iraq in the News: Past, Present, and Future,* p. 160; January, 2007, Deanna Romriell, review of *What Made the Wild West Wild,* p. 146, and Joel Bangilan, review of *Treasure Island,* p. 159; March, 2009, Sharon Morrison, review of *Anna's World,* p. 142.

ONLINE

Pat Perrin and Wim Coleman Home Page, http://www.playsonideas.com (January 10, 2010).*

*   *   *

PETERS, Bernadette 1948-

Personal

Born Bernadette Lazzara, February 28, 1948, in New York, NY; daughter of Peter (a truck driver) and Marguerite (a homemaker) Lazzara; married Michael Wittenberg (an investment advisor), July 20, 1996 (died 2005). *Education:* Attended Quintano's School for Young Professionals (New York, NY); studied acting with David Le Grant, tap dancing with Oliver McCool III, and singing with Jim Gregory.

Addresses

Home—New York, NY. *Agent*—Jeff Hunter, William Morris Agency, 1325 Avenue of the Americas, New York, NY 10019.

Career

Actor, singer, and dancer. Stage appearances include *The Most Happy Fella,* 1959; *Gypsy* (touring production), 1961-62; *This Is Google,* 1962; *Riverwind,* 1966; *The Penny Friend,* 1966-67; *The Girl in the Freudian Slip* (Broadway debut), 1967; *Johnny No-Trump,* 1967; *Curley McDimple,* 1967-68; *George M!,* 1968; *Dames at Sea,* 1968-69; *La Strada,* 1969; *W.C.* (touring production), 1971; *Nevertheless They Laugh,* 1971; *On the Town,* 1971-72; *Tartuffe,* 1972-73; *Mack and Mabel,* 1974; *Sally and Marsha,* 1982; *Sunday in the Park with George,* 1983, 1984-85; *Song and Dance,* 1985-86; *Into the Woods,* 1987-89; *The Goodbye Girl,* 1993; *Annie Get Your Gun,* 1999; *Gypsy,* 2003; and *A Night with Bernadette Peters* (touring production), 2009-10. Recording artist; recordings include *Bernadette,* 1980, *Now Playing,* 1981, *Sondheim: A Celebration at Carnegie Hall,* 1991; *Bernadette Peters Live at Carnegie Hall, I'll Be Your Baby Tonight,* 1996; *Sondheim, Etc.,*

Bernadette Peters (Photograph by Firooz Zahedi. Courtesy of EMI Classics/Angel Records.)

1997, *Bernadette Peters Loves Rodgers & Hammerstein,* 2002, *Sondheim, Etc., Etc.,* 2005, and *A Duck in New York City* (for children), 2006. Film appearances include *Ace Eli and Rodger of the Skies,* 1973, *The Longest Yard,* 1974, *W.C. Fields and Me,* 1976, *Silent Movie,* 1976, *The Jerk,* 1979, *Tulips,* 1981, *Pennies from Heaven,* 1981, *Pink Cadillac,* 1989, *Slaves of New York,* 1989, *Alice,* 1990, *Impromptu,* 1991, *Let It Snow,* 2001, and *It Runs in the Family,* 2003. Television appearances include numerous specials; special appearances on series, including *Ally McBeal;* and television films, including *What the Deaf Man Heard, Fall from Grace, The Last Best Year, Bobbie's Girl,* and *Prince Charming.* Advocate on behalf of organizations, including Broadway Cares/Equity Fights AIDS; cofounder, with Mary Tyler Moore, of Broadway Barks (annual animal adoption event), 1999.

Awards, Honors

Theatre World award, 1968; Drama Desk Award for outstanding performance, 1968, for *Dames at Sea;* Theatre World Award, 1968, for *George M!;* Antoinette Perry ("Tony") Award nomination for best actress in a musical, 1972, for *On the Town;* Best of Las Vegas Award, 1980; Golden Globe Award for best film actress in a musical/comedy, 1981, for *Pennies from Heaven;* Tony Award nomination, 1983, for *Sunday in the Park with George;* Tony Award, and Drama Desk Award for best actress in a musical, both 1986, both for *Song and Dance;* Distinguished Performance Award, Drama

League of New York, 1986; Hasty Pudding Woman of the Year Award, Harvard University, 1987; Tony Award nomination, 1992, for *The Goodbye Girl;* inducted into Theatre Hall of Fame, 1996; Drama Desk Award for outstanding actress, Outer Critics Circle Award for outstanding actress in a musical, and Tony Award for best actress in a musical, all 1999, for *Annie Get Your Gun;* named Police Athletic League Woman of the Year, 1999; Actors Fund of America Artistic Achievement Award, 1999; New York Heroes Award, National Academy of Recording Arts and Sciences, 2000; honorary doctorate, Hofstra University, 2002; inducted into Hollywood Bowl Hall of Fame, 2002; Drama Desk nomination, and Tony Award nomination, both 2003, both for *Gypsy;* Matrix Award, New York Women in Communications, 2004; honored by National Dance Institute, 2009; Sarah Siddons Actress of the Year Award; Grammy awards (with others) for original-cast albums, and nominations for *Bernadette Peters Loves Rodgers & Hammerstein, Bernadette Peters Live at Carnegie Hall,* and *I'll Be Your Baby Tonight.*

Writings

Broadway Barks (with CD), illustrated by Liz Murphy, Chronicle Books (Maplewood, NJ), 2008
Stella Is a Star (with CD), illustrated by Liz Murphy, Chronicle Books (Maplewood, NJ), 2010.

Vocalist on CD accompanying picture book *Dewey Doo-It Helps Owlie Fly Again,* illustrated by Jean Gillmore, Randall-Fraser Publishing (Irvine, CA), 2005.

Sidelights

In a career spanning over half a century, award-winning actress and singer Bernadette Peters rose from an early stint as a child star to her status as one of the most beloved performers on Broadway. In addition to her roles in Broadway musicals and in concert, Peters has appeared in films and on television—including an appearance with Jim Henson's Muppets—where her long, curly red hair and round-faced, wide-eyed enthusiasm has won her countless fans.

Peters grew up in New York City, where her father drove a bread truck. Her mother encouraged Peters to develop her performance skills, enrolling her in singing and tap-dancing lessons. By age ten Peters was appearing on local television programs, and she quickly moved to the stage. At age thirteen, she starred in a touring production of *Gypsy,* although she left acting to focus on her high-school academics and graduated from Quintano's School for Young Professionals in 1966. Her Broadway debut came the following year, in a production of *Johnny No-Trump,* and numerous other roles have followed. By the 1970s Peters had amassed credits both in film and on television, where she appeared on *The Muppet Show* and *The Carol Burnett Show.* Her

first movies included *The Jerk,* a comedy in which she played the wife of Steve Martin, as well as *Pennies from Heaven,* and she balanced her career on film with Broadway roles in musicals such as *Into the Woods, Annie Get Your Gun,* and *Gypsy,* as well as a successful career as a singer. Among her many awards are two Antoinette Perry ("Tony") awards, several Emmy Award nominations and a Golden Globe award; her performance in the 1999 revival of the popular musical *Annie Get Your Gun* earned Peters a Drama Desk award, an Outer Critics Circle award, and her second Tony award for best actress in a musical.

In 1999 Peters used her status as a celebrity to help the many animals confined in New York City's animal shelters. Together with actress Mary Tyler Moore, she founded Broadway Barks, an annual event that matches homeless dogs with loving families in the city. This work inspired Peters to write the children's books *Broadway Barks* and *Stella Is a Star,* both of which include a CD featuring a song performed by Peters. Portions of the proceeds of both books benefit the Broadway Barks charity.

In *Broadway Barks* readers meet a homeless terrier named Douglas, who lives in a city park and finds food and shelter where he can. Douglas sees his circumstances change when a friendly lady with curly red hair

*Performer Peters channels her creative talents into **Broadway Barks,** a picture book featuring multimedia artwork by Liz Murphy.* (Blue Apple Books, 2008. Illustration copyright © 2008 by Liz Murphy. Reproduced by permission.)

takes him for a ride in a taxi and he finds a new home and a new name: Kramer. In *Publishers Weekly* a contributor described *Broadway Barks* as "a sweet if slight story" that features "roughhewn, mixed-media collage" art by Liz Murphy, and a *Kirkus Reviews* writer commended Peters' picture book as "not-too-self-aggrandizing and wholly goodhearted." *School Library Journal* contributor Kathy Krasniewicz described canine character Douglas as "a cute concoction of gray flannel and a fine . . . mascot for [Peters'] . . . message."

Biographical and Critical Sources

PERIODICALS

Kirkus Reviews, May 15, 2008, review of *Broadway Barks.*
Publishers Weekly, May 5, 2008, review of *Broadway Barks,* p. 61.
School Library Journal, August, 2008, Kathy Krasniewicz, review of *Broadway Barks,* p. 100.

ONLINE

Bernadette Peters Home Page, http://www.bernadette peters.com (February 1, 2010).*

*   *   *

PHILBRICK, Rodman 1951-
(William R. Dantz, Chris Jordan, W.R. Philbrick)

Personal

Born 1951, in Boston, MA; married Lynn Harnett (a novelist and journalist), 1980. *Hobbies and other interests:* Fishing.

Addresses

Home—ME; Florida Keys. *Office*—P.O. Box 4149, Portsmouth, NH 03802-4149.

Career

Writer, 1987—. Formerly worked as a longshoreman and boat builder.

Awards, Honors

Best Novel award, Private Eye Writers of America, 1993, for *Brothers and Sinners;* Judy Lopez Memorial Award honor book designation, 1994, Nebraska Golden Sower Award, Wyoming Soaring Eagle Award, 1997, Charlotte Award, New York State Reading Association, and Best Young-Adult Book of the Year and Recom-

Rodman Philbrick (Photograph by Lynn Harnett. Reproduced by permission.)

mended Book for the Young-Adult Reluctant Reader designations, both American Library Association (ALA), all for *Freak the Mighty;* Best Young-Adult Book of the Year selection, ALA, Maine Lupine Award, Isinglass Teen Read Award, and Maryland Readers' Medal, all 2001, and YALSA 100 Best of the Best Books for the 21st Century, all for *The Last Book in the Universe.*

Writings

YOUNG-ADULT NOVELS

Freak the Mighty, Blue Sky Press (New York, NY), 1993, published as *The Mighty,* Scholastic, Inc. (New York, NY), 1997.
The Fire Pony, Scholastic, Inc. (New York, NY), 1996.
Max the Mighty, Scholastic, Inc. (New York, NY), 1998.
(With wife, Lynn Harnett) *Abduction,* Scholastic, Inc. (New York, NY), 1998.
REM World: Where Nothing Is Real and Everything Is about to Disappear, Scholastic, Inc. (New York, NY), 2000.
The Last Book in the Universe, Scholastic, Inc. (New York, NY), 2000.
The Journal of Douglas Allen Deeds: The Donner Party Expedition (historical fiction), Scholastic, Inc. (New York, NY), 2001.
The Young Man and the Sea, Blue Sky Press (New York, NY), 2004.

The Mostly True Adventures of Homer P. Figg, Blue Sky Press (New York, NY), 2009.

Also author of novel *The Tinycrawlers,* serialized in eight installments in *Boston Globe,* 2006. Adaptor of *Freak the Mighty* as one-and two-act plays.

"HOUSE ON CHERRY STREET" SERIES; FOR YOUNG ADULTS

(With Lynn Harnett) *The Haunting,* Scholastic, Inc. (New York, NY), 1995.
(With Lynn Harnett) *The Horror,* Scholastic, Inc. (New York, NY), 1995.
(With Lynn Harnett) *The Final Nightmare,* Scholastic, Inc. (New York, NY), 1995.

"VISITORS" SERIES; FOR YOUNG ADULTS

(With Lynn Harnett) *Strange Invaders,* Scholastic, Inc. (New York, NY), 1997.
(With Lynn Harnett) *Things,* Scholastic, Inc. (New York, NY), 1997.
(With Lynn Harnett) *Brain Stealers,* Scholastic, Inc. (New York, NY), 1997.

"WEREWOLF CHRONICLES" SERIES; FOR YOUNG ADULTS

Night Creature, Scholastic, Inc. (New York, NY), 1996.
Children of the Wolf, Scholastic, Inc. (New York, NY), 1996.
The Wereing, Scholastic, Inc. (New York, NY), 1996.

FOR ADULTS

Brothers and Sinners, Dutton (New York, NY), 1993.
Dark Matter, Xlibris (Philadelphia, PA), 2000.
Coffins, Forge (New York, NY), 2002.

ADULT MYSTERY NOVELS; AS W.R. PHILBRICK

Shooting Star, St. Martin's Press (New York, NY), 1982.
Slow Dancer, St. Martin's Press (New York, NY), 1984.
Shadow Kills: A J.D. Hawkins Mystery, Beaufort (New York, NY), 1985.
Ice for the Eskimo: A J.D. Hawkins Mystery, Beaufort (New York, NY), 1986.
The Neon Flamingo: A T.D. Stash Crime Adventure, New American Library (New York, NY), 1987.
The Crystal Blue Persuasion: A T.D. Stash Crime Adventure, New American Library (New York, NY), 1988.
Tough Enough: A T.D. Stash Crime Adventure, New American Library (New York, NY), 1989.
Paint It Black: A J.D. Hawkins Mystery, St. Martin's Press (New York, NY), 1989.
The Big Chip, illustrated by Bruce Jensen, Microsoft Press (Redmond, WA), 1990.
Walk on the Water: A J.D. Hawkins Mystery, St. Martin's Press (New York, NY), 1991.

UNDER PSEUDONYM WILLIAM R. DANTZ

Pulse, Avon (New York, NY), 1990.
The Seventh Sleeper, Morrow (New York, NY), 1991.
Hunger, Tor (New York, NY), 1992.
Nine Levels Down, Forge (New York, NY), 1999.

Author of unproduced screenplays *The Fire Pony, Stop Time,* and *Nine Levels Down,* based on his novels.

"RANDALL SHANE" SERIES; UNDER PSEUDONYM CHRIS JORDAN

Taken, Mira (Don Mills, Ontario, Canada), 2006.
Trapped, Mira (Don Mills, Ontario, Canada), 2007.
Torn, Mira (Don Mills, Ontario, Canada), 2008.

Adaptations

The motion picture *The Mighty* was adapted from Philbrick's novel *Freak the Mighty* and produced by Miramax, 1998. Several of Philbrick's novels have been adapted as audiobooks, including *The Mostly True Adventures of Homer P. Figg,* Listening Library, 2009.

Cover of Philbrick's young-adult novel **The Last Book in the Universe,** *featuring cover art by David Shannon.* (Jacket illustration © 2001 by David Shannon. Reproduced by permission of Scholastic, Inc.)

Sidelights

A prolific writer who has published under several pen names, Rodman Philbrick started his career as an author of adult thrillers before shifting his interest to young-adult fiction. Gaining national accolades for his debut YA novel, *Freak the Mighty,* Philbrick has gone on to lead something of a double life, continuing to pen adult mysteries under his own name as well as under the pseudonyms W.R. Philbrick, William R. Dantz, and Chris Jordan while also adding to his list of teen novels. Philbrick sometimes works in collaboration with his wife, journalist and author Lynn Harnett, and his young-adult novels include *Freak the Mighty, The Fire Pony, The Last Book in the Universe,* and *The Mostly True Adventures of Homer P. Figg.*

Born in Boston, Massachusetts, Philbrick grew up close to the New England coast, where one of his hobbies, fishing, is a prominent regional industry. Although he had completed a novel-length work by the time he was in high school, adulthood meant focusing on the day-to-day necessities of earning a living. Drawing his livelihood from the sea in traditional New England fashion, Philbrick worked as both a longshoreman and a boat builder, but still found enough time to complete several novels. Unfortunately those works were not accepted for publication. In 1982, however, the author made his literary debut with *Shooting Star,* published under the name W.R. Philbrick.

Philbrick's novel *Slow Dancer,* featuring female sleuth Connie Kale, was released two years later, and by 1987 the writer had left his other occupations behind to devote himself to novel writing full time. Working out the twists and turns of plots to mysteries and detective novels now became his stock in trade and resulted in books such as *Dark Matter* and *Brothers and Sinners,* the latter earning the Private Eye Writers of America's best novel award in 1993.

The move from adult whodunits to teen fiction happened, as Philbrick recalled, "more or less by accident," and was inspired by a boy from his neighborhood. "I used to see two kids walking down the street near our apartment. One of them was a big guy and he sometimes carried the small kid on his shoulders. Later my wife and I became friends with the small boy's mother. We discovered that the small boy had Morquio Syndrome, which meant he would never grow to be more than three feet tall. He was extraordinarily bright, had a love for words and books, and an interest in sci-fi and Arthurian legends. About a year after his tragic death, I got an idea for a story inspired by his very special personality. The story is fiction, but I never would have written it if I hadn't known the boy himself."

Inspired by the imagination and courage of this young neighbor, Philbrick's *Freak the Mighty* has been translated into numerous languages and read in classrooms throughout the world. The novel was described by *School Library Journal* contributor Libby K. White as

Cover of Philbrick's award-winning novel Freak the Mighty, *featuring artwork by David Shannon.* (Illustration copyright © 1993 by David Shannon. Reproduced by permission of Scholastic, Inc.)

"a wonderful story of triumph over imperfection, shame, and loss." In the book middle-school narrator Maxwell Kane feels doubly cursed. Not only is he clumsy, big boned, and condemned to an academic life of torment as a learning-disabled kid, but his dad is in prison for killing Maxwell's mom and the whole town knows about it. A loner, he spends much of his time in his room in the basement of his grandparents' house. Then something happens to change the dull despair of each passing day: a new boy moves in next door who Max recognizes from his day-care days. The new boy, Kevin, is wheelchair-bound due to a birth defect that has prevented him from growing physically; however, he has an imagination and an energy that allow him to soar mentally. Soon Max and "Freak"—Kevin's name for himself—are the best of friends. With Kevin sitting astride Max's broad shoulders, the two dub their joint self "Freak the Mighty," channeling the one's strength and the other's intelligence in order to confront the taunting of other children and get out and explore their world. Caught up in the legend of King Arthur and his noble knights, the two boys search for causes to battle, one of which proves scary: "Killer" Kane returns and kidnaps Max, who escapes only with Kevin's help. Sadly, the effects of Morquio Syndrome eventually overtake Kevin, and he finally dies. Now on his own, Max "is left with the memory of an extraordinary relationship," as well as a heightened sense of his own worth and a more optimistic outlook on his future, according to White.

The winner of numerous awards, *Freak the Mighty* has been lauded by reviewers for its sensitivity and appeal even among reluctant readers. *Bulletin of the Center for Children's Books* reviewer Deborah Stevenson praised Philbrick's novel as "a sentimental story written with energy and goofy humor instead of sentimentality," while *Horn Book,* contributor Nancy Vasilakis called it "a fascinating excursion into the lives of people whose freakishness proves to be a thin cover for their very human existence." Stephanie Zvirin labeled *Freak the Mighty* "both riveting and poignant, with solid characters, brisk pacing, and even a little humor to carry us along" in her *Booklist* review.

In addition to inspiring a feature film, *Freak the Mighty* also sparked a sequel, *Max the Mighty,* which was published in 1998. Reuniting with narrator Max Kane, readers are also introduced to Max's new friend, Rachel, a preteen who has escaped so far into her hobby of reading that fellow students refer to her as the "Worm." What prompts Rachel's reading is her need to mentally escape from the abusive household in which she has found herself since her mom's remarriage. Unfortunately, books cannot save her from her unstable stepdad, dubbed the "Undertaker" because of his creepy demeanor. The much older Max, now aged fourteen, eventually agrees to help Rachel run away and find her real father. On their way to Chivalry, Montana, in search of Rachel's real dad, the pair encounters a colorful cast of characters ranging from wild dogs to con artists, and has numerous adventures, all the while trying to elude both the Undertaker, who follows in pursuit, and the police, who are hunting Max in response to the kidnapping charges filed by Rachel's stepfather.

Noting that the ending of *Max the Mighty* is filled with "surprises" and is "more upbeat" than Philbrick's previous YA novel, a *Publishers Weekly* reviewer called the book a "rip-roaring, heartwarming escapade." Although Nancy Vasilakis wrote that several of the story's zany characters "sometimes threaten to stretch the reader's sense of reality to its limits," she concluded in her *Horn Book* review that Max and Rachel "grab our attention and engage your heart."

The Fire Pony also uses Montana as its setting and features a young man as its narrator. In the story, half-brothers Joe and Roy Dilly are on their own, having fled from ranch to ranch after the habits of arsonist Joe put an end to job after job. Now Joe has found work at the Bar None Ranch, where the owner, Nick Jessup, raises Arabian horses. The older of the two brothers, Joe has a talent for both blacksmithing and saddle-breaking horses and soon becomes a prized employee. While remaining concerned that his older brother's fascination with fire will ultimately force the two to go on

the run again, eleven-year-old Roy begins to settle in at the ranch. Trying to follow in Joe's footsteps, he attempts to break a palomino filly named Lady Luck, which Jessup has promised to Roy if he is successful. Ultimately, Roy rides Lady Luck to glory at a rodeo, despite the efforts of another man named Mullins to thwart the boy's success and get the horse for himself. Older brother Joe, angered at Mullins, first accosts the man, then goes into a hay field and sets a fire which quickly grows out of control and ultimately threatens the life of Roy and Lady Luck.

Noting the complex personalities of the two brothers in *The Fire Pony*, *Horn Book* contributor Martha V. Parravano commented that Philbrick's portrait of "the scarred but spirited Roy is near flawless," while Joe is "loving and funny and talented even as he is scary and unpredictable and disturbed." Praising Joe's rescue effort as the high point of the novel, *School Library Journal* contributor Christina Linz noted that *The Fire Pony* "has plenty of action and suspense and is a good choice for reluctant readers."

"The idea for *The Fire Pony* came while Lynn and I were driving across the Southwest," Philbrick once explained. "I loved the landscape, and when we got to

Philbrick mixes fantasy and adventure in his novel **REM** World, *featuring cover art by Greg Call.* (Cover illustration copyright © 2001 by Greg Call. Reproduced by permission of Scholastic, Inc.)

California the state was suffering from a rash of fires. The two ideas combined into a story about a boy and his older brother, who is not only a talented farrier, but a sometimes arsonist. The idea from that part may have been inspired by my love of Faulkner, in particular his story 'The Barn Burner.'"

While *The Fire Pony, Freak the Mighty,* and *Max the Mighty* are "issue-oriented" novels—learning disabilities, single parenting, and family violence are just a few of the subjects covered—Philbrick has also collaborated with his wife, Lynn Harnett, on several entertaining novels that also contain a salting of typical teen concerns in their plots. Because of the fast-paced action and the relatively simple vocabulary in such books as *The Haunting, Abduction,* and *Children of the Wolf,* they have been praised for their ability to motivate even reluctant readers to turn the page and see what happens next. Part of their success may be credited to Philbrick and Harnett's ability to devise a system of working together that seems to work well. As Philbrick explained, "Lynn and I discuss story ideas. Then I write an outline and Lynn does all the heavy lifting, writing the first draft of the chapters. After more discussion we polish up a finished draft."

"I don't have any 'lessons' in mind when I write about adolescent kids," Philbrick explained in response to a question regarding his opinion on the importance of inserting a "message" in books for young-adult readers. "Most of what I write, and the first person 'voice' I use, comes out of my own memories of being that age. The books Lynn Harnett and I collaborate on are intended to be easy-reading mass market paperbacks. My own work might be considered slightly more 'serious,' but, I hope, still entertaining enough to hold a reader's attention. For the most part I find that all young readers really want is a good story, of whatever type." However, Philbrick also expressed delight that the techniques he uses in creating his adult mysteries—"how to keep a reader turning pages to find out what happens next," for example—have been of value in his solo YA projects.

Philbrick's slightly "slightly more serious" return to solo projects include *The Last Book in the Universe* and *REM World: Where Nothing Is Real and Everything Is about to Disappear.* In the latter novel ten-year-old Arthur Woodbury has a weight problem that makes him the object of his classmates' jokes. He buys a weight-loss device from the REM World Products company, which promises that the contraption will help him slim down while he sleeps. However, Arthur does not follow the instructions for the new gadget properly, and he is instead transported to REM world, with little hope of getting back home. Arthur's arrival in REM world also disrupts the laws of the magical universe, placing its existence in jeopardy. In order to save the REM universe and return to his own world, Arthur embarks on a series of adventures involving a diverse group of fantastic creatures. With the help of these beings, Arthur is able to accomplish his twin goals, and in the process

loses weight and develops courage. A *Publishers Weekly* reviewer praised *REM World,* noting that its "imaginative characters" make it a "fun and fast-paced read." *School Library Journal* reviewer Nina Lindsay found the plot a bit thin, but praised the book for its "action-packed, cliff-hanging chapters."

The Last Book in the Universe is a science-fiction novel set in a dystopic future, where civilization as we know it has been destroyed by a major earthquake. A few people have created a new, better, isolated society called "Eden"; the unlucky individuals who remain behind and face deadly pollution and rule by brutal gangs. Many of those who live in the "Urbs," as the non-Eden part of the world is known, escape from reality through virtual-reality movies inserted directly into their brains via mind probes. The book's protagonist, Spaz, does not have this option—his epilepsy (the source of his nickname) prevents him from using them. A reluctant gang member, Spaz ends up befriending an old man named Ryter whom the teen was sent to rob, and together the two set out on a quest to save Spaz's critically ill foster sister, Bean. Their party picks up several other members along the way, including Lanaya, a resident of Eden; and Little Face, an orphan.

"Philbrick has created some memorable characters in this fast-paced adventure," Debbie Carton declared in *Booklist,* adding that *The Last Book in the Universe* "will leave readers musing over humanity's future." *School Library Journal* reviewer Louise L. Sherman also noted the "strong and provocative messages" in the book, while *Kliatt* contributor Paula Rohrlick thought that "Spaz's adventures and moral dilemmas in a strange and scary setting, vividly told from his viewpoint, make this an absorbing story with some depth to it." A *Publishers Weekly* critic praised other aspects of *The Last Book in the Universe,* noting that "Philbrick's creation of a futuristic dialect, combined with striking descriptions of a postmodern civilization, will convincingly transport readers to Spaz's world."

Philbrick branches out into historical fiction with *The Journal of Douglas Allen Deeds: The Donner Party Expedition.* While Douglas Allen Deeds was an actual member of the Donner Party, the infamous group of pioneers who were stranded in the Sierra Nevada mountains during the winter of 1846-47, the diary Philbrick creates for the fifteen-year-old orphan is fiction. Philbrick relates the well-known calamities that struck the party, including illness, starvation, and eventually cannibalism, but he also "show[s] the changes in people brought about by incredible hardships," as Lana Mills wrote in *School Library Journal.* The author generally "shows the action rather than merely telling about it," Kay Weisman commented in *Booklist,* with the fortunate exception of the incidents of cannibalism: Deeds, disgusted at the thought, heads off into the forest so that he will not have to watch while the others "take advantage of what has been provided."

Cover of Philbrick's middle-grade novel The Mostly True Adventures of Homer P. Figg, *featuring artwork by David Shannon.* (Jacket illustration © 2009 by David Shannon. Reproduced by permission of Scholastic, Inc.)

A young teen comes of age during the U.S. Civil War in *The Mostly True Adventures of Homer P. Figg,* but despite its dramatic backdrop, Philbrick's novel gains a lighthearted element due to the actions of its quirky titular hero. After older brother Harold Figg is strongarmed into the Union Army for suspicious reasons, twelve-year-old Homer decides to run away from the farm in dismal Pine Swamp, Maine, where the brothers have lived with heart-hearted Uncle Squinto Leach since their parents' death. On his journey south in search of Harold's regiment, Homer encounters slave hunters, spies, and abolitionists, befriends a naive young man of the cloth and a kindhearted professor, and flies in a hotair balloon, surviving due to his "courage, luck, and . . . talent for telling lies when needed," according to *School Library Journal* critic Steven Engelfried. The winding paths of both brothers intersect in the farmland near Gettysburg, Pennsylvania, where a pivotal battle is about to take place. In *Booklist* Carolyn Phelan praised Philbrick's novel, citing the "humor and folksy charm" that often characterizes Homer's first-person narration, and Betty Carter asserted in *Horn Book* that the young hero's colorful adventures "never obscure . . . the misfortunes of war and those who fought it." In a story designed to appeal to younger children, Philbrick weaves

information about the history and ethical issues of the U.S. civil-war era into a tale described by a *Kirkus Reviews* writer as "bursting with vividly voiced characters and [crisp] descriptions."

The Young Man and the Sea is "a rousing sea adventure with plenty of heart," Peter D. Sieruta declared in *Horn Book.* The young man of the title is Skiff Beaman, a twelve-year-old resident of coastal Maine. Skiff's mother has recently died, and his father, formerly a fisherman, now spends all of his time watching television and drinking, while his neglected boat slowly sinks in its moorings. Skiff makes raising and repairing the *Mary Rose* his mission, but fixing the waterlogged engine will cost over 5,000 dollars. The quickest way to make that much money is by catching just one of the massive, prized bluefin tuna that live in the ocean off Maine, so Skiff sets off in a tiny boat, determined to catch one of the 900-pound fish. Skiff's hunting of the tuna is related "in a 70-plus-page action sequence that inspires awe for both man and nature," noted a *Publishers Weekly* reviewer.

Philbrick's "excellent maritime bildungsroman has all of the makings of a juvenile classic," Jeffrey Hastings wrote in his *School Library Journal* review of *The Young Man and the Sea,* citing the novel's "wide-open adventure, heart-pounding suspense, and just the right amount of tear-jerking pathos." As several critics noted, Philbrick's novel has obvious parallels to early twentieth-century writer Ernest Hemingway's classic *The Old Man and the Sea,* including its spare language and reliance on inner dialogue. "I haven't read the Hemingway story since I was in high school," Philbrick told *Journal of Adolescent and Adult Literacy* interviewer James Blasingame, "but obviously it made a big impression."

As a writer, Philbrick remains constantly busy, reserving his mornings for his craft, and rewarding himself with a chance to go fishing in the afternoon. A voracious reader for many years, he counts among his favorite authors suspense novelist Elmore Leonard, as well as writers Mark Twain and Joseph Conrad. Perhaps because of his roots in the seafaring culture of the New England shoreline, Philbrick also enjoys the seagoing fiction of Patrick O'Brien. He and his wife divide their time between their home in Maine and the Florida Keys.

Biographical and Critical Sources

PERIODICALS

ALAN Review, winter, 1999; winter, 2001, Rodman Philbrick, "Listening to Kids in America," pp. 13-16.

Booklist, December 15, 1993, Stephanie Zvirin, review of *Freak the Mighty,* p. 748; June 1, 1998, Susan Dove Lempke, review of *Max the Mighty,* pp. 1749-1750;

December 15, 1998, Ilene Cooper, review of *Freak the Mighty,* p. 751; May 1, 2000, review of *REM World: Where Nothing Is Real and Everything Is about to Disappear,* p. 1670; November 15, 2000, Debbie Carton, review of *The Last Book in the Universe,* p. 636; August, 2001, Anna Rich, review of *The Last Book in the Universe,* p. 2142; January 1, 2002, Kay Weisman, review of *The Journal of Douglas Alan Deeds: The Donner Party Expedition,* p. 859; March 15, 2005, Patricia Austin, review of *The Young Man and the Sea,* p. 1313; January 1, 2009, Carolyn Phelan, review of *The Mostly True Adventures of Homer P. Figg,* p. 84.

Bulletin of the Center for Children's Books, January, 1994, Deborah Stevenson, review of *Freak the Mighty,* p. 165; April, 1998, Deborah Stevenson, review of *Max the Mighty,* p. 291; March, 2004, Elizabeth Bush, review of *The Young Man and the Sea,* p. 291; January, 2009, Elizabeth Bush, review of *The Mostly True Adventures of Homer P. Figg,* p. 212.

Childhood Education, winter, 2000, Barbara F. Backer, review of *REM World,* p. 109.

Horn Book, January-February, 1994, Nancy Vasilakis, review of *Freak the Mighty,* p. 74; July-August, 1996, Martha V. Parravano, review of *The Fire Pony,* p. 464; July-August, 1998, Nancy Vasilakis, review of *Max the Mighty,* p. 495; March-April, 2004, Peter D. Sieruta, review of *The Young Man and the Sea,* p. 187; January-February, 2009, Betty Carter, review of *The Mostly True Adventures of Homer P. Figg,* p. 100.

Journal of Adolescent and Adult Literacy, March, 2004, James Blasingame, interview with Philbrick, p. 518.

Kirkus Reviews, February 15, 1998, review of *Max the Mighty,* p. 272; January 15, 2004, review of *The Young Man and the Sea,* p. 87; December 1, 2008, review of *The Mostly True Adventures of Homer P. Figg.*

Kliatt, March, 1999, review of *Abduction,* p. 26; May, 2002, Paula Rohrlick, review of *The Last Book in the Universe,* p. 29; January, 2004, Claire Rosser, review of *The Young Man and the Sea,* p. 12.

Publishers Weekly, January 26, 1998, review of *Max the Mighty,* p. 91; March 27, 2000, review of *REM World,* p. 81; November 27, 2000, review of *The Last Book in the Universe,* p. 77; January 14, 2002, review of *Coffins,* p. 46; February 16, 2004, review of *The Young Man and the Sea,* p. 173; December 1, 2008, review of *The Mostly True Adventures of Homer P. Figg,* p. 58.

School Library Journal, December, 1993, Libby K. White, review of *Freak the Mighty,* p. 137; September, 1996, Christina Linz, review of *The Fire Pony,* p. 206; April, 1998, Marilyn Payne Phillips, review of *Max the Mighty,* p. 136; July, 1998, Brian E. Wilson, review of *Freak the Mighty,* p. 56; May, 2000, Nina Lindsay, review of *REM World,* p. 175; November, 2000, Susan L. Rogers, review of *The Last Book in the Universe,* p. 160; July, 2001, Louise L. Sherman, review of *The Last Book in the Universe,* p. 60; December, 2001, Lana Miles, review of *The Journal of Douglas Allen Deeds,* p. 142; February, 2004, Jeffrey Hastings, review of *The Young Man and the Sea,* p. 152; January, 2009, Steven Engelfried, review of *The Mostly True Adventures of Homer P. Figg,* p. 116.

ONLINE

Scholastic Web site, http://www2.scholastic.com/ (January 10, 2010), video interview with Philbrick.

Rodman Philbrick Home Page, http://www.rodman philbrick.com (January 10, 2010).*

*   *   *

PHILBRICK, W.R.
See PHILBRICK, Rodman

*   *   *

PINKNEY, Gloria Jean 1941-

Personal

Born September 5, 1941, in Lumberton, NC; daughter of Teed Daughtery (an insurance agent) and Ernestine (a seamstress) Maultsby; married Jerry Pinkney (an illustrator), March 19, 1960; children: Troy Bernardette Ragsdale, Brian, Scott, Myles. *Religion:* Christian.

Addresses

Home—Westchester County, NY.

Career

Children's book author and fashion designer. Jewelry by Gloria Jean (silversmith), Croton, NY, beginning 1980; Hats by Gloria Jean, Croton, beginning 1983. Jerry Pinkney Studio, production assistant, beginning 1968, publishing representative, beginning 1978. Star of Bethlehem Baptist Church, scholarship committee (president), Sunday school assistant superintendent.

Member

Society of Children's Book Writers and Illustrators, Authors Guild, Authors League of America, Black Women in Publishing.

Awards, Honors

Parent's Choice Award, 1992, Notable Children's Book citation, American Library Association, and New York Public Library 100 Titles for Reading and Sharing citation, all for *Back Home.*

Writings

Back Home, illustrated by husband, Jerry Pinkney, Dial (New York, NY), 1992.

The Sunday Outing, illustrated by Jerry Pinkney, Dial (New York, NY), 1994.

In the Forest of Your Remembrance: Thirty-three Goodly News Tellings for the Whole Family, illustrated by Jerry Pinkney and sons Brian Pinkney and Myles C. Pinkney, Phyllis Fogelman Books (New York, NY), 2001.

Music from Our Lord's Holy Heaven, illustrated by Jerry
     Pinkney, Brian Pinkney, and Myles C. Pinkney, intro-
     duction by daughter Troy Pinkney-Ragsdale, Harper-
     Collins (New York, NY), 2005.
(Reteller) *Daniel and the Lord of Lions,* illustrated by
     Robert Casilla, Abingdon Press (Nashville, TN), 2008.

Sidelights

Often illustrated by her husband, noted artist Jerry
Pinkney, Gloria Jean Pinkney's picture books for children draw on the author's reminiscences of her North
Carolina childhood and tap into her creative talents as
well as her strong spiritual beliefs. Pinkney's nostalgic
stories have been praised by critics for their depiction
of a loving, supportive, and realistic African-American
family. While her books *Back Home* and *The Sunday
Outing* are not strongly plot-driven, "Pinkney knows
how to play out a scenario," commented Betsy Hearne
in her review for the *Bulletin of the Center for Children's Books.* She also explores the stories of her Christian faith in *Daniel and the Lord of Lions,* a picture
book featuring artwork by Robert Casilla that a *Kirkus
Reviews* writer dubbed "a solid treatment" of an Old
Testament story. According to many critics, Pinkney's
stories warmly evoke the love of close-knit families and
appeal to children's sensibilities.

Pinkney was born in Lumberton, North Carolina, and
met her husband, illustrator Jerry Pinkney, while attend-

Gloria Jean Pinkney's biblical-themed picture book **Daniel and the
Lord of Lions** *features artwork by Robert Casilla.* (Illustration copyright ©
2008 by Robert Casilla. Reprinted by permission of the publisher, Abingdon Press.)

ing high school in Philadelphia. In addition to being a
mother to their four children—Myles, Brian, Troy, and
Scott—Pinkney helped her husband in his work and
also found her own creative outlet designing hats and
jewelry for her own boutique in Croton, New York. As
Jerry Pinkney's career expanded, so did that of sons
Brian and Myles: Brian is now an accomplished children's book illustrator who frequently collaborates with
his wife, writer Andrea Davis Pinkney, while Myles is a
talented photographer whose work also appears in books
for children. In fact, taken as a whole, the talented
Pinkney family has been involved in over one hundred
books.

Back Home, Pinkney's first children's book, "evolved
out of a family reunion in Lumberton, North Carolina,"
as the author once told *SATA.* "It rekindled some old
memories and I realized how much history there was in
my own family. When I came home and started thinking about it, I knew I was ready to write a book. The
story is based on a trip I took to Lumberton when I was
eight years old. I named the main character, Ernestine,
after my mother and dedicated the book to her."

Back Home recounts eight-year-old Ernestine's train
ride from Pennsylvania to North Carolina to visit her
relatives and see the place where she was born. The author contrasts ways of living in the city, where Ernestine lives, and the country, where she visits, and centers
on the friendship that gradually develops between the
girl and her teasing cousin. "Gloria [Jean] Pinkney's
text has a relaxed pace that is perfectly suited to the
summer setting," remarked a *Publishers Weekly*
reviewer. As Ann A. Flowers noted in *Horn Book, Back
Home* is "evocative of a gentle past," a past in which
rural poverty is less important than strong family ties.
Reflecting the views of more than one critic, Shirley
Wilton wrote in *School Library Journal* that *Back Home*
"celebrates the lives of an African-American family."

A prequel to Pinkney's award-winning first book, *The
Sunday Outing* centers on Ernestine's dream to travel
south to visit her relatives, a dream fed by weekly trips
to the train station with her great-aunt Odessa. As with
Back Home, The Sunday Outing features an emphasis
on a strong, loving family and passing on family history to the next generation. Odessa encourages Ernestine to help her parents save the price of a train ticket
to North Carolina, and soon the whole family is sacri-
ficing for the child's trip. Barbara Osborne Williams
praised the "realistic and moving" story and Pinkney's
true-to-life African-American dialogue in her *School Library Journal* review of *The Sunday Outing,* while *Horn
Book* contributor Hanna B. Zeigler concluded that "Gloria Jean Pinkney's quiet story and Jerry Pinkney's illustrations provide a portrait of a loving African-American
family working to make a dream come true."

Pinkney shares her strong Christian faith in her book *In
the Forest of Your Remembrance: Thirty-three Goodly
News Tellings for the Whole Family,* which features art-

work by her husband as well as by sons Brian and Myles Pinkney. The author pairs her reflections on the many instances where God has made his presence known in her life with a Bible verse that is relevant to the incident, and ranges in her focus from searching for a kitten for a child to reflecting on the color yellow. A *Publishers Weekly* contributor called *In the Forest of Your Remembrance* a "highly personal volume" featuring "graceful" illustrations, and *School Library Journal* contributor Kathryn Kosiorek predicted that Pinkney's work will be appreciated by people who experience "personal and family devotions" as "central to [their] . . . life."

Also illustrated by the three artistic Pinkneys, *Music from Our Lord's Holy Heaven* features an introduction by Gloria and Jerry's daughter, Troy Pinkney-Ragsdale. A collection of twenty-two African-American hymns and spirituals that is enhanced by distinctive artwork and Bible quotations, the book also includes a CD featuring Gloria Pinkney's vocal rendition of the music that has figured so strongly in her family life. In *School Library Journal* a contributor praised *Music from Our Lord's Holy Heaven* as a "superb collection" that features photographs as well as paintings enriched by "swirling shades of blue and gold."

Biographical and Critical Sources

PERIODICALS

Atlanta Journal-Constitution, July 22, 2005, Gracie Bonds Staples, "Artistry's All in the Family," p. G6.

Booklist, October 1, 2005, Ilene Cooper, review of *Music from Our Lord's Holy Heaven,* p. 70.

Bulletin of the Center for Children's Books, September, 1992, Betsy Hearne, review of *Back Home,* p. 21.

Horn Book, January, 1993, Ann A. Flowers, review of *Back Home,* p. 83; September, 1994, Hanna B. Zeigler, review of *The Sunday Outing,* p. 581.

Kirkus Reviews, September 15, 2005, review of *Music from Our Lord's Holy Heaven,* p. 1032; September 15, 2008, review of *Daniel and the Lord of Lions.*

Publishers Weekly, July 6, 1992, review of *Back Home,* p. 56; February 25, 2002, review of *In the Forest of Your Remembrance: Thirty-three Goodly News Tellings for the Whole Family,* p. 63; July 25, 2005, review of *Music from Our Lord's Holy Heaven,* p. 80.

School Library Journal, September, 1992, Shirley Wilton, review of *Back Home,* pp. 209-210; July, 1994, Barbara Osborne Williams, review of *The Sunday Outing,* pp. 86-87; September, 2001, Kathryn Kosiorek, review of *In the Forest of Your Remembrance,* p. 252; December, 2005, Linda L. Walkins, review of *Music from Our Lord's Holy Heaven,* p. 132.

ONLINE

Children's Literature Network Web site, http://www.clnetwork.org/ (January 10, 2010), "Gloria Jean Pinkney."*

POLACCO, Patricia 1944-

Personal

Born July 11, 1944, in Lansing, MI; daughter of William F. (a traveling salesman and television talk-show host) and Mary Ellen (a teacher) Barber; married c. 1962 (marriage ended); married Enzo Mario Polacco (a chef and cooking instructor), August 18, 1979; children: (first marriage) Traci Denise, Steven John. *Education:* Attended Ohio State University, California College of Arts and Crafts, and Lancy College; Monash University (Melbourne, Victoria, Australia), B.F.A. (painting), 1974; Royal Melbourne Institute of Technology, M.A., Ph.D. (art history), 1978; also studied in England, France, and Russia *Hobbies and other interests:* Travel, pets, painting, sculpture, egg art.

Addresses

Home—Union City, MI. *Agent*—Edythea Selman, 14 Washington Pl., New York, NY 10003.

Career

Author and illustrator, 1986—. Consultant on icon restoration; Babushka, Inc., founder. Speaker for school and reading organizations.

Member

Society of Children's Book Writers and Illustrators.

Awards, Honors

International Reading Association Award for Younger Readers, 1989, for *Rechenka's Eggs;* Sydney Taylor Book Award for Picture Books, Association of Jewish Libraries, 1989, for *The Keeping Quilt;* Commonwealth Club of California Award, 1990, for *Babushka's Doll,* and 1992, for *Chicken Sunday;* Boston Area Education for Social Responsibility Award, 1992; Golden Kite Award for Illustration, 1992, for *Chicken Sunday;* Jane Addams Award Honor Book designation, 1993 for *Mrs. Katz and Tush;* American Book of the Year Award nomination, 1995, and West Virginia Children's Book Award, 1997, both for *Pink and Say;* Jo Osborne Award for Humor, 1996; North Dakota Library Association Children's Book Award, 1996, and Missouri Show Me Readers' Award, 1997, both for *My Rotten Redheaded Older Brother;* Parents' Choice Honor designation, 1998, and Gold Award, 1999, both for *Thank You, Mr. Falker;* Mid-South Independent Booksellers Humpty Dumpty Award, 1998.

Writings

PICTURE BOOKS; SELF-ILLUSTRATED, EXCEPT AS NOTED

Meteor!, Dodd, Mead (New York, NY), 1987.
Rechenka's Eggs, Philomel (New York, NY), 1988.

Patricia Polacco (Photograph by Al Guiteras. Reproduced by permission of Guiteras Photography.)

Boat Ride with Lillian Two Blossom, Philomel (New York, NY), 1988.

(With Ernest Lawrence Thayer) *Casey at the Bat,* Putnam (New York, NY), 1988.

The Keeping Quilt, Simon & Schuster (New York, NY), 1988, tenth anniversary edition with eight new drawings, 1998.

Uncle Vova's Tree, Philomel (New York, NY), 1989.

Babushka's Doll, Simon & Schuster (New York, NY), 1990.

Just Plain Fancy, Bantam (New York, NY), 1990.

Thunder Cake, Philomel (New York, NY), 1990.

Some Birthday!, Simon & Schuster (New York, NY), 1991.

Appelemando's Dreams, Philomel (New York, NY), 1991.

Chicken Sunday, Philomel (New York, NY), 1992.

Mrs. Katz and Tush, Bantam (New York, NY), 1992.

Picnic at Mudsock Meadow, Putnam (New York, NY), 1992.

The Bee Tree, Putnam (New York, NY), 1993.

Babushka Baba Yaga, Philomel (New York, NY), 1993.

My Rotten Redheaded Older Brother, Simon & Schuster (New York, NY), 1994.

Pink and Say, Philomel (New York, NY), 1994.

Tikvah Means Hope, Doubleday (New York, NY), 1994.

Babushka's Mother Goose (collection of stories and poems), Philomel (New York, NY), 1995.

My Ol' Man, Philomel (New York, NY), 1995.

The Trees of the Dancing Goats, Simon & Schuster (New York, NY), 1996.

Aunt Chip and the Great Triple Creek Dam Affair, Philomel (New York, NY), 1996.

I Can Hear the Sun: A Modern Myth, Philomel (New York, NY), 1996.

In Enzo's Splendid Gardens, Philomel (New York, NY), 1997.

Uncle Isaaco, Philomel (New York, NY), 1997.

Mrs. Mack, Philomel (New York, NY), 1998.

Thank You, Mr. Falker, Philomel (New York, NY), 1998.

Welcome Comfort, Philomel (New York, NY), 1999.

Luba and the Wren, Philomel (New York, NY), 1999.

The Calhoun Club, Philomel (New York, NY), 2000.

The Butterfly, Philomel (New York, NY), 2000.

Betty Doll, Philomel (New York, NY), 2001.

Mr. Lincoln's Way, Philomel (New York, NY), 2001.

When Lightning Comes in a Jar, Philomel (New York, NY), 2002.

A Christmas Tapestry, Philomel (New York, NY), 2002.

The Graves Family, Philomel (New York, NY), 2003.

G Is for Goat, Philomel (New York, NY), 2003.

An Orange for Frankie, Philomel (New York, NY), 2004.

Oh, Look!, Philomel (New York, NY), 2004.

John Philip Duck, Philomel (New York, NY), 2004.

Mommies Say Shhh!, Philomel (New York, NY), 2005.

The Graves Family Goes Camping, Philomel (New York, NY), 2005.

Emma Kate, Philomel (New York, NY), 2005.

Something about Hensley's, Philomel (New York, NY), 2006.

Rotten Richie and the Ultimate Dare, Philomel (New York, NY), 2006.

Ginger and Petunia, Philomel (New York, NY), 2007.

The Lemonade Club, Philomel Books (New York, NY), 2007.

For the Love of Autumn, Philomel Books (New York, NY), 2008.

Someone for Mr. Sussman, Philomel Books (New York, NY), 2008.

In Our Mothers' House, Philomel Books (New York, NY), 2009.

January's Sparrow, Philomel Books (New York, NY), 2009.

Junkyard Wonders, Philomel Books (New York, NY), 2010.

Several of Polacco's works have been translated into Spanish.

OTHER

Firetalking (autobiography), photographs by Lawrence Migdale, Richard C. Owen (Katonah, NY), 1994.

Adaptations

Spoken Arts video adaptations of Polacco's books include *Rechenka's Eggs,* 1991, *Chicken Sunday,* 1992, *The Keeping Quilt,* 1993, *Aunt Chip and the Great Triple Creek Dam Affair,* 1996, *Pink and Say,* 1996, *Thank You, Mr. Falker,* 1999, *Christmas Tapestry,* 2004, *John Philip Duck,* 2005, *Rechenka's Eggs,* and *Thunder Cake.* Sound recordings of author's works include

Chicken Sunday, Scholastic, 1993; *Just Plain Fancy,* Bantam Doubleday Dell Audio, 1994; *Casey at the Bat,* Spoken Arts, 1994; *The Keeping Quilt,* Spoken Arts, 1998; *Meteor!; Thunder Cake;* and *Thank You, Mr. Falker.* Several of Polacco's works have been issued in book/cassette combinations. *The Butterfly* was adapted as a stage musical by Barbara Zinn Krieger and produced by Making Books Sing, 2008.

Sidelights

Author and illustrator Patricia Polacco is "as natural a storyteller as they come," according to Shannon Maughan in *Publishers Weekly.* The highly praised, award-winning Polacco has dozens of picture books to her credit, quite a feat in light of the fact that she did not start publishing until 1987, at the age of forty-one. A popular writer and artist, Polacco is lauded for transforming childhood memories, favorite episodes from family history, and elements from her Russian, Ukrainian, Jewish, and Irish heritage into books such as *My Rotten Redheaded Older Brother,* that are noted for their freshness, originality, warmth, panache, and universality. The characters in her picture books *The Keeping Quilt, Uncle Vova's Tree, Pink and Say, Welcome Comfort, The Butterfly,* and *In Our Mothers' House* reflect a variety of races, religions, sexual identities, and age groups, celebrating both diversity and

Polacco's evocative pencil art enhances her nostalgic story of childhood in **Betty Doll.** (Puffin Books, 2004. Reproduced by permission of Puffin Books, a division of Penguin Putnam Books for Young Readers.)

commonality. Several of Polacco's works retell stories that have been handed down for generations and feature Russian and Jewish customs and folklore, while others focus on African and Native Americans, the Irish, and the Amish. Whatever their subject, Polacco's tales are noted for their clear, fluid language and a text that makes them suitable for reading aloud.

As an illustrator, Polacco works in watercolor, gouache, charcoal, and collage, and she characteristically offsets images penciled on a stark white field with bright colors and patterned backgrounds. Praising Polacco's renderings of facial expressions as "priceless," *School Library Journal* reviewer Grace Oliff wrote in her review of *John Philip Duck* that the picture book's "artwork is simply beautiful as the artist orchestrates a harmonious symphony of color."

Polacco was born in Lansing, Michigan, in 1944, the daughter of William Barber, a salesman who became a television talk-show host, and Mary Ellen Barber, a teacher. Her father was of Irish descent and her mother was from a Russian/Ukrainian background. After her parents' divorce when she was three years old, Polacco and her older brother lived mostly with their mother on her grandmother's farm in Union City, Michigan. When she was five years old, her beloved *babushka* (grandmother) passed away, after which her mother moved the family to Coral Gables, Florida, for three years before settling in Oakland, California. Writing on her home page, Polacco recalled that living on the farm in Union City "was the most magical time of my life" and "my Babushka and other grandparents were some of the most inspirational people in my life."

Polacco inherited a natural storytelling voice from both sides of the family. Although stories—both oral and read from books—fascinated the introspective girl, she had problems reading on her own. At age fourteen Polacco was finally diagnosed with dyslexia; by this time, however, she had already suffered her classmates' taunts due to her lackluster progress in reading and math. Sketching and illustrating became her focus; her classmates were speechless when confronted with her fluid artwork. The world created by her own imagination became Polacco's refuge during adolescence.

Graduating from high school, Polacco received a college scholarship, but instead she decided to marry at age eighteen. She attended Ohio State University for a couple of terms, but eventually dropped out to go to work and have two children, Traci and Steven. After she and her first husband divorced, Polacco completed her undergraduate studies in California. She went to Australia for further education, earning an M.F.A. in painting from Monash University in Melbourne and a Ph.D. in Russian and Greek iconographic history from the Royal Melbourne Institute of Technology. While studying in Australia, Polacco met her second husband, Enzo Polacco, an Italian Jew from Trieste, Italy, who is a chef and cooking instructor as well as a Holocaust survivor.

Throughout her life, Polacco has been a maker of books. As she told Maughan in *Publishers Weekly,* "I've always made rough dummies, like thick greeting cards, for people in my life to celebrate any occasion." At the insistence of a friend who admired these efforts, Polacco joined her local chapter of the Society of Children's Book Writers and Illustrators and began adapting her family stories as picture books. In 1987, she and her mother went to New York City to shop around Polacco's eighty-pound portfolio, visiting sixty publishers in a single week. "I was too stupid to be frightened, and I just loved it," she recalled to Maughan. The same year, Polacco sold her first book, *Meteor!*

Meteor! is the "mostly true" tale about the events that occur after a fallen star crashes in the backyard of Grampa and Gramma Gaw in Union City, Michigan. After the meteor lands, the news buzzes through town, becoming more detailed and outlandish with every telling. Soon the farm becomes a carnival ground complete with a circus. When the festivities end, the townspeople who have touched the meteor feel that it has changed their lives. Called "an affectionate poke at small-town life" by a critic in *Kirkus Reviews, Meteor!* was praised by a *Publishers Weekly* critic as "an enchanting book [that] overwhelmingly expresses the magic that suddenly pervades a small town, from the funny, folksy way the story is told to the imaginative, full-color illustrations." Polacco produced *The Calhoun Club,* a sequel to *Meteor!,* in 2000. In this book, children's author Petra Penwrite sets out to prove that the meteorite in her hometown of Union City is real and that it grants wishes to children.

Rechenka's Eggs is a folkloric tale set in Russia before the communist revolution of 1917. In this work, old Babushka, who lives alone in her small country home, paints beautiful, prize-winning eggs that always win first place at the Easter Festival. Babushka rescues Rechenka, a goose shot and wounded by a hunter, nurses her back to health, and in so doing receives the gift of beautifully colored eggs which the goose lays for her. Noting the book's "beauty and authenticity," Shaun Traynor added in her *Times Educational Supplement* that *Rechenka's Eggs* is "the perfect Easter book for all seasons." Leonard Marcus stated in the *New York Times Book Review* that Polacco's book "is as much about friendship and the workmanlike small things of this life as it is about faith," while Marcus Crouch concluded in *Junior Bookshelf* that "this lovely book introduces a new and outstanding talent to the field of children's books. . . . It is a picture-book of outstanding quality."

In one of Polacco's most popular books, *The Keeping Quilt,* little Patricia narrates the story of a quilt that has been in her family for many years. The quilt ties together four generations of an immigrant Jewish family and becomes a symbol of their love and faith. Writing in *School Library Journal,* Lee Bock called *The Keeping Quilt* a "beautifully conceived book" and a "lovely story," while Denise M. Wilms concluded in *Booklist* that, in addition to being "useful for the sense of history

it presents to young viewers (especially in discussions of genealogy), this tale also carries a warm message on the meaning of family." In 1998, Polacco produced a revised, tenth-anniversary edition of *The Keeping Quilt.* The first edition ended with a picture of Polacco holding her newborn daughter; the revised edition expands the story with five new pages of text and eight illustrations that depict the author's two children and their use of the keeping quilt.

Polacco has published several other books that deal with her Jewish heritage and the history of Jews in the United States and abroad. In *Tikvah Means Hope* a Jewish family exhibits resilience after a devastating fire occurs in the hills of Oakland, California. A reviewer for *Publishers Weekly* wrote that Polacco's drawings for this book "skillfully and emotionally convey the anguish and suffering of the community, as well as its resilience and hopefulness." In *The Trees of the Dancing Goats* Polacco once again draws on family memory and stories to tell the tale of how a Jewish family in Michigan helps make their neighbors' Christmas memorable during an outbreak of scarlet fever. "Polacco's brightly colored, detailed paintings in marking pens and pencil show a child in a close, loving home that is bursting with energy and joy," wrote *Booklist* contributor Hazel Rochman in a review of *The Tree of the Dancing Goats.*

With *Uncle Isaaco,* Polacco focuses on the events surrounding World War II and the Holocaust. In the book she tells how her husband, Enzo, was expelled from his home in Trieste, Italy, by the Nazis as a little boy and how he missed his beloved uncle most of all. She also details the suffering of the Jews in World War II and the bravery of the French Resistance in *The Butterfly,* a story originally told to her by her aunt Monique. Monique's mother hides a Jewish family in her basement and tries to help them escape. Wendy Lukehart, writing in *School Library Journal,* called *Uncle Isaaco* a "perfect blend of art and story," while *Booklist* reviewer Rochman concluded that "what will hold grade-school kids is the truth of the friendship story and the tension of hiding to survive."

Thank You, Mr. Falker is based heavily on Polacco's own life. In this story, ten-year-old Trisha yearns to read, but has been teased constantly by her classmates because she stumbles over words and numbers. Although she has won respect for her artistic talent, Trisha still hides the fact that she cannot read. Finally, her fifth-grade teacher, Mr. Falker, turns a sympathetic eye to the girl's difficulty. Using his own money, he pays a reading specialist to work with Trisha until she overcomes her problem. Rochman, writing in *Booklist,* noted in a review of *Thank You, Mr. Falker* that Polacco's young heroine "isn't idealized; we see her messy and desperate, poring over her books. This will encourage the child who feels like a failure and the teacher who cares."

Polacco deals with contemporary social issues in several of her books. Three adopted children reflect on their childhood growing up with two mothers in *In Our Mothers' House,* while race is the focus of *Chicken Sunday,* a story in which neighborhood children help *get Miss Eula the Easter bonnet she likes and in so do-ing win over a local Jewish shopkeeper.* Praised by *School Library Journal* contributor Martha Simpson as a "gem of a book," *In Our Mothers' House* "can help youngsters better understand their world" and its diver-sity, while in *Booklist* Linda Perkins praised Polacco for pairing "energetic" pencil-and-magic marker artwork with the story's patchwork of "special moments" that "reveal . . . loving insight." Calling *Chicken Sunday* a "moving picture book," *Booklist* contributor Carolyn Phelan added that "the hatred sometimes engendered by racial and religious differences is overpowered by the love of people who recognize their common humanity." *Chicken Sunday* is "an authentic tale of childhood friendship," Dorothy Houlihan noted in *School Library Journal,* and Polacco's tale "resonates with the veracity of a personal recollection . . . replete with vivid visual and visceral images."

Polacco blends questions of race with another family tale that stands among her most highly regarded books. *Pink and Say* relates a poignant story set during the U.S. Civil War that was told by the author's great-great-great-grandfather on her father's side. In this book, fifteen-year-old Sheldon Russell Curtis (Say), an Ohio boy who has been left for dead in a Georgia battlefield, is rescued by gravedigger Pinkus Sylee (Pink), an African-American teen who is a fellow Union soldier. Pink drags Say to his home a few miles away. While the boy convalesces, he and Pink become friends and share their secrets: Pink can read—a knowledge forbid-den to slaves—and wants to fight slavery, while Say ad-mits that he is a deserter. Say also shook the hand of U.S. President Abraham Lincoln, and this becomes a talismanic handshake between Pink and Say. Pink teaches Say to read, and his fervor against slavery in-spires Say to rejoin his regiment. However, both boys are taken prisoners by the Confederates, who kill Pink's mother and send the friends to the notorious Anderson-ville prison camp. Due to his skin color, Pink is hung a few hours after entering the prison, while Say is re-leased several months later. As a reviewer noted in *Publishers Weekly,* "Polacco's "gripping story resonates with emotion as she details the chilling and horrible re-verberations of war and social injustice." Praising the book's illustrations as "a spectacular achievement," a *Kirkus Reviews* critic added that Polacco tells her story "carefully and without melodrama so that it speaks for itself." Writing in the *New York Times Book Review,* Henry Mayer concluded: "It is rare to find a children's book that deals so richly, yet gently, with the sober themes of slavery and freedom, martyrdom, and histori-cal memory."

The eponymous protagonist of *Welcome Comfort,* a lonely, overweight foster child, is taken under the wing—or rather in the sleigh—of a rather plump school custodian. Comfort has never known the joys of Christ-mas until the mysterious custodian and his wife initiate him. A reviewer for *Publishers Weekly* noted that "this warm blend of fantasy and reality delivers a satisfying surprise ending," and that Polacco's artwork "is even

more vibrant than usual." Reviewing the same title in the *Washington Post Book World,* Michael Patrick Hearn called *Welcome Comfort* "as warm as a down comforter and told with the conviction and cadences of a tall tale."

Other tales that draw from Polacco's Midwest family tradition include *When Lightning Comes in a Jar, Betty Doll, My Rotten Redheaded Older Brother, Christmas Tapestry,* and *An Orange for Frankie.* Two reunions of extended family are the focus of *When Lightning Comes from a Jar,* as relatives come from all over Michigan to gossip, share food, and talk about the latest news, both in the early twentieth century and again, three genera-tions later. In *Betty Dolly* Polacco's sensitive graphite drawings bring to life the story of a beloved handmade doll that, cherished by its first owner, is eventually packed away, only to be discovered by future generations. A poignant Christmas Eve from genera-tions past is the setting for *An Orange for Frankie,* which finds a young boy looking forward to waking up on Christmas morning to find the highly prized citrus perched on the family home's fireplace mantel. "With her usual narrative flair Polacco weaves a story of fam-ily remembrances and traditions," wrote Wanda Meyers-Hines in her *School Library Journal* review of *When Lightning Comes in a Jar,* while a *Publishers Weekly* contributor predicted that adult readers will "appreciate the [book's] . . . warm message of the importance of

Polacco takes a lighthearted look at the dark side in her picture book **The Graves Family.** (Philomel Books, 2003. Text and illustrations copyright © 2003 by Babushka, Inc. All rights reserved. Reproduced by permission of Philomel Books, a di-vision of Penguin Putnam Books for Young Readers.)

heritage." Similar praise was accorded the nostalgic holiday story *Christmas Tapestry,* which finds a boy and his minister father patching up a hole in the crumbling wall of their Detroit church with a wall-hanging that has unexpected tied to the past of an elderly friend. Reviewing the story, GraceAnne A. DeCandido wrote in *Booklist* that "Polacco is a master at intergenerational, interfaith stories that bring comfort and joy," and a *Kirkus Reviews* writer wrote that in *Christmas Tapestry* the author/illustrator "succeeds as always with her watercolor-and-pencil illustrations in creating unique, expressive characters."

In a family story with a twist, Polacco describes the experiences of two children who meet some interesting new neighbors in *The Graves Family.* The wife, Shalleaux Graves, kills every plant she touches and her Venus Fly trap gobbles up the hats of nearby ladies when she participates in a garden club tea, while husband Doug Graves distributes a hair restorative that causes its users to behave like the cats that serve as the concoction's secret ingredient. Just when it seems like the new family will never be accepted by the town, their spooky, blood-red house finds favor with a well-known interior decorator, spider webs and all. A trip to Lake Bleakmire, with its assorted creepy crawlies, is in store for both Doug and Shalleaux Graves, as well as readers of *The Graves Family Goes Camping,* until a pastry-loving, fire-breathing dragon cuts the couple's gruesome holiday short. Noting that Polacco's tale mixes "a little light horror" with "over-the-top hilarity," a *Publishers Weekly* reviewer added that in *The Graves Family* the author/illustrator "mines the theme of children nourished by unexpected friendships." Uncharacteristic of Polacco, *The Graves Family* "is lighter and less emotionally resonant than many of her other works," according to *School Library Journal* reviewer Rachel G. Payne, although Payne also noted that the author's "creative puns, and over-the-top descriptions" pair well with her "comic, cartoon" art.

Another imaginative tale by Polacco, *Ginger and Petunia,* introduces a pianist who teaches students in the home she shares with a pig named Petunia. When a solo performance requires Ginger's absence, and the pet sitter is a no-show, the clever swine masquerades as the fashion-conscious Ginger until the woman's return. Praising the "droll text and playfully hyperbolic art," a *Publishers Weekly* reviewer dubbed "Polacco's porcine protagonist" the star of an "endear[ing] and "light-hearted caper," while a *Kirkus Reviews* writer praised the author/illustrator's "vibrant signature artwork," which includes "expressive cameo portraits" as well as "more expansive compositions that spill over from one page to the next."

A kitten, rather than a pig, is the animal star of *For the Love of Autumn,* which also features Polacco's original art. In the story, a young teacher named Danielle adopts a lost kitten and when she move to a new home along the coast of Washington state, Autumn the kitten accompanies her. During a stormy night, Autumn disap-

Polacco's engaging illustrations and entertaining story combine in the picture book **Ginger Petunia.** (Copyright © 2007 by Babushka, Inc. All rights reserved. Reproduced by permission of Philomel Books, a division of Penguin Putnam Books for Young Readers.)

pears, but returns six weeks later, accompanied by a new friend for the lonely Danielle. Calling *For the Love of Autumn* "a lovely story," Susan E. Murray added in *School Library Journal* that the work also features the author/illustrator's "trademark" use of pattern and color. Although noting that the book's romantic ending will likely have greater adult appeal, a *Kirkus Reviews* writer predicted that youngsters "will doubtless respond to Autumn's genuinely vivid personality."

Whether writing about inter-generational relationships, the love shared by humans and their pets, history, cross-cultural friendships, Russian witches, or Jewish quilts, Polacco is happily at home in her created worlds and makes such worlds accessible for her readers as well. As she noted in her autobiography, *Firetalking,* "I am lucky . . . so very lucky! I love my life. Can you imagine doing what you love every day? . . . My thoughts boil in my head. They catch the air and fly. The images and stories come back with fury and energy. . . . My heart sings whenever I am drawing."

Biographical and Critical Sources

BOOKS

Children's Literature Review, Volume 40, Gale (Detroit, MI), 1996, pp. 175-201.

Polacco, Patricia, *Firetalking*, Richard C. Owen (Katonah, NY), 1994.

PERIODICALS

Booklist, December 1, 1988, Denise M. Wilms, review of *The Keeping Quilt*, p. 654; March 15, 1992, Carolyn Phelan, review of *Chicken Sunday*, p. 1388; November 1, 1996, Hazel Rochman, review of *The Trees of the Dancing Goats*, p. 509; May 1, 1998, Hazel Rochman, review of *Thank You, Mr. Falker*, p. 1522; November 15, 1998, Susan Dove Lempke, review of *Mrs. Mack*, p. 597; May 15, 1999, review of *Luba and the Wren*, p. 1700; April 4, 2000, Hazel Rochman, review of *The Butterfly*, p. 1479; August, 2000, Isabel Schon, review of *The Keeping Quilt*, p. 155; August, 2002, Julie Cummins, review of *When Lightning Comes in a Jar*, p. 1975; September 1, 2002, GraceAnne A. DeCandido, review of *Christmas Tapestry*, p. 138; May 1, 2003, GraceAnne A. DeCandido, review of *G Is for Goat*, p. 1606; September 15, 2003, Kay Weisman, review of *The Graves Family*, p. 248; March 1, 2004, Linda Perkins, review of *Oh, Look!*, p. 1198; August, 2004, Lauren Peterson, review of *John Philip Duck*, p. 1944; December 1, 2004, Terry Glover, review of *An Orange for Frankie*, p. 662; May 15, 2005, Ilene Cooper, review of *The Graves Family Goes Camping*, p. 1666; September 15, 2005, Gillian Engberg, review of *Emma Kate*, p. 75; April 15, 2006, Jennifer Mattson, review of *Rotten Richie and the Ultimate Dare*, p. 54; October 1, 2008, John Peters, review of *Someone for Mr. Sussman*, p. 48; May 1, 2009, Linda Perkins, review of *In Our Mothers' House*, p. 82.

Horn Book, March-April, 2004, Susan Dove Lempke, review of *Oh, Look!*, p. 174.

Grand Rapids Press, September 18, 2005, Maranda, interview with Polacco, p. J2.

Junior Bookshelf, June, 1988, Marcus Crouch, review of *Rechenka's Eggs*, p. 131.

Kirkus Reviews, April 1, 1987, review of *Meteor!*, p. 557; September 15, 1994, review of *Pink and Say*, p. 1279; May 1, 2002, review of *When Lighting Comes in a Jar*, p. 665; November 1, 2002, review of *Christmas Tapestry*, p. 1624; April 15, 2003, review of *G Is for Goat*, p. 610; August 15, 2003, review of *The Graves Family*, p. 1077; February 1, 2004, review of *Oh, Look!*, p. 137; May 1, 2004, review of *John Philip Duck*, p. 446; November 1, 2004, review of *An Orange for Frankie*, p. 1052; January 15, 2005, review of *Mommies Say Shhh!*, p. 124; April 15, 2005, review of *The Graves Family Goes Camping*, p. 479; August 1, 2005, review of *Emma Kate*, p. 856; April 15, 2006, review of *Rotten Richie and the Ultimate Dare*, p. 414; July 1, 2006, review of *Something about Hensley's*, p. 68; April 1, 2007, review of *Ginger and Petunia*; August 15, 2007, review of *The Lemonade Club*; July 15, 2008, review of *For the Love of Autumn*; October 15, 2008, review of *Someone for Mr. Sussman*.

New York Times Book Review, April 3, 1988, Leonard Marcus, review of *Rechenka's Eggs*, p. 16; November 13, 1994, Henry Mayer, review of *Pink and Say*, p. 42.

Publishers Weekly, April 10, 1987, review of *Meteor!*, p. 95; February 15, 1993, Shannon Maughan, interview with Polacco, pp. 179, 185; August 15, 1994, review of *Pink and Say*, p. 95; September 12, 1994, review of *Tikvah Means Hope*, p. 90; October 12, 1998, review of *Mrs. Mack*, p. 76, and *My Rotten Redheaded Older Brother*, p. 79; September 27, 1999, review of *Welcome Comfort*, p. 56; June 12, 2000, review of *The Butterfly*, p. 72; May 13, 2002, review of *When Lighting Comes in a Jar*, p. 70; August 4, 2003, review of *The Graves Family*, p. 79; March 29, 2004, review of *Oh, Look!*, p. 61; September 27, 2004, review of *An Orange for Frankie*, p. 63; August 8, 2005, review of *Emma Kate*, p. 232; July 5, 2004, review of *John Philip Duck*, p. 56; February 7, 2005, review of *Mommies Say Shhh!*, p. 58; April 9, 2007, review of *Ginger and Petunia*, p. 52; July 30, 2007, review of *The Lemonade Club*, p. 82.

School Library Journal, October, 1988, Lee Bock, review of *The Keeping Quilt*, p. 136; May, 1992, Dorothy Houlihan, review of *Chicken Sunday*, p. 92; August, 1994, Pamela K. Bomboy, review of *Firetalking*, p. 150; November, 1996, review of *The Trees and the Dancing Goat*, pp. 90-91; December, 1998, Christy Norris Blanchette, review of *Mrs. Mack*, p. 89; June, 1999, review of *Meteor!*, p. 119; May, 2000, Wendy Lukehart, review of *The Butterfly*, p. 151; June, 2002, Wanda Meyers-Hines, review of *When Lighting Comes in a Jar*, p. 108; October, 2002, Virginia Walter, review of *Christmas Tapestry*, p. 62; May, 2003, Nancy Call, review of *G Is for Goat*, p. 128; September, 2003, Rachel G. Payne, review of *The Graves Family*, p. 187; February, 2004, Gay Lynn Van Vleck, review of *Oh, Look!*, p. 121; June, 2004, Grace Oliff, review of *John Philip Duck*, p. 116; March, 2005, Rachel G. Payne, review of *Mommies Say Shhh!*, p. 186; June, 2005, Kathleen Kelly MacMillan, review of *The Graves Family Goes Camping*, p. 124; November, 2005, Kristine M. Casper, review of *Emma Kate*, p. 103; May, 2006, Eve Ottenberg Stone, review of *Rotten Richie and the Ultimate Dare*, p. 97; August, 2006, Kathleene Pavin, review of *Something about Hensley's*, p. 94; October, 2007, Susan Lissim, review of *The Lemonade Club*, p. 126; August, 2008, Susan E. Murray, review of *For the Love of Autumn*, p. 100; December, 2008, Beth Cuddy, review of *Someone for Mr. Sussman*, p. 100; May, 2009, Martha Simpson, review of *In Our Mothers' House*, p. 85.

Times Educational Supplement, March 25, 1988, Shaun Traynor, review of *Rechenka's Eggs*, p. 31.

Washington Post Book World, December 12, 1999, Michael Patrick Hearn, "Picturing the Holidays," p. 15.

ONLINE

Patricia Polacco Web site, http://www.patriciapolacco.com (January 10, 2010).

OTHER

Drawing with Patricia Polacco (short film), Art'SCool, 2005.*

R

RADZINSKI, Kandy 1948-

Personal
Born 1948. *Education:* East Texas State University, M.A., 1972.

Addresses
Home—Tulsa, OK. *E-mail*—kradzinski@yahoo.com.

Career
Illustrator, designer, and teacher. Central Washington University, instructor in printmaking and drawing, 1972-73; University of Tulsa, Tulsa, OK, assistant professor of art, 1973-78; K. Radzinski & Company (design firm), Tulsa, president and creator of gift items and art for greeting cards, catalogues, and other consumer products.

Member
Society of Children's Book Writers and Illustrators.

Writings

SELF-ILLUSTRATED

The Twelve Cats of Christmas, Chronicle Books (San Francisco, CA), 1992.
What Cats Want for Christmas, Sleeping Bear Press (Chelsea, MI), 2007.
What Dogs Want for Christmas, Sleeping Bear Press (Chelsea, MI), 2008.
Where to Sleep, Sleeping Bear Press (Chelsea, MI), 2009.

ILLUSTRATOR

Jane Chelsea Aragon, *Lullaby,* Chronicle Books (San Francisco, CA), 1989.

Kandy Radzinski (Photograph by Mark Radzinski. Reproduced by permission.)

Devin Scillian, *S Is for Sooner: An Oklahoma Alphabet,* Sleeping Bear Press (Chelsea, MI), 2003.
Marcia Schonberg, *I Is for Idea: An Inventions Alphabet,* Sleeping Bear Press (Chelsea, MI), 2005.

Sidelights
An entrepreneur, illustrator, artist, and Tae Kwon Do third-degree black belt, Kandy Radzinksi has done some of everything in the illustration field. In addition to teaching drawing and printmaking, she has also created artwork for everything from posters, note cards and Christmas cards to cat-food boxes and children's clothing catalogues. In the arena of children's literature,

Radzinski has also written and illustrated several picture books in addition to contributing artwork to books by writers such as Devin Scillian and Marcia Schoenberg.

Radzinski's first self-illustrated title, *The Twelve Cats of Christmas,* depicts several of her friend's cats. *What Dogs Want for Christmas,* another original self-illustrated picture book, features pictures of fourteen dogs of different breeds along with their wishes for appropriate Christmas gifts, such as a fur coat for a Chihuahua. A contributor to *Kirkus Reviews* commented that in *What Dogs Want for Christmas* "Radzinski's illustrations capture the expression and furry details of each dog, with careful attention to proportion and perspective."

Radzinski's story in *Where to Sleep* follows a cat around a farmyard as it looks for appropriate places to take a nap. Angela Reynolds, writing for *School Library Journal,* commented that the book's "rhymed text is simple enough for beginning readers," while *Booklist* critic Carolyn Phelan concluded that Radzinski's "pleasing, soporific rhythm makes [*Where to Sleep*] . . . a satisfying choice."

Biographical and Critical Sources

PERIODICALS

Booklist, April 1, 2009, Carolyn Phelan, review of *Where to Sleep,* p. 46.
Kirkus Reviews, November 1, 2008, review of *What Dogs Want for Christmas.*

Radzinski creates detailed, folk-styled artwork to pair with her original story in the picture book **Where to Sleep.** (Sleeping Bear Press, 2009. Illustration copyright © 2009 by Kandy Radzinski. Reproduced by permission.)

School Library Journal, May, 2009, Angela J. Reynolds, review of *Where to Sleep,* p. 86.

ONLINE

Kandy Radzinksi Home Page, http://www.kradzinski.com (January 21, 2010).

* * *

RANKIN, Joan 1940-

Personal

Born June 24, 1940, in Johannesburg, South Africa; daughter of Edward Baker (a surgeon) and Ada Lillie (a nurse) Trehair; married Anthony Mottram Rankin (a surgeon), November 25, 1961; children: Nicolette Rojas, Susan, Lorrain. *Education:* Attended Michaelis Art School, 1957-58; attended Johannesburg Technical College; studied painting with Sidney Goldblatt. *Hobbies and other interests:* Cats, dogs, birds, tropical fish, pottery, weaving.

Addresses

Home and office—7 Saint Pauls Rd., Houghton, Johannesburg 2198, South Africa.

Career

Artist, author, and illustrator. Shadow puppeteer; presenter at conferences and schools. *Exhibitions:* Work included in International Exhibitions of Children's Book Illustrations, Sarmede, Italy, 1987-93, 1995-96; Exhibition of International Children's Books, Japan, 1988; International Exhibition of Children's Book Illustrations, Catalonia, Spain, 1990, 1992; Biennale of Illustrations, Bratislava, Slovakia, 1993, 1995; South African Children's Book Illustrations; Flemish Book Fair, Antwerp, Belgium, 1997; Rand Afrikaans University, Johannesburg; University of South Africa, Pretoria; and numerous exhibitions in Johannesburg, Durban, and Cape Town, South Africa.

Member

Johannesburg Children's Book Forum, Union Internationale de la Marionette, Johannesburg Spinners and Weavers Guild, Society for Woman Writers and Journalists.

Awards, Honors

First place, HAUM-Daan Retief Publishers Competition for children's book illustration, 1986, for *The Far-Away Valley* by Jenny Seed; Katrine Harries Children's Book Illustration Award, 2001; Oppenheim Toy Portfolio Gold Award, 2003, for *A Frog in the Bog* by Karma Wilson.

Joan Rankin (Reproduced by permission.)

Writings

SELF-ILLUSTRATED

Peter's Dulcie Duck, Anansi (Cape Town, South Africa), 1993.

The Little Cat and the Greedy Old Woman, Margaret K. McElderry Books (New York, NY), 1995.

Come Quickly, Tafelberg (Cape Town, South Africa), 1996.

Hurry! Hurry!, Human & Rousseau (Cape Town, South Africa), 1996.

Scaredy Cat, Margaret K. McElderry (New York, NY), 1996.

Sorry, I Lost the Baby, Tafelberg (Cape Town, South Africa), 1996.

Fat Paws and Pit Wit, Tafelberg (Cape Town, South Africa), 1996.

Wow! It's Great Being a Duck, Bodley Head (London, England), 1997, Margaret K. McElderry (New York, NY), 1998.

Let's Make a House, Cambridge University Press (Cambridge, England), 1999.

You're Somebody Special, Walliwigs!, Margaret K. McElderry Books (New York, NY), 1999.

First Day, Margaret K. McElderry Books (New York, NY), 2002.

Oh, Mum!, Red Fox (London, England), 2002.

What Sam Said, Songololo Books (Pietermaritzburg, KwaZulu-Natal, South Africa), 2004.

ILLUSTRATOR

Moira Thatcher, *Tselane,* Tafelberg (Cape Town, South Africa), 1986.

M. Margoles and S. Hoffenberg, *Mandu and the Forest Guardian,* Tafelberg (Cape Town, South Africa), 1987.

Jenny Seed, *The Far-Away Valley,* translated by H.J.M. Retief, Daan Retief (Pretoria, South Africa), 1987.

Teddy Knoetze, *The Samurai without a Sword,* Daan Retief (Pretoria, South Africa), 1988.

P. Grobbelaar, *The House with the Seven Doors,* Daan Retief (Pretoria, South Africa), 1988.

The Twelve Days of Christmas, Daan Retief (Pretoria, South Africa), 1989.

Renee Deatlefs, *Ask Patricia,* Human & Rousseau (Cape Town, South Africa), 1989.

Ian Macdonald, *The Dancing Elephant,* Human & Rousseau (Cape Town, South Africa), 1990.

Mitzi Margoles, *Ten Are Too Many,* Human & Rousseau (Cape Town, South Africa), 1990.

Phyllis Savory, *The Little Wise One: African Tales of the Hare,* Tafelberg (Cape Town, South Africa), 1990.

Diane Pitcher, *Catch Me a River,* Tafelberg (Cape Town, South Africa), 1990.

Jenny Seed, *The Wind's Song,* Daan Retief (Pretoria, South Africa), 1991.

Dianne Hofmeyr, *The Magical Mulberry Blanket,* Tafelberg (Cape Town, South Africa), 1991.

Jay Heale, *Storyland,* Tafelberg (Cape Town, South Africa), 1991.

Kathleen Arnot, *Five Zulu Tales,* Anansi (Cape Town, South Africa), 1992.

Jenny Seed, *Old Grandfather Mantis: Tales of the San,* Tafelberg (Cape Town, South Africa), 1992.

Anne Clulow, *Pepper Pig,* Human & Rousseau (Cape Town, South Africa), 1993.

Anne Clulow, *Pepper Pig and the Robber,* Human & Rousseau (Cape Town, South Africa), 1993.

Anne Clulow, *Pepper Pig and the Bad Rats,* Human & Rousseau (Cape Town, South Africa), 1993.

Anne Clulow, *Bubble Gum Mess,* Human & Rousseau (Cape Town, South Africa), 1993.

Anne Clulow, *Help!,* Human & Rousseau (Cape Town, South Africa), 1993.

Judith Garratt, *Titch and Mitch Go to France,* Knowledge Unlimited (Sandton, South Africa), 1993.

Judith Garratt, *The Beautiful Chinese Balloon,* Knowledge Unlimited (Sandton, South Africa), 1993.

Judith Garratt, *The Green Umbrella,* Knowledge Unlimited (Sandton, South Africa), 1993.

Dianne Hofmeyr, *Hic Hic Hiccups,* R.E.A.D. (Johannesburg, South Africa), 1993.

Lindi Mahlangu and Lungi Maseka, *Scary Footsteps,* R.E.A.D. (Johannesburg, South Africa), 1993.

Mitzi Margoles, *King Fob,* Knowledge Unlimited (Sandton, South Africa), 1994.

Max Sed, *Princess, setshameki sa dibaesekapo!,* Oxford University Press (New York, NY), 1994.

John Mathibe, *John and the Porcupine,* Oxford University Press (New York, NY), 1994.

Julius Oelke, chronicler, *From the Heart of the Fire: Folk Tales and Legends,* Tafelberg (Cape Town, South Africa), 1995.

Elana Bregin, *Bert the Crusher,* Human & Rousseau (Cape Town, South Africa), 1995.

Nkululeko Lindi, *Three Fat Cats,* Cambridge University Press (Cambridge, England), 1998.

Alyssa Satin Capucilli, *Mrs. McTats and Her Houseful of Cats,* Margaret K. McElderry Books (New York, NY), 2001.

Karma Wilson, *A Frog in the Bog,* Margaret K. McElderry Books (New York, NY), 2003.

Deborah Ruddell, *Today at the Bluebird Café: A Branchful of Birds,* Margaret K. McElderry Books (New York, NY), 2007.

Wendy Hartmann, *Theo the Library Cat,* LAPA Publishers (South Australia, Australia), 2007.

Wendy Hartmann, *Theo and the Cat Burglar,* LAPA Publishers (South Australia, Australia), 2007.

Wendy Hartmann, *Theo and the Circus Act,* LAPA Publishers (South Australia, Australia), 2007.

Louise Borden, *Off to First Grade,* Margaret K. McElderry Books (New York, NY), 2008.

Deborah Ruddell, *A Whiff of Pine, a Hint of Skunk: A Forest of Poems,* Margaret K. McElderry Books (New York, NY), 2009.

Sidelights

South African author and illustrator Joan Rankin was born and raised in the city of Johannesburg, where she still lives today. After studying painting, weaving, and pottery in college, Rankin set out to become an illustrator, mostly gearing her work toward adults. In 1986, however, she began illustrating books for children, and one of her early works, *The Far-Away Valley,* won first place in the HAUM-Daan Retief competition for children's-book illustration. Rankin has gone on to illustrate her own books, as well as tales by other authors, such as Anne Clulow, Judith Garratt, Louise Borden, and Karma Wilson. Her favorite artistic mediums

Rankin's artwork adds a dose of humor to Alyssa Satin Capucilli's story in **Mrs. McTats and Her Houseful of Cats.** (Illustration copyright © 2001 by Joan Rankin. Reprinted with the permission of Margaret K. McElderry Books, an imprint of Simon & Schuster Macmillan.)

include water color, crayon, and pencil, although she sometimes uses airbrush, collage, and rubber stamps. Most of Rankin's books deal with young children and the real-life situations that they face.

One of Rankin's first self-illustrated books, *The Little Cat and the Greedy Old Woman,* finds an old woman spending her day preparing a delicious meal for herself while ignoring the mewling of her hungry little cat. The cat finally helps itself to some of the old woman's food and is thrown out into the rain as punishment. What happens next allows the cat to get sweet revenge. As a *Books for Keeps* reviewer wrote, *The Little Cat and the Greedy Old Woman* "has the feel of a cautionary tale, and could provide lots of interesting discussions." In *Wow! It's Great Being a Duck,* Lillee is a newborn duckling who still has a bit of shell stuck to her. Unfortunately, the shell covers the duckling's eyes. Her mother warns Lillee to stay away from Fox, but since Lillee cannot yet see, she allows the fox to befriend her without realizing who it is. In the nick of time, the shell falls off and Lillee scampers and swims to safety. *Booklist* critic April Judge predicted that children will enjoy the tale "because they will realize the case of mistaken identity before the duckling does."

In *You're Somebody Special, Walliwigs!* a parrot gets separated from his mother and ends up living with a flock of chickens. One of the hens, Martha, immediately adopts and loves colorful Walliwigs, but the other chickens make fun of him. Much to the sadness of Martha, Walliwigs is taken away to the Institute of Ornithology, where it is discovered that he is rare and, in fact, an endangered species. When she finds this out, Martha rejoices to learn that Walliwigs will be taken care of properly. In *Booklist* Shelle Rosenfeld commented that Rankin's "delightful, reassuring story celebrates the many meanings of family," while a *Publishers Weekly* reviewer called *You're Somebody Special, Walliwigs!* "endearing and uplifting."

Another tale by Ranking that features animal protagonists, *First Day* deals with Haybillybun and his first day at puppy school. Haybillybun begins to imagine all kinds of problems that might crop up in his day: his name is too long, his fuzzy ears will keep him from hearing his teacher, or his "slip-slidey-fluffy-feet" will stop him from being able to run and play. However, after none of his fears is realized, the young pup has great fun. Predicting that *First Day* will appeal to parents and children preparing for the beginning of school, a *Kirkus Reviews* critic found it "difficult to resist the beautiful watercolor illustrations that give such personality to the worried puppies and his friends."

Rankin's illustration work for other authors includes creating the art for Deborah Ruddell's *Today at the Bluebird Café: A Branchful of Birds,* which includes over twenty short verses about birds of all colors, shapes, and sizes. Calling Ruddell's poetry "neat," Joanna Rudge Long added in *School Library Journal*

that "Rankin's airy, light-filled watercolors pull it all together, real and fantastical alike." Another collaboration with Ruddell, *A Whiff of Pine, a Hint of Skunk: A Forest of Poems,* features the author and illustrator's signature "whimsical scenarios that will amuse" young readers while also introducing "basic zoological facts," according to *Booklist* critic Gillian Engberg. Bringing to life Louise Borden's A-to-Z free-verse poems in *Off to First Grade,* Rankin's "quirky watercolor cartoons are humorous and expressive," according to Lynne Mattern in *School Library Journal.* In her contribution to Karma Wilson's award-winning picture book *A Frog in the Bog* Rankin also adds a comic touch, contributing what a *Publishers Weekly* contributor described as "sassy, intricately composed watercolors that . . . look appropriately bog-spattered."

Rankin once told *SATA:* "I started as an abstract painter, then moved into weaving, making hand-woven puppets, and lastly children's book illustrating and writing. Being creative and using the imagination is a very important part of my life. It is something I wish to encourage in children. Through children's books and visiting schools, I hope to widen . . . children's horizons, by showing them book illustrations, drawing for them, and showing them shadow puppet theatre.

"Many of the books I have illustrated have been African folktales. These stories are of special value, I think. Through my writing, I try to address areas that are painful to small children. Often I use animals as the main characters. Humor and quality are essential ingredients."

Biographical and Critical Sources

PERIODICALS

Booklist, June 1, 1998, April Judge, review of *Wow! It's Great Being a Duck,* p. 1781; July, 1999, Shelle Rosenfeld, review of *You're Somebody Special, Walliwigs!,* p. 1954; September 1, 2001, Susan Dove Lempke, review of *Mrs. McTats and Her Houseful of Cats,* p. 113; June 1, 2002, Hazel Rochman, review of *First Day,* p. 1743; November 1, 2003, Kay Weisman, review of *A Frog in the Bog,* p. 508; January 1, 2007, Gillian Engberg, review of *Today at the Bluebird Café: A Branchful of Birds,* p. 110; March 15, 2009, Gillian Engberg, review of *A Whiff of Pine, a Hint of Skunk: A Forest of Poems,* p. 64.

Books for Keeps, January, 1999, Judith Sharman, review of *Scaredy Cat,* p. 18; September, 1999, review of *The Little Cat and the Greedy Old Woman,* p. 22.

Horn Book, May-June, 2007, Joanna Rudge Long, review of *Today at the Bluebird Café,* p. 297.

Kirkus Reviews, June 1, 2002, review of *First Day,* p. 809.

New York Times Book Review, April 27, 1997, review of *Scaredy Cat,* p. 29.

Publishers Weekly, December 22, 1997, review of *Wow! It's Great Being a Duck,* p. 58; May 3, 1999, review of *Scaredy Cat,* p. 78; June 7, 1999, review of *You're*

Somebody Special, Walliwigs!, p. 82; January 15, 2001, review of *Wow! It's Great Being a Duck,* p. 78; May 28, 2001, review of *Mrs. McTats and Her Houseful of Cats,* p. 87; May 27, 2002, review of *First Day,* p. 59; October 20, 2003, review of *A Frog in the Bog,* p. 52; December 11, 2006, review of *Today at the Bluebird Café,* p. 68.

School Library Journal, March, 1998, Patricia Pearl Dole, review of *Wow! It's Great Being a Duck,* p. 186; August, 1999, Alicia Eames, review of *You're Somebody Special, Walliwigs!,* p. 141; July, 2002, Lisa Gangemi Kropp, review of *First Day,* p. 97; December, 2003, Linda L. Walkins, review of *A Frog in the Bog,* p. 130; February, 2007, Grace Oliff, review of *Today at the Bluebird Café,* p. 112; August, 2008, Lynne Mattern, review of *Off to First Grade,* p. 84; April, 2009, Kirsten Cutler, review of *A Whiff of Pine, a Hint of Skunk,* p. 126.

ONLINE

University of South Africa Children's Literature Research Unit Web site, http://www.childlit.org.za/ (January 10, 2010), "Joan Rankin."*

*   *   *

RAWLINSON, Julia

Personal

Born in London, England; married; husband's name Neil; children: two sons. *Education:* Southampton University, degree (geography).

Addresses

Home—London, England.

Career

Children's book author.

Writings

FOR CHILDREN

Fred and the Little Egg, illustrated by Jane Massey, Good Books (Intercourse, PA), 2005.

A Surprise for Rosie, illustrated by Tim Warnes, Tiger Tales (Wilton, CT), 2005, published as *Rosie's Special Surprise,* Little Tiger (London, England), 2005.

Fletcher and the Falling Leaves, illustrated by Tiphanie Beeke, Greenwillow Books (New York, NY), 2006, published as *Ferdie and the Falling Leaves,* Gullane Children's (London, England), 2006.

Mule School, illustrated by Lynne Chapman, Gullane Children's (London, England), 2008, Good Books (Intercourse, PA), 2008.

Fletcher and the Springtime Blossoms, illustrated by Tiphanie Beeke, Greenwillow Books (New York, NY), 2009, review of *Ferdie's Sprintime Blossom,* Gullane Children's (London, England), 2009.

Contributor of poems to children's anthologies.

Author's works have been translated into French.

Sidelights

Julia Rawlinson's books for young readers include *Fred and the Little Egg, A Surprise for Rosie,* and *Fletcher and the Falling Leaves. Fred and the Little Egg,* focuses on a bear cub who hopes to help Mother Nature nurture new life by making a cozy nest for a fallen acorn, which he confusedly thinks is the oak tree's egg. Teaching her son a lesson about life, Fred's mother explains to the helpful cub that, because a seed is not an egg, planting is a better way to help the acorn grow. Another story of an animal with lessons to learn, *Mule School* introduces Stomper, a helpful mule who is unsuccessful in learning to stubbornly balk and slow things like a good mule should. Featuring illustrations by Lynne Chapman, *Mule School* was described by a *Kirkus Reviews* writer as a "quirky" tale in which Rawlinson's "humorous cast of characters and lively prose serves the timeless message well."

Another story dealing with a young nature lover, *Fletcher and the Falling Leaves,* was called a "potent synthesis of art and prose" by *School Library Journal* contributor Catherine Threadgill. Published in England as *Ferdie and the Falling Leaves,* the tale finds a young fox worried when the leaves on his favorite tree turn as

Julia Rawlinson's seasonal story Fletcher and the Springtime Blossoms *features gentle, evocative art by Tiphanie Beeke.* (Greenwillow Books, 2009. Illustrations copyright © 2009 by Tiphanie Beeke. Used by permisssion of HarperCollins Children's Books, a division of HarperCollins Publishers.)

brown as Fletcher's own foxy fur coat. When autumn leaves begin to fall, the fox tries to reattach them, but to no avail; by the time Fletcher needs to hibernate, most have blown away. Worry turns to wonder, however, when the fox emerges from his den in mid-winter to find his favorite tree glistening with strands of icicles. Praising *Fletcher and the Falling Leaves* as "a poetic tribute to winter and fall," a *Kirkus Reviews* writer cited Rawlinson's "warm and lyrical text," while Threadgill noted the "resplendent" water-color illustrations by Tiphanie Beeke.

Beeke and Rawlinson reunite for *Fletcher and the Springtime Blossoms,* in which Fletcher the fox emerges from his den to discover that the air is still full of floating objects that he concludes are snowflakes, even though the air is warm and buds and green shoots are emerging to greet the sun. He rushes to warn his woodland friends that snow is coming, but the young fox is quickly corrected: it is not snow he sees, but tree blossoms! Praising Beeke's artwork for its "signature naif style," a *Publishers Weekly* contributor also predicted that Rawlinson's "distinctive British lilt . . . should prove captivating for preschoolers." She "writes lyrically, almost poetically," noted Donna Cardon in her *School Library Journal* review of *Fletcher and the Springtime Blossoms,* the critic also praising the author's use of "rhythm, alliteration, and onomatopoeia."

In *A Surprise for Rosie* toddlers meet a curious young rabbit whose father has promised her a surprise. Rosie searches for her surprise with the help of her woodland animal friends, who provide her with clues, but she eventually gives up. Finally, her surprise is ultimately revealed in a foldout: a basket held aloft by a huge blue balloon, in which Rosie and her father can take a ride into the sky. In *School Library Journal* Wanda Meyers-Hines called *A Surprise for Rosie* "a great choice for a read-aloud or naptime story," while in *Kirkus Reviews* a critic predicted that Rawlinson's "readers will definitely share Rosie's delight."

Biographical and Critical Sources

PERIODICALS

Kirkus Reviews, March 1, 2005, review of *A Surprise for Rosie,* p. 294; August 1, 2006, review of *Fletcher and the Falling Leaves,* p. 794; May 15, 2008, review of *Mule School;* February 15, 2009, review of *Fletcher and the Springtime Blossoms.*

Publishers Weekly, February 14, 2005, review of *A Surprise for Rosie,* p. 75; January 5, 2009, review of *Fletcher and the Springtime Blossoms,* p. 48.

School Library Journal, May, 2005, Wanda Meyers-Hines, review of *A Surprise for Rosie,* p. 94; August, 2006, Catherine Threadgill, review of *Fletcher and the Falling Leaves,* p. 94; August, 2008, Catherine Threadgill,

review of *Mule School,* p. 100; April, 2009, Donna Cardon, review of *Fletcher and the Springtime Blossoms,* p. 115.*

*   *   *

RICH, Anna 1956-

Personal

Born 1956; married; children: one son. *Education:* Rhode Island School of Design, B.F.A.

Addresses

Home and office—Elmont, NY.

Career

Illustrator. Works for Graphic Artists Guild.

Illustrator

Dakari Hru, *Joshua's Masai Mask,* Lee & Low (New York, NY), 1993.

Barbara E. Barber, *Saturday at the New You,* Lee & Low (New York, NY), 1994.

Ellen Levine, *If You Lived at the Time of Martin Luther King,* Scholastic, Inc. (New York, NY), 1994.

Angela Shelf Medearis, *Annie's Gifts,* Just Us Books (East Orange, NJ), 1994.

Angela Shelf Medearis, *Dare to Dream: Coretta Scott King and the Civil Rights Movement,* Lodestar (New York, NY), 1994.

Angela Shelf Medearis, *Little Louis and the Jazz Band: The Story of Louis "Satchmo" Armstrong,* Lodestar (New York, NY), 1994.

Camille Yarbrough, *Tamika and the Wisdom Rings,* Random House (New York, NY), 1994.

A.R. Flowers, *Cleveland Lee's Beale Street Band,* Bridgewater (Mahwah, NJ), 1995.

Olive Wong, *From My Window,* Silver (Parsippany, NJ), 1995.

Cheryl and Wade Hudson, compilers, *Kids' Book of Wisdom: Quotes from the African-American Tradition,* Just Us Books (East Orange, NJ), 1996.

Karen English, *Just Right Stew,* Boyds Mills (Honesdale, PA), 1998.

Dee Boyd, *Only the Stars,* Scholastic, Inc. (New York, NY), 2004.

Amy Lundebrek, *Under the Night Sky,* Tilbury House (Gardiner, ME), 2008.

Sidelights

Known for creating artwork that features multicultural themes, Anna Rich developed a love of drawing as a young child, and by high school she knew she wanted to make illustration her career. After graduating from the Rhode Island School of Design, Rich began providing illustrations for magazines and newspapers, along with working for the Graphic Artists Guild. In 1993, the first picture book illustrated by Rich, Dakari Hru's

Anna Rich creates dramatic that capture the beauty of the Northern Lights in her art for Amy Lundebrek's **Under the Night Sky.** (Tilbury House, 2008. Illustration copyright © 2008 by Anna Rich. Reproduced by permission.)

Joshua's Masai Mask, was published. A *Publishers Weekly* critic said of the title that "children may well take pride in recognizing themselves in Rich's bold artwork, bursting with bright hues and humor."

In her more-recent work, Rich continues to produce images that reflect diverse cultures and ethnicities. A beauty parlor in an African-American neighborhood is the setting for *Saturday at the New You,* a story by Barbara E. Barber in which Rich "paints with joie de vivre, imparting kindliness to every face," according to a *Publishers Weekly* reviewer. Olive Wong's *From My Window* is told from the perspective of a young African-American boy who also lives in a multicultural neighborhood, and here Rich's combined close-ups and panoramic scenes feature bright colors and "bold outlines" that "coalesce into a visually engaging whole," according to a *Publishers Weekly* contributor.

An African-American family tries to recreate Victoria's grandmother's oxtail stew in *Just Right Stew,* a story by Karen English. Although her mother and aunts do their best, only Victoria knows the secret ingredient. Susan Dove Lempke, writing in *Booklist,* noted the "expressive faces and the deftly observed body language" in Rich's illustrations for the tale, and a writer for *Publishers Weekly* commented that the "boldly hued, tex-tured oil paintings add an extra dash of humor" to English's family-centered tale. Featuring a text by Amy Lundebrek, *Under the Night Sky* takes place in a northerly environment, as a mother wakes up her son to show him the aurora borealis. A *Kirkus Reviews* contributor felt that Rich's "paintings tremble with a feeling of anticipation and a sense that magic is in the air."

Biographical and Critical Sources

PERIODICALS

Booklist, September 15, 1994, Kay Weisman, review of *Tamika and the Wisdom Rings,* p. 138; December 1, 1994, Hazel Rochman, review of *Saturday at the New You,* p. 684; February 15, 1998, Susan Dove Lempke, review of *Just Right Stew,* p. 1019.

Kirkus Reviews, September 15, 2008, review of *Under the Night Sky.*

Publishers Weekly, May 10, 1993, review of *Joshua's Masai Mask,* p. 71; September 19, 1994, review of *Saturday at the New You,* p. 68; July 3, 1995, review of *From My Window,* p. 59; January 12, 1998, review of *Just Right Stew,* p. 59.

School Library Journal, August, 2008, Martha Simpson, review of *Under the Night Sky,* p. 97.

ONLINE

Lee & Low Web site, http://www.leeandlow.com/ (January 19, 2010), "Anna Rich."*

*   *   *

ROBERTS, Marion 1966-

Personal

Born 1966, in Australia. *Education:* Studied alternative medicine and psychotherapy; attended RMIT University (Melbourne, Victoria, Australia); postgraduate study at Melbourne University.

Addresses

Home—Victoria, Australia.

Career

Writer. Previously worked as a naturopath and counselor; formerly ran a whole-foods cooking school.

Writings

Sunny Side Up, Wendy Lamb (New York, NY), 2009.

Sidelights

Australian writer Marion Roberts worked as a naturopath and counselor, and also ran a whole-foods cooking school, before she turned to writing and followed her interest in fiction-writing. Roberts had no plans to become a writer until she stumbled upon a writing course at RMIT University in Melbourne, Victoria, and eventually produced her first novel, *Sunny Side Up.*

Sunny Side Up recounts a pivotal summer for Australian teen Sunny. Although Sunny's parents are divorced, the family has remained emotionally placid and the separation was amicable. Now, however, Sunny has to adjust to her mother's boyfriend moving in with his two children, as well as her stepmother's pregnancy and an invitation to visit her estranged grandmother. Beyond these family concerns, Sunny's best friend and partner in the Friday-night Pizza-a-Go-Girl business has become boy crazy, crushing on a boy who Sunny dislikes.

"Roberts's glib, tangential, first-person narrative promises—and delivers—moments of charming girlhood transition and pathos," wrote a *Kirkus Reviews* critic in appraising *Sunny Side Up.* Sunny's "authentic first-person voice" was cited by Monika Schroeder in *Book-* *list,* and Jennifer Ralston called the heroine's running commentary "precocious and funny" in her *School Library Journal* review of the novel. Along with her story's humorous tangents and lighthearted tone, "Roberts raises potent questions about honesty and forgiveness," added a *Publishers Weekly* contributor, concluding that *Sunny Side Up* offers teens more than just entertainment.

Biographical and Critical Sources

PERIODICALS

Booklist, January 1, 2009, Monika Schroder, review of *Sunny Side Up,* p. 86.
Kirkus Reviews, December 1, 2008, review of *Sunny Side Up.*
Publishers Weekly, January 19, 2009, review of *Sunny Side Up,* p. 60.
School Library Journal, February, 2009, Jennifer Ralston, review of *Sunny Side Up,* p. 108.

Cover of Marion Roberts' middle-grade novel Sunny Side Up, *featuring artwork by Allen Crawford.* (Jacket art © 2009 by Allen Crawford/Plankton Art Co. Used by permission of Wendy Lamb Books, an imprint of Random House Children's Books, a division of Random House, Inc.)

ONLINE

Booked Out Web site, http://www.bookedout.com.au/
(January 19, 2010), "Marion Roberts."*

* * *

ROBERTUS, Polly M. 1948-

Personal

Surname is pronounced "row-bert-us"; born January 16, 1948, in Denver, CO; daughter of John Clinton Mohler (a journalist) and Dorothy May Schell; married Jon D. Robertus (a professor of chemistry), August 28, 1971; children: David, Clare, Kate. *Education:* University of California, San Diego, B.A. (with honors), 1970; attended University of Texas at Austin, beginning 1991.

Addresses

Home—Austin, TX.

Career

Writer. Girl Scout leader; member of neighborhood association board.

Member

Society of Children's Book Writers and Illustrators.

Writings

The Dog Who Had Kittens, illustrated by Janet Stevens, Holiday House (New York, NY), 1991.
The Richest Doll in the World, Holiday House (New York, NY), 2008.

Contributor of stories to *Cricket.*

Sidelights

Texas-based writer Polly M. Robertus published her first children's book, *The Dog Who Had Kittens,* in the early 1990s, and it would be over fifteen years before her second book, *The Richest Doll in the World,* was released. "I always wanted to be a writer, but for many years that's as far as I got," Robertus once told *SATA.* "I didn't know how authors worked. I thought that I had to have the whole idea in my head before I started, and that I should start with 'Chapter One' and write in complete, perfectly grammatical sentences all the way to 'The End.' Now I know that I have to start writing in order to *discover* what I'm going to write about, and that I can do draft after draft after draft, each one representing a larger discovery of what a piece is to become."

A picture book featuring illustrations by Janet Stevens, *The Dog Who Had Kittens* features a story based on one Robertus first published in *Cricket* magazine. "One day I was casting about for an idea," she once noted,

Polly M. Robertus's story in **The Dog Who Had Kittens** *is brought to life in detailed artwork by* **Janet Stevens.** (Illustration copyright © 1991 by Janet Stevens. Reproduced by permission of Holiday House, Inc.)

explaining the story's origins. "I decided to make a list of made-up titles without thinking about it very much—just writing fifteen or so titles very quickly. When I was done, I read back over the list . . . [and] was most surprised to see 'The Dog Who Had Kittens.' I liked the sound of it, and immediately was reminded of an incident that I had entirely forgotten about.

"I'd gone to pick up my oldest daughter at her friend's house, and they'd invited me in to see their new kittens. When I got in, their little dog wouldn't let me anywhere near the kittens; he or she jumped in the box with them and barked at me. My daughter's friend said, 'Our dog is a better mother to those kittens than their own mother!'"

In her middle-grade novel *The Richest Doll in the World*, Robertus introduces Emily, a girl who lives with her grandmother now that her parents have been tragically killed in an accident. Grandma Rose works as a companion to Mrs. Bigley, a crotchety elderly woman who has a mind of her own. After the wealthy Mrs. Bigley tells Emily about the presents she gives to Delilah, the beautiful porcelain doll that she keeps in the basement of her house, the girl's curiosity about the woman's strange fascination with the toy is piqued. When Emily leaves daycare in order to sneak into Mrs. Bigley's basement and scout out Delilah's whereabouts, Grandma Rose is notified and becomes alarmed. Meanwhile Mrs. Bigley decides to find Delilah the smallest dog in the world, and her fixation on the doll begins to appear unhealthy. Calling *The Richest Doll in the World* a "fast-paced novel," Debbie Whitbeck added in her *School Library Journal* that Robertus mixes "intrigue" and "suspense" as she follows both Emily and Mrs. Bigley as their paths intersect on a snowy Christmas Eve.

Discussing her work as a writer, Robertus admitted: "I love writing. I'm finally accomplishing my dream of writing a lot, every day, without worrying what the product will be. I trust the process and all my experience as a human being, a reader, and a writer to take care of the end result; I just show up and get to work."

Biographical and Critical Sources

PERIODICALS

Booklist, April 15, 1993, Lolly Gepson, review of *The Dog Who Had Kittens*, p. 1529.

Kirkus Reviews, March 15, 2008, review of *The Richest Doll in the World*.

School Library Journal, March, 1993, Fay L. Matsunaga, review of *The Dog Who Had Kittens*, p. 154; October, 2008, Debbie Whitbeck, review of *The Richest Doll in the World*, p. 120.*

ROONEY, Ronnie 1970-

Personal

Born 1970. *Education:* Attended University of Massachusetts, Amherst; Savannah College of Art and Design, M.F.A.

Addresses

Home—Plymouth, MA. *Agent*—Bernadette Szost, Portfolio Solutions, 136 Jameson Hill Rd., Clinton Corners, NY 12514.

Career

Illustrator.

Illustrator

L.A. Murphy, *Heavensbee,* Little Friend Press (Scituate, MA), 1996.

William Boniface, *Christmastime Is Cookie Time,* Price Stern Sloan (New York, NY), 2001.

Lin Quinn, *The Best Mud Pie,* Children's Press (New York, NY), 2001.

William Boniface, *Santa's Sleigh Is Full!: A Top This! Book,* Price Stern Sloan (New York, NY), 2002.

Cathy Goldberg Fishman, *Soup,* Children's Press (New York, NY), 2002.

William Boniface, *What Do You Want in Your Cereal Bowl?,* Price Stern Sloan (New York, NY), 2002.

William Boniface, *Easter Bunnies Everywhere: A Top This! Book,* Price Stern Sloan (New York, NY), 2003.

Susan Blackaby, *Bess and Tess,* Picture Window Books (Minneapolis, MN), 2005.

Christianne C. Jones, *How the Camel Got Its Hump,* Picture Window Books (Minneapolis, MN), 2005.

Chiristianne C. Jones, *Around the Park: A Book about Circles,* Picture Window Books (Minneapolis, MN), 2006.

Nick Fauchald, *Batter Up! You Can Play Softball,* Picture Window Books (Minneapolis, MN), 2006.

Nick Fauchald, *Bump! Set! Spike! You Can Play Volleyball,* Picture Window Books (Minneapolis, MN), 2006.

Terri Dougherty, *Emily's Pictures,* Picture Window Books (Minneapolis, MN), 2006.

Nick Fauchald, *Face Off! You Can Play Hockey,* Picture Window Books (Minneapolis, MN), 2006.

Christianne C. Jones, *Four Sides the Same: A Book about Squares,* Picture Window Books (Minneapolis, MN), 2006.

Christianne C. Jones, *Party of Three: A Book about Triangles,* Picture Window Books (Minneapolis, MN), 2006.

Larry Dane Brimner, *Rumble Bus,* Child's World (Chanhassen, MN), 2006.

Nick Fauchald, *Tee Off! You Can Play Golf,* Picture Window Books (Minneapolis, MN), 2006.

Lisa Konzen, *The Great Catch of Fish: Luke 5:1-11 for Children,* Concordia Pub. House (St. Louis, MO), 2006.

Christianne C. Jones, *Two Short, Two Long: A Book about Rectangles,* Picture Window Books (Minneapolis, MN), 2006.

Jill L. Donahue, *Danny's Birthday,* Picture Window Books (Minneapolis, MN), 2007.

Charnan Simon, *Officers Everywhere!,* Child's World (Chanhassen, MN), 2007.

Nick Healy, *The Big Pig,* Picture Window Books (Minneapolis, MN), 2007.

Shirley Raye Redmond, *The Princesses' Lucky Day,* Picture Window Books (Minneapolis, MN), 2007.

David Michael Slater, *Comin' Through,* Magic Wagon (Edina, MN), 2008.

Amanda Doering Tourville, *Get Up and Go: Being Active,* Picture Window Books (Minneapolis, MN), 2008.

Trudi Strain Trueit, *Memorial Day,* Child's World (Mankato, MN), 2008.

Janice Kramer, *The Christmas Baby: The Story of Christmas from Luke 2 for Children,* Concordia Pub. House (St. Louis, MO), 2008.

Marcie Aboff, *The Pool Party,* Picture Window Books (Minneapolis, MN), 2008.

Molly Blaisdell, *Up, Up in the Air,* Picture Window Books (Minneapolis, MN), 2008.

Amanda Doering Tourville, *Brush, Floss, and Rinse: Caring for Your Teeth and Gums,* Picture Window Books (Minneapolis, MN), 2009.

Amanda Doering Tourville, *Fuel the Body: Eating Well,* Picture Window Books (Minneapolis, MN), 2009.

Nick Fauchald, *Funky Chicken Enchiladas and Other Mexican Dishes,* Picture Window Books (Minneapolis, MN), 2009.

Amanda Doering Tourville, *Go Wash Up: Keeping Clean,* Picture Window Books (Minneapolis, MN), 2009.

Nick Fauchald, *On-the-go Schwarmas, and Other Middle-Eastern Dishes,* Picture Window Books (Minneapolis, MN), 2009.

Nick Fauchald, *Roly-poly Ravioli and Other Italian Dishes,* Picture Window Books (Minneapolis, MN), 2009.

The Wheels on the Bus, Child's World (Mankato, MN), 2009.

Nick Fauchald, *Wrap-n-bake Egg Rolls, and Other Chinese Dishes,* Picture Window Books (Minneapolis, MN), 2009.

Melinda Melton Crow, *Mud Mess,* Stone Arch Books (Minneapolis, MN), 2010.

Mari Kesselring, *November,* Magic Wagon (Edina, MN), 2010.

Mari Kesselring, *October,* Magic Wagon (Edina, MN), 2010.

Melinda Melton Crow, *Road Race,* Stone Arch Books (Minneapolis, MN), 2010.

Mari Kesselring, *September,* Magic Wagon (Edina, MN), 2010.

Melinda Melton Crow, *Snow Trouble,* Stone Arch Books (Minneapolis, MN), 2010.

Melinda Melton Crow, *Truck Buddies,* Stone Arch Books (Minneapolis, MN), 2010.

Biographical and Critical Sources

PERIODICALS

School Library Journal, February, 2008, Sarah O'Holla, review of *Memorial Day,* p. 110; August, 2008, Martha Topol, review of *Comin' Through,* p. 102.

ONLINE

Portfolio Solutions Web site, http://www.portfoliosolutions llc.com/ (January 18, 2010), "Ronnie Rooney."*

S

SELLIER, Marie 1953-

Personal
Born 1953, in France. *Education:* College degree.

Addresses
Home—Nogent sur Marne, Paris, France. *E-mail*—toulne@aol.com.

Career
Journalist, editor, scriptwriter, and author of books for children. Bayard Press, Paris, France, editor for ten years.

Awards, Honors
Prix Sorcière and prix Octogone, both 2001, both for *L'Afrique petit Chaka.*

Writings

T comme Toulouse-Lautrec (board book), Réunion des Musées Nationaux/Seuil (Paris, France), 1992.

M comme Matisse (board book), Réunion des Musées Nationaux/Seuil (Paris, France), 1993, translated by Claudia Zoe Bedrick as *Matisse from A to Z,* Peter Bedrick Books (New York, NY), 1995.

C comme Chagall (board book), Réunion des Musées Nationaux/Seuil (Paris, France), 1993, translated by Claudia Zoe Bedrick as *Chagall from A to Z,* Peter Bedrick Books (New York, NY), 1996.

B comme Bonnard (board book), Réunion des Musées Nationaux/Seuil (Paris, France), 1993, translated by Claudia Zoe Bedrick as *Bonnard from A to Z,* Peter Bedrick Books (New York, NY), 1997.

(With Elisabeth Delange) *C comme Chardin* (board book), Réunion des Musées Nationaux/Seuil (Paris, France), 1993.

M comme Manet (board book), Réunion des Musées Nationaux/Seuil (Paris, France), 1994.

C comme Cézanne (board book), Réunion des Musées Nationaux/Seuil (Paris, France), 1995 translated by Claudia Zoe Bedrick as *Cézanne from A to Z,* Peter Bedrick Books (New York, NY), 1996.

R comme Rodin (board book), Réunion des Musées Nationaux/Seuil (Paris, France), 1996.

M comme Monet (board book), Réunion des Musées Nationaux/Seuil (Paris, France), 1997.

E comme Egypte (board book), Réunion des Musées Nationaux/Seuil (Paris, France), 1997.

D comme Delacroix (board book), Réunion des Musées Nationaux/Seuil (Paris, France), 1998.

B comme Bruegel (board book), Réunion des Musées Nationaux/Seuil (Paris, France), 1998.

V comme Van Gogh (board book), Réunion des Musées Nationaux/Seuil (Paris, France), 1999.

Le peinture entrée libre, Éditions Nathan (Paris, France), 2000.

L'Afrique petit Chaka, illustrated by Marion Lesage, Réunion des Musées Nationaux (Paris, France), 2001.

My Little Orsay, Réunion des Musées Nationaux (Paris, France), 2001.

Zadkine: des mains pour Créer, Chez Paris-Musée (Paris, France), 2001.

Mon petit Louvre (board book), Réunion des Musées Nationaux (Paris, France), 2001.

Mon petit Picasso (board book), Réunion des Musées Nationaux (Paris, France), 2002.

Mais où est donc passé Yvon?, illustrated by Béatrice Giffo, Éditions du Télélegramme, 2002.

Le réve de Louis (board book), illustrated by Luc Gauthier, Réunion des Musées Nationaux (Paris, France), 2002.

Maillol: Des mains pour créer (board book), Chez Paris-Musée (Paris, France), 2003.

My Little Cluny (board book), Réunion des Musées Nationaux (Paris, France), 2004.

Le douze manteaux de Maman, illustrated by Nathalie Novi and Miriam Mafou Métisse, Adam Biró-Jeunesse, 2005.

Marie Sellier's Asian-themed picture book **What the Rat Told Me: A Legend of the Chinese Zodiac** *features Catherine Louis' graphic-styled illustrations.* (North-South, 2009. Used with permission of North-South Books, Inc., New York, NY.)

L'histoire sans fin des Mafous et des Ratafous, illustrated by Diagne Chanel, Chez Paris-Musée (Paris, France), 2005.

Mon carnet vietnamien, illustrated by Cécile Gambini, 2006.

La lune nue, illustrated by Hélène Rajcak, Baron Perché, 2006.

Arts décoratifs entrée libre, Éditions Nathan (Paris, France), 2006.

Arts primitifs, entrée libre, Éditions Nathan (Paris, France), 2006.

(With Wang Fei) *La naissance du dragon,* illustrated by Catherine Louis, 2006, translated by Sibylle Kazeroid as *Legend of the Chinese Dragon,* NorthSouth Books (New York, NY), 2008.

My Little Pompidou Centre (board book), Réunion des Musées Nationaux (Paris, France), 2007.

What the Rat Told Me: A Legend of the Chinese Zodiac, illustrated by Catherine Louis, calligraphy by Wang Fei, NorthSouth (New York, NY), 2009.

Renoir's Colors, J. Paul Getty Museum (Los Angeles, CA), 2010.

Author or collaborator on art-related book series for Chez Paris-Musée and Réunion des Musées Nationaux.

Author of five scripts for French-language television series *Artistes,* produced by Michaël Gaumnitz.

Biographical and Critical Sources

PERIODICALS

Booklist, December 15, 2007, Linda Perkins, review of *Legend of the Chinese Dragon,* p. 47; March 15, 2009, Linda Perkins, review of *What the Rat Told Me: A Legend of the Chinese Zodiac,* p. 68.

Kirkus Reviews, April 1, 2008, review of *Legend of the Chinese Dragon*; December 1, 2008, review of *What the Rat Told Me.*

Publishers Weekly, November 20, 1995, review of *Matisse from A to Z,* p. 76.

School Library Journal, December, 2007, Margaqret A. Chang, review of *Legend of the Chinese Dragon,* p. 100; April, 2009, C.J. Connor, review of *What the Rat Told Me,* p. 126.

ONLINE

Repertoire Web site, http://charte.repertoir.free.fr/ (January 15, 2010), "Marie Sellier."*

*   *   *

SLATER, David Michael 1970-

Personal
Born May 8, 1970, in Pittsburgh, PA; son of Harvey (a burn surgeon) and Beverly (a teacher) Slater; married; wife's name Heidi (a library media specialist); children: Maxwell. *Education:* University of Michigan, B.A., 1992; Carnegie-Mellon University, M.A., 1994; Lewis and Clark College, M.A.T., 1995.

Addresses
Home—Portland, OR. *Agent*—Jennifer Carlson, Dunow, Carlson & Lerner, 27 W. 20th St., Ste. 1007, New York, NY 10011; Robin Kaver, Robert A. Freedman Dramatic Agency, 1501 Broadway, Ste. 2310, New York, NY 10036.

Career
Educator and author. Seventh-grade language arts teacher in Portland, OR, 1995—.

Awards, Honors
New Talent award, Great American Novel Contest, 2000, for *Selfless;* Cascadia Exchange Award, Pacific Northwest Playwrights Guild, 1996; honor book selection, Society of School Librarians International, for *The Ring Bear.*

Writings

FOR CHILDREN

Cheese Louise!, illustrated by Steve Cowden, Whitecap Books (Vancouver, British Columbia, Canada), 2000.

The Ring Bear: A Rascally Wedding Adventure, illustrated by S.G. Brooks, Flashlight Press (New York, NY), 2004.

Jacques and Spock, illustrated by Debbie Tilley, Clarion Books (New York, NY), 2004.

Ned Loses His Head, illustrated by S.G. Brooks, Abdo Publishing (Edina, MN), 2007.

Flour Girl: A Recipe for Disaster, illustrated by S.G. Brooks, Abdo Publishing (Edina, MN), 2007.

The Sharpest Tool in the Shed, illustrated by Brandon Reibeling, Abdo Publishing (Edina, MN), 2007.

Missy Swiss, illustrated by Brandon Reibeling, Abdo Publishing (Edina, MN), 2007.

7 Ate 9, illustrated by Zachary Trover, Abdo Publishing (Edina, MN), 2007.

Comin' Through, illustrated by Ronnie Rooney, Abdo Publishing (Edina, MN), 2007.

The Bored Book, illustrated by Doug Keith, Simply Read Books (Vancover, British Columbia, Canada), 2008.

A Wrench in the Works, illustrated by Andres Martinez Ricci, Magic Wagon (Edina, MN), 2009.

Battle of the Books, illustrated by Jeff Ebbeler, Magic Wagon (Edina, MN), 2009.

Milo and the Monster, illustrated by Jeff Ebbeler, Magic Wagon (Edina, MN), 2009.

Ned Breaks His Heart, illustrated by S.G. Brooks, Magic Wagon (Edina, MN), 2009.

Ned's Nose Is Running!, illustrated by S.G. Brooks, Magic Wagon (Edina, MN.), 2009.

On the Level, illustrated by Andres Martinez Ricci, Magic Wagon (Edina, MN), 2009.

"SACRED BOOKS" YOUNG-ADULT NOVEL SERIES

The Book of Nonsense, Volume I, Blooming Tree Press, 2008.

The Book of All Things, Blooming Tree Press, 2008.

The Book of Nonsense, Volume II, Blooming Tree Press, 2009.

The Book of Maps, Blooming Tree Press, 2010.

FOR ADULTS

Selfless (novel), Absey (New York, NY), 2008.

The Book of Letters (short stories), Evermore Books 2010.

Sidelights

The titles of David Michael Slater's books, which include *Cheese Louise!, Flour Girl: A Recipe for Disaster,* and *A Wrench in the Works,* hint at the whimsical approach he takes to writing for children. In *Missy Swiss,* for example, the secret world inside the average refrigerator comes to life in a story about a chunk of Swiss cheese that looks for fame but winds up starting a great thaw when she accidentally pulls the plug and the 'fridge warms up. Turning to older readers, Slater follows the adventures of siblings Daphna and Dexter Wax as they shoulder the destiny of saving the entire world in his "Sacred Books" series.

In his humorous stories, Slater features characters that, whether actual humans or human stand-ins, "are grappling with inner conflict," as *School Library Journal* contributor Martha Topol observed. In *Flour Girl* Sophie misinterprets her father's announcement that he is marrying his girlfriend Maggie and Sophie will be the flower girl at the upcoming wedding. Jealous that Maggie has joined the baking time she and her father share, Sophie sprinkles flour on all her future mom's belongings, even dumping flour into the woman's purse. The title characters of *Jacques and Spock* are a pair of matching orange socks . . . at least until Jacques is tossed in with a load of whites and bleached to a paler hue. Now mismatched, the socks are separated until the shy Spock finds a way to reunite them. Featuring what James K. Irwin described in *School Library Journal* as a "upbeat ending," *Jacques and Spock* was recommended by the critic as "a good choice for storytimes on feelings and . . . separation anxiety."

"What first got me interested in writing was probably the play *Rosencrantz and Guildenstern Are Dead,* by Tom Stoppard," Slater once noted. "I first read it in high school, then again in college. I was inspired to write my own version of two characters having absurd philosophical conversations." Among his favorite writers Slater counts Jorge Louis Borges.

"Usually, I don't know where my stories are going, and consequently I tend to use a rather circular style. I write until I'm stuck, then simply begin revising from the start until I can inch the story forward. When I'm stuck again, I start again. And so on.

"The most surprising thing I've learned as a writer is that it takes an ungodly, possibly pathological, persistence to get your work published. Exhibit A: my three giant binders stuffed with rejection letters."

Biographical and Critical Sources

PERIODICALS

Children's Bookwatch, August, 2004, review of *The Ring Bear: A Rascally Wedding Adventure,* p. 7.

Resource Links, April, 2000, review of *Cheese Louise!,* pp. 6-7.

School Library Journal, December, 2004, James K. Irwin, review of *Jacques and Spock,* p. 122; August, 2008, Martha Topol, reviews of *Flour Girl: A Recipe for Disaster* and *Missy Swiss,* both p. 102.

ONLINE

David Slater Home Page, http://www.davidmichaelslater.com (January 10, 2010).*

*   *   *

SPANGLER, Brie

Personal

Born in MA; married; husband's name Matt. *Hobbies and other interests:* Going to clambakes, watching baseball, spending time with her dog.

Addresses

Home—NH. *E-mail*—cbriespangler@gmail.com.

Career

Writer and illustrator.

Writings

SELF-ILLUSTRATED

Peg Leg Peke, Alfred A. Knopf (New York, NY), 2008.
The Grumpy Dump Truck, Alfred A. Knopf (New York, NY), 2009.

ILLUSTRATOR

Jodi Carse and Maria Gallagher, *Enough Is Enough!,* Grosset & Dunlap (New York, NY), 2004.
Jodi Carse and Maria Gallagher, *Winner Takes All!,* Grosset & Dunlap (New York, NY), 2005.
Jodi Carse and Maria Gallagher, *Gotta Have It!,* Grosset & Dunlap (New York, NY), 2005.
Zoe Quinn, *Cabin Fever,* Yearling (New York, NY), 2006.
Zoe Quinn, *The Caped Sixth Grader: Lightning Strikes!,* Yearling (New York, NY), 2006.

Brie Spangler creates an amusing cartoon story geared for toddlers in her picture book The Grumpy Dump Truck. (Copyright © 2009 by Brie Spangler. Used by permission of Alfred A. Knopf, an imprint of Random House Children's Books, a division of Random House, Inc.)

Zoe Quinn, *The Caped Sixth Grader: Totally Toxic!,* Yearling (New York, NY), 2006.

Zoe Quinn, *The Caped Sixth Grader: Happy Birthday, Hero!,* Yearling (New York, NY), 2006.

Sidelights

Massachusetts-raised author and illustrator Brie Spangler graduated from the Rhode Island School of Design. Since graduation, she has provided artwork for several books by other authors in addition to crafting her own self-illustrated stories. Her first illustration assignments pair her cartoon-style art with stories by Jodi Carse and Maria Gallagher, and Spangler has also provided illustrations for Zoe Quinn's "Caped Sixth Grader" series of middle-grade novels about a girl who discovers that she is a superhero.

Spangler's first self-illustrated title was inspired by her pet, a Pekingese named Lola. In *Peg Leg Peke,* a small, sad Pekingese has broken his leg. With the help of an unnamed speaker, however, little Peke realizes that his imagination is not broken. His broken leg transforms into the peg leg of a pirate, and as Peke begins his imaginative adventures, Spangler's text grows smaller while her illustrations of the pup's adventures begin to dominate the pages. Calling Peke a "sweet and comical" doggy protagonist, *School Library Journal* reviewer Maura Bresnahan predicted that *Peg Leg Peke* is "sure to be a hit" among early readers. A *Publishers Weekly* contributor called the book a "cartooned charmer" featuring artwork that is "sweet and chummy," while a *Kirkus Reviews* critic concluded that *Peg Leg Peke* captures "the fun of creative play to lift anyone's spirit."

Another picture book by Spangler, *The Grumpy Dump Truck,* introduces Bertrand, a grouchy, anthropomorphized dump truck that is the scourge of the construction site. Bernard is mean to his coworkers and complains loudly about his job. When he nearly runs into a porcupine construction worker named Tilly, she shoots her quills at Bertrand's rubber tire in alarm. The dump truck is furious at first, until Tilly removes not only the prickly quills but also assorted other items that have gotten stuck in Bertrand's tire treads. After he begins to feel better, Bertrand realizes that being nice can actually be fun. Reviewing *The Grumpy Dump Truck, Booklist* contributor Shelle Rosenfeld commented on Spangler's "lively cartoon-style art," with its "simply drawn, expressive characters." A *Publishers Weekly* critic, while finding the change in Bertrand's temperament overly dramatic, acknowledged that Spangler "knows how to create a compelling comic antihero" and noted that the "narrative never slackens."

Biographical and Critical Sources

PERIODICALS

Booklist, June 1, 2009, Shelle Rosenfeld, review of *The Grumpy Dump Truck,* p. 72.

Kirkus Reviews, May 15, 2008, review of *Peg Leg Peke.*

Publishers Weekly, June 16, 2008, review of *Peg Leg Peke,* p. 47; June 22, 2009, review of *The Grumpy Dump Truck,* p. 43.

School Library Journal, September, 2006, Cheryl Ashton, review of *The Caped Sixth Grader: Happy Birthday, Hero!,* p. 216; August, 2008, Maura Bresnahan, review of *Peg Leg Peke,* p. 102; June, 2009, Martha Simpson, review of *The Grumpy Dump Truck,* p. 100.

ONLINE

Brie Spangler Home Page, http://www.briespangler.com (January 19, 2010).

Peg Leg Peke Web site, http://www.peglegpeke.com/ (January 19, 2010), "Brie Spangler."

T

TALBOTT, Hudson 1949-

Personal

Born July 11, 1949, in Louisville, KY; son of Peyton (a mortgage loan officer) and Mildred (a dress shop manager) Talbott. *Education:* Attended University of Cincinnati, 1967-69; Tyler School of Art (Rome, Italy)/ Temple University, B.F.A., 1971. *Politics:* Democrat. *Religion:* Siddha yoga. *Hobbies and other interests:* Skiing, playing tennis, horse riding, gardening.

Addresses

Home—New York, NY. *Office*—119 5th Ave., Ste. 500, New York, NY 10003. *E-mail*—info@hudsontalbott. com.

Career

Freelance illustrator, beginning 1974. Clients include Metropolitan Museum of Art, Museum of Modern Art, Metropolitan Opera Guild, Bloomingdale's Department Store, and Easy Street, Inc. Member of board of directors of Art Awareness (a nonprofit arts-presenting organization), Lexington, NY.

Member

Society of Children's Book Writers and Illustrators.

Awards, Honors

Book of the Year selection, Library of Congress, 1987; Notable Book selection, National Council for the Social Studies/Children's Book Council, 2000; Orbis Pictus Recommended Book designation, National Council of Teachers of English, and Henry Bergh Children's Book Award, American Society for the Prevention of Cruelty to Animals, 2002, both for *Safari Journal;* Newbery Honor Book designation, 2005, for *Show Way* by Jacqueline Woodson; New York Library Association selection for national book festival, and Hudson Valley Hero designation, Scenic Hudson Envirnmental Organization, both 2009, and Notable Book Designation, American Library Association, 2010, all for *River of Dreams.*

Hudson Talbott (Reproduced by permission.)

Writings

SELF-ILLUSTRATED

How to Show Grown-ups the Museum, Museum of Modern Art (New York, NY), 1986.
The Lady at Liberty, Ishihara, 1987.
We're Back! A Dinosaur's Story, Crown (New York, NY), 1987.
(Adaptor) *Into the Woods* (novelization of the musical by Stephen Sondheim and James Lapine), Crown (New York, NY), 1988.
Going Hollywood: A Dinosaur's Dream, Crown (New York, NY), 1989.
King Arthur: The Sword in the Stone, Morrow (New York, NY), 1991.
Your Pet Dinosaur: An Owner's Manual, Morrow (New York, NY), 1992.
Excalibur, Morrow (New York, NY), 1996.
(With Mark Greenberg) *Amazon Diary: The Jungle Adventures of Alex Winters,* Puffin (New York, NY), 1997.
O'Sullivan Stew: A Tale Cooked up in Ireland, Putnam (New York, NY), 1999.

Lancelot, Morrow (New York, NY), 1999.

Forging Freedom: The True Story of Heroism during the Holocaust, Putnam (New York, NY), 2000.

Safari Journal: The Adventures in Africa of Carey Monroe, Harcourt (San Diego, CA), 2002.

United Tweets of America: Fifty State Birds, Putnam (New York, NY), 2008.

The Story of the Hudson River, Putnam (New York, NY), 2009.

ILLUSTRATOR

Jean Fritz, *Leonardo's Horse,* Putnam (New York, NY), 2001.

Jean Fritz, *The Lost Colony of Roanoke,* Putnam (New York, NY), 2004.

Jacqueline Woodson, *Show Way,* Putnam (New York, NY), 2005.

Adaptations

We're Back! A Dinosaur's Story was adapted into a full-length animated feature film by Steven Spielberg for Universal, 1993. *River of Dreams* was adapted as a musical play funded by the Henry Hudson Quadricentennial Committee, 2009.

Sidelights

New Yorker Hudson Talbott got his start in writing and illustrating children's books when a major U.S. museum commissioned him to create a book for children that would inspire an interest in fine art. In the years since, Talbott has produced books ranging in subject from dinosaurs to history to Renaissance art, all featuring his detailed paintings. In his humorous *United Tweets of America: Fifty State Birds* he introduces the top birds in each of the fifty states, while *Into the Woods* combines a retelling of the popular Broadway musical with Talbott's evocative paintings. His award-winning paintings for Jacqueline Woodson's picture book *Show Way,* which captures the history of Woodson's African-American family, uses a quilt motif to good effect, creating "a potent symbol of the hope, courage, and perseverance that light this handsome book," according to *Horn Book* contributor Joanna Rudge Long.

A native of Louisville, Kentucky, Talbott earned a fine-arts degree from Temple University and began working as a freelance illustrator in New York City in 1974. His first book, *How to Show Grown-ups the Museum,* was written for young Museum of Modern Art visitors. Talbott found commercial success with *We're Back! A Dinosaur's Story,* which follows the comical return of dinosaurs to live among humans in the modern age. In the story a talking Tyrannosaurus Rex and his pals disrupt New York City's Thanksgiving Day parade and hide out at the Museum of Natural History, among other adventures. The book's charms lured Steven Spielberg into making *We're Back!* the basis of an animated film.

Talbott has written two other dinosaur books, including a spoof on the household pet-care genre, *Your Pet Dinosaur: An Owner's Manual.* Humorous illustrations and text provide advice for the care, feeding, and training of various breeds of dinosaur. A contributor to *Pub-*

Talbott pairs his detailed art with a fascinating story from World War II history in **Forging Freedom.** (Copyright © 2000 by Hudson Talbott. Reproduced by permission of G.P. Putnam's Sons, a division of Penguin Putnam Books for Young Readers.)

lishers Weekly liked the "dexterously drawn images of preppie families romping with their pets in immaculate suburban settings." In addition to his dinosaur books, Talbott has also penned several adaptations of the King Arthur legend and has illustrated them as well. In *King Arthur: The Sword in the Stone* he recounts Arthur's boyhood times in early medieval London, while *Excalibur* tells the story of young King Arthur and his reckless disregard of Merlin's advice. Ignoring his wizard's caution, he leads his army into battle and loses spectacularly. "Talbott's retelling of this celebrated story emphasizes Arthur's youthful hunger for adventure," noted *Booklist* critic Karen Morgan in a review of the second book. A *Publishers Weekly* reviewer found the artist/author to be "at his vivid best with animals: rearing horses, eager dogs and a miraculous Questing Beast."

Talbott, whose commercial-illustration clients have included the Metropolitan Museum of Art and Bloomingdale's department stores, has earned praise for the unique format used in several of a few of his books. The first of these to attract attention was a project with Mark Greenberg. *Amazon Diary: The Jungle Adventures of Alex Winters* is purported to be the scrapbook

Talbott's illustration projects include creating artwork for Jean Fritz's historical picture book **Leonardo's Horse.** (Copyright © 2001 by Hudson Talbott, illustrations. Used by permission of G.P. Putnam's Sons, a division of Penguin Putnam Books for Young Readers.)

of a youngster who has accompanied his anthropologist parents to the South American rainforest. A plane crash leads them to the Yanomami, an indigenous people who have had almost no contact with the modern world. Alex is at first stunned by their primitive way of life, and the Yanomami are in turn fascinated by some of his gadgets, such as his Polaroid camera. As Alex adjusts he begins to appreciate the Yanomami's simpler way of life. A *Publishers Weekly* reviewer found that "the book's design and graphics are inventive," and particularly liked *Amazon Diary*'s text, which the writer described as "hand-lettered in a credible sixth-grade scrawl." *School Librarian* reviewer Angela Redfern also commended the book as "a wonderful mixture of photos, annotated sketches, drawings, and maps."

Talbott turns the famed Arabian Nights saga into an Irish fable in *O'Sullivan Stew: A Tale Cooked Up in Ireland.* The story is set in an Irish coastal town, Crookhaven, where residents live in fear of a local witch. When her horse is stolen one day by the king's army, her neighbors do nothing to help, and she retaliates by casting spells on the elements that wreak havoc on the local economy. Crookhaven's fishermen fail to bring back any fish, the cows have no milk to give, and famine seems imminent. Clever Kate O'Sullivan and her brothers decide to return the horse to the witch to save the town, but their plan goes awry, and they are arrested. Like Scheherazade of the 1,001 Arabian Nights, Kate saves herself by telling fantastical tales that captivate her listeners. Hers concern leprechauns, fairy folk, and serpents, and by her talent she saves each one of her brothers; then the king falls in love with her. "Several clever turns of plot add spice to this appetizing concoction," noted a contributor to *Publishers Weekly,* who also deemed *O'Sullivan Stew* "visually and verbally inventive in its details and its broader storytelling." In *Booklist* Kay Weisman also commended Talbott's effort in the book, declaring that his "colorful illustrations complement the exaggerated text and add to the tall tale flavor."

In *United Tweets of America* Talbott presents a colorful parade of the birds that rank number one in each of the United States, pairing each profile with information about the state and its history. He also includes bird-focused parodies of state songs, and a whimsical mix of state-related facts. In a *Kirkus Reviews* a critic predicted the book's popularity among "trivia fans" and *Booklist* critic Hazel Rochman dubbed it a "sly, comic, and irreverent book" that is "loaded with hilarious puns and parodies." Characterizing *United Tweets of America* as "a hoot," Ellen Heath added in *School Library Journal* that Talbott's "rollicking romp through the states" features cartoon art and a trivia-filled text that will appeal to both children and adults.

Talbott turns to Europe during World War II in his self-illustrated *Forging Freedom: The True Story of Heroism during the Holocaust,* which recounts the wartime heroics of his friend Jaap Penraat. "The author's personal connection to and affection for Penraat is evident

Talbott focuses on a region that is close to his home and his heart in his self-illustrated picture book River of Dreams: The Story of the Hudson River.

in the warmth of his descriptions," wrote *School Library Journal* critic Kathleen Isaacs wrote, calling *Forging Freedom* a "compelling biography." Jaap was a young man living in Amsterdam in the 1930s and had many Jewish neighbors; when German Nazis invaded the Netherlands in 1940, the climate became increasingly hostile, and Dutch Jews began to be deported to concentration camps. Jaap was a student of art and architecture, and he employed his artistic skills as a forger of identity and travel papers to help his Jewish friends and neighbors. In 1942, as *Forging Freedom* recounts, he launched an ingenious scheme: first, he created documents for a fictitious German construction company and papers for himself as its official representative. He then applied for travel permits to take Dutch "workers" to an alleged construction site in France, from which his Jewish charges were then smuggled into Spain and out of Nazi jurisdiction. The clever two-year ruse helped more than 400 Dutch Jews escape to freedom.

Talbott's illustrations of Jaap's heroics included images of a teenaged Jaap visiting his neighbors on the Shabbas, collages of the skillfully forged papers, and images of Amsterdam under Nazi rule. "Text and pictures both have a boyish enthusiasm that nevertheless acknowledges the real human cost of the war," stated a reviewer for *Horn Book*. A *Publishers Weekly* contributor praised the "freshly conceived and powerfully rendered paintings," and remarked that in his illustrations of crowd scenes depicting Nazi parades and Dutch sympathizers of fascism, "Talbott uses indistinct gray tones to imply the crowd mentality and reserves color for resisters like Jaap." In *Booklist* Hazel Rochman also commended the book's images, singling out one that shows a barbed-wire-bedecked map of Europe under Nazi occupation. "Always present is the horror of what the refugees are escaping, as well as the exciting action and [Jaap's] . . . heroism," Rochman wrote.

Another true story, Jean Fritz's *Leonardo's Horse,* also features Talbott's illustrations. This book recounts the long history of the massive bronze equine sculpture once sketched by famed Italian Renaissance artist Leonardo da Vinci. A commission for the duke of Milan, the horse was modeled in clay in 1493, but before work in bronze could begin, French troops invaded this part of northern Italy and Leonardo's model was destroyed. The duke was forced to use his store of bronze to make armaments instead. The never-realized project was said to have haunted Leonardo until his death. Centuries, in 1977, American art collector Charles Dent decided to revive the project. Dent planned to have the sculpture completed by a contemporary artist and then presented to the people of Italy as a gift. Dent died in 1994, but "Leonardo's Horse" was unveiled in Milan in 1999. In *Booklist* Carolyn Phelan commended the book's illustrations, noting that "Talbott makes good use of the irregularly shaped pages in his pleasing and occasionally dramatic illustrations." A *Kirkus Reviews* contributor offered similar praise. Talbott's drawings, the reviewer noted, "range from utterly recognizable scenes of Florence to the ghostly horses at Leonardo's deathbed," and images depicting the contemporary part of *Leonardo's Horse* are "drawn with as much spirit and vitality as the Renaissance ones."

Talbott rejoins Fritz in *The Lost Colony of Roanoke,* which combines a history of the English colony that disappeared from North Carolina's Roanoke Island shortly after arriving there in 1587. Together with Fritz's fact-filled text about the mystery surrounding the dozens of men, women, and children whose true fate has never been learned, Talbott's "fluid, expressive watercolors enhance the writing" and recall the work of "sixteenth-century portrait artists." according to Phelan. In both smaller, spot images and full-page paintings, the artist "give[s] each player a face," noted *Horn Book* critic Betty Carter, and Talbott's larger paintings allow readers "to pause while reading the brisk narrative" and contemplate the intriguing history by "perus[ing] . . . maps, diagrams, and setting." *The Lost Colony of Roanoke* is "studded with facts, anecdotes and historical asides," according to a *Publishers Weekly* critic, and Talbott's "detailed watercolors" enhance Fritz's text by adding "miniature portraits of the principals as well as dramatic, sprawling scenarios."

Another self-illustrated book by Talbott, *River of Dreams: The Story of the Hudson River,* shares the history and beauty of the area in New York state that has long captivated the artist. The beautiful, wooded Hudson River running north of New York City was a key waterway during the Revolutionary War. It continued to be of key importance during the industrialization of New York and New England, connecting with the Erie Canal and also providing water power to fuel the region's early industry. In this "fascinating book," the author pairs his mix of history and legend with what *Horn Book* critic Monica Edinger praised as "large, lush paintings," while Gillian Engberg called *River of Dreams* a "compelling blend of political and natural history" that pairs "delicate watercolor-and-pencil illustrations with

accessible text." The book "presents a staggering amount of information about the Hudson River without ever overwhelming or confusing readers," according to a *Publishers Weekly* critic.

Talbott once noted: "I came into book authorship through my artwork. David Allender, an editor at Crown Publishers, saw my art on a calendar and called to ask if I would be interested in writing and illustrating a book. Although I'm still principally a visually oriented person, I am very excited by the new challenge of exploring the verbal portion of my creativity."

Biographical and Critical Sources

PERIODICALS

Booklist, November 15, 1996, Karen Morgan, review of *Excalibur,* p. 585; February 1, 1999, Kay Weisman, review of *O'Sullivan Stew: A Tale Cooked up in Ireland,* p. 983; July, 2000, Hazel Rochman, review of *Forging Freedom: The True Story of Heroism during the Holocaust,* p. 2026; October 15, 2001, Carolyn Phelan, review of *Leonardo's Horse,* p. 394; April 1, 2004, Carolyn Phelan, review of *The Lost Colony of Roanoke,* p. 1362; September 15, 2005, Hazel Rochman, review of *Show Way,* p. 63; April 1, 2008, Hazel Rochman, review of *United Tweets of America: Fifty State Birds,* p. 43; December 15, 2008, Gillian Engberg, review of *River of Dreams: The Story of the Hudson River,* p. 43.
Books for Keeps, March, 1998, Clive Barnes, review of *Amazon Diary: The Junble Adventures of Alex Winters,* p. 23.
Entertainment Weekly, December 10, 1993, Steve Daly, reviews of *Going Hollywood: A Dinosaur's Dream* and *Your Pet Dinosaur: An Owner's Manual,* both p. 86.
Horn Book, January, 2001, review of *Forging Freedom,* p. 119; September, 2001, review of *Leonardo's Horse,* p. 609; May-June, 2004, Betty Carter, review of *The Lost Colony of Roanoke,* p. 344; November-December, 2005, Joanna Rudge Long, review of *Show Way,* p. 712; March-April, 2009, Monica Edinger, review of *River of Dreams,* p. 215.
Kirkus Reviews, December 15, 1998, review of *O'Sullivan Stew,* p. 1804; September 15, 2001, review of *Leonardo's Horse,* p. 1357; April 15, 2008, review of *United Tweets of America.*
New York Times Book Review, November 13, 2005, Jenny Allen, review of *Show Way,* p. 30.
Publishers Weekly, October 18, 1991, review of *King Arthur: The Sword in the Stone,* p. 60; August 3, 1992, review of *Your Pet Dinosaur,* p. 72; July 22, 1996, review of *Excalibur,* p. 240; August 12, 1996, review of *Amazon Diary,* p. 83; January 11, 1999, review of *O'Sullivan Stew,* p. 72; October 23, 2000, review of *Forging Freedom,* p. 77; May 17, 2004, review of *The Lost Colony of Roanoke,* p. 52; September 12, 2005, review of *Show Way,* p. 67; May 19, 2008, review of *United Tweets of America,* p. 53; January 5, 2009, review of *River of Dreams,* p. 49.

School Librarian, summer, 1998, Angela Redfern, review of *Amazon Diary,* p. 96.

School Library Journal, October, 1999, Virginia Golodetz, review of *Lancelot,* p. 143; November, 2000, Kathleen Isaacs, review of *Forging Freedom,* p. 176; May, 2008, Ellen Heath, review of *United Tweets of America,* p. 118; March, 2009, Margaret Bush, review of *River of Dreams,* p. 170.

ONLINE

Hudson Talbott Home Page, http://www.hudsontalbott.com (January 10, 2010).

*   *   *

THOMSON, Sarah L.

Personal

Born in Ames, IA. *Education:* Oberlin College, B.A. (English); attended Oxford University.

Addresses

Home—Portland, ME. *E-mail*—slthomson@earthlink. net.

Career

Writer and editor. HarperCollins Children's Books, New York, NY, former senior editor; Simon & Schuster, New York, NY, former editor; freelance writer, beginning c. 2001.

Awards, Honors

Bank Street College Best Children's Books of the Year designation, and Cooperative Children's Book Council Choice designation, both 2001, both for *The Dragon's Son;* Bank Street College Best Children's Book of the Year designation, 2003, for *Imagine a Night,* and 2005, for *Amazing Gorillas;* Oppenheim Toy Portfolio Gold Seal Award, 2005, for *Tigers;* Great Early Elementary Reads designation, American Library Association/ ALSC, 2006, for *Amazing Snakes!;* Maine Lupine Award in Juvenile/Young-Adult category, 2007, for *Dragon's Egg; Smithsonian* magazine Notable Book for Children Designation, 2009, for *What Lincoln Said.*

Writings

FICTION

The Dragon's Son (stories; based on the Mabinogion), Orchard Books (New York, NY), 2001.

Imagine a Night, illustrated by Rob Gonsalves, Atheneum (New York, NY), 2003.

Sarah L. Thomson (Photograph by Mark Mattos. Reproduced by permission.)

(Adaptor) *The Nutcracker* (based on the play by E.T.A. Hoffmann), Seastar Books (New York, NY), 2003.

(Adaptor) Fritz Lieber, *Gonna Roll the Bones,* illustrated by David Wiesner, Milk & Cookies, 2004.

(Translator and adaptor) Jimmy Liao, *The Sound of Colors: A Journey of the Imagination,* illustrated by Liao, Little, Brown (New York, NY), 2005.

Imagine a Day, illustrated by Rob Gonsalves, Atheneum (New York, NY), 2005.

The Manny, Dutton (New York, NY), 2005.

The Secret of the Rose, Greenwillow (New York, NY), 2006.

Dragon's Egg, Greenwillow Books (New York, NY), 2007.

Imagine a Place, Atheneum Books for Young Readers (New York, NY), 2008.

Pirates, Ho!, illustrated by Stephen Gilpin, Marshall Cavendish Children (Tarrytown, NY), 2008.

(Translator and adaptor) Jimmy Liao, *The Blue Stone: A Journey through Life,* illustrated by Liao, Little, Brown (New York, NY), 2008.

(Translator and adaptor) Jimmy Liao, *When the Moon Forgot,* illustrated by Liao, Little, Brown (New York, NY), 2009.

NONFICTION

Robert Cormier (biography), Rosen (New York, NY), 2003.

Gary Paulsen (biography), Rosen (New York, NY), 2003.

Stars and Stripes: The Story of the American Flag, illustrated by Bob Dacey and Debra Bandelin, HarperCollins (New York, NY), 2003.

Tigers, photographs by Wildlife Conservation Society, HarperCollins (New York, NY), 2004.

Amazing Gorillas!, photographs by Wildlife Conservation Society, HarperCollins (New York, NY), 2005.

Amazing Whales!, photographs by Wildlife Conservation Society, HarperCollins (New York, NY), 2005.

Amazing Sharks!, photographs by Wildlife Conservation Society, HarperCollins (New York, NY), 2005.

Amazing Dolphins!, photographs by Wildlife Conservation Society, HarperCollins (New York, NY), 2006.

Amazing Snakes!, photographs by Wildlife Conservation Society, HarperCollins (New York, NY), 2006.

Extreme Stars Q & A, HarperCollins (New York, NY), 2007.

Extreme Dinosaurs Q & A, HarperCollins (New York, NY), 2007.

My Flag Book, HarperCollins (New York, NY), 2007.

Astronauts and Other Space Heroes, HarperCollins (New York, NY), 2007.

American Flag Q & A, HarperCollins (New York, NY), 2008.

(Adaptor) David Mendell, *Obama: A Promise of Change,* Amistad/HarperCollins (New York, NY), 2008.

(Adaptor) Greg Mortenson and David Oliver Relin, *Three Cups of Tea: One Man's Mission to Promote Peace . . . One School at a Time,* Dial Books for Young Readers (New York, NY), 2009.

(Coauthor) Tom and Allie Harvey, *Tiger Pups,* photographs by Tom Harvey and Keith Philpott, HarperCollins (New York, NY), 2009.

What Lincoln Said, illustrated by James Ransome, HarperCollins (New York, NY), 2009.

Where Do Polar Bears Live?, illustrated by Jason Chin HarperCollins (New York, NY), 2010.

Sidelights

After working for several years as an editor for New York City publishers, Sarah L. Thomson decided to embark on a writing career in 2001, with the publication of her young-adult novel *The Dragon's Son.* In addition to producing other novels for teens, Thomson has branched out into series nonfiction, biographies, and picture-book texts, all combining her interests in history, fantasy, and the natural world.

In *The Dragon's Son* Thomson draws from the medieval Welsh story collection known as the Mabinogion as well as from Thomas Malory's *Le Morte d'Arthur.* Featuring characters such as King Arthur, Morgan le Fay, Mordred, and Nimue, her "affecting" fiction debut sheds a light of realism on Arthurian Briton, according to *Booklist* contributor Sally Estes. "Fantasy and historical-fiction readers alike will enjoy the new perspective offered by this gritty, substantial novel," Cheri Estes added in her review of *The Dragon's Son* for *School Library Journal.*

Once again drawing on her interest in historic England, Thomson focuses on the court of Queen Elizabeth I in her young-adult novel *The Secret of the Rose.* The story focuses on fourteen-year-old Rosalind Archer. A Roman Catholic, Rosalind and her younger brother find themselves homeless and alone following their father's imprisonment and ultimate death in prison as a martyr for his faith. Disguising herself as a boy, Rosalind finds a way to support herself and her brother by entering the service of Elizabethan playwright Christopher Marlowe. Through Marlowe, Rosalind is quickly drawn into the exciting world of the London stage, but she also realizes that her secretive and mercurial employer must never be trusted with her true identity. In *Kirkus Reviews* a contributor dubbed *The Secret of the Rose* "fast-paced and accessible." *Kliatt* reviewer Claire Rosser praised Thomson for including "detail[s] of life in the Elizabethan theatre" in her novel and concluded that "suspense . . . grips the reader from the first pages."

In *The Manny* Thomson sets her story in contemporary New York City as sixteen-year-old Justin Blakewell casts about for a summer job that will allow him to get out of the city and mingle with interesting—and wealthy—people. And find a girlfriend. A job in the swanky Hamptons as a male nanny, or "manny," taking care of the four-year-old daughter of a wealthy couple seems to be perfect. When Justin makes a disaster of juggling friendships with the beautiful but condescending Serafina and the down-to-earth Liz, however, the teen realizes that he needs to rethink his priorities. Noting that the humor in *The Manny* will appeal to teens, a *Kirkus Reviews* writer added that "Thomson's flowing writing style keeps her reader interested" in *The Man-*

Thomson creates the evocative text that links Rob Gonsalves' intriguing paintings in **Imagine a Day.** (Illustration copyright © 2005 by Ron Gonsalves. Reprinted with the permission of Atheneum Books for Young Readers, an imprint of Simon & Schuster Macmillan.)

ny's "well-developed characters" and "insightful" story. Dubbing the novel a "breezy read" that contains "moments of social commentary" about class distinctions, Karyn N. Silverman predicted in *School Library Journal* that the book will find fans among "girls who wish there were more guys like Justin."

Thomson again turns to fantasy in *Dragon's Egg,* a middle-grade novel set in a medieval-esque world where small, tame dragons live among humans much as dogs do. As a dragon keeper, twelve-year-old Mella helps to care for her kingdom's dragons, which are valued for their eggs. Then, from a knight visiting her family's inn, she learns about a different breed of dragon, the legendary "true" dragon that is now hunted as a threat. When the girl encounters a true dragon that is close to death, she learns the truth about the species and takes up the challenge of transporting the unhatched egg of a true dragon to safety in the Dragontooth mountains. Comparing *Dragon's Egg* to the fiction of Lloyd Alexander and Christopher Paolini, *Booklist* critic Debbie Carton wrote that the novel's "richly descriptive" text introduces a "fantasy world readers will want to revisit," while in *School Library Journal* Eva Mitnick called Mella "a likeable character" whose journey helps her to develop both "self-confidence and [the] strength . . . to keep her word." In *Kirkus Reviews* a contributor praised the "spunk" of Thomson's young heroine, adding that the story's "descriptive scenes lend character to the unusual fantasy elements."

In addition to her fiction for older readers, Thomson has also created poetic texts that pair with intriguing oil paintings by Rob Gonsalves in the picture books *Imagine a Day, Imagine a Night,* and *Imagine a Place.* Gonsalves's Dali-esque images envision a world in which imagination can transform reality; as Carolyn Phelan wrote in her *Booklist* review of *Imagine a Day.* Each of the three books provides young readers with "an intriguing introduction to the surreal in art" through Thomson's "lyrical text" and the artist's "remarkable paintings," added Phelan, while *School Library Journal* critic Marianne Saccardi called *Imagine a Night* "a fascinating foray into the imagination and a fine discussion starter for older children." Calling *Imagine a Place* a "book to ponder and pore over," Kathy Krasniewicz added in another *School Library Journal* review that Thompson's "lyrical" text and Gonsalves' art encourage readers to "stretch their imaginations and question perspective and perception."

American history has also provided Thomson with subjects for her work, resulting in the nonfiction titles *Stars and Stripes: The Story of the American Flag* and *What Lincoln Said.* A history of the flag of the United States of America, *Stars and Stripes* spans historic moments that have inspired the flag's prominent display, from its use as a symbol of revolution in colonial America to one honoring the nation in the weeks and months following the September 11, 2001 attacks on New York City and Washington, DC. In addition to praising the "vivid" illustrations by Bob Dacey and Debra Bandelin, Nancy Menaldi-Scanlan wrote in *School Library Journal* that *Stars and Stripes* serves as a "solid choice for introducing the history of both our flag and our country."

The presidency of Abraham Lincoln inspired Thompson's *What Lincoln Said,* a book that features the dramatic paintings of noted artist James Ransome. In what *Booklist* critic Laura Tillotson described as a "concise" text that is studded with quotes from the sixteenth president of the United States, the picture-book biography follows Lincoln from his rural Illinois childhood through to his signing of the Emancipation Proclamation that ended the institution of slavery following the U.S. Civil War. Thomson writes "with admirable simplicity," Tillotson added, citing her efforts to explain the social, ethical, and political issues that shaped Lincoln's life. *What Lincoln Said* serves as a "solid introduction" to a pivotal presidency, concluded a *Kirkus Reviews* writer, and Janet S. Thompson praised the book's pairing of a wealth of quotes with Thomson's brief text as an "engaging" and "worthy introduction" in her *School Library Journal* review.

Presenting simple introductions for budding naturalists who are still mastering reading skills, Thomson's contributions to the "Amazing" series include *Amazing Snakes!, Amazing Whales!,* and *Amazing Dolphins!,* among others. Full-color photographs from the Wildlife Conservation Society pair with texts covering the habitat, characteristics, and behaviors of several fascinating species. Kathleen Meulen discussed *Amazing Sharks!* for *School Library Journal,* writing that Thomson's "highly readable title explains basic facts of shark life and elaborates on the diversity of different species," while Hazel Rochman noted in *Booklist* that the book's "short sentences are clear and informative." Also praising Thomson's contribution to the "Amazing" nonfiction series, Phelan described the text of *Amazing Dolphins!* as "short, clear, and precise," and deemed *Amazing Gorillas!* "simply written but informative." In *Kirkus Reviews,* a critic called *Amazing Snakes!* "an engrossing introduction to a perennially fascinating subject." In *Extreme Dinosaurs Q & A,* another nonfiction effort, Thompson profiles over twenty prehistoric creatures in what *School Library Journal* critic Patricia Manning described as "a simple text" that will "surely appeal to most young dinophiles."

Reflecting on her move from editor to writer, Thomson once told *SATA:* "When I'm asked why I decided to leave my editing job and write books for a living, I often answer that it's quite simple: I like being in charge. I've always been a passionate reader, but even when I'm immersed in a novel, I can't stop my mind from taking its own path. Pretty soon I'm thinking 'Hey, what about this character? Why aren't we hearing more about her? Wait, would the hero really do *that?* No, I don't like that ending; why not end it *this* way?' In the end, I think that's why I write my own books: I want to decide what happens. Being a reader is wonderful, but being a writer is even better because I get to be the one making the choices.

"All my life I've spent at least as much time in books as in the real world—indeed, I'd be hard pressed to define one of those worlds as more real than the other. But today some of the imaginary worlds I get to spend time in are my own."

Biographical and Critical Sources

PERIODICALS

Booklist, May 1, 2001, Sally Estes, review of *The Dragon's Son,* p. 1675; September 15, 2003, Carolyn Phelan, review of *Stars and Stripes: The Story of the American Flag,* p. 243; January 1, 2005, Carolyn Phelan, review of *Imagine a Day,* p. 862; May 1, 2005, Carolyn Phelan, review of *Amazing Gorillas!,* p. 1588; May 15, 2005, Kay Weisman, review of *Amazing Whales!,* p. 1662; October, 1, 2005, Hazel Rochman, review of *Amazing Sharks!,* p. 60; December 15, 2005, Carolyn Phelan, review of *Amazing Snakes!,* p. 49; May 1, 2006, Jennifer Mattson, review of *The Secret of the Rose,* p. 47; July, 2006, Lynda Ritterman, review of *Amazing Dolphins!,* p. 95; October 1, 2007, Debbie Carton, review of *Dragon's Egg,* p. 52; September 15, 2008, Gillian Engberg, review of *What Lincoln Said,* p. 52.

Bulletin of the Center for Children's Books, July, 2001, review of *The Dragon's Son,* p. 425; September, 2005, Karen Coats, review of *The Manny,* p. 49; September, 2006, Deborah Stevenson, review of *The Secret of the Rose,* p. 38.

Canadian Review of Materials, November 14, 2003, review of *Imagine a Night.*

Horn Book, July-August, 2006, Jeannine M. Chapman, review of *The Secret of the Rose,* p. 452.

Kirkus Reviews, July 15, 2004, review of *Tigers,* p. 694; January 1, 2005, review of *Imagine a Day,* p. 58; May 1, 2005, review of *The Manny,* p. 547; May 15, 2005, review of *Amazing Gorillas!,* p. 597; January 1, 2006, review of *Amazing Snakes!,* p. 45; May 1, 2006, review of *Amazing Dolphins!,* p. 469; June 15, 2006, review of *The Secret of the Rose,* p. 638; September 15, 2007, review of *Dragon's Egg;* July 15, 2008, review of *Pirates, Ho!;* September 1, 2008, review of *Imagine a Place;* December 1, 2008, review of *What Lincoln Said.*

Kliatt, May, 2005, Janis Flint-Ferguson, review of *The Manny,* p. 18; July, 2006, Claire Rosser, review of *The Secret of the Rose,* p. 15.

Publishers Weekly, May 26, 2003, review of *Stars and Stripes,* p. 70; June 9, 2003, review of *Imagine a Night,* p. 50; February 27, 2006, review of *The Sound of Colors: A Journey of the Imagination,* p. 60.

School Library Journal, July, 2001, Cheri Estes, review of *The Dragon's Son,* p. 114; July, 2003, Nancy Menaldi-Scanlan, review of *Stars and Stripes,* p. 119; August,

2003, Beth Jones, review of *Gary Paulsen,* p. 186; October, 2003, Marianne Saccardi, review of *Imagine a Day,* p. 205; September, 2004, Lynda Ritterman, review of *Tigers,* p. 194; January, 2005, Mary Hazelton, review of *Amazing Whales!,* p. 116; April, 2005, Catherine Threadgill, review of *Imagine a Day,* p. 114; June, 2005, Karyn N. Silverman, review of *The Manny,* p. 170; August, 2005, Susan Lissim, review of *Amazing Gorillas!,* p. 118; January, 2006, Kathleen Meulen, review of *Amazing Sharks!,* p. 124; July, 2006, Lynda Ritterman, review of *Amazing Dolphins!,* p. 95; December, 2007, John Peters, review of *Astronauts and Other Space Heroes,* p. 158; January, 2008, Eva Mitnick, review of *Dragon's Egg,* p. 128; March, 2008, Patricia Manning, review of *Extreme Dinosaurs Q & A,* p. 191; October, 2008, Susan Weitz, review of *Pirates, Ho!,* p. 128; December, 2008, Kathy Krasniewicz, review of *Imagine a Place,* p. 104, and Janet S. Thompson, review of *What Lincoln Said,* p. 116.

Voice of Youth Advocates, June, 2001, review of *The Dragon's Son,* p. 136; August, 2005, Rollie Welch, review of *The Manny,* p. 227; December, 2006, Jane G. Van Wiemoldy, review of *The Secret of the Rose,* p. 435.

ONLINE

Sarah L. Thomson Home Page, http://www.sarahlthomson. com (January 10, 2010).

*   *   *

TICKLE, Jack
See CHAPMAN, Jane

*   *   *

TODD, Pamela 1950-

Personal

Born February 22, 1950, in Chicago, IL; daughter of George L. (an engineer) and Audrey (an artist) Brown; married Donn D. Todd (a contractor), October 9, 1971; children: three daughters, one son. *Education:* Purdue University, B.S. (psychology; cum laude). *Politics:* Democrat. *Religion:* Lutheran. *Hobbies and other interests:* Camping, hiking, violin, biking, swimming, prairie gardening.

Addresses

Home—IL. *Agent*—Erin Malone, William Morris Agency, 1325 Avenue of the Americas, New York, NY 10019. *E-mail*—pam@pamelatodd.com.

Career

Writer. Scott, Foresman, Chicago, IL, psychology textbook editor, 1970-72; freelance magazine and newspaper writer, and technical writer for corporations, begin-

Pamela Todd (Photograph by Nancy Neal. Reproduced by permission.)

ning 1972. Siren Interactive, lead content strategist, beginning 2006. Teacher of journal writing; core teaching artist for Ragsdale Foundation. Presenter at schools and conferences.

Member

Companions (prison ministry; board member, beginning 1997), Society of Children's Book Writers and Illustrators (network representative, 1996-2001).

Awards, Honors

Work-in-progress grant, Society of Children's Book Writers and Illustrators (SCBWI); Mary France Shura Award, SCBWI—Illinois; Ragdale Foundation residency; Illinois Arts Council grant; Green Earth Book Award, Sigurd Olson Nature Writing Award, and Great Lakes Book Award, all 2009, all for *The Blind Faith Hotel.*

Writings

YOUNG-ADULT NOVELS

Pig and the Shrink, Delacorte Press (New York, NY), 1999.
The Blind Faith Hotel, Margaret K. McElderry Books (New York, NY), 2008.

Contributor to periodicals, including *Writer, Chicago Tribune Magazine,* and *Runner's World.*

Sidelights

In her award-winning novels *Pig and the Shrink* and *The Blind Faith Hotel,* Pamela Todd focuses on young characters who come to terms with personal challenges while also discovering their personal passions and gaining a sense of self. Based in Illinois, Todd shares her own passions for both writing and the environment by teaching, hosting workshops on writing and prairie ecology, and speaking at schools and other gatherings. Among her awards, Todd has earned the Green Earth Book Award and the Sigurd Olson Nature Writing Award for *The Blind Faith Hotel.*

Pig and the Shrink, Todd's first young-adult novel, is the story of a science-fair project that yields some unexpected results. Narrator Tucker Harrison—nicknamed "the Shrink" for his small stature—is under pressure from his divorced parents to do well in the upcoming science fair in order to win a place at a prestigious math and science academy. When the school principal disapproves of his first project, Tucker decides to cast his fellow classmate, Angelo Pighetti—called "Pig" by some—as the subject in a science experiment on nutrition and obesity. Tucker studies up on fat and exercise and tries a variety of diets on his subject, but Pig actually gains weight. When Tucker visits Pig at his family's pizzeria, he begins to understand why. However, the budding scientist also discovers the warmth and acceptance Pig gets from his family, something that Tucker has never received from his overachieving and emotionally distant parents.

"Readers struggling to accept others and themselves will be affirmed by this comedy of human foibles," predicted a *Publishers Weekly* critic in appraising Todd's novel. "Tucker's wisecracking voice keeps the action clipping along, and his gradual realization that body shape does not necessarily correlate with happiness is a point well made," observed *Bulletin of the Center for Children's Books* critic Elizabeth Bush in another review of *Pig and the Shrink.*

Todd's second novel, *The Blind Faith Hotel,* was published after a span of nine years. Told in a series of flashbacks, the coming-of-age story introduces fourteen-year-old Zoe, the daughter of a fisherman. After their parents' relationship breaks down, Zoe and her siblings move with their mother from their Seattle home to a run-down family farm in Minnesota. This new environment feels alien to the teen, and she also misses her father. When her anger translates into acting out by shoplifting, Zoe gets caught and is ordered to make good by participating in a work program at a prairie preserve. While learning to appreciate the prairie ecosystem, Zoe also meets an unusual friend with whom she can share her interest in nature. In *Booklist* Michael Cart noted that the environmental aspects of Todd's novel are balanced by "her careful exploration of . . . a family in transition," while Claire Rosser wrote in *Kliatt* that *The Blind Faith Hotel* "captures the tension and love and fury and hurtin a family in crisis." Todd's use of "language . . . makes every page a treasure," Rosser added, and a *Kirkus Reviews* contributor cited her "homespun tone" and her novel's "themes of home, family, memory, and loss."

"When I was growing up, I wanted to be either a writer or a child psychologist," Todd once told *SATA,* "and I think both of those aspirations led me to write *Pig and the Shrink.* I had fun writing that book, but I also thought a lot about what it means to be a friend, how we come to accept ourselves and other people, how we can best be of service to others, and how we learn to forgive. I hope people reading it will find themselves laughing and thinking about these things too.

"That's the best part about having a book published: that you can have this sort of conversation with people you will never meet. But I would write anyway, even if I knew my books would never be published, because writing helps me pay attention to the world, to learn

about myself and my relationships with other people, to slow down and really see. I write every day, mostly because it makes my life happier, and I divide my time between writing in my journal, working on books, reading other people's work and thinking about what I admire in it, and staring out the window. Even though it may not seem like it, I consider all of these things essential to making my books.

"Here's my advice for aspiring writers. Don't settle for passive entertainment. Go out and live your life. Laugh, cry, get messy, fall down, and get up again. And keep a journal. Not the 'today I did this. . .' kind, but whatever pops into your head and needs to be said. Let it all spill out of you, and when you're done, read it over and write again. Because the best conversation of all is the lifelong conversation you have with yourself in the pages of your journal."

Biographical and Critical Sources

PERIODICALS

Booklist, October, 1999, Carolyn Phelan, review of *Pig and the Shrink,* p. 358; October 15, 2008, Michael Cart, review of *The Blind Faith Hotel,* p. 35.
Bulletin of the Center for Children's Books, November, 1999, Elizabeth Bush, review of *Pig and the Shrink.*
Herald Review (Decatur, IL), December 15, 2008, Arlene Mannlein, interview with Todd.
Kirkus Reviews, June 1, 1999, review of *Pig and the Shrink,* p. 890; September 15, 2008, review of *The Blind Faith Hotel.*
Kliatt, November, 2008, Claire Rosser, review of *The Blind Faith Hotel,* p. 18.
Publishers Weekly, August 2, 1999, review of *Pig and the Shrink,* p. 85.
School Library Journal, September, 1999, Elaine Baran, review of *Pig and the Shrink;* December, 2008, Brandy Danner, review of *The Blind Faith Hotel,* p. 140.

ONLINE

Pamela Todd Home Page, http://pamelatodd.com (January 15, 2010).
Society of Children's Book Writers and Illustrators—Illinois Web site, http://www.scbwi-illinois.org/ (January 15, 2010), "Pamela Todd."

Cover of Todd's middle-grade novel **The Blind Faith Hotel,** *which finds a young teen dealing with an unwanted family move.* (Jacket photograph copyright © by Little Blue Wolf Productions/Corbis. Reproduced by permission of Margaret K. McElderry Books, an imprint of Simon & Schuster Macmillan, and Corbis.)

*   *   *

TOPAZ, Ksenia

Personal

Born in Moscow, USSR (now Russia); immigrated to Israel, 1991; children: two daughters. *Education:* Strogonoff Academy of Art (Moscow, USSR), degree. *Religion:* Jewish.

Addresses

Home—Jerusalem, Israel. *E-mail*—studio@kseniatopaz.com.

Career

Illustrator, graphic designer, and fine artist.

Illustrator

Tami Lehman-Wilzig, *Lase Lotty's Tablecloth,* Gefen Publishing (Israel), 2007.

Tami Lehman-Wilzig, *Levi Mayer and His Lemon Tree,* Gefen Publishing (Israel), 2007.

Anna Levine, *Jodie's Hanukkah Dig,* Kar-Ben Publishing (Minneapolis, MN), 2008.

Tami Lehman-Wilzig, *Zvuvi's Israel,* Kar-Ben Publishing (Minneapolis, MN), 2009.

Raanan Levy, *Who Needs a Hug?,* Yediot Publishing (Israel), 2009.

Ofra Gelbart-Avni, *Itai: A Sweet Story,* Matar Publishing (Israel), 2009.

Vered Shlauzer-Ida, *Sheleg Is Toffy,* Agam Publishing (Israel), 2010.

Contributor to periodicals, including *Sukariot* (newspaper).

Biographical and Critical Sources

PERIODICALS

Booklist, November 1, 2008, Kay Weisman, review of *Jodie's Hanukkah Dig,* p. 46.

Kirkus Reviews, November 1, 2008, review of *Jodie's Hanukkah Dig.*

School Library Journal, October, 2008, Teri Markson, review of *Jodie's Hanukkah Dig,* p. 95.

ONLINE

Ksenia Topaz Home Page, http://www.kseniatopaz.com (January 15, 2010).

* * *

TRUESDELL, Sue 1959-

Personal

Born 1959. *Education:* Pratt Institute, B.F.A. (communication design—illustration), 1981.

Addresses

Home—Tenafly, NJ.

Career

Illustrator.

Awards, Honors

Theodor Seuss Geisel Award Honor Book designation, 2009, for *Chicken Said, "Cluck!"* by Judyann Ackerman Grant.

Illustrator

Dennis Haseley, *The Pirate Who Tried to Capture the Moon,* HarperCollins Children's (New York, NY), 1983.

Alvin Schwartz, *Unriddling: All Sorts of Riddles to Puzzle Your Guessery,* HarperCollins Children's (New York, NY), 1983.

Mitchell Sharmat, *The Seven Sloppy Days of Phineas Pig,* Harcourt Brace (New York, NY), 1983.

Anne Leo Ellis, *Dabble Duck,* HarperCollins Children's (New York, NY), 1984.

Betsy C. Byars, *The Golly Sisters Go West,* HarperCollins Children's (New York, NY), 1985.

Joan Robins, *Addie Meets Max,* HarperCollins Children's (New York, NY), 1985.

Phyllis Root, *Soup for Supper,* HarperCollins Children's (New York, NY), 1986.

Susan Shreve, *Lily and the Runaway Baby,* Random House Books for Young Readers (New York, NY), 1987.

Bill Grossman, *Donna O'Neeshuck Was Chased by Some Cows,* HarperCollins Children's (New York, NY), 1988.

Jocelyn Stevenson, *O'Diddy,* Random House Books for Young Readers (New York, NY), 1988.

Jean Little, *Hey World, Here I Am!,* HarperCollins Children's (New York, NY), 1989.

Amy Hest, *Travel Tips from Harry: A Guide to Family Vacations in the Sun,* William Morrow (New York, NY), 1989.

Joan Robins, *Addie Runs Away,* HarperCollins Children's (New York, NY), 1989.

Betsy C. Byars, *Hooray for the Golly Sisters!,* HarperCollins Children's (New York, NY), 1990.

Laura Geringer, *Look Out, Look Out, It's Coming!,* HarperCollins Children's (New York, NY), 1992.

Alvin Schwartz, *And the Green Grass Grew All Around,* HarperCollins Children's (New York, NY), 1992.

Barbara M. Joosse, *Wild Willie and King Kyle, Detectives* ("Wild Willie Mystery" series), Clarion (New York, NY), 1993.

Joan Robins, *Addie's Bad Day,* HarperCollins Children's (New York, NY), 1993.

Betsy C. Byars, *The Golly Sisters Ride Again,* HarperCollins Children's (New York, NY), 1994.

Barbara M. Joosse, *The Losers Fight Back* ("Wild Willie Mystery" series), Clarion (New York, NY), 1994.

Nola Buck, *Creepy Crawly Critters, and Other Halloween Tongue Twisters,* HarperCollins Children's (New York, NY), 1995.

Nola Buck, *Santa's Short Suit Shrunk, and Other Christmas Tongue Twisters,* HarperCollins Children's (New York, NY), 1997.

Barbara M. Joosse, *Nugget and Darling,* Clarion (New York, NY), 1997.

Barbara M. Joosse, *Ghost Trap* ("Wild Willie Mystery" series), Clarion (New York, NY), 1998.

Roberta Karim, *This Is a Hospital, Not a Zoo!*, Clarion (New York, NY), 1998.

Linda L. Strauss, *A Fairy Called Hilary*, Holiday House (New York, NY), 1999.

Jean Craighead George, *How to Talk to Your Dog*, Harper-Collins (New York, NY), 1999.

Barbara M. Joosse, *Alien Brain Fryout* ("Wild Willie Mystery" series), Clarion Books (New York, NY), 2000.

Andrew Clements, *Circus Family Dog*, Clarion Books (New York, NY), 2000.

Jean Craighead George, *How to Talk to Your Cat*, Harper-Collins (New York, NY), 2000.

Elizabeth Winthrop, *Halloween Hats*, Henry Holt (New York, NY), 2002.

Judyann Ackerman Grant, *Chicken Said, "Cluck!"*, HarperCollins (New York, NY), 2008.

Sue Stainton, *I Love Dogs*, Katherine Tegen Books (New York, NY), 2010.

Sidelights

Sue Truesdell is the illustrator of dozens of books for children. Her illustrations appear alongside texts by numerous writers, among them acclaimed authors Betsy C. Byars, Joan Robins, Andrew Clements, Alvin Schwartz, Elizabeth Winthrop, and Barbara M. Joosse, the last for whom Truesdell has illustrated the "Wild Willie Mystery" series of early-grade readers. In one of her early illustration projects, Dennis Haseley's *The Pirate Who Tried to Capture the Moon*, her imaginative black-and-white cartoon drawings feature a centerpiece: the glowing golden moon, the hue of which is intensified on every page. Reviewing Joosse's *Alien Brain Fryout*, Linda Plevak wrote in *School Library Journal* that Truesdell's "cartoon characters" in the "Wee Willie Mystery" series, "with their big eyes and comical investigative ways have surefire appeal."

Nonfiction writer Nola Buck teams up with Truesdell on a number of children's books, including *Creepy Crawly Critters, and Other Halloween Tongue Twisters*. For this preschool-age reader, Truesdell contributes watercolor illustrations that depict children's celebrations of the scary holiday and feature a bevy of witches, goblins, bats, and other creatures cavorting across the pages. Pamela K. Bomboy, writing in *School Library Journal*, declared that Truesdell's drawings "add to the amusement" of Buck's text in *Creepy Crawly Critters, and Other Halloween Tongue Twisters*.

For their collaboration on *Santa's Short Suit Shrunk, and Other Christmas Tongue Twisters*, Truesdell and Buck once again return to the delight of verbal-dexterity testers, and the pleasant nature of the season provides ample opportunity for Truesdell's pen. Humor and recurring characters, including dogs and a boy named Sam, reappear throughout the book's pages. A *School Library Journal* assessment by Jane Marino found that "Truesdell's lively illustrations are well suited to the material," while *Horn Book* critic Roger Sutton wrote that the art-filled pages in *Santa's Short Suit Shrunk, and Other Christmas Tongue Twisters* possesses "a pleasing unity."

Sue Truesdell's illustration projects include Nola Buck's **Santa's Short Suit Shrunk, and Other Christmas Tongue Twisters.** (Illustration © 1997 by Susan G. Truesdell. Reproduced by permission of HarperCollins Publishers, Inc.)

Truesdell's collaborations with Joosse include the elementary-grade reader *Nugget and Darling*. Nugget is Nell's beloved dog, but their relationship is dramatically altered when Nugget finds a kitten and Nell adopts it. A series of minor jealousies erupts, but in the end all find that there is more than enough love for everybody. While some reviewers noted that Joosse's story delves into rather coy, heart-tugging territory, Truesdell's characterizations of the pets' faces "are a hoot, smoothly tempering the inherent sentimentality of the story," declared Stephanie Zvirin in *Booklist*. A *Publishers Weekly* reviewer termed both text and art for *Nugget and Darling* to be "full-bodied and pleasingly idiosyncratic."

Joosse's "Wild Willie Mystery" series of detective fiction begins with *Wild Willie and King Kyle, Detectives* and introduces the two neighborhood pals. The adventures continue in *The Losers Fight Back, Ghost Trap*, and *Alien Brain Fryout*. In *Wild Willie and King Kyle* Kyle's family moves back into Willie's neighborhood but buys an older home in great need of repair. Willie's new friend Lucy finds herself resenting Kyle, but the decrepit state of the house—and its treasure-filled attic—gives all three ample opportunity for potential detective work. When Lucy discovers that the previous owner died in Kyle's very bedroom, tensions escalate until a clever parrot and Willie's graciousness help end the conflict. Susan Hepler, writing in *School Library Journal,* praised "Truesdell's big-nosed, large-eyed, loosely limned characters." In *Alien Brain Fryout* Kyle, Lucy, and Willie find themselves worried about neighborhood bully Chuckle. Here "Truesdell's playful . . . illustrations show the exaggerated emotions" that fuel the story's humor, according to *Booklist* contributor Shelley Townsend-Hudson.

Whimsical drawings by the accomplished Truesdell also help tell the story in Roberta Karim's beginning reader *This Is a Hospital, Not a Zoo!* and Judyann Ackerman Grant's *Chicken Said, "Cluck!,"* the latter the saga of a farming couple whose trusty chicken helps to save their pumpkin patch from hungry insects. In *This Is a Hospital, Not a Zoo!* Truesdell's illustrations depict a little boy who confounds the medical professionals when he metamorphoses into various animals according to which animal cracker he eats. Stephanie Zvirin, writing in *Booklist,* praised "Truesdell's funny, irresistible artwork" for *This Is a Hospital, Not a Zoo!,* while the art in *Chicken Said, "Cluck!"* "support[s] the reading with simple clarity," according to *School Library Journal* critic Teresa Pfeifer.

In Clements' picture book *Circus Family Dog* a grouchy old circus dog finds itself upstaged by a younger pup, and here the artist contributes "vibrant" watercolor-and-pen art that reflects the "realistic mood" of Clements' "funny and warm story," according to *School Library Journal* critic Wanda Meyers-Hines.

Biographical and Critical Sources

PERIODICALS

Booklist, March 1, 1997, Stephanie Zvirin, review of *Nugget and Darling,* p. 1172; March 1, 1998, Stephanie Zvirin, review of *This Is a Hospital, Not a Zoo!,* p. 1140; June 1, 2000, Ilene Cooper, review of *Circus Family Dog,* p. 1905; September 15, 2000, Shelley Townsend-Hudson, review of *Alien Brain Fryout,* p. 241; September 15, 2002, Stephanie Zvirin, review of *Halloween Hats,* p. 24.

Horn Book, November-December, 1997, Roger Sutton, review of *Santa's Short Suit Shrunk, and Other Christmas Tongue Twisters,* p. 695; January-February, 2009, Martha V. Parravano, review of *Chicken Said, "Cluck!",* p. 92.

Kirkus Reviews, August 1, 2002, review of *Halloween Hats,* p. 1146; September 15, 2008, Judyann Ackerman Grant, review of *Chicken Said, "Cluck!"*

New York Times Book Review, May 14, 2000, Adam Liptak, review of *How to Talk to Your Dog,* p. 29.

Publishers Weekly, February 24, 1997, review of *Nugget and Darling,* p. 91; January 10, 2000, reviews of *How to Talk to Your Dog* and *How to Talk to Your Cat,* both p. 68.

School Library Journal, November, 1995, Pamela K. Bomboy, review of *Creepy Crawly Critters, and Other Halloween Tongue Twisters,* p. 88; October, 1997, Jane Marino, review of *Santa's Short Suit Shrunk, and Other Christmas Tongue Twisters,* pp. 45-46; June, 1998, Susan Hepler, review of *Ghost Trap,* p. 111; August, 2000, Wanda Meyers-Hines, review of *Circus Family Dog,* p. 146; September, 2000, Linda L. Plevak, review of *Alien Brain Fryout,* p. 200; October, 2002, Piper L. Nyman, review of *Halloween Hats,* p. 136; November, 2008, Teresa Pfeifer, review of *Chicken Said, "Cluck!",* p. 88.

ONLINE

HarperCollins Web site, http://www.harpercollins.com/ (January 10, 2010), "Sue Truesdell."*

W-Z

WANG, Gabrielle

Personal

Born in Melbourne, Victoria, Australia; married; children: Ren (son), one daughter. *Education:* Royal Melbourne Institute of Technology, degree (graphic design); Melbourne University, degree (Chinese language); attended Zhejiang Academy of Fine Art (Hangzhou, China). *Hobbies and other interests:* Singing.

Addresses

Home—Melbourne, Victoria, Australia. *E-mail*—gabrielle@gabriellewang.com.

Career

Author and educator. Rum Jungle (design studio), cofounder; Royal Melbourne Institute of Technology, Melbourne, Victoria, Australia, teacher of Chinese language.

Awards, Honors

Aurealis Award for best children's long fiction, 2002, for *The Garden of Empress Cassia;* Aurealis Award shortlist, 2004, for *The Pearl of Tiger Bay,* and nomination, 2009, for *A Ghost in My Suitcase.*

Writings

Chinese Calligraphy: A Beginner's Manual, privately published (Melbourne, Victoria, Australia), 1985.
The Garden of Empress Cassia, Puffin (Ringwood, Victoria, Australia), 2002.
The Pearl of Tiger Bay, Puffin (Camberwell, Victoria, Australia), 2004.
The Hidden Monastery, Penguin (Camberwell, Victoria, Australia), 2006.
The Lion Drummer, illustrated by Andrew McLean, Penguin (Camberwell, Victoria, Australia), 2008.
A Ghost in My Suitcase, Puffin (Camberwell, Victoria, Australia), 2009.
The Chinese Zodiac, illustrated by Sally Rippin and Regine Abos, Black Dog Books (Fitzroy, Victoria, Australia), 2010.
Little Paradise, Penguin (Camberwell, Victoria, Australia), 2010.

Biographical and Critical Sources

PERIODICALS

Magpies, September, 2002, review of *The Garden of Empress Cassia,* p. 22; July, 2006, Chloe Mauger, review of *The Hidden Monastery,* p. 38; March, 2009, Sharon Greenaway, review of *A Ghost in My Suitcase,* p. 16.

ONLINE

Gabrielle Wang Home Page, http://www.gabriellewang.com (January 10, 2010).*

* * *

WILLIAMS, Carol Lynch 1959-

Personal

Born September 28, 1959, in Lincoln, NE; daughter of Richard T. (affiliated with the U.S. Air Force) and Anne Y. (a college teacher) Lynch; married Andrew G. Williams (an Internet security-writer), August 13, 1985; children: Sarah Elise, Laura Anne, Kyra Leigh, Caitlynne Victoria, Carolina Grace. *Education:* Attended Vermont College of Fine Arts. *Religion:* Church of Jesus Christ of Latter-Day Saints (Mormon). *Hobbies and other interests:* Movies, baking bread, cross stitching, going to garage sales, spending time with family.

Carol Lynch Williams (Photograph by Drew Williams. Reproduced by permission.)

Addresses

Home—Springville, UT. *Agent*—Steve Fraser, Jennifer DeChiara Literary Agency, 31 E. 32nd St., Ste. 300, New York, NY 10016.

Career

Author of children's books, beginning 1993. Brigham Young University, Provo, UT, part-time instructor in creative writing.

Member

Society of Children's Book Writers and Illustrators.

Awards, Honors

Two-time winner, Utah Original Writing Competition; Best Book for Young Adults designation, American Library Association, and Nebraska Golden Sower Award, both 1997, both for *The True Colors of Caitlynne Jackson;* Teacher's Choice designation, International Reading Association/Children's Book Council, 1999, for *If I Forget, You Remember;* Outstanding Book for Young People with Disabilities award, 2009, for *Pretty like Us;* PEN/Phyllis Naylor Working Writer fellowship, 2009.

Writings

FOR CHILDREN

Kelly and Me, Delacorte (New York, NY), 1993.
Adeline Street, Delacorte (New York, NY), 1995.

The True Colors of Caitlynne Jackson, Delacorte (New York, NY), 1997.
If I Forget, You Remember, Delacorte (New York, NY), 1998.
My Angelica, Delacorte (New York, NY), 1999.
Carolina Autumn, Delacorte (New York, NY), 2000.
Christmas in Heaven, Putnam (New York, NY), 2000.
A Mother to Embarrass Me, Delacorte (New York, NY), 2002.
Walk to Hope, Spring Creek Book Co. (Provo, UT), 2004.
24 Games You Can Play on a Checkerboard, Gibbs Smith, Publisher (Layton, UT), 2007.
Pretty like Us, Peachtree (Atlanta, GA), 2008.
Beware in Delaware, Peachtree (Atlanta, GA), 2009.
Secret in Pennsylvania, Peachtree (Atlanta, GA), 2009.
The Chosen One, St. Martin's Griffin (New York, NY), 2009.

"LATTER-DAY DAUGHTERS" SERIES

Anna's Gift, Aspen Books (Salt Lake City, UT), 1995.
Laurel's Flight, Aspen Books (Salt Lake City, UT), 1995.
Sarah's Quest, Aspen Books (Salt Lake City, UT), 1995.
Esther's Celebration, illustrated by Paul Mann, Aspen Books (Salt Lake City, UT), 1996.
Marciea's Melody, illustrated by Paul Mann, Aspen Books (Salt Lake City, UT), 1996.
Catherine's Remembrance, Aspen Books (Salt Lake City, UT), 1996.
Caroline's Secret, Deseret Book Company (Salt Lake City, UT), 1997.
Victoria's Courage, Deseret Book Company (Salt Lake City, UT), 1998.
Laura's Box of Treasures, Bookcraft (Salt Lake City, UT), 1999.

Sidelights

Carol Lynch Williams writes middle-grade and young-adult novels in Utah where she shares a home with her husband and five daughters. An award-winning writer, Williams has authored several novels in the "Latter-Day Daughters" series published by Aspen Books and Deseret Book Company in Salt Lake City. She has also received enthusiastic praise from reviewers for her other works of fiction, which include *The True Colors of Caitlynne Jackson, The Chosen One,* and *A Mother to Embarrass Me.*

Williams's first novel, *Kelly and Me,* is geared for older elementary-grade readers. The story centers on sisters Leah and Kelly, whose Florida household suddenly expands when their eccentric but beloved grandfather, "Papa," moves in. As narrated by eleven-year-old Leah, Papa draws Leah and ten-year-old Kelly into a series of comic adventures as well as several near-dangerous mishaps. Conflict intensifies in the Orton family when the sisters and their elderly confidente come up against sensible parents. These conflicts come to an abrupt halt when Kelly fatally collapses at the breakfast table, the result of an undiagnosed aneurysm. In shock, Leah blames Papa for her sister's death, but as Carolyn Noah observed in her *School Library Journal* review of *Kelly and Me*, "within the space of twelve pages, the family nearly tears apart, then begins to knit together as they share their memories and grief." Writing in the *Bulletin of the Center for Children's Books,* Deborah Stevenson noted that the novel's "dialogue and family dynamics are authentic, humorous, and restrained," while a *Kirkus Reviews* writer deemed *Kelly and Me* "a capable first novel that views both boisterous comedy and wrenching loss with a perceptive eye."

A sequel to *Kelly and Me, Adeline Street* presents a month-by-month chronicle of how the Ortons, and especially Leah, deal with the loss of a young family member. Now twelve years old, Leah again narrates, describing the changes in her life that have been wrought by both the past trauma as well as because of her emerging adolescence. The mischievous Papa is still present, although his antics have become less outrageous, and the book ends with the revelation that Mrs. Orton is expecting another child. "Williams again displays an easy gift for evocation of place and voice," remarked Stevenson in her review of *Adeline Street.*

Cover of Williams' young-adult novel The True Colors of Caitlynne Jackson. (Cover photographs by Michael Kornafel/FPG and Rob Cage/FPG. Used by permission of Yearling, an imprint of Random House Children's Books, a division of Random House, Inc.)

Another pair of close siblings provide the focus for *The True Colors of Caitlynne Jackson,* Williams's novel for young adults. Caitlynne and Cara are half sisters as well as joint victims of an emotionally and physically abusive mother. One day, their mother announces that she is leaving the girls alone at their isolated rural home so that she can be alone and write a book. Her departure is almost a relief, and the older, artistically gifted Caitlynne learns much about herself over the next few weeks as she assumes the role of caretaker of the household. When the girls finally run out of food, they are helped by Caitlynne's supportive boyfriend. Ultimately, melodrama ensues after they seek the help of their grandmother and the authorities intervene. *The True Colors of Caitlynne Jackson* "is gripping and believable," opined Stevenson in her review of the novel for the *Bulletin of the Center for Children's Books,* the critic adding that "the desperation and up-close parental menace are originally and powerfully depicted" by Williams.

Williams returns to the subject of aging grandparents in *If I Forget, You Remember.* In this middle-grade novel, the much-anticipated summer vacation of preteen Elyse, an aspiring writer, and older sister Jordyn is disrupted when their grandmother moves in with the sisters and their widowed mother. Granny has Alzheimer's disease, and her increasing dementia both upsets Elyse and Jordyn and forces them to confront troubling, adult-sized issues. In addition, Elyse is uncomfortable with the fact that her mother is beginning to date, and she herself struggles with new feelings for a boy who was once just a playmate. While "Elyse's distress . . . has the mournful knell of authenticity," remarked a *Kirkus Reviews'* critic, a *Publishers Weekly* review praised Williams' novel for culminating with "a credible and uplifting conclusion that may help readers as much as the protagonist."

In *My Angelica,* Williams again presents the world through the eyes of another preteen literary hopeful. Sage Oliver is intensely involved in writing her first novel, *Angelica and the Seminole Indians,* and her first draft of the historical novel is full of exclamation points and tortured, romance-novel prose. Sage's best friend, George, thinks that her friend's book is terrible, but he cannot summon the courage to tell her. George also does not know how to admit to Sage that he has a secret crush on her, despite her penchant for purple prose. Comic results ensue when Sage's novel is entered in a school writing competition and George decides to hide part of the manuscript to save its author from certain embarrassment. In *School Library Journal* Janet Hilbun remarked of *My Angelica* that Williams' "strength of characterization again shines" in her "truly enjoyable novel." Roger Sutton, writing in *Horn Book,* declared that, "truth be told, the generous excerpts from Sage's writing are the best part."

Williams also addresses middle graders in *A Mother to Embarrass Me,* which finds twelve-year-old Laura

Cover of Williams' young-adult novel Carolina Autumn, *featuring cover art by Matt Manley.* (Jacket illustration copyright © 2000 by Matt Manley. Used by permission of Laurel-Leaf, an imprint of Random House Children's Books, a division of Random House, Inc.)

Stephan mortified by her mother's penchant for totally out-of-style music and clothes. When the woman announces that she is pregnant with a second child, the preteen is even more mortified, but Laura's tendency to over-dramatize her plight and take everything personally gradually changes over the course of the months and weeks leading up to the birth of her new sibling. Recommending the book to fans of writer Phyllis Reynolds Naylor, Terrie Dorio added in her *School Library Journal* review that *A Mother to Embarrass Me* is an "amusing novel" in which Williams addresses typical 'tween behavior with "a gentle and humorous touch," and a *Kirkus Reviews* writer predicted that "middle-grade girls will nod in recognition" of Laura's frustrations.

Fourteen-year-old Carolina McKinney has more substantial worries in *Carolina Autumn:* she is coping with a tragic loss and those she would talk to have become distant or are no longer around. Although she has Garrett, her new boyfriend, the teen is hesitant about sharing her emotional burdens, and her best friend Mara shows herself not to be trusted. Hoping to move beyond

her sadness, Carolina uses letter-writing and the creative hobby of photography that she shared with her father to come to terms with a future that is far different than the one she had taken for granted. Praising Williams for avoiding sentimentality in her coming-of-age story, *Booklist* critic Shelle Rosenfeld added that *Carolina Autumn* is nonetheless "heart-felt and sympathetic," and the author uses "simple, descriptive prose" to bring to life her likeable ninth-grade heroine. A *Publishers Weekly* critic had special praise for Carolina, calling her "an honestly wrought" character "whom readers will understand and respect," while *School Library Journal* contributor Kit Vaughan described *Carolina Autumn* as "a finely crafted novel" that uses "spare, lyrical prose" to portray "an adolescent blossoming into a thoughtful . . . young woman."

An introverted sixth grader living in small-town Florida is introduced to readers in *Pretty like Us.* As far as Beauty McElwrath is concerned, the first day of a new school year is just another day of being an outcast. Then she meets Alane, a new student who also seems destined for outsider status. Alane has a disease that makes her age rapidly, and while Beauty is first put off by the girl's shriveled skin, and frailty, she soon sees beyond appearances to Alane's upbeat, typical preteen personality. To protect her new friend, Beauty takes a more assertive approach at school, ultimately putting herself at risk to save her friend. Describing *Pretty like Us* as "a bittersweet tale," a *Publishers Weekly* contributor added that Williams' unusual theme "will be recognizable to readers as their own social conflicts writ large." Beauty is a typical teen, according to *School Library Journal* contributor Amelia Jenkins: "she is as moody and self-conscious as any girl her age." In *Kirkus Reviews* a contributor praised the "delightful twist" that Williams uses to lighten the novel's ending, calling *Pretty like Us* "a lovely story that will reach many middle-school girls."

Based on a true incident—the forced marriages of underaged girls at a Texas cult in the spring of 2008—*The Chosen One* is a suspenseful story that takes readers into the world of a young girl growing up in a strict polygamist community. Raised in a communal nursery as one of twenty-one children born to a man with three wives, thirteen-year-old Kyra seems to follow the required path of those in her Apostolic community. However, now she has come of age and cult leader Prophet Childs commands her to become the seventh wife of her own father's sixty-year-old brother. Her revulsion signals to the teen that something is not right with life among the Chosen Ones, and these feelings grow stronger when she discovers a bookmobile while straying outside the fenced confines of her desert community. While searching for a way to escape from the upcoming marriage and her oppressive life, Kyra is punished when Prophet Childs discovers her budding romance with Joshua, a fellow member her age. In *The Chosen One* Williams tells "a fast-moving story" featuring "sympathetic characters" and a suspenseful ending, according

Cover of Williams' young-adult novel Pretty like Us, *in which two girls forge an unlikely friendship.* (Peachtree Publishers, 2008. Reproduced by permission.)

to *Horn Book* contributor Chelsey Philpot, while a *Kirkus Reviews* critic dubbed the novel "intensely gripping and grippingly intense." In *Booklist* Ilene Cooper noted that, although Kyra's problems are worlds away from those of the average teen, her "yearnings and fears . . . will still seem familiar and close." In her review for the *New York Times Book Review,* Jessica Bruder praised Williams' "spare, evocative writing" in *The Chosen One,* the critic adding that the author's "honest sense of character . . . helps bridge the rift between Kyra's world and ours."

Biographical and Critical Sources

PERIODICALS

Booklist, June 1, 2000, Ilene Cooper, review of *Christmas in Heaven,* p. 1899; September 1, 2000, Shelle Rosenfeld, review of *Carolina Autumn,* p. 109; February 15, 2009, Ilene Cooper, review of *The Chosen One,* p. 71.
Bulletin of the Center for Children's Books, March, 1994, Deborah Stevenson, review of *Kelly and Me,* p. 238; April, 1995, Deborah Stevenson, review of *Adeline Street,* p. 289; February, 1997, Deborah Stevenson, review of *The True Colors of Caitlynne Jackson,* p. 226.

Horn Book, January-February, 1999, Roger Sutton, review of *My Angelica,* p. 72; May-June, 2009, Chelsey Philpot, review of *The Chosen One,* p. 311.
Kirkus Reviews, November 1, 1993, review of *Kelly and Me,* p. 1400; December 15, 1997, review of *If I Forget, You Remember,* p. 1844; February 1, 2002, review of *A Mother to Embarrass Me,* p. 192; September 1, 2008, review of *Pretty like Us;* April 1, 2009, review of *The Chosen One.*
Publishers Weekly, January 5, 1998, review of *If I Forget, You Remember,* p. 68; July 10, 2000, review of *Christmas in Heaven,* p. 64; August 21, 2000, review of *Carolina Autumn,* p. 74; January 14, 2002, review of *A Mother to Embarrass Me,* p. 60; September 29, 2008, review of *Pretty like Us,* p. 82.
School Library Journal, September, 1993, Carolyn Noah, review of *Kelly and Me,* p. 236; January, 1999, Janet Hilbun, review of *My Angelica,* p. 134; June, 2000, Ronnie Krasnow, review of *Christmas in Heaven,* p. 156; September, 2000, Kit Vaughan, review of *Carolina Autumn,* p. 239; March, 2002, Terrie Dorio, review of *A Mother to Embarrass Me,* p. 239; January, 2009, Amelia Jenkins, review of *Pretty like Us,* p. 124; July, 2009, Carolyn Lehman, review of *The Chosen One,* p. 96.

ONLINE

Cynsations Web log, http://cynthialeitichsmith.blogspot.com (May 12, 2009), Cynthia Leitich Smith, interview with Williams.*

*   *   *

WOOD, David 1944-

Personal

Born February 21, 1944, in Sutton, Surrey, England; son of Richard Edwin and Audrey Adele Wood; married Sheila Ruskin, 1966 (marriage dissolved, 1970); married Jacqueline Stanbury (an actress), January 17, 1975; children: Katherine, Rebecca. *Education:* Worcester College, Oxford, B.A. (with honors), 1966. *Hobbies and other interests:* Writing, conjuring, collecting old books.

Addresses

Home—England. *Agent*—(For plays) Casarotto Ramsay & Associates, Waverly House, 7-12 Noel St., London W1F 8GQ, England; (for children's books) Eunice McMullen, Low Ibbotsholme Cottage, Off Bridge La., Troutbeck Bridge, Windermere, Cumbria LA23 1HU, England.

Career

Actor, composer, producer, director, playwright and author. W.S.G. Productions Ltd., director, 1966—; Whirligig Theatre (touring children's theatre company), co-founder, with John Gould, and director, beginning 1979; Verronmead Limited (television production company), founder and director, beginning 1983; Westwood Theatre Productions, founder and director, 1986-94; W2 Productions Ltd., cofounder and director, beginning 1995. Presenter at schools and workshops; lecturer. Member of Arts Council of Great Britain drama advisory panel, 1978-80; chair of Action for Children's Arts, 1997—member of board, Polk Children's Theatre, 1979—; trustee of Wimbledon Theatre, 1996-2003, and Story Museum, 2006—.

Member

British Actors Equity Association, Society of Authors, Inner Magic Circle.

Awards, Honors

Nottinghamshire Children's Book of the Year Award, 1990, for *Sidney the Monster;* Distinguished Playwriting Award, American Alliance of Theatre and Education, 2003, for *Spot's Birthday Party,* 2007, for *Danny the Champion of the World;* named to Order of the British Empire, 2004; authored plays have earned several production awards.

Writings

CHILDREN'S PLAYS

The Tinder Box (two-act; adaptation of a story by Hans Christian Andersen), produced in Worcester, England, 1967.

(Author of lyrics) *Cinderella,* book by Sid Collin, music by John Gould, produced in Glasgow, Scotland, 1968.

(With Sheila Ruskin) *The Owl and the Pussycat Went to See. . .* (two-act musical; adaptation of works by Edward Lear; produced in Worcester, 1968, and in London, England, 1969; also see below), Samuel French (London, England), 1970.

(With Sheila Ruskin) *Larry the Lamb in Toytown* (two-act musical; adaptation of stories by S.G. Hulme Beaman; produced in Worcester, England, 1969, and in London, England, 1973), Samuel French (London, England), 1977.

The Plotters of Cabbage Patch Corner (two-act musical; produced in Worcester, England, 1970, and in London, England, 1971; also see below), Samuel French (London, England), 1972.

Flibberty and the Penguin (two-act musical; produced in Worcester, England, 1971, and in London, England, 1977), Samuel French (London, England), 1974.

Tickle (produced on tour in England, 1972, and in London, England, 1977), Samuel French (London, England), 1978.

The Papertown Paperchase (two-act musical; produced in Worcester, England, 1972, and in London, 1973), Samuel French (London, England), 1976.

Hijack over Hygenia (two-act musical; produced in Worcester, England, 1973), Samuel French (London, England), 1974.

Old Mother Hubbard (two-act musical; produced in Hornchurch, Essex, England, 1975; also see below), Samuel French (London, England), 1976.

Old Father Time (two-act musical; produced in Hornchurch, Essex, England, 1976), Samuel French (London, England), 1977.

The Gingerbread Man (two-act musical; produced in Basildon, Essex, England, 1976, and in London, England, 1977; also see below), Samuel French (London, England), 1977.

Mother Goose's Golden Christmas (two-act; produced in Hornchurch, Essex, England, 1977; also see below), Samuel French (London, England), 1978.

Nutcracker Sweet (two-act; produced in Farnham, Surrey, England, 1977, and in London, England, 1980), Samuel French (London, England), 1981.

Babes in the Magic Wood (two-act; produced in Hornchurch, Essex, England, 1978), Samuel French (London, England), 1979.

There Was an Old Woman . . . (two-act; produced in Leicester, England, 1979), Samuel French (London, England), 1980.

Cinderella (produced in Hornchurch, Essex, England, 1979; also see below), Samuel French (London, England), 1980.

The Ideal Gnome Expedition (produced as *Chish and Fips,* Liverpool, England, 1980; produced as *The Ideal Gnome Expedition,* on tour and in London, England, 1981; also see below), Samuel French (London, England), 1982.

Aladdin (produced in Hornchurch, Essex, England, 1980), Samuel French (London, England), 1981.

(With Dave and Toni Arthur) *Robin Hood* (produced in Nottingham, England, 1981, and in London, England, 1982), Samuel French (London, England), 1985.

Meg and Mog Show (adaptation of stories by Helen Nicoll and Jan Pienkowski; produced in London, England, 1981), Samuel French (London, England), 1984.

Dick Whittington and Wondercat (produced in Hornchurch, Essex, 1981), Samuel French (London, England), 1982.

Jack and the Giant (produced in Hornchurch, Essex, England, 1982), Samuel French (New York, NY), 1987.

Magic and Music Show (one-man show), produced in London, England, 1983.

The Selfish Shellfish (produced in London, England, 1983), Samuel French (New York, NY), 1986.

(With Dave and Toni Arthur) *Jack the Lad,* produced in Manchester, England, 1984.

The Old Man of Lochnagar (adaptation of the story by Prince Charles; produced in London, England, 1986), Amber Lane Press, 1986.

Dinosaurs and All That Rubbish (music by Peter Pontzen; adaptation of the story by Michael Foreman; produced in Denbigh, Wales, 1986, and in London, England, 1988), Amber Lane Press, 1986.

The See-Saw Tree (produced in Farnham, Surrey, England, 1986, and in London, England, 1987), Amber Lane Press, 1987, Samuel French (New York, NY), 1987.

(With Dave and Toni Arthur) *The Pied Piper* (based on the tale by Robert Browning; produced at Yeovil, England and on tour, 1988.

Save the Human (adapted from the story by Toni Husband and David Wood; produced in London, England, 1990), Samuel French (New York, NY), 1990.

(Adaptor) *The BFG (Big Friendly Giant)* (adapted from the book by Roald Dahl; produced in London, England, 1991, produced in Philadelphia, PA, 2006; also see below), Samuel French (London, England), 1991, published in picture-book format as *The BFG: Plays for Children,* illustrated by Jane Walmsley, Puffin (Harmondsworth, England), 1993.

(Adaptor) *The Witches* (adapted from the book by Roald Dahl; produced in London, England, 1992), Samuel French (New York, NY), 1994.

Noddy (adapted from stories by Enid Blyton; produced in London, England, 1993), Samuel French (New York, NY), 1995.

Rupert and the Green Dragon (adaptation of the "Rupert Bear" stories by Mary Tourtel and Alfred Bestall; produced on tour, 1993), Samuel French (New York, NY), 1996.

Meg and Mog: Four Plays for Children (adaption of stories by Helen Nicoll and Jan Pienkowski), Puffin (Harmondsworth, England), 1994.

More Adventures of Noddy (adapted from stories by Enid Blyton; produced on tour, 1995), Samuel French (New York, NY), 1996.

Babe, the Sheep-pig (based on the book by Dick King-Smith), Samuel French (New York, NY), 1997.

Plays I (includes *The Gingerbread Man, The Seesaw Tree, The Ideal Gnome Exhibition,* and *Mother Goose's Golden Christmas*), Methuen Drama (London, England), 1999.

Plays II (includes *Quadrille, The Owl and the Pussycat Went to See . . . , The BFG, The Plotters of Cabbage Patch Corner,* and *Save the Human*), Methuen Drama (London, England), 1999.

Tom's Midnight Garden (based on the book by Philippa Pearce; produced in New York, NY, 2001), Samuel French (New York, NY), 2001.

Spot's Birthday Party (musical; based on the "Spot" books by Eric Hill), Samuel French (New York, NY), 2002.

The Twits (based on the story by Roald Dahl), Puffin (London, England), 2003.

Fantastic Mr Fox (based on the book by Roald Dahl), Samuel French (New York, NY), 2003.

(Author of libretto) *James and the Giant Peach* (adapted from the book by Roald Dahl), music by Stephen McNeff, Samuel French (New York, NY), 2004.

Clock Work (based on the story by Philip Pullman), produced in London, England, 2004.

Danny the Champion of the World (based on the book by Roald Dahl; produced in Cardiff, England, 2004), Samuel French (London, England), 2006.

Lady Lollipop (adapted from the book by Dick King-Smith), illustrated by Jill Barton, Walker (London, England), 2005.

Fimbles Live (adaptation of television program), produce in London, England), 2005.

The Lighthouse Keeper's Lunch (musical; based on the book by Ronda and David Armitage), Josef Weinberger (London, England), 2006.

The Tiger Who Came to Tea (adapted from the book by Judith Kerr), produced in London, England), 2008.

George's Marvelous Medicine (based on the book by Roald Dahl), produced in London, England, 2009.

Contributor of plays to books, including *Robin Hood and Friar Tuck* and *Marian and the Witches' Charm,* in *Playstages,* edited by John Alcock, Methuen (London, England), 1987.

CHILDREN'S FICTION

The Operats of Rodent Garden, illustrated by Geoffrey Beitz, Methuen (London, England), 1984.

The Gingerbread Man (from Wood's play), illustrated by Sally Anne Lambert, Pavilion (London, England), 1985.

The Discorats, illustrated by Geoffrey Beitz, Methuen (London, England), 1985.

(With Don Seed) *Chish 'n' Fips,* Boxtree, 1987.

Play Theatre (includes *Nativity Play* and *Jack and the Beanstalk*), two volumes, illustrated by Richard Fowler, Pavilion (London, England), 1987.

Sidney the Monster, illustrated by Clive Scruton, Walker (London, England), 1988.

Happy Birthday, Mouse! A First Counting Book, illustrated by Richard Fowler, Hodder & Stoughton (London, England), 1990.

Save the Human! (from Wood's play), illustrated by Toni Husband, Hamish Hamilton (London, England), 1991.

Baby Bear's Buggy Ride (To the Shops/To the Park), illustrated by Richard Fowler, Hazar, 1993.

Kingfisher Pop-up Theatre: Cinderella, illustrated by Richard Fowler, Kingfisher (London, England), 1994.

Bedtime Story: A Slip-in-the-Slot Book, illustrated by Richard Fowler, Doubleday (New York, NY), 1995.

The Magic Show, illustrated by Richard Fowler, Hazar, 1995.

Silly Spider!, illustrated by Richard Fowler, Harcourt Brace (San Diego, CA), 1998.

The Toy Cupboard (interactive book), illustrated by Richard Fowler, Pavilion (London, England), 2000.

Funny Bunny's Magic Show (lift-the-flap book), illustrated by Richard Fowler, Doubleday (London, England), 2000.

The Phantom Cat of the Opera (based on a novel by Gaston Leroux), illustrated by Peters Day, Pavilion (London, England), 2000, Watson-Gutpill (New York, NY), 2001.

Under the Bed!, illustrated by Richard Fowler, Barrons Educational Series (Hauppauge, NY), 2006.

It Wasn't Me!, illustrated by Richard Fowler, Over the Moon (Burgess Hill, England), 2006.

Mole's Bedtime Story, illustrated by Richard Fowler, Doubleday (London, England), 2007.

A Present for Santa Claus (pop-up book), illustrated by Dana Kubrick, Candlewick Press (Cambridge, MA),

2008, published as *A Present for Father Christmas,* Walker (London, England), 2008.

ADULT PLAYS

(With David Wright) *Hang Down Your Head and Die* (two-act), produced in London, England, and in New York, NY, 1964.

(With John Gould) *Four Degrees Over* (two-act), produced in London, England, 1966.

(With Mick Sadler and John Gould) *And Was Jerusalem,* produced in Oxford, England, 1966; produced as *A Present from the Corporation* in London, England, 1967.

(With David Wright) *A Life in Bedrooms* (two-act), produced in Edinburgh, Scotland, 1967; produced as *The Stiffkey Scandals of 1932* in London, England, 1968.

(With John Gould) *Three to One On* (two-act), produced in Edinburgh, Scotland, 1968.

(With John Gould) *Postscripts* (two-act), produced in London, England, 1969.

(With John Gould) *Down Upper Street* (two-act), produced in London, England, 1971.

(With John Gould) *Just the Ticket* (two-act), produced in Leatherhead, Surrey, England, 1973.

Rock Nativity (two-act musical; music by Tony Hatch and Jackie Trent; produced in Newcastle-upon-Tyne, England, 1974; produced as *A New Tomorrow* in Wimbledon, England, 1976), Weinberger, 1977.

(With Iwan Williams) *Maudie* (two-act), produced in Leatherhead, Surrey, England, 1974.

(With Bernard Price and Julian Sluggett) *Chi-Chestnuts* (two-act), produced in Chichester, England, 1975.

(With John Gould) *Think of a Number* (two-act), produced in Peterborough, England, 1975.

(Co-author) *More Chi-Chestnuts* (two-act), produced in Chichester, England, 1976.

(With John Gould) *Bars of Gould* (two-act revue), produced in Exeter, England, 1977.

(With John Gould) *The Luck of the Bodkins* (two-act; adaptation of a work by P.G. Wodehouse), produced in Windsor, England, 1978.

Abbacadabra (music by Bjorn Ulvaeus and Benny Andersson, lyrics by Don Black, Mike Batt, and Ulvaeus), produced in London, England, 1983.

Lyricist for stage performances, including *Have You Seen Manchseter?,* 1969, *Dead Centre of the Midlands* (revue), 1970, *Turn Your Own Sod* (revue), 1972, and *The Forest Child* (children's opera), 1998.

OTHER

Swallows and Amazons (screenplay), Anglo EMI Ltd., 1974.

Tide Race (screenplay), 1990.

People and Places: Activities and Assessments, Hodder & Stoughton (London, England), 1998.

(With Janet Grant) *Theatre for Children: A to Writing, Adapting, Directing, and Acting,* Ivan R. Dee (Chicago, IL), 1999.

Also writer for television, including the series *Playaway,* 1973-77, *Emu's Christmas Adventure,* 1977, *Writer's Workshops,* 1978, *Chish 'n' Fips,* 1984, *Chips' Comic,* 1984, *Seeing and Doing,* 1986, *The Old Man of Lochnagar* (based on the book by HRH the Prince of Wales), 1987, *Back Home* (adaptation of the story by Michelle Magorian), 1989, *Watch,* 1992, and *The Gingerbread Man* (animated series), 1992. Contributor of articles to *Drama* and *London Drama.*

Adaptations

Wood's stage adaptation of Enid Blyton's books was adapted into the video production *Noddy,* BBC Video, 1994.

Sidelights

Honored by Queen Elizabeth for his work in children's theatre, David Wood is a writer, director, actor, and playwright whose touring company, Whirligig Theatre, is devoted entirely to sharing his love of drama with children throughout England. Several of Wood's plays, such as *The Gingerbread Man* and *The Owl and the Pussycat Went to See . . . ,* give a new spin to old tales while others, such as *Flibberty and the Penguin* and *The See-Saw Tree,* introduce original stories to young audiences. Wood's *Theatre for Children: A Guide to Writing, Adapting, Directing, and Directing* has also contributed to the growth of children's theatre, both in England and the United States. The playwright's "musical plays appeal to children's love of action, movement, colour, and spectacle," asserted Colin Mills in *Twentieth-Century Children's Writers,* and a *Plays and Players* contributor dubbed Wood England's "first, and only children's dramatist."

Although he began his life in the theatre as a teen by performing at children's parties, Wood began to write seriously while a student at Oxford University. His first play as a co-writer, *Hang Down Your Head and Die,* was produced at the Comedy Theatre in 1964 while Wood was still a student. Since the 1970s, Wood has written, directed, and acted in dozens of plays, both for children and adult audiences. He has also written for film and television, and in the late 1980s he began collaborating with artist and paper engineer Richard Fowler on books for children. While his books have gained Wood fans in North America, his children's plays have earned him renown in his native United Kingdom. According to Mills, Wood's plays are enriched by "an actor's instinct for their impact, as well as a gifted storyteller's feel for character, plot, and theme."

In plays such as *Robin Hood* and *Old Mother Hubbard,* Wood bases his drama on well-known stories that have a reassuring quality because they are familiar to children. His original plays also work to instill a comfort for the theatre environment by utilizing traditional stock characters such as friendly dragons, well-intentioned but bumbling characters, and evil villains.

Wood's "original plays are vital and unflagging," asserted Mills. As the critic further observed, the British playwright "is a superb creator of names that capitalise upon children's love of word play: Blotch and Carbon, Kernel Walnut, Herr Von Cuckoo. In his dialogue and songs, he exploits the fun to be had from the topsy-turvy and the illogical."

Discussing his work with Whirligig Theatre, Wood noted in an interview with *Plays and Players* that "the dream was to form a company to tour the shows, one that was not four actors and a hamper, that would sit upon the set that happened to be there. We give a fully staged show, with 60 or 70 lighting cues. . . . The mere phrase 'children's theatre,' in this country, has always had a second division tag on it. But these are tomorrow's theatregoers: they deserve more."

Featuring the same drama and vivid characters as his plays, Wood's picture books include *The Phantom Cat of the Opera,* a retelling of French writer Gaston Leroux's *The Phantom of the Opera* that features a bewhiskered feline cast. Modeled on a play, the picture book tells its story of the beautiful Christine and the mysterious phantom in four acts, and *School Library Journal* critic Rosalyn Pierini asserted that Wood's "flowing narrative style authentically re-creates the drama, mystery, and magic" of the well-known tale. An original

David Wood's interactive picture book A Present for Santa Claus *features detailed illustrations by British artist Dana Kubick.* (Illustration copyright © 2008 by Dana Kubick. Reproduced by permission of the publisher Candlewick Press, Inc., Cambridge, MA.)

story "with a twist," according to Maryann H. Owen in the same periodical, *Under the Bed!* finds a small bear looking for parental help in ousting an under-bed monster. The action in *Under the Bed!* carries through in Fowler's pop-up illustrations, and Owen predicted that young readers "will get a kick out of the [book's] surprise ending."

On his home page, Wood reflected on his decades-long career in children's theatre. "It never gets easier!," he noted. "My plays are usually written for professional adult actors to perform in theatres for audiences of children in family and school parties; but an increasing number of schools put on productions of their own. I write original plays and adaptations of popular books. For musical plays I often write the music and lyrics of the songs."

"My aims haven't changed," Wood added. "I am trying to give children an exciting, memorable theatre experience by triggering their imaginations, making them laugh and sometimes cry, emotionally involving them in a really good story. I want to use the magic of theatre—the lighting, the sound, the scenery, the costumes, the music, the movement—to provide a unique, special event."

Biographical and Critical Sources

BOOKS

Twentieth-Century Children's Writers, 4th edition, St. James Press (Detroit, MI), 1995, pp. 1038-1040.

PERIODICALS

Kirkus Reviews, November 1, 2008, review of *A Present for Santa Claus.*
New Statesman, March 29, 2004, Michael Portillo, "Saved by a Song," p. 133.
Plays and Players, December, 1987, interview with Wood, pp. 8-9.
School Library Journal, November, 2001, Rosalyn Pierini, review of *The Phantom Cat of the Opera,* p. 139; July, 2006, Maryann H. Owen, review of *Under the Bed!,* p. 90.

ONLINE

David Wood Home Page, http://www.davidwood.org.uk (January 10, 2010).*

*   *   *

WU, Donald

Personal

Born in Hong Kong; immigrated to United States. *Education:* California College of the Arts.

Addresses

Home—Alameda, CA. *Office*—757 Santa Clara Ave., No. 9, Alameda, CA 94501. *Agent*—MB Artists, 10 E. 29th St., 40G, New York, NY 10016. *E-mail*—donald@donaldwu.com.

Career

Illustrator and fine artist.

Member

Society of Children's Book Writers and Illustrators.

Illustrator

Maribeth Boelts, *Dogerella,* Random House (New York, NY), 2008.
Gene Fehler, *Change-up: Baseball Poems,* Clarion Books (New York, NY), 2009.
Denise Brennan-Nelson, *J Is for Jack-o-Lantern: A Halloween Alphabet,* Sleeping Bear Press (Chelsea, MI), 2009.
Carolyn Crimi, *Principal Fred Won't Go to Bed,* Marshall Cavendish (New York, NY), 2010.

Biographical and Critical Sources

PERIODICALS

Booklist, March 15, 2009, John Peters, review of *Change-up: Baseball Poems,* p. 56.
Bulletin of the Center for Children's Books, March, 2009, Deborah Stevenson, review of *Change-up,* p. 28.
Kirkus Reviews, January 15, 2009, review of *Change-up.*
School Library Journal, August, 2008, Farinda S. Dowler, review of *Dogerella,* p. 83; February, 2009, Marilyn Taniguchi, review of *Change-up,* p. 91; September, 2009, Donna Atmur, review of *J Is for Jack-o-Lantern,* p. 139.

ONLINE

Donald Wu Home Page, http://www.donaldwu.com (January 10, 2009).*

*   *   *

YATES, Philip 1956-

Personal

Born September 6, 1956, in Darby, PA; son of Edward J. (a former director of *American Bandstand*) and Teresa Yates; married Maria Beach, June 9, 1996. *Education:* Widener University, B.A. (with honors), 1989; Villanova University, M.A. (theatre arts and playwriting), 1994.

Philip Yates (Reproduced by permission.)

Addresses

Home—Austin, TX. *E-mail*—pfyates@yahoo.com.

Career

Widener University, instructional media specialist, 1990-96; stand-up comedian and performer with comedy troupe, the Laugh-a-Roni Institute, 1991-93; teacher of elementary and middle-school workshops on writing and performing jokes, beginning 1993; writer, beginning 1993; Austin Public Library, library assistant at Will Hampton Branch at Oak Hill, 1996—.

Member

Society of Children's Book Writers and Illustrators (Austin chapter), Authors League, American Library Association.

Awards, Honors

Pennsylvania Council on the Arts grant for one-act play.

Writings

JOKE BOOKS; WITH MATT RISSINGER

Great Book of Zany Jokes, illustrated by Lucy Corvino, Sterling Publishing (New York, NY), 1994.

Biggest Joke Book in the World, illustrated by Jeff Sinclair, Sterling Publishing (New York, NY), 1995.
World's Silliest Jokes, illustrated by Jeff Sinclair, Sterling Publishing (New York, NY), 1997.
Best School Jokes Ever, illustrated by Jeff Sinclair, Sterling Publishing (New York, NY), 1998.
Greatest Jokes on Earth, illustrated by Jeff Sinclair, Sterling Publishing (New York, NY), 1999.
Totally Terrific Jokes, illustrated by Jeff Sinclair, Sterling Publishing (New York, NY), 2000.
Nutty Jokes, illustrated by Steve Harpster, Sterling Publishing (New York, NY), 2001.
It's Not My Fault Because . . . : The Kids' Book of Excuses, illustrated by Jeff Sinclair, Sterling Publishing (New York, NY), 2001.
Greatest Giggles Ever, illustrated by Jeff Sinclair, Sterling Publishing (New York, NY), 2002.
Greatest Kids' Comebacks Ever, illustrated by Jeff Sinclair, Sterling Publishing (New York, NY), 2003.
Wacky Jokes, illustrated by Steve Harpster, Sterling Publishing (New York, NY), 2003.
Kids' Quickest Comebacks, illustrated by Rob Collinet, Sterling Publishing (New York, NY), 2004.
(With Michael J. Pellowski) *Kids' Bathroom Book Knock-Knocks,* Sterling Publishing (New York, NY), 2004.
The Little Giant Book of Laughs, Sterling Publishing (New York, NY), 2004.
Cleverest Comebacks Ever, illustrated by Rob Collinet, Sterling Publishing (New York, NY), 2005.
Silly Jokes and Giggles, illustrated by Ed Shems, Sterling Publishing (New York, NY), 2005.
Galaxy's Greatest Giggles, Sterling Publishing (New York, NY), 2008.
Nuttiest Knock-knocks Ever, illustrated by Ethan Long, Sterling Publishing (New York, NY), 2008.

OTHER

Ten Little Mummies: An Egyptian Counting Book, illustrated by G. Brian Karas, Viking (New York, NY), 2003.
A Pirate's Night before Christmas, illustrated by Sebastía Serra, Sterling Publishing (New York, NY), 2008.

Also author of plays, including *Splitting Image* (radio play), performed in Philadelphia, PA, 1988, and *REM,* produced in Philadelphia, 1993.

Sidelights

Although most of Philip Yates' writing time is spent collaborating with colleague Matt Rissinger to craft books designed to entertain children with jokes, excuses, and snappy responses, he sometimes takes a break into story. Filled with the same humor and wordplay that highlight his joke books, Yates' children's picture books include *Ten Little Mummies: An Egyptian Counting Book* and *A Pirate's Night before Christmas.* In addition to his work as a writer, Yates has also worked as a stand-up comic, teacher, and librarian, all of which have allowed him to share his talents with children.

In *Ten Little Mummies* the title characters are bored spending time buried in a tomb, so they go out to play in the deserts along the Nile. As the mummies cavort, various misfortunes befall them: one is arrested for trying to paint the Sphinx, another is blown away by a sandstorm, and a third simply unravels. "The misadventures here will draw chortles from young readers," commented a *Kirkus Reviews* contributor in a review of Yates' story. In *Horn Book* Peter D. Sieruta found *Ten Little Mummies* to be "a cheerfully offbeat addition to the genre," while in *Booklist* Gillian Engberg called Yates's story "an excellent read-aloud, even for youngsters who have already mastered one through ten."

In *A Pirate's Night before Christmas* Yates teams up with artist Sebastía Serra to tell a holiday story with a salty twist. A rhyming verse chronicles Sir Peggedy's travels throughout the pirate world on Christmas Eve, carried aloft by flying seahorses and filling up the tattered sailor stockings hanging alongside ships. Praising *A Pirate's Night before Christmas* as "a swashbuckling version of the classic Christmas poem" by Clement C. Moore, Kitty Flynn added in *Horn Book* that Serra's colorful, "retro-looking" art captures the humor in the story's "festive band of brigands." In *Kirkus Reviews* a critic dubbed the book a "pitch-perfect parody" of Moore's poem, adding that Yates' "witty" verses are "expertly rhymed" and "packed full of pirate jargon."

"I stumbled into writing humor books for children quite by accident," Yates once told *SATA*. "My friend (and eventual coauthor) Matt Rissinger and I met in a com-

Yates' high-energy story for **A Pirate's Night before Christmas** *is highlighted by Sebastía Serra's colorful artwork.* (Sterling Publications, 2008. Illustration © by Sebastía Serra. Reproduced by permission.)

edy writing group. Several of us got together once or twice a week to write and perform jokes for each other. Eventually, we stopped performing for each other and hit the comedy club circuit, to mixed success. There was a mixture of comedy types in the group—some of us did straight stand-up, some did song parodies, others did improvisational bits. . . . Matt and I hit it off right away, eventually becoming known as the 'writers' of the group. We started writing and performing in our own sketches. We also took a class taught by Joe Medeiros, Jay Leno's head writer.

"Eventually, our comedy-writing group broke up, but Matt Rissinger and I kept in touch. . . . Since Matt and I were kind of tired of the whole adult comedy performing scene, we tossed around the idea of writing a children's joke cookbook. Lots of food jokes and funny recipes. We had lots of rejections until Sheila Barry at Sterling Publishing sensed our potential and offered us a contract for a joke book. We wrote over 2,000 jokes for the first book, although only about 600 were really required. Our second book, *Biggest Joke Book in the World,* required us not only to come up with more original jokes, but to collect and rewrite some old ones, giving them a new twist.

"We try to approach each joke as if it's a story with a beginning, middle, and end. That's the impossible goal of joke writing: you have to create a setting, evoke a character, and deliver a socko punch line all in the context of a few sentences. Picture books are great, but with humor sometimes the only picture available is the one the hearers will create in their heads when they hear a joke. Matt and I both love words—love experimenting with words and twisting them inside out until a joke comes squirming into the world.

"Believe it or not, some of our best jokes were written while driving in the car—long distances, of course. Matt always drives while I write the jokes. Sometimes it's very random writing, other times we have specific subjects in mind. You're very relaxed in the car, and your mind is free to roam over all kinds of subjects. We once wrote a hundred or so jokes in the car on our way to a book signing at a library. Sometimes we write our jokes separately, and then get together and help to fix each other's one-liners, riddles, and knock-knocks. We're very honest with each other. You have to be when you write humor for children, because when you end up telling them out loud, you either sink or swim.

"We think it's important for children to learn that words can be the magic ingredient in the joke, especially in their alternative meanings. Like when you hear the word 'order': The judge slams the gavel and shouts, 'Order, order in the court.' Naturally, everyone understands the judge is talking decorum. But when some smart aleck shouts, 'I'll have a cheeseburger with fries,' suddenly 'order' takes on a new meaning. It's so important to select the proper word for best effect. The right word means the difference between laughter and silence."

Yates concluded to *SATA:* "Victor Borge, I think, once said, 'Laughter is the shortest distance between two people,' and I think he hit the nail on the head."

Biographical and Critical Sources

PERIODICALS

Booklist, November 15, 2003, Gillian Engberg, review of *Ten Little Mummies: An Egyptian Counting Book,* p. 604.
Horn Book, September-October, 2003, Peter D. Sieruta, review of *Ten Little Mummies,* p. 605; November-December 2008, Kitty Flynn, review of *A Pirate's Night before Christmas,* p. 654.
Kirkus Reviews, August 15, 2003, review of *Ten Little Mummies,* p. 1081; November 1, 2008, review of *A Pirate's Night before Christmas.*
Publishers Weekly, August 4, 2003, review of *Ten Little Mummies,* p. 79; October, 2008, Anne Connor, review of *A Pirate's Night before Christmas,* p. 99.

ONLINE

Society of Children's Book Writers and Illustrators—Austin Chapter Web site, http://www.austinscbwi.com/ (January 10, 2010), "Philip Yates."
Cynsations Web log, http://cynthialeitichsmith.blogspot.com/ (November 6, 2008), Cynthia Leitich Smith, interview with Yates.
Philip Yates Home Page, http://www.mattandphilipjoke books.com (January 15, 2010).

*   *   *

ZELLAN, Audrey Penn
See PENN, Audrey

DATE DUE

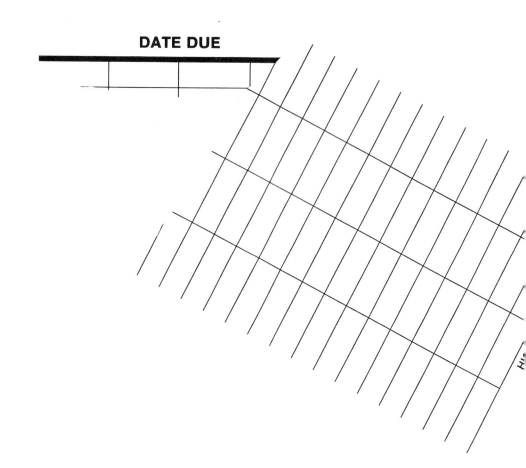